The
Robert Sheppard
Companion

The Robert Sheppard Companion

edited by

James Byrne &
Christopher Madden

with a preface by
Charles Bernstein

Shearsman Books

First published in the United Kingdom in 2019 by
Shearsman Books Ltd
50 Westons Hill Drive
Emersons Green
BRISTOL
BS16 7DF

Shearsman Books Ltd Registered Office
30–31 St. James Place, Mangotsfield, Bristol BS16 9JB
(this address not for correspondence)

ISBN 978-1-84861-625-7

CONTENTS

Aesthetic Justice

Charles Bernstein

So much of the aesthetically radical poetry of our time closes in on itself, hoarding its virtue or harboring the secret of its style.

Virtue, in the last word, is corrosive to style.

Aesthetic justice is when 'form becomes reform,' to quote one of Robert Sheppard's suite of poems published here. In Sheppard's poetics, reform doesn't mean ameliorative improvement. Reform is a mark of poetry's capacity to reformulate without final conclusion, to think outside formulation.

In Sheppard's writing, essays and poems, we hear the clang of discourse: the warp, but also the whoop, of everyday life. His work will never stand for election. It resists even the self-election that is the sign of a poet's despair of (or for) polis.

Aesthetic justice is the onward movement of the imaginary smashing into the possible. But aesthetic justice is also *dwelling in a now* that burrows ever deeper into its refusal of thematic deliverance.

Sheppard's voices (discrepant discursive registers, transcreations, heteronyms) don't call out to us as readers, as in a well-mannered lyric, nor do they call out to each other, as in a story. Rather the voices, the textual shards, call out to themselves, self-reflexively, as in — a poem is the cry of its vocations and the measure of its resistances.

Forms calls us out to ourselves: *calls out to*, a kind of aesthetic hailing; but also *calls us out*, exposing us, laying us bare, vulnerable, guilty as charged, without defense.

Sheppard has been a champion of British poetry that actively resists the complacent and the convenient, the merely competent. That has meant evading bullies who would 'banish us,' to use Dickinson's phrase. Sheppard's aesthetic justice has never been *just* for him; his social imagination is at one with poems, essays, teaching, and editing. His work is restlessly agile, generous at heart. Or so the essays in this book propose in their various insistences.

Otherwise innovation is just a fancy new saddle at the mind's rodeo.

August 15th 2018,
Provincetown, Mass.

Introduction: A Sheppardian Social Poetics

JAMES BYRNE

Most writers make a contribution to literature but the great ones extend the literary tradition. Robert Sheppard belongs to the latter group as one of the most influential poets of his generation, someone who has been able to further our understanding of innovative poetry and poetics in a remarkable writing life spanning over forty years.

The present volume is a collection of thirteen chapters on Sheppard's writing. This structure intentionally reveals him as one who works in several modes – mostly as poet, but also as critic, editor, teacher, inventor (as Pessoa did before him, Sheppard has invented several heteronymic authors). We include key interviews, a roundtable discussion between contemporary poets about the writings and legacy of Sheppard's work, a comprehensive bibliography, reference index and a brief selection of the author's most recent and unpublished poems.

Sheppard's poetry can be read as 'linguistically innovative', emanating from the British Poetry Revival of the 1960s and 1970s. Barely out of school shorts, Sheppard sought to develop his sphere of influence early, tracking down Bob Cobbing in November 1973 and Lee Harwood (September '74), thus beginning lifelong correspondences with both poets and all this before attending the University of East Anglia where he studied English Literature. He interviewed Robert Creeley in 1984, six years before publishing a full collection of his own. Crucially, however, Sheppard's aesthetic remains distinct from the poets he sought out and is different to other linguistically innovative poets he met early on, such as Gilbert Adair, Maggie O'Sullivan and Adrian Clarke. His hearing for the poetic line and musical ear – sharp as any poet I've known – remains unique.

One of the ways Sheppard has extended the poetic tradition in England (where he has lived all his life) is via a complex reworking of poetic forms – or, rather, a 'reforming' of forms, as Charles Bernstein highlights in his Preface to this book. For Sheppard, as it was for Creeley and Charles Olson before him, 'form is content' and this melding is made possible, once again, because of the importance of musicality in his writing.[1] For Sheppard, there always has to be an element of swing in the language. It's not that he puts language under pressure as such; language *is* pressure. Enjambed lines frequently work as hinges, which often allows for multiple readings of individual poems. In the opening chapter of this volume, Robert Hampson considers Sheppard's early poetics via influences such as Cobbing and Harwood (but also Roy Fisher and John Seed), exploring how form and/as content involve(s) a necessary (more organic) fracturing or disruption, a dislocated sense of narrative.

As Bernstein has noted, Sheppard's poetics is social, open, generous. One of many rapid-fire statements in *The Necessity of Poetics* asserts that a 'reason to make your poetics public is to test it, to build a community of writers'.[2] His approach to poetry encourages collagic, communal ways of reading. At the end of *Empty Diaries* (1998) he alludes to 'strands' which operate through individual poems to produce constellations of meaning(s). In *The Poetry of Saying*, he extends Valentin Vološinov's social theory to suggest that utterance, but also thinking itself, is essentially a dialogue with the world.[3] Crucially for Sheppard's poetics, the poem *is* social, a space where the reader is able to enter as an active participant. *Complete Twentieth Century Blues* – one of three Selected Poems to date – affirms this in a section entitled 'Poetic Sequencing and the New', which states: '[t]he aim [is] to activate the reader into participation, into relating differences, to sabotage perceptual schema, to educate desire.'[4] *Complete Twentieth Century Blues* provides the reader with a non-linear way to read Sheppard, playing with the idea of the 'Complete' or 'Selected', as often reinforced by publishers. This navigational way of reading Sheppard forms the basis of Mark Scroggins's chapter in this book (along with Alison Mark's, one of two writings revised specifically

---

[1] This idea of 'form as content' was written down by Charles Olson in 'Projective Verse', who attributes it to Robert Creeley. See 'Projective Verse', *Poetry Foundation* <https://www.poetryfoundation.org/articles/69406/projective-verse> [accessed 18 August 2018]. (Interestingly, as mentioned in *The Wolf* interview republished in this book, Sheppard scrutinises Olson's manifesto: 'Olson has always seemed too literal to me, and like most prosody, his looks less clear the more you look at it.' '*The Wolf* Interview' [with Christopher Madden], *The Wolf*, 29 [Winter 2013], pp. 59-68 [p. 62]).

[2] Robert Sheppard, *The Necessity of Poetics*, Edge Hill Ormskirk edn (Liverpool: Ship of Fools, 2003; originally 2002), p. 4.

[3] Robert Sheppard, *The Poetry of Saying* (Liverpool: Liverpool University Press, 2005), p. 7.

[4] Robert Sheppard, *Complete Twentieth Century Blues* (Cambridge: Salt, 2008), p. 83.

for inclusion in this volume). Within these various dialogic networks, Sheppard's poetry is what some would call 'difficult'. But the writing is no less socially recognisable for this. Sheppard has never compromised his poetry with overarching concerns of accessibility, of being understood. Instead, he is wary of the artificiality or insincerity that might arrive from the completeness of thought. His thinking here is foregrounded in Veronica Forrest-Thomson's theory of 'poetic artifice', which he has written about in each of his three major critical works, *The Poetry of Saying: British Poetry and its Discontents, 1950-2000* (2005), *When Bad Times Made for Good Poetry* (2011), and *The Meaning of Form in Contemporary Innovative Poetry* (2016). The opening chapter of *The Meaning of Form*, 'Poetic Artifice and Naturalization in Theory and Practice', is as clear an explication of Thomson's ideas as has been written. Introducing *When Bad Times Made for Good Poetry*, Sheppard clarifies his position towards (in)completeness in relation to his own personal aesthetic when he writes: 'Poems are coherent deformations and reformations of the matter of history into the manner of poetry, and it is their transformative, disruptive, power [...] that characterises the force of art.'[5]

Along with 'the education of desire', the 'matter of history' reformed/deformed is explored in many of Sheppard's poems. History, generative of the Latin 'historia' (to enquire), provides a frame through which to read several of his books, particularly *Warrant Error* (2009) and *Berlin Bursts* (2011), two of the poet's most impressive single volume collections. In the month before collecting materials for this introduction, it was interesting to note that parts of *Warrant Error* are being translated into Spanish and 'Prison Camp Violin, Riga' from *Berlin Bursts* has been selected as *Guardian* 'poem of the week'.[6] This, to the passing observer, might suggest a resurgence of interest in Sheppard's work. But the fact is he's a meticulously prolific poet who has never been away from the cutting edge of British poetry. Sheppard cares little for the corporate circus of prizes and mainstream jostling for position and this recent interest, though overdue perhaps, acknowledges how Britain is often slow to catch up with its practitioners writing ahead of the zeitgeist.

[5] Robert Sheppard, *When Bad Times Made for Good Poetry* (Bristol, Shearsman Books, 2011), p. 12.

[6] The *Guardian* republication, with a commentary by Carol Rumens, was published on 23rd July, 2018: www.theguardian.com/books/booksblog/2018/jul/23/poem-of-the-week-prison-camp-violin-riga-by-robert-sheppard.

Interestingly, *Warrant Error* ('war on terror' – Cobbing's sonic influence working here) is revealed by Adam Hampton as deploying a 'political language [that] seeks subterfuge, conceals its true depths, cloaks its ideology by appealing to the interlocutor as a political being, preying upon their ideological biases'. This, again, reveals a writer who requires something of the reader. *Warrant Error* is a socio-political text, but one that is, like history itself, interruptive (of itself) and on the move.

The creative work published at the end of this volume opens with selections from Sheppard's 'The English Strain', a satiric yet fierce response to BREXIT and some of his most polemical writing to date. But there is no departure from some of the linguistic 'subterfuge' of previous collections. Given his subject matter, the temptation here might be to carefully chronicle Britain's decision to leave the European Union. This kind of passivity for Sheppard wouldn't do. Whether ventriloquizing Boris Johnson via Thomas Wyatt or awakening Elizabeth Barrett Browning's 'Sonnets from the Portuguese' to the ongoing political horrors of the twenty-first century, Sheppard is able to form activist responses to the times through which we live without sacrificing his linguistic range: 'The roof of our love-nest hosts noisome finches; /it's infested with mice scratching at your cricket bat. / On Sky News you applaud the Shithole President.'

Throughout his eleven full collections, we find a serious poet with a terrific sense of humour. This is rare among British poets of Sheppard's generation, many of whom remain chained to the bland social realism (or what I might call self-indulgent lyric miserablism) that comes from a nation still in love with Larkin. Sheppard, by contrast, celebrates language (even when serious) without ever forsaking the ethical. Smut, sex or sexual innuendo are able to act as a mirror tilted back to the violence that emanates from within our shared sense of history. Sheppard is willing to reveal the language of sexual power. Again, readerly participation is important here: he presents his findings – (over)hearings, observations – and, if we choose, we might add a layer of thinking, of desire enacted. There is dare in operating like this, depending on who or what is being observed. Sheppard is a breaker of taboos. At The University of Liverpool, soon after the paedophile disc-jockey Jimmy Savile died, I heard him read a poem as if written in Savile's own voice. The audience faced themselves facing the unspeakable (this poem is mentioned in Tom Jenks' chapter 'God's not too pleased with me': Robert Sheppard's Poetics of Transformative

Translation', which also considers Sheppard's reimaginings of Petrarch). Elsewhere, Sheppard has dug up The Earl of Rochester from his sadist grave in *Fucking Time* (1994), as the title suggests never holding back on the erotic. Parts of *Empty Diaries* narrate the lives of female characters and 'Wiped Weblogs', a recent series of poems, is written through the female voice. However, it would be wrong to think Sheppard's intensity and sensitivity to his subjects dips in any way. Presenting a range of examples from both of these texts, Joanne Ashcroft documents 'an alternative vision of female subjectivity, one which offers women another way of being seen and, more importantly, of *seeing.*'

This last point about the seen and the seeing is important to Sheppard's poetics, from the point of view of how he constellates observation alone – the eye as an active recorder, unblinking. Sheppard is non-stop, a writer on high alert. In countering the sharpness of the blank page, he doesn't wait for the misnomer of 'inspiration'. Instead, he prefers to write daily, notationally, is a considerable diarist, twitterer, blogger.[7] During one of our many dialogues about writerly process at Edge Hill University, where I worked with him for four years, Sheppard told me that he often writes (sculpts?) from a large block of text, from which individual poems might emerge. Since retiring as Professor of Poetry and Poetics at Edge Hill, he is busy as ever, a fact unsurprising to anyone that knows him, not so much *retired*, more a full-time writer.

The seeing and the seen also bring up Sheppard's sensitivities towards the self and other, in which he cleverly reckons with the idea of a poetry of saying alongside that which is said. In *When Bad Times Made for Good Poetry*, he quotes Emmanuel Levinas: 'Language as *saying* is an ethical openness to the other; as that which is *said* – reduced to a fixed identity or synchronised presence – it is an ontological closure of the other.'[8] For Sheppard it's more complicated than this since 'the *saying* must exist in the said, as ghost to its host'. This interrelationship suits his open, social poetics which, though not looking to close down his writing into 'saidness', acknowledges the relationship between what is written (saying) and what is read (said).[9] The reader is on hand, creative,

---

[7] His blog, a large archive of materials related to his work and frequently referred to in the chapters of this book, can be found at: www.robertsheppard.blogspot.com.

[8] Emmanuel Levinas, 'Dialogue with Emmanuel Levinas: Emmanuel Levinas and Richard Kearney', in *Face to Face with Levinas* (Albany, NY: State University of New York Press, 1986), pp. 13-34 (p. 29).

[9] Sheppard, *The Poetry of Saying*, p. 13.

part of the commune. Nikolai Duffy explores these ideas of saying/said, self/other, detailing why Sheppard, ultimately, prefers the concept of 'unfinishing'. Like Allen Fisher in a later chapter, Duffy also focuses on Sheppard and his interest in music. For Fisher, Sheppard is, above all, a 'blues man', who carries through his poems the trace of damage and/or disruption, something that inevitably affects both the form and content of his poems. Duffy, relating Sheppard's writings to the importance of rhythm and musicality (as well as Levinas and Jacques Derrida and a questioning of self and other in relation to form), prefers to amalgamate Sheppardian musicality with the discordance of modern jazz.[10] These themes of musicality, self-other, form-content (especially regarding lineation) are also picked up by Christopher Madden, who turns his critical attention to the possibilities of Sheppard as 'Anti-Orpheus', exploring the idea of the lyric in his work and bringing together a myriad of key thinkers relevant to Sheppard's own poetics, such as Derrida, Maurice Blanchot and Theodor Adorno, among others.

Although this book has been edited to include stand-alone chapters, there are, as we have seen, many links and threads, networks, strands. Various chapters in this volume look beyond the act of writing poetry. Scott Thurston had produced a nuanced history of *Pages*, edited by Sheppard, which published a who's-who of linguistically innovative (mostly UK) poets from 1987-1990, and has been recently republished on *Jacket2*.[11] Sheppard's editorial activity is another important strand to his modus operandi as a communal poet. After editing a transatlantic anthology of poetry and poetics with myself, a few months later he brought together the 'European Union of Imaginary Authors' – invented poets written through collaborations with several leading poets in the UK, a project conceived before Britain's European referendum had indeed taken place, perhaps somehow anticipating it.[12] Sheppard's dual interest in translation and heteronyms is brought into view here, and is

---

[10] Sheppard is a huge music fan. He is also a musician (guitar, harmonica) who played various gigs in Sussex, where he was born, before moving to UEA, London and Liverpool, where he has lived for many years.

[11] See 'Pages, 1987–1990, ed. Robert Sheppard', *Jacket2* <www.jacket2.org/reissues/pages> [accessed 18 August 2018].

[12] The two anthologies referred to here are *Atlantic Drift: An Anthology of Poetry and Poetics* (Todmodern and Ormskirk: Arc Publications and Edge Hill University Press, 2017) and *Twitters for a Lark: Poetry of the European Union of Imaginary Authors* (Bristol: Shearsman Books, 2017).

explored in Zoë Skoulding's chapter, 'European Fictions', which looks at the reasons why a writer would produce 'fake' poets from underneath the fading horizon of the EU. Two further chapters discuss different kinds of collaboration. Patricia Farrell has written about Sheppard's work with the artist Pete Clarke, the 'expressive tension' between text and image and the production of meaning in these works, rather than the 'donation' of a fixed or specific meaning. Ailsa Cox writes a portrait of her former colleague at Edge Hill where, as she outlines, he was a pedagogic game-changer, someone who never compromised in over twenty years of teaching innovative poetry and poetics.

I would like to thank my co-editor Christopher Madden for his expert eye in all our editorial exchanges, for the many conversations we've had about Sheppard's work in which I've learnt a great deal and, above all, for bringing this book to life. Also, a massive thank you to our contributors for their dedication and know-how in exploring Sheppard's work. The backstory of this *Companion* began in September 2015 when I realised it was likely to be the last year of Sheppard's teaching.[13] The following year myself, Madden, Ashcroft and Jenks arranged for a 'Robert Sheppard Symposium' at Edge Hill which, on 8th March, saw four panels rotate throughout a full day with an evening reading at the Arts Centre. Many people who have worked with or been taught by Sheppard were in attendance.[14] Of course, Sheppard himself started things off, with trademark high velocity. All that occurred has been impressively documented by Joey Francis.[15] Apart from the reading, Sheppard himself decided to keep out of the panels, which he did in a typically dignified manner, offering a short note.[16] We are grateful

---

[13] In this case I mean full-time academic teaching. Sheppard has been retained by Edge Hill as a Professor Emeritus, where he still supervises Ph.Ds.

[14] These events were supported by Edge Hill's department of English, History & Creative Writing. Thanks also to Izzy Lamb, the RSS intern who worked tirelessly on the day.

[15] Joey Francis, 'Conference Report: Robert Sheppard Symposium', *Journal of British and Irish Innovative Poetry* <http://doi.org/10.16995/biip.40>. Francis, instrumental to the reissuing of *Pages* on *Jacket2*, has also interviewed Sheppard about his editorial of the magazine. See 'On *Pages*: An interview between Robert Sheppard and Joey Frances', *Jacket2* <http://jacket2.org/commentary/pages> [accessed 18 August 2018].

[16] The note that was read was as follows: 'I am extremely grateful that this symposium is happening – and I suppose I should explain why I am absent from the room during its sessions (though I am hanging about the rest of the time!). For one, I would find it almost unendurable to witness the full critical apparatus turned upon my work (which I hope is what will occur). I have heard today described as a 'celebration' of my work,

to all who presented for the Symposium – those not included in this volume and those who are. Myself and my co-Chairs always hoped that what began as the Symposium would culminate in producing a book of this quality. Finally, thank you Robert – innovator, catalyst – for your extraordinary approach to poetry and poetics, for the way you continue to move the tradition forwards.

17th August, 2018
Liverpool

but I hope it will be an interrogation of it. Secondly, I have no wish to take part in it (even subliminally, by sheer silent presence). I provide the headache (in Beckett's memorable metaphor) but it is not my job to provide the aspirin. My commitment to poetics as a speculative, writerly discourse is in part predicated on the belief that a writer cannot 'read' his or her work, or better had not, that 'explanation' is neither the business of poet or poetics. Thirdly, I am taking a cue from the late Tom Raworth who, when I was about to deliver a paper on his work at the Sound Eye Festival in Cork, told me he was going to explore the city. I have heard of symposia on writers that have been policed by the presence and intervention of the writer. I like to think Tom was telling me what I am telling you all now: that my absence will allow you freedom to express yourselves exactly as you see fit. As it should be. See you later.'

Convergences:
Robert Sheppard's Early Poetry
and English Traditions

ROBERT HAMPSON

Robert Sheppard has always argued that what Gilbert Adair called 'Linguistically Innovative Poetry' had its roots in an indigenous UK poetry tradition. This chapter explores the indigenous roots of Sheppard's early poetry – and shows the importance of poets like Lee Harwood, Roy Fisher, Allen Fisher and Bob Cobbing, in particular, to the development of Sheppard's poetics through the early 1980s. The chapter concludes with the 1993 publication of *Transit Depots/Empty Diaries* with its alternation of texts by Sheppard and John Seed.[1] This publication marked a convergence of two English poetry traditions and another turning point in Sheppard's poetry and poetics.

'Recognition and Discovery in the 1980s', Sheppard's 1990 account of his response to 'language writing' provides a brief outline of his early poetic development and also gives insight into his development of a poetics during this period.[2] In this essay, Sheppard notes how the work of 'Roy Fisher, Lee Harwood, Tom Raworth, Bob Cobbing, and J H Prynne' (p. 60) was the context for his own early poetry. He notes also how he moved from 'modernist defamiliarisation and self-consciousness' (p. 60), through a study of the critical works of Peter Ackroyd and Veronica Forrest-Thomson and the writings of Allen Fisher, to a rejection of 1970s' 'open field' poetics (which was the dominant mode in 1970s' late-modernist poetry in the UK and elsewhere) and the development of a particular politics of form.[3] In doing so, he follows, by different means and with different (British) points of reference, a process similar to that mapped out in Charles Bernstein's *Content's Dream* (1986), where Bernstein articulates a 'language poetry' poetics through engagements with Ezra Pound, Gertrude Stein, William

---

[1] Robert Sheppard and John Seed, *Transit Depots/Empty Diaries* (London: Ship of Fools, 1993).

[2] Robert Sheppard, 'Recognition and Discovery in the 1980s', *Fragmente*, 2 (1990), 60-61. Further references to this edition are given after quotations in the text.

[3] See, for example, *Alembic*, 4 (Winter 1975/1976), the 'open field' issue.

Carlos Williams, Louis Zukofsky, Charles Olson, Clarke Coolidge, and others.[4] This politics of form Sheppard described as 'using new forms of poetic artifice and formalist techniques to defamiliarise the dominant reality principle, in order to operate a critique of it' (p. 60). These techniques involved using 'indeterminacy and discontinuity', and, as one particular form of indeterminacy and discontinuity, in these writings, subjectivity became 'a question of linguistic position, not of self-expression' (p. 60). In particular, he defines his post-1985 practice, partly influenced by 'language writing', as moving from 'polyphonic lyric and interfering narratives to the multiply coherent text' (p. 61). As the Bibliography included in the present volume shows, Sheppard has been an active and influential reviewer of poetry (and critical work on poetry) since 1975, writing for specialist poetry magazines such as *Iron*, *Chock*, *Kudos*, *Rock Drill*, but also for more widely disseminated journals such as *PN Review*, the *TLS*, and the *New Statesman*. An early review in *Poetry Information* 14 (1975/1976), for example, written when he was still an undergraduate student at the University of East Anglia, engaged with Peter Redgrove's early selected poems, *Sons of My Skin* (1975). However, more typical of Sheppard's reviewing practice is 'Reading Prynne and Others', which appeared in Ken Edwards's *Reality Studios* in 1979.[5] This approaches Prynne's *Down Where Changed* (1979) through recent critical books by two other Cambridge poets, Veronica Forrest-Thomson's *Poetic Artifice: A Theory of Twentieth-Century Poetry* (1978) and Peter Ackroyd's *Notes for a New Culture: Essays on Modernism* (1976). From Forrest-Thomson, Sheppard takes up the idea of poetry as 'a special form of discourse' not engaged in 'the language-game of information', but rather foregrounding artifice and resisting naturalisation.[6] However, Ackroyd's reading of Prynne's work as a poetry of written surfaces with no meaning beyond their written form leads Sheppard to question whether such a 'formalist anti-humanism' was not like throwing the baby out with the bathwater.

Sheppard returned to this question in *Reality Studios* in his essay 'The Bath-water and the Baby: A Formalist Humanism'. In this essay, Sheppard begins by proposing Barry MacSweeney's *Odes* (1978) as

---

[4] Charles Bernstein, *Content's Dream: Essays 1975-1984* (Los Angeles, CA: Sun & Moon Press, 1986).

[5] 'Robert Sheppard, 'Reading Prynne and Others', *Reality Studios*, 2.2 (October-December 1979), 25-27.

[6] Ibid., p. 25.

an example of 'formalist-humanism' to set against the formalist anti-humanism of Ackroyd's account of Cambridge poetry. (In his own revaluation of Prynne's work in this essay, he claims that Ackroyd's account of the poetry as 'pure surface' occludes Prynne's 'deeply humanist concerns'.) While maintaining 'the operational autonomy of the imagination', Sheppard foregrounds the idea of 'the poet as maker'[7] – that is, he foregrounds the poet as maker of forms rather than as a self-expressive lyric voice. In his attempt to negotiate MacSweeney's relation to Ackroyd's particular account of Cambridge poetry, Sheppard then draws on Russian Formalism to propose a necessary tension between formalist absoluteness and humanist significance through which the poem produces a liberation from the habitual world of perceptions. The asserted autonomy of the imagination, through an alignment with Herbert Marcuse's 'aesthetic dimension', now has the potential for radical critique through the transformative effects of the poem's formal elements. In the same issue of *Reality Studios*, Sheppard also offered a review of MacSweeney's *Odes*, which focusses on quite other concerns.[8] Here he begins with a consideration of the horizontal and vertical vectors of the page as a result of MacSweeney's use of a central axis in the layout of the odes. He proceeds through MacSweeney's 'rigorous condensation' and his resistance to 'reading at the informational level' to propose that this practice, with its 'gestures towards the referential' (p. 31), makes 'potential readers more acutely responsive' to the language (p. 30) and to 'the patterning of the artifice' (p. 31). Finally, he considers the speed of MacSweeney's odes, produced by this 'rigorous condensation', and its political implications. Here he suggests, perhaps with Raworth in mind as well, that: '[c]elerity is a guerrilla tactic against a language that belongs increasingly to the controllers of our society' (pp. 31-2). In these two essays, then, we see a clear performance of the two modes of Sheppard's critical writings: the pioneering critical review and the serial formulation of a poetics.

As this brief account suggests, through reviews, essays and critical books, Sheppard has worked throughout his career to produce a critical

[7] Robert Sheppard, 'The Bath-water and the Baby', *Reality Studios*, 3.2 (1981), 53-55 (p. 53).

[8] Robert Sheppard, 'Far Language', *Reality Studios*, 3.2 (1981), 30-2. Further references to this edition are given after quotations in the text. 'Far Language' was collected with other essays by Sheppard in *Far Language: Poetics and Linguistically Innovative Poetry 1978-1997* (Exeter: Stride, 1999).

and theoretical discourse around the innovative poetry emerging at the time but also to develop his own working poetic. Accordingly, in Sheppard's early reviews, prior to his 1990 summative essay, 'Recognition and Discovery in the 1980s', it is possible to trace the evolution of this poetic during this period. His 1983 review of Marjorie Perloff's *The Poetics of Indeterminacy: Rimbaud to Cage* (1999), for example, focussed on the title's keyword 'indeterminacy'. He notes that 'Perception itself, phenomenology teaches us, is an indeterminate realm', and, more radically, he quotes David Antin: 'phenomenological reality is itself "discovered" and "constructed by poets."'[9] Sheppard's 1985 review of Andrew Kingsley Weatherhead's *The British Dissonance: Essays on Ten Contemporary Poets* (1983), a pioneering study of the 'other tradition' in UK poetry, picks up on 'the structural indeterminacy' of Harwood, which is 'directed towards the potential reader, who is expected to enter into its play', and on the different ways in which Raworth and Roy Fisher work to 'defamiliarise the world of custom and habit [...] to break habitual patterns of thought and association'.[10] In the case of Fisher's *Matrix*, for example, he argues that 'Monolithic perceptions are broken down, and given autonomous life within the context of the poem; the purpose of this freedom is to make "dislocative effects" in the reader's mind' (p. 3). Sheppard's 1986 review of Allen Fisher's *Unpolished Mirrors*, *Brixton Fractals*, and *Necessary Business* picks up on both the 'expansive semantic indeterminacy' of Fisher's production, the 'jagged polyphony' which requires the reader's 'participatory invention', creating 'temporary coherence line-by-line', and Fisher's theoretical endorsement of polyphony and indeterminacy, the continual invention of fresh meaning, as a Blakean strategy to avoid 'the imagination's "co-option by the State"'.[11] Sheppard's attention to Harwood's 'pseudo-narratives' and to Allen Fisher's 'interfering narratives' leads fairly directly into his own early poetic practice, while his analysis of Roy Fisher's representation of cultural discontinuities in the topological transformations of Birmingham in *City* (1961) and of Allen Fisher's

---

[9] Robert Sheppard, 'The Other Tradition', *PN Review* 32, 9.6 (July-August 1983), 63; reprinted in *Reviews 1979-86* (London: Ship of Fools, 1987), pp. 1-2.

[10] Robert Sheppard, 'Discovering The British Dissonance', *PN Review* 44, 11.6 (July-August 1985), 65; reprinted in *Reviews 1979-1986* (London: Ship of Fools, 1987), pp. 2-3.

[11] Robert Sheppard, 'Irregular Actions', *PN Review* 53, 13.3 (January-February 1987), 95-96; reprinted in *Reviews 1979-86* (London: Ship of Fools, 1987), p. 5.

Olsonian engagement with a similarly palimpsestic London in *Place* lead into his own engagements with history and culture.

In the light of these statements, it is possible to consider Sheppard's own early poetic development, emerging from an engagement with the work of a previous generation of English poets. In this chapter, I will focus particularly on Sheppard's relation with Bob Cobbing. The final section will consider how Sheppard's early poetry converges with the contemporary work of John Seed, who was following a different poetic trajectory, in the poets' joint publication *Transit Depots/Empty Diaries* (1993). This volume, with its charcoal-drawn images by Patricia Farrell, is another example of Sheppard's remarkable interest in collaboration. As mentioned above, it marked the convergence of two distinct poetic trajectories. More importantly, it was the beginning of Sheppard's move in the 1990s from a disjunctive poetics to his own distinctive engagement with history and culture. In 'Recognition and Discovery', he describes his post-1985 poetic development as a move 'from polyphonic lyric and interfering narratives to the multiply coherent text', but he also expresses his concern that this came at a price: the 'turning away from history, perception, sense-data, memory and narrative' (p. 61). *Empty Diaries* and the collaboration with Seed can be seen as a response to this perceived loss.

Recognition and Discovery

Returns (London: Textures, 1985), Sheppard's fourth poetry pamphlet, shows very clearly his early involvement in modernist defamiliarisation and self-consciousness – and his indebtedness to an earlier generation of English poets – in particular, to Roy Fisher.[12] The title poem, for example, which was written in 1982, works through a range of devices and motifs familiar from Fisher's work: the cool, depersonalised objective style whose abstraction is suddenly disrupted by the striking metaphor ('a wonder / of discriminations cutting / upon a knife-edge of sunlight'); the playful literary self-consciousness:

---

[12] *Returns* lists three earlier publications: *Dedicated to you but you weren't listening* (London: Writers Forum, 1979); *The Frightened Summer* (Durham: Pig Press, 1981); and *Of Appearances* (Brighton: Supranormal/Rock Drill Press, 1983).

> Slothfully
> an idiot paperboy is moving along the wet street.
> Time and again he's erased from the drafts
> of my poems, but is now allowed
> to stay   (p. 4)

Sheppard has picked up from Fisher the interrogation of the perceptual; the interplay of the public and the private, explored through the spaces of private rooms and public parks, which also expresses the poem's own ambiguous status, poised between private experience and public statement; the concern with 'psychological environments'; the attention to the measured, to the liminal (as in the blurred border between dream and waking), and to what goes beyond boundaries:

> Somebody
> is practising on a drum,
> a rolling, intermittent, persistence; somewhere
> just out of range, lies perfect chaos. (p. 7)

or

> You step out of this grid, return
> to the public spectrum of plain eyes,
> and are gone about your business -
> which is not the business of the poem. (p. 6)

In these last two instances, as often in Fisher, Sheppard draws attention to limits, to what is outside the range of vision or knowledge, as an alienation device to produce in the reader both an awareness of indeterminacy and an awareness of themselves as reader.

As Sheppard suggests in 'Recognition and Discovery', 1985 marked a watershed in his poetic practice. 'Mesopotamia', written September/ October 1985, is a good example of the new direction Sheppard's work was taking. The titles for each of the seven sections derive from notes on the back of contact prints sent during the First World War. As Scott Thurston also highlights in the present volume, these titles – and the specific, identifiable register they use – create expectations in the reader, which the work itself then plays with. A comparison can be made with Harwood's *The Sinking Colony*, which begins with what seem to be fragments from a memoir of the Raj: 'At the time being a young geologist with the British Raj in India I was somewhat limited in the actions I could take, you see'; 'Back at the bungalow my young wife was wearing her long white dress', and so on.[13] The photograph on the front cover of the original Fulcrum Press edition played up this ironised colonial nostalgia. Harwood uses colonial narrative as the key to which the poem keeps returning, but the location shifts from India to Canada, and other kinds of narrative are brought in:

> *The mansion was set in magnificent grounds*
> *The trees were heavy with rain*
> *and the fields of barley beaten down by summer storms*

Haven't we been here before?[14]

The interweaving and interrupted narratives create a generalised location, which can be read as a structure of feelings, a state of mind, the exploration of a relationship. At the same time, the constant shifting of the geographical location (and the concomitant shifts in the narration) creates a sense of gaps, dislocations, and instability, which, in turn, encourages simultaneously an actual openness and an active searching for connection on the part of the reader. Sheppard has written of how Harwood's poetry works with 'the potentialities of fragmented narrative structures' and asserts the 'interconnectedness of apparently unrelated experiences'.[15] The narratives function, in the poem's own words, 'like a mould made to hold the final object and then be destroyed or forgotten once the real purpose was achieved', except that the 'final object' remains elusive, while the narrative fragments and their emotional associations resonate in the memory. The reader is encouraged to complete 'the unfinished utterance, guided by its context', while Harwood's own risk-taking emotional openness and acceptance of incompleteness is offered to his readers as the basis of a co-created community.[16]

---

[13] Lee Harwood, *The Sinking Colony* (London, Fulcrum Press, 1970), p. 25.

[14] Harwood, *The Sinking Colony*, p. 28.

[15] Robert Sheppard, 'British Poetry and its Discontents', in *Cultural Revolution? The Challenge of the Arts in the 1960s*, ed. by Bart Moore-Gilbert and John Seed (London: Routledge, 1992), pp. 160-80 (p. 167).

[16] Robert Sheppard, Review of *Monster Masks* and *Dream Quilt*, *Reality Studios*, 8 (1986), 90-92 (p. 91).

In 'Mesopotamia', Sheppard similarly interweaves various narratives (the war in Mesopotamia; stories about Buffalo Bill – or various Buffalo Bills), while the orientalist narrative of Mesopotamia attracts to it other colonial narratives. The underlying narrative, however, is that of a viewer looking through a peepshow machine, where the image is produced by the flicker effect of separate cards, and this points up the difference between Harwood's work and Sheppard's. Harwood uses narrative elements which maintain a narrative function. Thus, in the title poem, 'The Sinking Colony', there is the suggestion of an on-going narrative that connects 'the heavy iron gates' in the second section, that 'swung open revealing beyond / a rich countryside at dusk', with the mansion 'set in magnificent grounds' in the fourth section. This phantom narrative concludes in the final section, when

> The rusted iron gate at last fell from its hinges
> – someone *had* been tampering with the padlock[17]

Similarly, there seems to be a colonial narrative which runs from the security of the 'young geologist' and his wife in the first section, through the 'time of waiting while the rains lasted' and the ominous note, 'The maple tappers were passing through the district but no one was expecting trouble', to the final section, when 'They stumbled out into the clearing' and 'everything was thrown into confusion'.[18] In 'Mesopotamia', with the exception of the peepshow framing device, there is no sense of narrative progression, and this is because the narrative materials are much more fragmented and dislocated; indeed, as Thurston observes, Sheppard's combination of discontinuity and creative linkage represents his model of innovative poetic practice at the time. The sections progress through a series of discrete sentences, and not only is there cutting between sentences but also (progressively) within sentences:

> Her back arched in steam, as if printed to defend it within a few lines, as Sweeney Todd is sketched in around her sufficiently for me to date the event in a dream in which she is shot by a sniper.[19]

---

[17] Harwood, *The Sinking Colony*, p. 30.

[18] Ibid., pp. 25, 27, 29, 30.

[19] Sheppard, 'Mesopotamia', in *The Flashlight Sonata* (Exeter: Stride, 1993), pp. 8-11 (p. 10).

In addition, as the sections proceed, there is the sense that Sheppard has
cut and re-cut some of the same material within the separate sections.
Thus the first section begins:

> Adventures are few: a storm during which a chap became so
> sea-sick they had to remove his future memoirs down the
> rubber tube, though I couldn't then recognise them as such.
> Blank cards flicker before my eyes: the ritual Arab girl, shot by
> a sniper, now bones and tattered uniform.[20]

Here the alternately extended and impacted syntax of the passage
signals its derivation through cut-up, but, as we read on, the material
that constitutes this passage also seems to be cut again into the material
of later sections. Thus we find, in subsequent sections:

> The Death Arab speaks to him in a dream in which she becomes
> snake-nippled Cleopatra: the crumpling and smoothing of
> oriental silks! They remove this mess from your world so you
> won't have a map of the British Empire in the 1909 Atlas
> (Section 2) (p. 8)

> He dictates blank cards, the mess pianola slowing down, unfleshed
> dances before the sinking night sounds (Section 3) (p. 9)

> A third soldier chanced a futile dash to the well; after the battle
> he would enter blank course remains because of the flies. The
> woman stood staring at me as though I were a problem to be
> solved, but then I sensed myself slowing down (Section 4) (p. 9)

> Blink above the snaking looking pianola I can rubber restless
> floats back to the blinding sand, returning to find a man
> looking through an empty courtyard (Section 5) (p. 10)

> Arab girl shot leave in India. Click of his fingers, the suture of
> the sky splits in a flash-blink: shot by a sniper. My eyes blink
> above the snaking Transvaal (Section 6) (p. 10)

As this suggests, the sequence develops through a process of accretion

---

[20] Ibid., p. 8.

and erosion. This produces the recurring motifs of 'the dream'; the snake; the 'Arab girl, shot by a sniper'; the 'blank cards' that morph into various blinks; the peepshow machine that finds a technological echo in the pianola. The words circulate in shifting patterns and shifting senses within different contexts and configurations in a verbal equivalent of visual flicker. They do not settle into a recoverable narrative, but repeatedly disrupt and dislocate any possibility of stable representation.

The interrogation of visual images (in this case, contact prints from Mesopotamia and, perhaps also, peepshow images), the shifting narrative position, the engagement with narrative materials as historically weighted and not just narrative material, and the attention to sexuality, all look forward to Sheppard's next watershed moment – the 'Empty Diaries' project of the nineties.

Letter from the Blackstock Road (London: Oasis, 1988), written November 1985, similarly suggests the boundary that Sheppard had crossed and was conscious of crossing that year (in that reference to his 'post-1985 practice'). The title gestures towards the genre of the poetic letter and works like Auden's 'Letter to Lord Byron' and 'New Year Letter', but the generic expectations of a stable subject and an addressee are not fulfilled. Although there is an 'I' as a source for occasional utterances, most of the text derives from other subject positions. In addition, halfway through, the text responds to the phrase 'A Dictionary of Evil' by running in order through most (but not all) of the letters of the alphabet, enforcing a different reading of the work's title. However, the epistolary implications of the title also suggest a fixed time and place, and the text indeed makes various references to 'November' and to a very precise area of North London radiating out from the Blackstock Road, Brownwood Road, and Seven Sisters Road area of Finsbury Park. However, *Letter from the Blackstock Road* is not the kind of montage of notations that one might have found in 1970s English 'open field' writings of 'place'. Time is disrupted and opened out by references to mythic and historical figures: the etiolated, fragmented, and inconclusive narrative of George and Pearl and Roger in Finsbury Park around the time of the riots also includes Hrothgar and Robin Hood and Guy Fawkes:

> Hood and George print leaflets on petrol bombing, poster Tottenham, but they're not to be seen when the shit hits the fan. [...] When Fawkes is arrested he is given bail, so long

as he resides at a friend's, in Hampstead. [...] Hood and Fawkes smash up the house, make the rich young couple fuck, whimpering, in front of them.[21]

Place is similarly ruptured by verbal plays and the knowing inclusion of the already written:

> 'Do we get to win this time, sir?' Sgt Bilko will ask. Pearl's husband became punched. George takes the protective guard off of his fire, and uses it as an out-tray, stencils R.Mutt on his forehead.[22]

or:

> Sometime soon I shall shout All fall down! and we all will. Roger would be ill at his own funeral, pentecostal glossalalia behind 60s frosted glass. Bob would be bobbing. To de-anglicize England, submit it to a 'coherent deformation'.[23]

Like 'Mesopotamia', the poem deploys what it refers to as 'paratactic tactics' (p. 13). As in Language Poetry works of this period, Lyn Hejinian's *My Life* (Burning Deck, 1980) or Bob Perelman's *a.k.a.* (The Figures, 1984), Sheppard's text builds up through a montage of decontextualised sentences. To produce this text, Sheppard followed a pre-set (but flexible) procedure. He assembled various pages of writing – new observations, bits of narrative, liftings from older writings (particularly writing about November) – and spread them in arrays of six pages. He then used throws of the dice to select the particular page, and then relied on intuition to select particular sentences or parts of sentences (with the default position of moving on to the next page if intuition failed to find appropriate matter). As a result of this combination of chance procedures and intuitive selection, there is a move, in the text produced by this process, towards the 'continual torquing of sentences' that Ron Silliman (in 'The New Sentence') has analysed in *a.k.a.* as a device 'to enhance ambiguity and polysemy' – a device that has moved poetic form directly into the

---

[21] Sheppard, *Letter from the Blackstock Road* (London: Oasis Books, 1988), pp. 12-13.

[22] Ibid., p. 19.

[23] Ibid.

grammar of the sentence.[24] In Sheppard's case, however, Fisher's *Matrix* or *The Ship's Orchestra*, with its peristaltic textual progression, is as likely to be the encouragement for this practice as Hejinian or Perelman, or, rather, Hejinian and Perelman would have reinforced lessons already learned from Fisher. Also, as the last quotation from *Letter from the Blackstock Road* suggests, Sheppard's work is self-consciously engaged in a specifically English political project, and part of that self-consciousness is through the citation and recycling of material from Sheppard's critical engagement with the political task of the poet in England in the 1980s.

The third text by Sheppard from this period that I want to consider, *Codes and Diodes* (London: Writers Forum, 1991), throws further light on this project. It also shows, again, how Sheppard's early poetic development takes place within a specifically English poetic tradition, though one which situates itself within a larger European movement. In this case, the text is produced through collaboration with another major figure from that rhizomatic poetic network of English 1970s experimentalists. *Codes and Diodes*, Sheppard's collaboration with Bob Cobbing, takes off from Cobbing's *Processual* series: the cover and the first page are both visual poems from parts of the *Processual* series, while the first poem by Sheppard, 'The Micro-Pathology of the Sign', written in July 1987, responds to Cobbing's *Processual*.[25] It offers a description of Cobbing's work which is both multiply impressionistic in visual terms and also acknowledges the text's status as score for voice and movement:

> Turinshrouded in voice-print drizzle
> Tumbled black and space language dripped
> Elevator inkclouds on multiple horizons
> Claws of lightning fissure the black
> Into sand-rippled sea-light
> In decalcomanic daybreak[26]

---

[24] Ron Silliman, 'The New Sentence', extracted in *In the American Tree*, ed. by Ron Silliman (Maine: National Poetry Foundation, 1986), pp. 561-75 (pp. 572, 573). For more on Silliman, see Thurston, p. 55 n. 41, in this volume.

[25] The cover is from *Prosexual* (Writers Forum, 1984); the visual poem is from *Processual Double Octave* (Writers Forum, 1984); and Sheppard's poem, 'The Micro-Pathology of the Sign', first appeared as an introduction to Bob Cobbing, *Processual: Collected Poems*, vol. 10 (London: New River Project, 1987).

[26] Sheppard, 'The Micropathology of the Sign', in Bob Cobbing, *Processual*, unpaginated.

That allusion to Max Ernst's technique of 'decalcomania', a blotting process involving paint or ink trapped between two surfaces, not only picks up the registering of body and voice in the material of the Turin shroud and the visual display of the spectogram and links this registration to the natural signs of lightning flashes or ripples left on the sand by the sea, but also, like the reference to 'R. Mutt' and the Duchampian tradition of the ready-made in *Letter from the Blackstock Road*, situates Cobbing's work in a tradition of European avant-garde practice. The poem then builds towards a theory of the work's political function:

> Desire flows into the matrix between
> Biomorphic alphabets on stone desiring
> Eye desires body constructs its music
> Flaming hieroglyph in a burnt-out world
> Each looking is a performance a reading
> Of flash-cards spelling a new desire.[27]

Where Cobbing reads his texts as scores for voice and body, Sheppard begins with a translation of Cobbing's text, a discursive response to *Processual*, that ends by placing it within a politics of reading and performance grounded in desire, which has its roots in the surrealist cultivation of desire for personal liberation and world-transformation, but also draws on Sheppard's reading of Jean-François Lyotard.[28] In his essay 'Re-Working the Work: Pausing for Breath', Sheppard explains this reading of Lyotard as follows: 'The reader's desire, in terms of fluxes of objectless energy, is activated by the formal techniques of the text, but is not fulfilled [...] The reader's desires, in terms of societal awareness, perhaps not even hitherto recognised, are hopefully aroused during this affirmative moment.'[29] In short, the poem, as it is read,

---

[27] Sheppard, 'The Micropathology of the Sign', unpaginated.

[28] See Robert Sheppard, *The Education of Desire* (London: Ship of Fools, 1988). In this pamphlet, Sheppard presents his poetics and the corresponding reading experience in terms of 'an education of activated desire'. The pamphlet is reprinted in *Far Language* with an 'Afterword'. Here he relates his thinking on desire to Lyotard's essay, 'The Critical Function of the Work of Art', and cites two further essays where the argument is extended: Chris Beckett's 'Anxiety and Desire in the Poetic Machine', *First Offense*, 5; and Sheppard's response, 'Re-Working the Work: Pausing for Breath', *First Offense*, 6 (1990).

[29] Sheppard, 'Re-Working the Work'.

'projects a future in its very refusal to mean *this* world'.[30]

Codes and Diodes is both Sheppard's homage to Cobbing, a trace of Cobbing's extended interaction with Sheppard, and a processual, process-showing production extending over a four-year collaboration. Thus, the second poem by Sheppard, 'Verse and Perverse', written a year later in July 1988, offers a second take on Cobbing's work. The ur-text for 'Verse and Perverse', the set of notes from which the poem was written, was sent to Cobbing and cut up to provide the word-source for Cobbing's response 'Non-verse and Perverse', which emphasises the materiality of the sign, through its attention to other languages, scripts, and sign-systems. 'The Magnetic Letter' and 'Seventy Lines', Sheppard's third and fourth poem are then written each of the following years, in 1989 and 1990 respectively, using 'Non-Verse and Perverse' as their word-source. The last two poems in the volume are Cobbing's 'At the Level of Song' and Sheppard's 'Codes and Diodes are both Odes', both written in December 1990. In these last poems, Cobbing goes back to the start of the series, 'The Micro-Pathology of the Sign' and 'Verse and Perverse,' but also engages with Sheppard's recently published essay, 'Recognition and Discovery in the 1980s'. Sheppard, in turn, goes back to the last term in his series, 'The Magnetic Letter', for his form, but engages with both 'At the Level of Song' and 'Recognition and Discovery in the 1980s' by taking them as his word-source. Sheppard, in this final poem, re-affirms a poetics (and a politics of form) grounded in desire, fractured syntax, and polyphony: 'Desire / dances in the polyphonic / sentence'; 'particle syntax admitting / intertexts' produces 'enough revealed delight to design / us all'.[31] As Sheppard put it (in deliberately simplified terms) in a pamphlet designed for A-level students, 'Poetry is the education of desire' and '[t]o change the wants and desires of the people of the world would be a revolution of sorts'.[32] A final exchange of letters reveals that 'Verse and perverse' derives from a schoolteacher's response to a letter Sheppard received from Cobbing in 1973: since 'verse and perverse' provides the title for the first poem in the sequence and is echoed in 'Codes and Diodes are both Odes', the title for the last poem in the sequence, the whole sequence can be seen

---

[30] Ibid.

[31] Sheppard, 'Codes and Diodes are both Odes', in Robert Sheppard/Bob Cobbing, *Codes and Diodes* (London: Writers Forum, 1991), unpaginated.

[32] Robert Sheppard, *The Education of Desire* (London: Ship of Fools, 1988), unpaginated.

as the celebration of a choice of masters and the acknowledgement of a seventeen-year apprenticeship.

History's Membrane

John Seed's work, over the same period already discussed, followed a very different trajectory. Seed's first hesitant explorations of contemporary poetry involved attending readings at the Morden Tower in Newcastle upon Tyne and the purchase of Donald Allen's influential anthology, *The New American Poetry 1945-1960* (1960). However, it was the Objectivists (and George Oppen, in particular) who left the strongest mark on Seed's early practice. Seed's *History labour night* (Durham: Pig Press, 1984), for example, seems to have been derived from a process similar to the 'imagist intensity of vision' of Oppen's poetry; at the same time, as in Oppen's work, Seed's attentiveness to the moment of experience also involves an awareness of the historical past. In Seed's words, Oppen's poems are 'located in complex ways in the historically specific relations of social and economic life';[33] they contain 'a historical sense of the world as a human construct, in part; not to be taken for granted, vulnerable and incomplete'.[34] In Seed's next volume, *Interior in the Open Air* (London: Reality Street, 1993), however, there is a shift from 'History' as 'a directly accessible unitary past' to a new historical hermeneutics of texts and discourses, and a new literary self-consciousness. Thus, instead of following the Oppenesque model, with its authorising consciousness and its attention to 'the actual moment [...] moments of conviction', the poem 'Novel' (from the title onwards) flaunts its fictionality. The volume represents a paradigm shift in Seed's poetry: from an empirical subject and an objective reality to the split subject, the self as a construct, the self as a space traversed by codes encountering another network of codes and discourses. With this volume, with its textualised history and its use of montage, he has also swung closer to the poetic practices of Robert Sheppard.

In 1993 John Seed and Robert Sheppard published *Transit Depots / Empty Diaries* (Ship of Fools), with images by Patricia Farrell. Seed began work on *Transit Depots* in 1989: during this year he began a

---

[33] John Seed, 'Living the Storm: George Oppen's "Songs of Experience"', in *Not Comforts / But Visions: Essays on the Poetry of George Oppen*, ed. by John Freeman (Budleigh Salterton: Interim Press, 1985), pp. 10-25 (p. 19).

[34] Ibid., p. 23.

reading programme and started filing quotations, details, and so on, under the appropriate year (year of reference or year of publication). This then provided the raw material for a sequence of poems, working year by year through the century, with each text made up of words, phrases, and sentences supplied by the reading. Sheppard was working on a similar project, 'Empty Diaries', again working year by year through the century, constructing each poem from notes relating to that particular year. In the joint publication, the two sequences (from 1919 to 1940) are put in dialogue.

An analogue to Seed's project would perhaps be Humphrey Jennings's *Pandemonium*, a history of the impact of the machine presented through eye-witness accounts organised chronologically.[35] Charles Madge's 'Bourgeois News', however, would be closer to Seed's method of collage.[36] Seed combines his fragments to produce de-centred narratives, different voices played critically against each other. For example, the second stanza for 1923 reads:

> Centralization is inevitable. What's it got to do with you that people are starving. They divided the country in the way they thought best.[37]

The challenging middle sentence gives an obvious charge to the surrounding sentences, so that the final sentence (which, out of context, might have appeared as neutral as the first sentence) now has the force of othering, of alienation, and resentment. The second stanza for 1924 plays a similarly critical eye on the political culture of the time through collage:

> Motoring up yesterday he had an idea for a revue. The King obligingly relaxed the rule that Cabinet Ministers should wear knee-breeches and white silk stockings at Royal levees. It's pleasant that there are so many of them and that they're interchangeable. The courts are working feverishly.

---

[35] See Humphrey Jennings, *Pandemonium 1660-1886: The Coming of the Machine as Seen by Contemporary Observers*, ed. by Mary-Lou Jennings and Charles Madge (London: André Deutsch, 1985).

[36] Charles Madge, 'Bourgeois News', in *The Disappearing Castle* (London: Faber, 1937); reprinted in *Alembic*, 6 (Summer 1977), 3-5.

[37] Sheppard and Seed, *Transit Depots/Empty Diaries*, unpaginated.

The juxtaposed sentences present Court life as performance and cabinet ministers as interchangeable, while, with the transition from Court to courts, Seed points to the occluded but functional linkage between royal display and social mechanisms of oppression.

In Sheppard's poems, as is often the case, some of the source material was photographic and Cindy Sherman's artworks provided one of the models. Rosi Braidotti has cited Sherman's work as 'a perfect example of nomadic engagement with historical essences':

> In her *History Portraits*, she enacts a series of metabolic consumptions of different historical figures, characters, and heroes, whom she impersonates [...] Through a set of parodic self-portraits in which she appears in different guises as many different 'others', Sherman couples shifts of location with a powerful political statement about the importance of locating agency precisely in shifts, transitions, and mimetic repetitions.[38]

Sheppard's *Empty Diaries* similarly involves transgendered impersonations. Thus, 'Empty Diary 1924' includes the following transgendered vignette:

> This cigarette
> card Empire, where an Arab
> in pearls drags me to his soft
> bed, collapses at my feet.
> The beauty of his parted
> lips: he has only to speak
> and I will disappear

The brief evocation of period cigarette cards (with their sets of actresses, sportsmen, military heroes) is quickly displaced by the cinema, with the idea of empire as the common link. The 'Arab', presumably the Italian American Rudolph Valentino in the 1921 film *The Sheik*, draws in another kind of 'othering', another kind of impersonation and disguise, while the desire to hear him 'speak' resonates ironically in the context of silent films. Similarly, Sheppard begins 'Empty Diary 1939', his penultimate poem in the pamphlet, with another female voice:

---

[38] Rosi Braidotti, *Nomadic Subjects* (New York, NY: Columbia University Press, 1994), pp. 169-70.

He handed me coins, notes, a rustle
of affluence in my palm. I counted
the change, slowly, powerless. Once, I could
have worked miracles on dirty table cloths;
tea, a mash of fish, crumbled over,
over the picture of Goebbels.

In these transgendered impersonations, gender becomes a cultural performance: naturalised and reified notions of gender that support masculine hegemony are defamiliarised and displaced through the act of impersonation. Curiously, as the sequence proceeds, it is Sheppard's work which is less fragmented and more discursive, more obviously involved in the detail of English social history, whereas Seed, from start to end, consistently produces collages of juxtaposed sentences. Thus 'Empty Diary 1939' ends with a vignette of evacuees:

Platform tickets, trains, toy aeroplanes scraping my
knees, bags slung round our necks; signs
we cannot read, destinations we can't erase.

This final poem moves from the woman's economic powerlessness relative to the man to this different powerlessness before other forces of history.

Conclusion

Through the 1980s, Robert Sheppard developed a writing practice and a poetics that was influenced, in particular, by the work of Roy Fisher and Lee Harwood – a poetics that involved an interrogation of the perceptual and a collaging of interrupted narratives. However, by the time of 'Mesopotamia' and *Letter from the Blackstock Road*, he had begun to explore the use of procedures – chance methods to fragment and permutate textual material. By the time of *Codes and Diodes*, his collaboration with Bob Cobbing, he had begun to engage with the processual as a way of making poetry. However, as 'Recognition and Discovery' makes clear, by 1990 he was experiencing this focus on text and textual permutation as a 'turning away from history, perception, sense-data, memory and narrative'.[39] At this point, he was also in dialogue with John Seed, who was developing his own poetics, working out of a concern with history, memory, narrative, and sense-data. Starting with quite different poetics and quite different poetic allegiances, they arrived in 1993 in a collaborative publication. First, we see in both poets, despite their different poetics, a use of disjunction and dislocation as a major device, but, in each case, what is important is the way disjunction is used to forge new relations and the way that these new relations are used as part of a cultural critique.[40] Secondly, this convergence also has implications for the question of groups and groupings in recent English poetry. Sheppard, in terms of both location and affiliations, was clearly a member of the 'London group' at the time of the collaboration: his co-editing of *Floating Capital: New Poets from London* (1991) put the seal on this. Seed, in his earliest work, could be linked with a loose north-east England grouping – his interest in objectivism is not unconnected with the presence of Basil Bunting in Newcastle upon Tyne, and his first two books were published by Ric Caddell's Pig Press in Durham – but his subsequent career could be associated with either London or Cambridge groupings.[41] This is not to suggest that such groupings were not important in this period, but it also points to the rhizomatic networks that were also an important feature of the multiple disorganisation of this poetic practice in England. Finally, in the background to these groupings is not just an alternative system of publishing, but also various alternative institutions. *Floating Capital* present Bob Cobbing and Allen Fisher as the two tutelary spirits, the forerunners, of the poets in the anthology. In his Afterword, Sheppard mentions Gilbert Adair's long-running SubVoicive poetry reading series as one of the alternative institutions that supported and sustained the poets in the anthology. He also mentions Bob Cobbing's Writers Forum workshop, an even longer-running institution, and the more recent RASP workshop, which Allen Fisher had taken over from Paul Brown. What should be added to this list of alternative London institutions in

---

[39] Sheppard, 'Recognition and Discovery', p. 61.

[40] See Robert Sheppard, 'Creative Linkage: The Poetics of Recent British Linguistically Innovative Poetries', *Assembling Alternatives*, University of New Hampshire, August 1996, and 'Adhesive Hymns: Creative Linkage in the Recent Work of Ulli Freer' in *Far Language*, pp. 56-60

[41] His work, for example, appears in *A Various Art*, ed. by Andrew Crozier and Tim Longville (London: Paladin, 1990).

this period is Sheppard's own Thursday evening workshop, run once a month out of his house in Tooting from August 1991 to April 1994, for the discussion of poetry and poetics. This brought together a sizable group of London-based poets – including John Seed, Ken Edwards, cris cheek, Johan de Wit, and myself. Unsurprisingly, there are obvious continuities between the interests of this workshop and the subjects through which Sheppard developed his poetics. In June 1993, for example, the workshop included discussion of new poems by John Seed and Ken Edwards – and Seed's 'Some notes on poetry, poetics, politics'; in August, a recent essay by Prynne, 'Stars, Tigers and the Shape of Words'; in September, new poems by Peter Middleton and myself; in October, Prynne's *High Pink on Chrome* (1975) and recently-published *Not-You*; in January 1994, Seed's essay on Bunting, 'Before *Briggflatts*', and cris cheek on writing about the other. There was also discussion of work by Barry MacSweeney, Colin Simms, and some of Sheppard's *Empty Diaries* as work in progress. The combination of attention to recent poetry and engagement with recent criticism follows Sheppard's established practice as a critic. It was also, as we have seen, the motor for his developing poetics and practice as a poet.

'For which we haven't yet a satisfactory name': The Birth of Linguistically Innovative Poetry and the Practice of a Collective Poetics in Robert Sheppard's *Pages* and *Floating Capital*

Scott Thurston

In July 1987 Robert Sheppard published the first issue of a little magazine called *Pages*. The magazine was a humble affair, comprised of four folded A4 sheets to give eight printed pages per issue. Typescript material was pasted into camera ready copy format and photocopied.[1] The editorial opens:

> Anybody concerned for a viable poetry in Britain must be depressed by the persistence of the Movement Orthodoxy from the 1950s into the late 80s; by its consolidation of power for a bleak future; by its neutralising assimilation of the surfaces of modernism; by its annexation of the increasingly fashionable term postmodernism; and by its ignorance – real or affected – of much of the work of the British Poetry Revival.[2]

This is very much a downbeat tone on which to begin a new enterprise. The editorial goes on to reflect on the loss of a 'power base' at the Poetry Society ten years earlier, the contribution of universities to this problem, and the relative merits of postmodernism as a viable term for the new work beginning to emerge. Sheppard permits some hopes for the yet unpublished *The New British Poetry* (1988), asking whether the reviewers of Orthodoxy will 'oppose, assimilate, annex or ignore these important publications' (p. 2). The editorial concludes:

---

[1] This mode of production is visible in digital scans from the original copy that Joseph Frances (a Ph.D candidate researching innovative poetry and poetics at the University of Salford since 2017) has digitised for publication on *Jacket2*: https://jacket2.org/reissues/pages. Frances' interview with Sheppard about *Pages* is also on the site: https://jacket2.org/commentary/pages.

[2] Robert Sheppard, 'Prescript', *Pages 1-8* (July 1987), 1-2 (p. 1). Further references to this issue are given after quotations in the text.

> It is not the spirit of optimism that fuels this project, but a
> knowledge that the one necessary thing to do is to keep working,
> to set up processes that may have unforeseeable results. *Pages* is
> probably not going to affect this situation greatly. (p. 2)

The use of the word 'necessary' here alludes to Allen Fisher's conception
of poetry as 'necessary business' (mentioned elsewhere in the editorial)
and, if not overtly optimistic, Sheppard concedes that each issue of
his new magazine might be 'potentially exciting' and that 'my own
depression is assuaged by my enthusiasm at receiving the first few
manuscripts through the post' (p. 2). Sheppard is hoping for 'active
engagement' that will lead to 'cumulative understanding' – and it
is important to note just how much cumulative understanding of
innovative poetry and poetics has followed from this modest starting
point, leading to his sustained theoretical, critical, and creative work
during the subsequent thirty years.

In January 1988, Sheppard published an editorial in the seventh
issue of *Pages* which establishes a number of key themes that not only
constitute the first clear theorisation of what later became known
as Linguistically Innovative Poetry, but also the distinctive attitude
of Sheppard towards the role of community in driving aesthetic
development, hinted at in the earlier editorial. Under the pointedly
punning title of 'Beyond Revival', Sheppard reflects on Blake Morrison's
article 'Young Poets in the 1970s'[3] noting Morrison's grudging
acknowledgement and dismissal of two important strands of the British
Poetry Revival.[4] Sheppard alludes to his previous reflections that the
latter group's withdrawal from the activities of the *Poetry Society* in a
mass walkout in 1977 had led to the 'loss of an effective power-base'.[5]
For Sheppard, this marked-off the poets who emerged under Mottram's
influence (he names Allen Fisher, Ken Edwards, and Bill Griffiths)

---

[3] In Peter Jones and Michael Schmidt, eds, *British Poetry since 1970: A Critical Survey*
(Manchester: Carcanet, 1980).

[4] Eric Mottram coined the term British Poetry Revival for the period 1960-1975:
the two strands referred to by Morrison were the group of poets associated with J.
H. Prynne at the University of Cambridge and those associated with Eric Mottram
at the University of London. See Mottram, 'The British Poetry Revival, 1960-75' in
New British Poetries: The Scope of the Possible, ed. by Robert Hampson and Peter Barry
(Manchester and New York, NY: Manchester University Press, 1993), pp. 15-50.

[5] Robert Sheppard, 'Beyond Revival', *Pages 49-56* (January 1988), 49-51 (p. 49).

from those that followed who 'had to operate in fragmentation and incoherence'.[6] Sheppard reflects: 'I have sensed the difference myself, since as a publisher, I've experienced both periods; as a poet, only the latter',[7] thus establishing the context for his own intervention with *Pages* (alongside other enterprises such as Ken Edwards' *Reality Studios* magazine and Gilbert Adair's Sub-Voicive poetry reading series) and the recognition of a new poetry emerging under these more difficult conditions.[8] Sheppard articulates the shared 'operational axioms' of this group of writers as follows:

> that poetry must extend the inherited paradigms of 'poetry'; that this can be accomplished by delaying a reader's process of naturalisation; by using new forms of poetic artifice and formalist techniques to defamiliarise the dominant reality principle, in order to operate a critique of it; and that it must use indeterminacy and discontinuity as major devices of this politics of form. The reader thus becomes an active co-producer of these writers' texts, and subjectivity becomes a question of linguistic position, not of self-expression.[9] [10]

This is a crucial statement which reappeared in the jointly-written

---

[6] Ibid., p. 49.

[7] Ibid., p. 49.

[8] Later in the editorial Sheppard draws on the list of poets published or forthcoming in *Pages* as a way of delineating this group operating in 'fragmentation and incoherence': 'Gilbert Adair, Adrian Clarke, Virginia Firnberg (the youngest, featured in this issue), Harry Gilonis, Peter Middleton, Maggie O'Sullivan, Valerie Pancucci and Hazel Smith. Outside London, associated *Pages* contributors include Kelvin Corcoran, Alan Halsey and Andrew Lawson. This list is, of course, not exhaustive, and is – I emphasize – drawn from the contents list of this publishing project' (*Pages 49-56*, p. 50).

[9] Ibid., p. 50.

[10] In his later work *The Poetry of Saying: British Poetry and its Discontents, 1950-2000* (Liverpool: Liverpool University Press, 2005), Sheppard usefully glosses poet and critic Veronica Forrest-Thomson's concept of delayed/suspended naturalisation (from her important work *Poetic Artifice* (Manchester: Manchester University Press, 1978. A new edition, edited by Gareth Farmer, was published by Shearsman Books in 2017) as follows: 'her theory elevates artifice over poetry's referential function but offers a model of reading that presents naturalisation – the reading of the text as a statement about the external world – as a process that is best suspended to encourage concentration upon the poem's artifice' (p. 67).

'Afterword' of *Floating Capital: New Poets from London*,[11] the anthology that Sheppard edited with poet Adrian Clarke in 1991, and which constitutes the first comprehensive public articulation of the poetics of Linguistically Innovative Poetry. In the *Pages* editorial, Sheppard acknowledges Allen Fisher as an important mentor figure for this younger generation of writers and describes how he deliberately launched *Pages* with extracts from Fisher's *Gravity as a Consequence of Shape*.[12] Sheppard outlines a poetics of community that might sustain these developments:

> It's not enough that these similarities be enumerated, these names listed; it is also crucial for such poets to recognise and use their shared poetics, and to begin to exchange their insights and discoveries, to foster debate. [...] To become visible to others, the poets must first see each other clearly. The poetry also demands accompanying documentation, poetics and criticism (something lacking in *A Various Art*[13]). The significance, but not the strength, of much artistic practice is demarcated by the coherence of the discourses that surround it.[14]

Here Sheppard reveals his underlying commitment to the multiple forms of a 'shared poetics', later defining poetics as 'the product of the process of reflection upon writings, and upon the act of writing, gathering from the past and from others, and casting into the future, speculatively'.[15] Although he often uses the term to refer to the (non-academic) documents that writers produce about their practice (see below), he seems to include, at least potentially, critical writing here as part of the desired documentation. His distinction between significance

---

[11] Adrian Clarke and Robert Sheppard, 'Afterword', in *Floating Capital: New Poets from London*, ed. by Adrian Clarke and Robert Sheppard (Elmwood Connecticut: Potes and Poets Press Inc, 1991), pp. 121-25. Further references to this edition are given after quotations in the text.

[12] A complete version of which was published by Reality Street in 2016.

[13] *A Various Art* was an anthology edited by Andrew Crozier and Tim Longville first published by Carcanet in 1987 and then under the Paladin imprint of Grafton Books in 1990. It counts one woman (Veronica Forrest-Thomson) amongst its 17 contributors.

[14] *Pages 49-56*, pp. 50-51.

[15] See Robert Sheppard, *The Poetry of Saying: British Poetry and its Discontents, 1950-2000* (Liverpool: Liverpool University Press, 2005), pp. 195-96.

and strength in regard to the potential fate of emerging artistic practices shows him recognising the value of a coherent discourse around this poetry: an approach which North American Language Poetry pursued much more effectively than its British peers,[16] although one which Sheppard has sought to emulate throughout his ongoing career whether as a reviewer, academic researcher, editor, or producer of manifold manifesti, statements, and pedagogical interventions. *Pages* itself later became a creative and critical project with a series of single author publications which included creative work followed by critical and creative responses and bibliographical information.[17] More recently Sheppard has reinvented *Pages* as an Internet weblog (or 'blogzine' as he refers to it) which, although its primary focus is on his own developing creative, critical and poetics writing, also showcases and links to the work of many other contemporary innovative poets. Sheppard's European Union of Imaginary Authors (EUOIA) project, a collaboration with 23 contemporary poets to write the fictional translated works of 28 imagined European authors, albeit in quite a different fashion, also demonstrates his ongoing engagement in collective modes of creative activity.[18]

---

[16] Some of the major poetics works of Language Poetry include: Charles Bernstein, *Content's Dream: Essays 1975-1984* (Los Angeles, CA: Sun and Moon, 1986) and *A Poetics* (Cambridge MA and London: Harvard University Press, 1992); Bruce Andrews, *Paradise and Method: Poetics and Praxis* (Evanston, IL: Northwestern University Press, 1996); Ron Silliman, *The New Sentence* (New York: Roof Books, 1987); Steve McCaffery, *North of Intention: Critical Writings 1973-1986* (New York, NY: Roof Books; Toronto: Nightwood Editions, 1986); Bob Perelman, *The Marginalization of Poetry: Language Writing and Literary History* (Princeton, NJ: Princeton University Press, 1996) and Barrett Watten, *Total Syntax* (Carbondale and Edwardsville, IL: Southern Illinois University Press, 1985). Some of the key poetics publications of Linguistically Innovative Poetry in the same period are: Allen Fisher, *Necessary Business* (London: Spanner, 1985); Robert Sheppard, *Far Language: Poetics and Linguistically Innovative Poetry 1978-1997* (Exeter: Stride Publications, 1999); John Wilkinson, 'Imperfect Pitch' in *Poets on Writing: Britain 1970-1991*, ed. by Denise Riley (London: Macmillan, 1992), pp. 154-72; Adrian Clarke, *Millennial Shades and Three Papers* (London: Writers Forum, 1998). The number and scale of the British contributions are far outweighed by their American counterparts.

[17] Series Two of *Pages* was subtitled 'resources for the linguistically innovative poetries' and ran from April 1994 to May 1998. The 12 issues covered the work of Adrian Clarke, Ulli Freer, Gilbert Adair, Eric Mottram, Hazel Smith, John Wilkinson, cris cheek, Peter Middleton, Rod Mengham, Virginia Firnberg, Ken Edwards, Alan Halsey, and Maggie O'Sullivan.

[18] See Robert Sheppard et al, *Twitters for a Lark: Poetry of the European Union of Imaginary Authors* (Bristol: Shearsman Books, 2017).

In the ninth issue of *Pages* dated March 1988, Sheppard published four statements of responses to his January editorial of that year under the heading 'Theoretical Practice':

> Responses to my January editorial, 'Beyond Revival', have been varied: from cryptic approval to lengthy qualification; from admonishments from an older writer for suggesting artistic change without the evidence, to a plea from a younger writer to start a literary movement![19]

These remarks, and the publication of these statements (alongside two of Sheppard's own parodic poems in the pseudonymous guise of Wayne Pratt which act like mini-manifesti in themselves) illustrate Sheppard's openness to collective thinking on poetics. He approvingly cites Ken Edwards' review of *In the American Tree* (1986), the first book-length anthology of Language Poetry edited by Ron Silliman, in which Edwards speculates on the significance of Language Poetry for contemporary British writing, remarking: 'I have a sense of a poetry as yet largely unwritten, one which will move the terms of agreement on from the great burst of energy of the early 70s' (p. 65). Sheppard sees 1988 as a 'crucial point', on the eve of the publication by Paladin of selected poems by Lee Harwood and Tom Raworth and the appearance of the anthology *The New British Poetry* from the same publisher.[20] While Sheppard acknowledges that it is time for a 'proper literary critical assessment of the British Poetry Revival', he is more concerned for the production of an 'active poetics to begin to help delineate a poetry that is "as yet largely unwritten", to encourage writers to take up its challenges' (p. 66). As suggested above, Sheppard's commitment to the discourse of poetics is a key aspect of his critical and theoretical thought. He defines it here, almost incidentally, as 'not a literary critical activity, not a theory of poetry, but [...] a necessary sorting out of what Ken [Edwards] calls "the terms of agreement" between the writers' (p. 66). Indeed, this issue of *Pages* is an ideal example of poetics in action, containing as it does short position statements by the poets Adrian

[19] Robert Sheppard, 'Theoretical Practice', *Pages 65-72* (March 1988), 65-66 (p. 65). Further references to this issue are given after quotations in the text.

[20] Lee Harwood, *Crossing the Frozen River: Selected Poems* (1988); Tom Raworth, *Tottering State: Selected Poems 1963-1987* (1988); *The New British Poetry 1968-1988*, edited by Gillian Allnutt, Fred D'Aguiar, Ken Edwards, and Eric Mottram (1988).

Clarke, Gilbert Adair, Andrew Lawson, and Virginia Firnberg: taken together, they reveal the becoming of a collective poetics.

The focus of the debates in this issue is summarised by Sheppard through the question: 'how can a radical poetics engage a radical politics while either negotiating, by-passing or eradicating the language of representation?' (p. 65) and they are worth addressing in turn.

Adrian Clarke reflects that the new poetry is united by 'the example of Modernism in its most pertinent radical thrusts – Russian Futurism and Dada to I novissimi, OuLiPo and L=A=N=G=U=A=G=E' arguing that this cannot be responded to in terms of continuing a tradition, but only by 'adapting and inventing strategies for a similarly "critical" art – in the sense defined by Lyotard [...] [that can] release the demystified potential of language' (p. 67). Gilbert Adair's statement starts by describing how the cultural conditions for this new work developed during the years of Thatcher's premiership:

> Fewer opportunities to look at and buy books; decreasing publishing opportunities; wide gaps in continuations of public (i.e. small-magazine) discussions; a one-way 'dialogue' with oppositions that largely expunge us from more public discussions. [...] The context is [...] the high level of conflict accepted by 80s government along with hegemony of consumerist and instrumentalist views of art inside competitive stimulations. (p. 68)

It is in this context that Adair coins the term 'linguistically innovative poetry', immediately followed by the remark in parentheses: '(for which we haven't yet a satisfactory name)' (p. 68). Given the currency of this term extended until the first few years of the twenty-first century, with occasional revivals, this almost accidental naming is resonant not least because of Adair's critique of some of Sheppard's 'operational axioms' for innovative writing. For Sheppard's 'delaying naturalization' Adair advocates '*eradicating* it' and also takes Sheppard to task on his role for discontinuity as a means to resist the 'dominant reality principle' (p. 68). As an alternative formulation to the latter problem, Adair also draws on Jean-François Lyotard, in this case Lyotard's focus on the '"false abstract universality" of exchange (via all-translating money), and work relations', Adair commenting that this constitutes 'a grating between experience and universality that any number of discourses fall over themselves to bridge and exonerate' (p. 68). For Adair, the dominant reality principle cannot be equated with '"realistic" discourse', noting how even advertisements are 'ample in "discontinuities"', and therefore that radical poetry, in its 'cutting across formations categorised as discrete' is only discontinuous 'if it makes *other* relations; or else it is mimesis of actual informational chaos' (p. 68).[21] Andrew Lawson recognises a similar problem when he argues that:

> To privilege what a work 'does and incites' over its meaning may be indeterminate in a reactionary sense in that it reproduces capitalism's imposed trajectory through consumer images and the bizarre farrago of an imaginary history (p. 69).

As with Adair's call to Sheppard to recognise 'the varied positivities of the forms being made in the 80s', Lawson also seeks a less overtly negative poetics when he suggests that

> the way through might be to try and articulate these crippling multiple determinations (economic, sexual, political) on the body of the socius and the self [...] and pose against them not indeterminacy [...] but nodal points of coherence that *can* be grasped and worked through. (p. 69)

Virginia Firnberg, the last of the four respondents, registers her discomfort in having her poetic work placed in the issue in which Sheppard's editorial appeared:

> By virtually setting precedents (which, incidentally, it took me half a day to understand, and I would never say to myself – I 'must extend the inherited paradigms of "poetry"'...... by delaying a reader's process of naturalisation, by using new

---

[21] This interest in making other relations is developed by Sheppard in a later statement 'Linking the Unlinkable' in Sheppard, *Far Language: Poetics and Linguistically Innovative Poetry 1978-1997* (Exeter: Stride, 1999), pp. 54-55, in which his discussion of Lyotard's 'Discussions, or phrasing "after Auschwitz"' leads to a theorising of 'creative linkage' as a form of juxtaposition that is both disruptive but also emphasises new continuities: 'the links so melted into the materials that they disappear' (p. 55). This approach for Sheppard contains an ethical imperative to link to the components of the daily catastrophe, along with all its ecstasies, that we live' (p. 54) – ultimately a resolve to 'link the unlinkable' (p. 55). See discussion below.

formalist techniques to defamiliarise the dominant reality
principle, in order to operate a critique of it; and that it
must use indeterminacy and discontinuity as major devices
of this politics of form.') – and placing me straight after
them, I felt rather strange and full of CONTRADICTORY
THOUGHTS. (p. 70)

Firnberg's response to Sheppard's position-setting is to attempt to resist
the act of taking a position itself: 'as soon as a name is given to the
essence of poetry and a marquee is erected with flags and speeches you
lose the essence' (p. 70). As a composer and performer as well as a writer,
Firnberg posits a poetics of space as an alternative way of thinking about
radical writing: 'surely the most exciting interaction of all time is that
between space and what crosses it, and that slight perception of what
space might be creates a tension which is the third element that makes a
poem' (p. 70). Nevertheless, despite her initial resistance to the practice
of poetics as exemplified by Sheppard's approach, Firnberg discloses a
'series of things that I might say to myself, but never would actually'
which seem compatible with Sheppard's 'critical' poetics and even
Adair's interest in making '*other* relations', for example in the statement:
'find new juxtapositions – to wake the word up – thereby constructing
an independent language with its own particular parameters' (p. 70).

This picture reveals a complex state of affairs – with respondents
registering their critical disagreement with the details of Sheppard's
argument as well as with the discourse in which it is presented. Never-
theless, Sheppard's decision to reproduce these statements in their entirety
reflects a tolerance and openness to these different points of view, and a
complex curatorial role, as he reflects in the editorial to this issue:

> One correspondent suggested that *Pages* become the mouth-
> piece of this poetry and its poetics, but I feel that *Pages* should be a
> variable forum, however useful its frequency is to the immediate
> dissemination of ideas (but there's unfortunately only space
> enough for assertion, not analysis). Hopefully, another journal
> might see itself as an anthology of this writing. It is my business
> to encourage and present, and to maintain a sense of community;
> to exclude, say, post-Objectivist writers is unproductive. Indeed,
> their elected agnosticism can be instructive. Tony Baker, as a
> 'student of Bunting', complains that I 'give too much weight

to the various critical apparatuses that follow in the wake of "artistic practice'". (p. 66)

These remarks immediately precede Sheppard's definition of poetics quoted earlier 'as not a literary critical activity' although interestingly his regret that there is not space enough for analysis of ideas suggests, to a degree, a commitment to critical, if not explicitly literary-critical, practice. Nevertheless, here Sheppard provides a useful reflection on his exchange with the poet Tony Baker which reveals how he treats different points of view as instructive, thus maintaining, rather than fracturing, a sense of community. Sheppard concludes the editorial by once again valorising the role of poetics in this context:

> Importantly, it is time for an active poetics to begin to help delineate a poetry that is 'as yet largely unwritten', to encourage writers to take up its challenges, and to pay detailed attention to the little of its poetry that is already written. (p. 66)

Despite Adair's reservations about the term 'linguistically innovative', the above-mentioned afterword to the *Floating Capital* anthology that Sheppard co-wrote with Adrian Clarke was the first to use 'linguistically innovative' as a critical term. From the outset, the afterword signals the oppositional politics of the earlier statements by Sheppard, Clarke, and Adair from the perspective of the early nineties:

> The eighties in Britain was a time of divisive and decisively negative social measures, blatant cynical manipulation of official information, continuing support for US military interventions and a small war of our very own in the South Atlantic. If British state policy is unchanged, there has been a change in the perception of it across the media. (p. 121)

This summary of the editors' view of the years under the Thatcher government – including a reference to the Falklands War in 1982 – immediately gives way, however, to a consideration of how these circumstances and the change in perception of them influenced the production of poetic work in the period:

The suspicion that this mediation amounts to something like Baudrillard's 'hyperreality' may explain some strategies in the texts we have selected for FLOATING CAPITAL, for example: the virtual disappearance of citation, testimony and varieties of 'unacknowledged legislation' in favour of a warier engagement with their materials, a politics of the sign.

The references to citation, testimony and Shelleyan 'unacknowledged legislation' suggest a version of the stereotypical modernist poem that an engagement with a postmodern theorist such as Baudrillard would displace, whilst the invocation of a 'politics of the sign' alludes to the poetics of Language Poetry. Indeed, the introduction to the book is provided by Bruce Andrews – the co-editor of $L=A=N=G=U=A=G=E$ magazine with Charles Bernstein and one of the pre-eminent poets and critics of Language Poetry. As Andrews argues, the arrival of the anthology represents a 'transatlantic communiqué, reflecting & anticipating a more attractive cross-fertilisation' between innovative American and British poetries, leading to a feel of 'some of the same *barriers* being dismantled', such as:

> the assumption that radicalism is mere 'experiment'; that the social-political claims of poetry (& its grasp of a social order in need of change) are mere embarrassments; that constructivist method & artifice should be confined to well-mannered incremental moves within a regime of stylistic niceties; that the sign system & the conventions of discourse holding the status quo together are absolute horizons rather than materials to challenge and defamiliarise.[22]

Andrews' remarks resonate with some of the debates unfolding in *Pages* three years previously. He comments: 'only a drastic adventurousness of language can articulate the crises facing poetry on *both* sides of Atlantic. Foreword as Afterword – Afterword as Kickstand. Questions – Responses.'[23] Following this last phrase Andrews' introduction develops into a series of paragraphs, each opening with a single word question,

---

[22] Bruce Andrews, 'Transatlantic', in *Floating Capital: New Poets from London*, ed. by Adrian Clarke and Robert Sheppard (Elmwood, CT: Potes and Poets Press Inc, 1991), pp. i-v (p. i).

[23] Ibid., p. ii.

followed by a sequence of responding sentences:

> Radicalism? The Old is not New. Stop. Give the old engines
> a holiday – no more the slow, outdrawing & unfolding of
> continuities, exclusive traditions & necessities. Refusal rips,
> accepts crisp scathe page – cut-up-ish swoon experimentation
> Language shines through. Surprise potentiometer.[24]

This style of writing is very much in Andrews' typical mode of
critical response: a kind of hybrid of poetry and poetics familiar
from his contributions to *L=A=N=G=U=A=G=E* magazine, which
counterpoints the more analytical and theorised approach of Sheppard
and Clarke's afterword, although both texts share reference points and
recognise the same key issues. That said, in the above passage Andrews
seems to valorise a poetics of discontinuity that Sheppard and Clarke
– following the earlier exchanges in *Pages* – are slightly more cautious
about (see below).[25]

To return to Sheppard and Clarke's afterword, they explain their
decision to include the work of Bob Cobbing and Allen Fisher in a
separate opening section to pay tribute to 'their various and substantial
productions before the period covered by the anthology and their
importance, in a variety of ways, for many of the writers who follow'
(p. 122). Whilst associating Cobbing with Dada experimentation,
Sheppard and Clarke note how Allen Fisher's major large-scale work
of the eighties and nineties, *Gravity as a Consequence of Shape*, 'both
confirmed and accelerated a shift away from ideals prevalent in the 60s
and 70s in favour of approaches that attend more closely to the paving
slabs than to "open field" poetics' (p. 122). This rejection of 'open field'
poetics represents the same sort of rejection as that expressed earlier
by Clarke in *Pages* of the influences of poets significant for the British

---

[24] Ibid., p. ii.

[25] In terms of the transatlantic exchange represented here it is pertinent to note Sheppard's
co-editorship of *Atlantic Drift: An Anthology of Poetry and Poetics* (Todmorden and
Ormskirk: Arc Publications and Edge Hill University Press, 2017) many years later. The
anthology contains many poets associated with Language Poetry (Charles Bernstein,
Lyn Hejinian) and (Linguistically) Innovative Poetry (Allen Fisher, Geraldine Monk)
and, although its introductions by Sheppard and Byrne are not devoted to analysing,
theorising or promoting innovative poetry per se (at this point in literary history, this
seems no longer necessary), Sheppard's editorial is devoted to theorising and promoting
the discourse of poetics, making a link back to his earlier preoccupations in *Pages*.

Poetry Revival such as Charles Olson.[26] Fisher was associated with the Revival at the beginning of his career and his previous large-scale work *Place* explored Olson's method in *The Maximus Poems*, although, from Sheppard and Clarke's perspective in the early nineties, the fascination with place in the seventies is described as 'deadening' (p. 122). Instead Sheppard and Clarke identify a new poetics more willing 'to deal with the materials that are readily to hand or impose themselves in the act of writing' (p. 122). Later in the afterword, they describe the 'expanded range of critical strategies in texts whose writers have relinquished claims to proprietorial control of meaning' as a less 'overtly utopian' poetics: thus registering the more negative poetics that Adair and Lawson reacted to in 1988 (p. 123).

An extended passage of the afterword actually reworks Sheppard's 'Beyond Revival' editorial, and offers the most developed statement of poetics for Linguistically Innovative Poetry at the time:

> The poets included hold at least some of these operational axioms in common: that poetry must extend the inherited paradigms of 'poetry'; that this can be accomplished by delaying, or even attempting to eradicate, a reader's process of naturalisation; that new forms of poetic artifice and formalist techniques should be used to defamiliarise the dominant reality principle in order to operate a critique of it; and that poetry can use indeterminacy and discontinuity to fragment and reconstitute text to make new connections so as to inaugurate fresh perceptions, not merely mime the disruption of capitalist production. (p. 124)

Comparing this statement with the previous version reveals how Sheppard has incorporated not only Adair's insistence that the process of naturalisation could, at least potentially, be eradicated, but also his concerns that the use of discontinuity should not simply imitate 'informational chaos' (here rendered as the 'disruption of capitalist production') but make 'other relations' (here rendered as 'new connections'). This is a wonderfully clear illustration of Sheppard's

---

[26] Clarke discusses the Revival poets as 'at the mercy of the inane schoolboy enthusiasm for tendentious "explanation" of Pound and Olson, the souped-up, head-free Romanticism of Ginsberg, the camp fashion-consciousness of certain New Yorkers or the less-than-fashionable (though not for lack of advocates) languid provincial neo-Romanticism of post-war England' (*Pages 65-72*, p. 67).

commitment to the process of working out a collective poetics. The statement concludes with a focus on the reader's role:

> The reader thus becomes an active co-producer of these writers' texts, and subjectivity becomes a question of linguistic position, not of self-expression or narration. Reading this work can be an education of activated desire, not its neutralisation by means of a passive recognition. (p. 124)

These last remarks in turn utilise ideas Sheppard articulated in a previous short poetics piece called 'The Education of Desire', written for students of A-level English literature in 1988.[27] *Floating Capital* therefore can be seen to represent the first maturing of a poetics of Linguistically Innovative Poetry: now fully distinguishing itself not only from the 'official "new" poetry of 80s Britain' (p. 124) but also from the poetics and politics of the British Poetry Revival.

Poet and critic Andrew Duncan reviewed *Floating Capital* in the year of its publication alongside Sheppard's book of poems *Daylight Robbery* (1990). Duncan introduces the anthology as a portrait of 'an overlapping group of poets [that] has patrolled the routes around Writers Forum, Spanner magazine and workshops, Eric Mottram's reading series at King's [College London], and the Sub-Voicive readings'[28] during the previous fifteen years. This sociology reflects the activity of Bob Cobbing's Writers Forum press, Allen Fisher's Spanner magazine, and Gilbert Adair and Patricia Farrell's Sub-Voicive reading series, which was also co-run in the mid-nineties by Sheppard, Clarke, and Ulli Freer. In the course of the review, Duncan offers the term 'Pulse' to describe the new style in British poetry he finds in the anthology. In response to the 'stripping down of language to noun strings' (p. 93) in poets such as Paul Brown and Maggie O'Sullivan, he includes an account of the use of metrical stress in Linguistically Innovative Poetry:

> The most basic insight of the group is that long constructions act to enfeeble the word-beat; stress, the propulsive force of poetry,

---

[27] Reprinted in *Far Language* (1999), pp. 28-31.

[28] Andrew Duncan, '"Pulse strings out beat of intermittent presence": Robert Sheppard, *Daylight Robbery*' (Stride, 1990); *Floating Capital: New Poets from London*; edited by Adrian Clarke and Robert Sheppard (Potes & Poets Press, 1991), in *fragmente*, 4 (Autumn/Winter 1991), 91-97 (p. 92). Further reference to this edition are given after quotations in the text.

is delayed and so continuously denied by the 'long cadence' presented by long clauses, long forms, and polysyllables. Rather than thinking of writing essays/articles and overlaying a metric pattern, one should think of absolute stress, dominating an empty space; and later hang formed words on it. (p. 93)

This characterisation partly derives from the distinctive performance style, particularly of London poets associated with Linguistically Innovative Poetry, which emphasised an accentual, stress-based metre. For Duncan, this focus on the pulse of the line is political: 'the "long cadence" of the discourse of the state and professions is replaced by Pulse, something to do with blood and breathing. Something sensuous emerges from beneath the shattered orders of learning' (p. 93).[29] Duncan sees Pulse poetry as a 'blast[ing] away [of] obsolete structural materials', suggesting that one could create 'a fake-Pulse poem by taking an existing poem and just deleting words and syllables until the bare pulse was there [...] forcibly freeing the poem of the deathly grip of social manners and refined usage' (p. 94). Pulse poetry is therefore inherently critical of the contemporary cultural alternatives which Duncan characterises as:

> Blasted genres: prefab Socialism; Marxist alienation; moralizing; religion; bourgeois guardianship; soap operas about people with A-levels; wet lyricism; complacent sensiblerie; National Trust reverence poems; and all the other crap which is killing us. (p. 94)

Pulse poetry, as Duncan conceives of it, is a kind of energetic, embodied poetics with an emphasis on 'a personal energy, and word-stress comes out of the poet's vital pulses' (p. 93). In other poetic tendencies, the personality is reduced to 'the prison of the poem [...] a tautology' but reappears in Pulse poetry as 'simply a rhythm of blanks and pulses: the word-beat is the total trace of personality [...] Language as a wire

---

[29] The reference to breathing suggests a possible connection to Charles Olson's 'Projective Verse' (1950). Despite the rejection of Olsonian poetics by poets associated with Linguistically Innovative Poetry, some of the central tenets of Olson's poetics, such as the directive that 'ONE PERCEPTION MUST IMMEDIATELY AND DIRECTLY LEAD TO A FURTHER PERCEPTION' are nevertheless suggestive of the kinds of formal strategies employed by Sheppard, Clarke and others.

connected to the muscles' (p. 94). Duncan's vivid and enthusiastic characterisations of this writing convey the excitement this work generated in the eighties and nineties: a tense, explosive and relentless poetry in some way akin to the spirit of Punk from a decade earlier. In his review, Duncan acknowledges Allen Fisher's importance as a founding figure for this group, whilst noting that his 'approach to the beat is totally different' (p. 96). He claims to have developed 'the whole "pulse" theory' in response to Ulli Freer and Maggie O'Sullivan's poetry but acknowledges that Freer is not in *Floating Capital* and admits that he 'can't date the events or name the innovators' (p. 96). Duncan's coining of 'Pulse poetry' appears to have been the only serious contemporary alternative to the term Linguistically Innovative Poetry, but, despite the the latter's infelicity, it became the one most widely adopted to describe the work of these writers.

Floating Capital contains an extract from Sheppard's long poem 'Daylight Robbery' published in the book of the same title (also reviewed by Duncan alongside the anthology).[30] In its sustained sequence of continuous short lines un-coordinated by punctuation and working the dynamics of continuity and discontinuity across the line break, the poem epitomises the energy and fragmentation of Duncan's characterisation of Pulse poetry, as well as Sheppard's own description of Linguistically Innovative poetics. Duncan describes the 'atomistic, pulsed, fragments' into which the poem is divided as 'reflecting the barrage of data coming from the TV screen: along with the viewer's fantasies and reactions' (p. 91-92):

> Whitewashed thought
> Flashing articulations
> Those transparencies
> Into the daylight modern
> Intermittent outbursts of unique
> Movie mind flying skating on
> Nobody's dream
> This dodge into synaesthesia
> Writing provides feet core
> Tremble and
> Skating on a frozen world

---

[30] A radically revised version of the poem was published as 'Living Daylights' in Sheppard's selected poems *History or Sleep* (Bristol: Shearsman Books, 2015), pp. 33-37.

I speak rest my thoughts speak at war with
Video rhyme[31]

However, given Sheppard's awareness of the risk of discontinuity
leading to an aping of the capitalist spectacle warned of by Adair, one
might sound a notion of caution in following Duncan's interpretative
approach in assertions such as:

> the force of the form (the consistent refusal to continue any idea
> for more than a line) is to exclude the human personality; the
> poem speaks from a pre-conscious level, trapping reality before
> a filter reshapes it into part of the personality. (pp. 91-92)

Although the onward momentum of Sheppard's line is forceful and
compelling, there is a constant interplay between the possibilities
of fragmentation and continuity. Rather than the poem refusing to
continue any idea for longer than a line, its phrasal units build up a
series of associations so that one starts to sense an argument forming
about the experience of contemporary media saturation. The 'modern /
Intermittent outbursts of unique / Movie mind' emanated by television,
cinema, and video are critiqued as 'whitewashed' and 'skating on
/ Nobody's dream' whilst writing seems to provide a kind of stable
instability in engaging with this 'frozen world' by providing both metrical
and actual feet: 'core / Tremble and / Skating'.[32] If, according to Duncan,
the poem excludes personality by speaking from a pre-conscious level,
a narrator does nevertheless appear to articulate a clear statement of the
poetics of the poem, as in the lines: 'I speak rest my thoughts speak at
war with / Video rhyme,' if qualified by the irony of the interruptive
phrase 'rest my thoughts' in this restless poem. If Duncan's readings
initially seem broadly compatible with the politics of Sheppard's writing,
the characterisation of this work as a kind of pre-conscious, instinctual
and unfiltered response to reality risks underplaying the very deliberate
and conscious critique of contemporary culture enacted here. The poem
is haunted by images of violence at the same time as it recognises such
images as manipulative and coercive:

---

[31] Robert Sheppard, 'from *Daylight Robbery*', in Clarke and Sheppard, *Floating Capital*,
pp. 105-07 (p. 105).

[32] One might, just about, detect an allusion to the ice-skating scene in Wordsworth's
The Prelude (1850) (Book One, ll. 425-463).

Each story must have
Binocular voices
A small boy was knifed meaning from doing
Street flaked out and puking guts
In strings left below the audible
Pool of blood above the visible
Morality of the lowlife
Invisible from the helicopter[33]

Here a possible news story about street violence seems coupled to a more abstract, analytical vocabulary in phrases like 'each story must have / binocular voices', 'meaning from doing', 'below the audible', 'above the visible' which feel like they might belong to the discourse of media theory. This interrupts the image of the knifed boy in the street from re-enacting its manipulative shock on the reader, instead leading to a more nuanced critique in which the narrator recognises the danger of the distancing effect of police helicopter surveillance. The poem reflects further on the poetics of its critique:

Logopoeia world in a stolen book
Between the capital letter and the doubted word
Which is speech wind which
Is voice image which way now[34]

The use of the term *logopoeia*, an ancient Greek term used most famously by Ezra Pound in his poetics to describe the effect of visual and sonic elements in poetry interacting with meaning,[35] is posited against a 'stolen book' and 'doubted word' and a 'capital letter', which all suggest a poetry aware that it too in turn becomes co-opted by the system that it rejects. This leads to a radical doubt with the implied questions 'which is speech [...] which / Is voice image which way now',

---

[33] Sheppard, 'from *Daylight Robbery*', p. 106.

[34] Ibid., p. 106.

[35] Ezra Pound, *ABC of Reading* (London: Faber and Faber, 1973), p. 63. In his scheme, Pound defines Phanopoeia as 'throwing the object (fixed or moving) on to the visual imagination' and Melopoeia as 'inducing emotional correlations by sound and rhythm of the speech'. Thus, logopoeia in poetry is responsible for: 'inducing both of the effects by stimulating the associations (intellectual or emotional) that have remained in the receiver's consciousness in relation to the actual words or word groups employed.'

which tangle with the intricacies of Pound's poetics in the references to speech and image whilst also suggesting a more general existential doubt. Later the poem recognises the cost of this activity, of pitting its 'wits against the shreds of chatter', and critiques its own practice: 'expressive gestures stolen from the news.'[36]

If at odds, to a degree, with Duncan's account, Sheppard's poetry is productively read back against the poetics outlined in the afterword of *Floating Capital*. The new forms of poetic artifice and formalist techniques that seek to fragment and reconstitute text to create critical 'fresh perceptions' are those of the phrasal poetics employed in *Daylight Robbery*, an innovation as important to Linguistically Innovative Poetry as the 'new sentence' was to Language Poetry. Both Sheppard and Clarke theorised a phrasal poetics in their responses to Jean-François Lyotard's work, whose influence on the poetics of Linguistically Innovative Poetry should by now already be clear. Clarke initiated this engagement in a paper entitled 'Listening to the Differences',[37] delivered to the first Sub-Voicive Colloquium in 1991. In keeping with Clarke's attitude to modernism indicated above, at the outset of his paper he rejects the proposal of the colloquium to debate poetics under the banner of the "'tradition of *Make It New*'":

> [*Make It New* is] a phrase that as it raises the spectre of Ezra Pound and grants it proprietorial rights over a 'tradition' into which we are summarily inserted excludes almost all my current concerns.[38]

Positing an 'alternative modernism' whose prerogative is a 'radical challenge to any attempt to ground a tradition', he finds Lyotard's book *The Differend: Phrases in Dispute*[39] particularly pertinent to this end:

> The way in which Lyotard attempts to subvert such totalizing concepts [tradition, the 'New', genre] is by a resort to the

---

[36] Sheppard, 'from *Daylight Robbery*', p. 106.

[37] Adrian Clarke, 'Listening to the Differences' in Adrian Clarke, *Millennial Shades & Three Papers* (London: Writers Forum, 1998), unpaginated.

[38] Ibid., unpaginated.

[39] Jean-François Lyotard, *The Differend: Phrases in Dispute*, trans. by Georges Van Den Abbeele (Minneapolis, MN: University of Minnesota Press, 1988). Clarke quotes from p. 11 (para. 17), p. 66 (para. 102), p. xiii (para. 'Stakes') and p. 181 (paras. 260, 262-63).

phrase, in a sense – wider than that of the grammatical unit – that is contextually defined, but the strategic significance of which is as a linguistic instance that cuts across genres and categories as it evades closure. [...] With phrases we are set adrift from narrative and logic to struggle with what they present without hope of return to safe ground: 'for a phrase to be the last phrase, another phrase is necessary to declare this, and thus it is not the last one.' Further, 'That there not be a phrase is impossible. It is rather *And a phrase* is necessary. It is necessary to link. [...] The linkage of one phrase with another is problematic, and this problem is politics'.[40]

Thus Lyotard's work enables Clarke to assert a politics based on a linguistic unit, in a way comparable to Language poet Ron Silliman's account of the 'new sentence' as a device based on the recognition that 'the sentence, hypotactic and complete, was and still is an index of class in society'.[41] For Lyotard, 'thought, cognition, ethics, politics, history or being, depending on the case, are in play when one phrase is linked onto another.'[42] Although Clarke acknowledges that the term 'phrase' in Lyotard is actually used in a sense wider than that of the grammatical unit, his claims for its 'strategic significance' are clearly creatively enabling.

Sheppard in turn was to later revisit similar remarks from Lyotard, and Clarke's own paper, in the poetics statement 'Linking the Unlinkable' (see footnote 43). In Sheppard's account he is interested

[40] Clarke, 'Listening to the Differences', unpaginated.

[41] Ron Silliman, *The New Sentence* (New York, NY: Roof Books, 1987), p. 79. For Silliman, the new sentence is a formal intervention which proposes that a sentence has 'become equivalent to a line' (p. 90). He describes the formal properties of the new sentence in the following terms:

1) The paragraph [rather than the stanza] organizes the sentences;

2) The paragraph is a unit of quantity, not logic or argument;

3) Sentence length [rather than the line] is a unit of measure;

4) Sentence structure is altered for torque, or increased polysemy/ambiguity;

5) Syllogistic movement is (a) limited (b) controlled;

6) Primary syllogistic movement is toward the paragraph as a whole, or the total work;

7) Secondary syllogistic movement is toward the paragraph as a whole, or the total work;

8) The limiting of syllogistic movement keeps the reader's attention at or very close to the level of language, the sentence level or below. (p. 91)

[42] Lyotard, *The Differend*, pp. xii-xiii.

in Derrida's response to Lyotard, which reveals Derrida to be less interested in phrases than 'in the processes of essential linkage' which become an 'ethical imperative'.[43] In the context of Derrida's argument, the ethical imperative is connected, as for Lyotard, to the Holocaust: 'if there is today an ethical or political question and if there is somewhere a *One must* it must link up with a *one must make links with Auschwitz*' (p. 54). Sheppard seeks a broadening of this axiom in both technical and ethical terms to conceive of a practice he calls 'creative linkage' – a way of talking about juxtaposition and discontinuity that offsets the 'Adornoesque negativity' that Adair and Lawson warn of in the earlier discussions in *Pages* (pp. 54-5). Sheppard acknowledges that his own approach is allied to Clarke's poetics, and adds that 'linguistically innovative writers momently create new "rules" for linkage, for what suits the particular "case": the disparate materials in need of procedural linkage' (p. 55). That the underlying motivation of this approach is to 'link the unlinkable' (p. 55) provides a key into the central aspect of Sheppard's writing which is perhaps not overtly declared in these statements of poetics (except perhaps implicitly in the interest in Lyotard and Derrida's discussion of writing after the Holocaust), that is, his engagement with history and historical documents in particular.

It is perhaps surprising that the politically-engaged poetics of Linguistically Innovative Poetry and Language Poetry should not overtly discuss the role of history. Yet, as Robert Hampson similarly argues in the present volume in relation to one of Sheppard's most significant early poems, 'Mesopotamia' – the final section of which is excerpted in *Floating Capital* – provides a model for innovative poetic practice through its use of discontinuity in harness with creative linkage whilst adopting the sentence and prose paragraph in a way akin to Language Poetry, rather than the phrasal poetics illustrated above. Its originality also lies, as Hampson acknowledges, in its engagement with historical documents – namely the contact prints from the First World War, which Sheppard describes in the note to the poem's later publication in *The Flashlight Sonata* (1993):

---

[43] Robert Sheppard, 'Linking the Unlinkable: an answer to the question "why do you do what you do?"', in Robert Sheppard, *Far Language: Poetics and Linguistically Innovative Poetry 1978-1997* (Exeter: Stride Publications, 1999), pp. 54-55 (p. 54). Further references to this edition are given after quotations in the text.

the titles derive from notes on the verso of contact prints and, in one case, an army Christmas card sent from Hugh Lopus Alway to his sister, my great aunt, Gina, during the First World War.[44]

In the section included in *Floating Capital*, the discontinuities that occur are also part of how the poem ethically attempts to link to the unlinkable narratives of colonial history:

Budhists Temple

A figure was leaning against the wall, owl eyes of the death-sport flickering at her fists, affording a view of the jumping scene. Did you suspect, stiffening in your pose, how might that blur of moving flesh have appeared on your face? Buffalo Bill stabbed by seductress, the death on London pavements. I turn the handle and the cards begin to flick, recapturing the Garden of Eden, the flies, mosquitoes and the heat.[45]

These evocative sentences function quite differently to the 'new sentence', generating a kind of ghostly narrativity, despite the discontinuities. In contrast to a poem like *Daylight Robbery*, which is readable as a response to a contemporary experience of society and culture, 'Mesopotamia' appears to derive meaning from the absent context of the historical images that were used in its production. In making links with the unlinkable, we are offered images of moments and events lost in time and space – ancient frescoes, Buffalo Bill, London pavements and a metonymical garden of Eden, full of insects and heat. We are also introduced here to a device that Sheppard developed later in *Empty Diaries* (1998) – the use of female narrators 'each one of whom "knows" she is narrated by a man'[46] in the sentence 'You step behind my eyes and enter the tunnel of her gaze'.[47] This section also contains a phrase which became the title of a 'strand' ('History of Sensation') in the complex architectural network of Sheppard's major work *Complete*

[44] Robert Sheppard, *The Flashlight Sonata* (Exeter: Stride, 1993), p. 51.

[45] Robert Sheppard, 'from "Mesopotamia"', in Clarke and Sheppard, *Floating Capital*, p. 102.

[46] Robert Sheppard, *Empty Diaries* (Exeter: Stride, 1998), back cover note.

[47] Sheppard, 'from "Mesopotamia"', p. 102.

Twentieth Century Blues (2008): 'no, that was somebody trying to locate the morning – my chest covered with flies – a history of sensation on the streets.'[48] This powerful conjunction of embodied experience with the narrative of history is emblematic of the overall thematic trajectory of Sheppard's work over the subsequent twenty years.

Sheppard's convening of spaces to develop a collective discourse of poetics, alongside his creative practice, was decisive in developing the poetics of Linguistically Innovative Poetry. The poetry discussed here represents an inventive and challenging alternative to the official verse culture of the 80s and 90s, and a sustained political critique of the Thatcher era, rooted in a shared set of practices emphasising the power of language in condensed, yet fragmentary, forms to de-familiarise perceptions and inaugurate new visions of reality, whilst, in Sheppard's case in particular, engaging with what I have called elsewhere the nightmare intersection of history, ethics and desire. The legacy of Linguistically Innovative Poetry is considerable, with many of the writers associated with it continuing to be active as its critical reception has developed. As Linguistically Innovative Poetry has matured and broadened out from its origins, the overarching term 'linguistically innovative' has been shortened to simply 'innovative', although it has been revived recently in the subtitle of the anthology *Out of Everywhere 2: Linguistically Innovative Poetry by Women in North America and the UK* (2015), itself a sequel to an anthology edited by Maggie O'Sullivan in 1996.[49] To the extent that this body of work now has an academic journal devoted to it in the form of the *Journal of British and Irish Innovative Poetry*, co-founded by Sheppard and myself in 2009, it may now also face a new challenge to resist academic institutionalisation. Sheppard's ongoing work as poet, critic, editor, educator, and blogger – and his continued commitment to a collectively unfolding poetics – nevertheless continues to offer challenges to conservative modes of poetic production and reception by drawing on this complex history of radical poetic practice.

---

[48] Ibid.

[49] *Out of Everywhere: Linguistically Innovative Poetry by Women in North America & the UK* (London: Reality Street Editions, 1996).

BIBLIOGRAPHY

Andrews, Bruce, 'Transatlantic', in *Floating Capital: New Poets from London*, ed. by Adrian Clarke and Robert Sheppard (Elmwood, CT: Potes and Poets Press Inc, 1991), pp. i-v

Clarke, Adrian and Sheppard, Robert, 'Afterword', in *Floating Capital: New Poets from London*, ed. by Adrian Clarke and Robert Sheppard (Elmwood, CT: Potes and Poets Press Inc, 1991), pp. 121-125

Clarke, Adrian, 'Listening to the Differences', in Adrian Clarke, *Millennial Shades & Three Papers* (London: Writers Forum, 1998)

Duncan, Andrew, '"Pulse strings out beat of intermittent presence": Robert Sheppard, *Daylight Robbery*' (Stride, 1990); *Floating Capital: New Poets from London*; edited by Adrian Clarke and Robert Sheppard (Potes & Poets Press, 1991), in *fragmente*, 4 (Autumn/Winter 1991), 91-97

Lyotard, Jean-François, *The Differend: Phrases in Dispute*, trans. by Georges Van Den Abbeele (Minneapolis, MN: University of Minnesota Press, 1988)

Pound, Ezra, *ABC of Reading* (London: Faber and Faber, 1973)

Sheppard, Robert, 'Beyond Revival', *Pages 49-56* (January 1988), 49-51

—— *Empty Diaries* (Exeter: Stride, 1998)

—— 'from *Daylight Robbery*', in *Floating Capital: New Poets from London*, ed. by Adrian Clarke and Robert Sheppard (Elmwood, CT: Potes and Poets Press Inc, 1991), pp. 105-107

—— 'from "Mesopotamia"', in *Floating Capital: New Poets from London*, ed. by Adrian Clarke and Robert Sheppard (Elmwood, CT: Potes and Poets Press Inc, 1991), p. 102

—— 'Linking the Unlinkable: an answer to the question "why do you do what you do?"', in Robert Sheppard, *Far Language: Poetics and Linguistically Innovative Poetry 1978-1997* (Exeter: Stride Publications, 1999), pp. 54-55.

—— 'Prescript', *Pages 1-8* (July 1987), 1-2

——*The Flashlight Sonata* (Exeter: Stride, 1993)

—— *The Poetry of Saying: British Poetry and its Discontents, 1950-2000* (Liverpool: Liverpool University Press, 2005)

Silliman, Ron, *The New Sentence* (New York, NY: Roof, 1987)

Unfinish: The Politics of Literary Experiment in Robert Sheppard

Nikolai Duffy

Throughout Robert Sheppard's poetry and criticism there is an unerring engagement with the politics of literary experiment, together with the wider aesthetic sense that such a politics may well be in fact one of the primary functions of experimental poetry. Such writing challenges received notions of what poetry might be, of course, but on a broader scale, it challenges the ways in which narratives – all narratives – are put together. This is no small feat. Words weigh, and weigh heavy; language grounds and guarantees, even when it risks the opposite, which is to say that language also, therefore, encloses. The trick is to speak in a language that hesitates, that 'lightens' meaning, suspends its weight.

In a short essay on Jacques Derrida's sense of *différance*, Jean-Luc Nancy terms this aesthetic strategy the 'lightening of meaning'. It refers, Nancy writes in somewhat enigmatic prose, to the 'knowledge of a condition of possibility that gives nothing to know'.[1] Nancy goes on to suggest that, in such a situation, 'meaning lightens itself [...] *as meaning*, at the cutting edge of its appeal and its repeated demand for meaning'.[2] Nancy's point is that politically-engaged writing must destabilise thematisation in favour of a kind of quivering openness, or what Emmanuel Levinas terms the 'meanwhile' or *l'entretemps* and which Gerald Bruns describes as 'the interval between neither and nor (neither one nor the other) – not a present, not a moment or an instant, but a pause, a setting of time to one side, a spacing of time'.[3]

In the context of these frameworks, my argument in this chapter is that Robert Sheppard's poetry and criticism aims towards a disturbance of common principles (of grammar, of existence, of the political), and that this disturbance produces what we might term a lightening of meaning. As I read it, Sheppard's work is about disrupting language, rethinking it, changing its shape, redrawing it in the present and

---

[1] Jean-Luc Nancy, 'Elliptical Sense', trans. by Peter Connor, in *Derrida: A Critical Reader*, ed. by David Wood (Oxford: Blackwell, 1992), pp. 36-51 (p. 41).

[2] Ibid., p. 42.

[3] Gerald Bruns, *Maurice Blanchot: The Refusal of Philosophy* (Baltimore, MD and London: Johns Hopkins University Press, 1997), p. 19.

arriving at a sense – hard to express – of gaps and inconsistencies. For instance, the first stanza of 'Living Daylights' begins with 'Whitewashed thought flashing articulations those / transparencies / in the daylight skating / on / nobody's dream' before the syntax spirals downwards, into 'synaesthesia' and a voice speaking in a 'frozen world'.[4] Throughout the poem inconsistent phrasing, unexpected line breaks, and a lack of punctuation open up the possibility of multiple readings. The poem appears specifically to invite this plural engagement, allowing different readings to co-exist both on the page and in the mind. Take for example the following lines from the poem's final stanza:

> Logopoeia world in a stolen
> book
> its nodes glisten identity
> which
> is speech wind
> which is voice image
> which street flaked
> out
> puking guts audible
> pool of blood above
> the visible morality of the low
> life –
> invisible from the helicopter's mirage (p. 37)

The pull towards multiple readings is announced at the outset of this stanza with the use of the term 'logopoeia' and its direct invocation of one of the three pillars of Ezra Pound's notion of how to read poetry. As Pound puts it, logopoeia is:

> 'the dance of the intellect among words,' that is to say, it employs words not only for their direct meaning, but it takes count in a special way of habits of usage, of the context we expect to find with the word, its usual concomitants, of its

---

[4] Robert Sheppard, *History or Sleep: Selected Poems* (Bristol: Shearsman Books, 2015), p. 33. Quotations from Sheppard's poems are taken from *History or Sleep* alone unless otherwise indicated. Further references to this edition are given after quotations in the text.

known acceptances, and of ironical play.[5]

For Pound, logopoeia leads to phanopoeia ('a casting of images upon the visual imagination', which is to say, what Pound also terms 'imagism') and melopoeia ('wherein the words are charged, over and above their plain meaning, with some musical property, which directs the bearing or trend of that meaning').[6] In Sheppard's poem, the play of words, phrases and lines constantly pushes at the limits of signification. '[I]ts nodes glisten identity' may refer to the 'book' in the previous line, or it may refer to 'logopoeia', or it may well refer to both 'book' and 'logopoeia'. Either way, the identity that glistens is more than one thing: images and metaphors are layered one on top of the other: it is 'speech wind', 'voice image', even possibly a 'street flaked / out' that is 'puking guts'. This gut vomit may be audible, or there may be a 'pool of blood' audible 'above' the retching. Equally, does the low possess a 'visible morality' that opens out into 'life', or are we meant to assume that 'low-life' breaks convention and has a moral core 'invisible' to the authoritarian gaze of the 'helicopter' that only criminalises dissent and despondency? And does mirage call back, as a kind of failed anagram that can be half seen but not heard, to the 'image' of the sixth line that names the structural procedure of the stanza as a whole? Is an image a mirage, a word 'charged, over and above [its] plain meaning, with some musical property, which directs the bearing or trend of that meaning'?[7]

However the stanza is read, the point is that in 'Living Daylights', as elsewhere across Sheppard's oeuvre more broadly, each line spills into the next, casting light and shadow simultaneously. Yet more interesting than simply being an example of a reframing of Poundian modernism into postmodern multiplicity and the infinite play of competing meanings, in Sheppard, each multiple strand or layer actually opens the poem towards what might be termed 'unreading'. Experiencing a poem like 'Living Daylights' is not so much about trying to stitch various phrases and images together, as it is about letting those units of text stand as they are, teetering between potential and dismantlement. It is not necessarily an easy space for a reader to occupy, but it is an important one; it is about resisting the pull towards thematisation and

[5] Ezra Pound, 'How to Read,' in *Literary Essays of Ezra Pound*, ed. by T. S. Eliot (London: Faber and Faber, 1954), pp. 50-40 (p. 25).

[6] Ibid.

[7] Ibid.

closure, and it is about establishing a poetics that begins to engage, in a direct and foundational way, with the political.

In the short essay from 1988, 'The Education of Desire', Sheppard names such writing 'revolutionary'. It is a form of radical praxis, Sheppard argues, because it seeks to resist the superficial and commodified language and form of advertising that Sheppard claims is parroted by prize-winning poetry:

> If you think of all the things that are said to make poetry what it is – things like rhythm, rhyme, alliteration, etc – then you will today find them on any list of tricks used by advertising agencies in making adverts.[8]

Such poetry, Sheppard argues, 'sells not a product [...] but a moral ("What survives of us is love")' (p. 28). In opposition to this, '[t]he writer who wants to do something different has to write in new ways' (p. 28). As a result:

> The poetry may seem strange. It may be difficult to understand.
> There may seem to be bits of it missing. There may be problems in putting all its parts together; things may not seem to follow on.
> It may be difficult to see who's speaking.
> It may seem as though there should be a story there, but there isn't.
>
> (p. 28)

Crucially, Sheppard goes on to add that such difficulties are not the kind that 'can be solved with the dictionary or encyclopaedia' but that 'stop the process of reading, or upset your reading habits' (p. 28). Elsewhere Sheppard describes such a practice as 'the disruption of the authority of the sentence by the micro-judgements of the phrase' (p. 28). It is not simply a question of learning to read 'difficult' poetry so as to be able to piece it back together; in Sheppard's terms, such a reading would simply arrive back at the simplified conclusions of advertising by way of a

---

[8] Sheppard, 'The Education of Desire', in *Far Language: Poetics and Linguistically Innovative Poetry 1978-1997* (Devon: Stride Publications, 1999), p. 28. Further references to this edition are given after quotations in the text.

convoluted path. The task, rather, is to read – or 'unread' – in such a way as the writer writes: 'independently of the controls of our society,' that privileges easily digestible message and the maintenance of bottom lines, favouring instead a committed attention to a 'few disconnected words' that may or may not make 'a new combination' (p. 29). 'This,' Sheppard adds, 'is part of the positive, revolutionary function of this writing,' what Sheppard terms 'the education of desire' because '[t]o change the wants and desires of the people of the world would be the beginning of a revolution of sorts' (p. 30).

In Sheppard's work, such a sense of radical praxis owes something to the influence of Russian Formalism. Indeed, the flow and work of a poem like 'Living Daylights' owes much to Viktor Shklovsky's essay 'Art as Device' and the importance of poetry, or 'formed speech', to the prevention of 'over-automitisation' which causes an individual to 'function as though by formula'.[9] As Shklovsky expands, 'In studying poetic speech in its phonetic and lexical structure as well as in its characteristic distribution of words and in the characteristic thought structures compounded from the words, we find everywhere the artistic trademark – that is, we find material obviously created to remove the automatism of perception; the author's purpose is to create the vision which results from that deautomatized perception.'[10] Sheppard says as much himself in *The Meaning of Form in Contemporary Innovative Poetry*, writing that he has:

> always concurred […] with the Russian Formalists, in the definition of defamiliarisation offered by Shklovsky, that 'the technique of art is to make objects 'unfamiliar', to 'make forms difficult', where the former relies upon the latter for the purpose of 'impart(ing) the sensation of things as they are perceived'.[11]

In an interview with Christopher Madden, Sheppard argues that, in order to be successful, the process of de-automotisation or defamiliari-

[9] *Viktor Shklovsky: A Reader*, ed. and trans. by Alexandra Berlina (London: Bloomsbury, 2017), p. 16. Sheppard himself quotes this aspect of Shklovsky's work in the 'Introduction' to *The Poetry of Saying: British Poetry and its Discontents, 1950-2000* (Liverpool: Liverpool University Press, 2005), pp. 4-5. Further references to this edition are given after quotations in the text.

[10] Ibid., p. 19

[11] Robert Sheppard, *The Meaning of Form in Contemporary Innovative Poetry* (London: Palgrave, 2016), p. 3.

sation 'must involve some necessary recognition of the object treated, estranged, distanced, transformed'.[12] This is the double bind of radical praxis: in order to challenge the processes of automotisation it is necessary to engage with the terms and structures that perpetuate it. The risk is that any attempted contestation will simply reinscribe the terms of hegemony and standardisation. This is why Sheppard writes in the final chapter of *The Meaning of Form* that 'it is easier to talk politics [...] than to interrogate form'.[13] As Derrida illustratively comments, 'as soon as there is inscription there is necessarily selection and, as a consequence, deletion, censorship, exclusion.'[14] This is why poetic form must be both formed and reformed in the same instant.

It is what Sheppard describes as 'the politics and poetics of "creative linkage"', or what he goes on to describe as 'a matter of accelerated forms of *montage*' (*The Poetry of Saying*, p. 3).[15] The aim, Sheppard explains, quoting Jacques Rancière, 'involves organising a clash, presenting the strangeness of the familiar, in order to reveal a different order of measurement that is only uncovered by the violence of a conflict.'[16] It is important to bear in mind that for Sheppard such a different order is about technique rather than statement. Technique, 'the collision and conflict of creative linkage,' opens up the possibility of imagining and living in the world in new, more fluid or open ways.

In his important 2005 study, *The Poetry of Saying: British Poetry and Its Discontents, 1950-2000*, Sheppard outlines the ways in which linguistically innovative poetry has three levels: the technical, the social and political, and the ethical. As he summarises in the 'Introduction' of that work, for Sheppard:

1. The technical concerns 'techniques of indeterminacy and discontinuity, of collage and creative linkage, of poetic artifice and defamiliarisation';

---

[12] '*The Wolf* Interview: Robert Sheppard', *The Wolf*, 29 (Winter 2013), 59-68 (p. 60).

[13] Sheppard, *The Meaning of Form in Contemporary Innovative Poetry* (London: Palgrave, 2016), p. 213.

[14] Jacques Derrida, *D'Ailleurs, Derrida*, dir. by Safaa Fathy (New York, NY: First Run/Icarus Films, 1999) <https://www.youtube.com/watch?v=JMQDUrQ6ctM&t=0s&index=19&list=WL> [accessed 26 March 2018].

[15] See also Robert Sheppard, *When Bad Times Made for Good Poetry: Episodes in the History of the Poetics of Innovation* (Exeter: Shearsman Books, 2011), p. 141.

[16] Jacques Rancière, *The Future of the Image* (London and New York, NY: Verso, 2007), p. 51; quoted in Sheppard, *When Bad Times*, p. 141.

2.   the social and political concerns 'a reading of the necessary dialogic nature of all utterance',

3.   and the ethical 'extends from the first two levels into an understanding of the varieties of openness to the other implied by the techniques and social orientation of the work.' (p. 1)

Arguably it is this latter level that occupies critical primacy in Sheppard's work. 'Varieties of openness to the other' plays out in various ways: from the sense of a poem as dialogue (on the most basic level, for example, many of Sheppard's poems are 'for' other poets, artists, and thinkers), to a constant documentation of and engagement with social and political error, much of Sheppard's poetry is concerned with creating 'a new space for thinking and feeling' that foregrounds what Sheppard terms 'unfinish'.

Sheppard's 2009 collection *Warrant Error*, playing on and responding to the so-called 'war on terror', provides a good illustration of what is at stake here. Each of the sonnets of this collection exhibits compression at the levels of both form and semantics, and much is left for the reader to fathom and/or finish. Take, for example, the sonnet 'Afghanistan':

Night vision green flecked with sparks
And clouds of vectoral vapour pouring across
Sun-baked gravel where a human head severe
And severed scarved in crackling plastic.[17]

There is a clear narrative here in which the violence of the imagery conveys the poem's own political position, but it is also a poem whose discourse, while noun-heavy, lacks connectives. Words are layered, often by alliteration, but they are also left in a kind of suspense. Although it may well be the case, it is not incontrovertibly clear, for instance, that the 'severe' 'human head' is itself 'severed', or whether the verb picks up and plays with the prevalence of violence that resulted from the invasion of Afghanistan. In many ways, deciding on a specific reading is beside the point. The poem's form and structure work to push the closure of definitive statements into the margins.

In this context, 'unfinish' is related to a fairly common sense of an open field poetics developed from Charles Olson onwards, but it is also

---

[17] Robert Sheppard, *Warrant Error* (Exeter: Shearsman Books, 2009), p. 106.

rooted in Sheppard's understanding of Levinas's notion of the openness of 'saying'. For Levinas, saying is a form of language that is 'an ethical openness to the other'.[18] It is, in other words, a form of language that doesn't close itself off, that refuses to be 'reduced to a fixed identity or synchronised presence'.[19] As Sheppard writes, '[s]aying is the call of, the call to, the other, the fact of the need and obligation to respond to, and become responsible for, the other' (p. 12). The difficulty is that, in order for saying to appear, to become active, it must become said, which is to say, bounded, thematised, closed off. In relation to this, Sheppard quotes Robert Eaglestone:

> It is impossible to say the saying because at the moment of saying it becomes the said, betrayed by the concrete language which is the language of ontology. The saying, which is unthematizable, impossible to delimit, becomes limited, thematised, said.[20]

This is why Sheppard favours the term 'unfinish'. It denotes a perpetually incomplete present, what Derrida would term the temporality of *l'avenir* or to come. An ethically-grounded politics, Derrida argues, issues a promise to the future, 'a promise that risks and must always risk being perverted into a threat'.[21] For Derrida, the common manifestation of so-called democracy is little more than a form of governance, of political administration and decision-making. Derrida's invocation of the 'not yet', however, or what Sheppard calls 'unfinish', relocates democracy – and the political more generally – away from administration towards the *promise* of its *idea*. To think the idea of a democracy to come is to remember the promise of the Enlightenment yet to be fulfilled, which is to say, no doubt somewhat simply, emancipation for all, which would

---

[18] Emmanuel Levinas and Richard Kearney, 'Dialogue with Emmanuel Levinas', in *Face to Face with Levinas*, ed. by Richard A. Coen (Albany, NY: State University of New York Press, 1986), pp. 13-44 (p. 29).

[19] Emmanuel Levinas, 'Ethics of the Infinite', in *States of Mind: Dialogues with Contemporary Thinkers on the European Mind*, ed. by Richard Kearney (Manchester: Manchester University Press, 1995), pp. 177-99 (p. 194).

[20] Robert Eaglestone, *Ethical Criticism: Reading After Levinas* (Edinburgh: Edinburgh University Press, 1997), p. 147; quoted in Sheppard, *The Poetry of Saying*, p. 12.

[21] Jacques Derrida, 'Autoimmunity: Real and Symbolic Suicides—A Dialogue with Jacques Derrida', in *Philosophy in a Time of Terror: Dialogues with Jürgen Habermas and Jacques Derrida*, ed. by Giovanna Borradori (Chicago, IL and London: The University of Chicago Press, 2003), pp. 85-136 (p. 120).

mean for everyone. It is also, therefore, to remember the injunction of this promise, to welcome it, and by so doing to attend to the task of trying – and failing – to bring it into the present. The critical point is that the non-arrival of the promise of democracy decentres political structures and foundations precisely because it inscribes a hiatus, an element of uncertainty or 'unfinish' that destabilises the authority of each and every political system. Derrida's point is that in order for the political to remain not only faithful to this specifically ethical responsibility of the future, but also to make it politically active, the political can never possess, neither today nor tomorrow, a pre-given programme or course of action. 'Democracy to come' fails, but this failure is necessary: failure reignites the need to try again. In rather reduced terms, Derrida's point is that it is necessary to decide, but that it is also necessary to critique, that we simultaneously perform both tasks, and that we do so without authority, from the displacement and dispossession of the time of *l'avenir*, or in Sheppard's parlance, the 'unfinish'.

As Sheppard puts it in interview, '"unfinish" has turned into an ethical-formal amalgam',[22] a way of leaving things open even while 'Immensity's blade rushes the wind and / grieves a full deck of bad luck' (p. 112). Or as Sheppard notes, quoting Jill Robbins: 'We should not take for granted that we know what we mean by the saying.'[23] 'Writing as saying,' Sheppard continues, 'is ethical, processual, interhuman, dialogic in Bakhtin's sense. Writing as said is ontological and fixed, even violent; a closure of the other, monologic in Bakhtin's terms' (p. 13). Sheppard's frame of reference here is broad and eclectic and this critical breadth mirrors the broad development of his poetics over the years. As the term 'unfinish' foregrounds, it is a poetics that strives to be always more than itself: sometimes difficult, in-turned, and yet always recognisable and engaged with the various worlds around it. It also often mimes a double discourse between lines, a space of doubling more often than not constructed by a rhythm, syntax, and line-break that complicates where one phrase ends and another begins. This complication aims to be the point of saying in Sheppard's poetry, the impossible but necessary dual space of ethical consideration and political decision.

---

[22] '*The Wolf* Interview: Robert Sheppard', p. 61.

[23] Robert Sheppard, 'Robert Sheppard: The Poetry of Saying: The Point of Poetry: Ethics, Dialogue and Form' <http://robertsheppard.blogspot.co.uk/2015/09/robert-sheppard-poetry-of-saying-point.html> [accessed 28 March 2017].

In Sheppard, such an ethico-political notion of 'unfinish' also finds a formal corollary in Sheppard's indebtedness to jazz, particularly to a free jazz structure that encompasses a central melody that is constantly being opened up to digression, deviation, and re-patterning. For instance, in 'Round Midnight', written as a tribute to Theolonious Monk, a 'jagged chord' is pricked with 'stray notes' that 'flesh an illusion', everything in counter-balance, just as the poem figures the pianist's hands being mirrored by a 'ghost's hands', 'a left / knuckling his right, exactly' (p. 9). The comma before 'exactly' is vital to the pitch of the poem: it spaces the line, but it also draws opposites together, and with great precision. In this respect, even in its shifts and folds, the syncopation and disrupted phrasing of 'Round Midnight' is into a coherent weave. It performs what Gertrude Stein describes as 'keeping two times going at once'.[24] A strand begins, shifts, moves off, before being reclaimed by the same recognisable melody, quietly insistent. Sheppard knows there is risk with such an aesthetic, but he also knows poetry has the potential to open up into something more generous and far-reaching when it runs this risk. As the ending of 'Round Midnight' has it:

> if one played a sharp where the other
> played a flat
> we might witness chaos – or invention. (p. 9)

It might be worth hearing the Latin etymology of invention in the final word of this poem in the sense that the poem does not end on the possibility of some epiphanic discovery but rather that experimentation and improvisation might lead to more casual or colloquial observances and ways of thinking: *invenire*, to come upon. Invention here is imbued with all the potential and freedom of happenstance, things that may well be desired, but which cannot be planned or willed into existence. In this context, invention is about being open to what happens, to being responsive. Of course, there is nothing simple about such openness. It is infinitely demanding, and takes place in an infinite present. Crucially, the linguistic evocation of such a mode of being is about expression rather than illustration.

This double-time technique is evident across much of Sheppard's work to the extent that it might legitimately be considered one of the abiding features of his poetic. It is often conceptualised via the figure of

---

[24] Gertrude Stein, *Lectures in America* (New York, NY: Random House, 1935), p. 180.

the 'twin'. In an early poem, 'Returns', Sheppard plays on a constantly shifting sense of doubleness, partly through the image of a 'twin rainbow' but also through the shifting ground of the poem's own meta-narrative:

> When I'm with you
> I think about the poem. When I'm
> writing I'm thinking of you
> as palpable as memory, somewhere
> the other side of sense. (p. 11)

All the while 'an idiot paperboy' shifts in and out of the poem. Here doubleness is about the arbitrary nature of 'discriminations' and how all such classifications themselves teeter on a 'knife-edge'. There is always more than one way of reading things. This is also one of the reasons why Sheppard privileges the notion of the poem being a dialogue, between poem and reader, but also between language and sociality more broadly. Following Vološinov, Sheppard writes how '[t]here is no escape from this process of dialogue' (p. 7). 'A word is a bridge thrown between myself and another,' Sheppard quotes Vološinov, '*Word is a two-sided act... As word, it is precisely the product of the reciprocal relationship between speaker and listener, addresser and addressee.*'[25] And as Sheppard continues, '[e]ven thinking, or inner speech, is conceived as a dialogue with the world' (p. 7).

Sheppard's 'Twin Poem' makes this dialogic or doubling aesthetic even more explicit, picking up as it does on the 'twin rainbows' from 'Returns' and relocating it into the folds of 'Twin Poem's' rhetoric that begins 'A gloss between the lines / Identical to ours' before quickly shifting to 'Fragmentary pauses and shifts / Carried into the mind make credible things' (p. 17). Such 'credible things', however, are as elusive and intangible as 'light shimmering in the heat'. This is a poetic landscape in flux, in which things do not happen as they appear, and vice versa. Nothing quite meshes to the extent that 'twinning' is not so much about identicality or even a looser sense of similarity, but rather adjacency. 'There cannot be a poetry of pure saying,' Sheppard writes, 'the saying must exist in the said, as ghost to its host.'[26]

---

[25] Valentin Vološinov, *Marxism and the Philosophy of Language*, trans. by Ladislav Matejka and I. R. Titunik (Cambridge, MA: Harvard University Press, 1986), p. 86; quoted in Sheppard, *The Poetry of Saying*, p. 7.

[26] Sheppard, 'Robert Sheppard: The Poetry of Saying: The Point of Poetry: Ethics,

In other words, this is a poetry about contiguity rather than equivalence. Equivalence is a closed field. Rather than necessarily illuminating the world, contiguity caters for doubt: as a relation between terms it makes no totalising claim. In *Being Singular Plural*, Nancy develops this sense of contiguity, arguing that contiguity establishes a discrete chain of singularities which are non-continuous with one another. 'From one singular to another,' Nancy writes, 'there is contiguity but not continuity. There is proximity, but only to the extent that extreme closeness emphasises the distancing it opens up.'[27]

Sheppard's more immediate points of context are the legacies of British modernism of the late 1960s and early 1970s, that is more commonly referred to under the umbrella term of the British Poetry Revival, and that developed into the London Sub Voicive reading series that ran from 1978-2000. Building on this tradition, for Sheppard a committed poem has repeatedly been one that shows that the world can be reconfigured. This is a technical question, but it is also political and ethical. In many of Sheppard's poems, the real and the imagined happen alongside each other, never quite blending, but never quite separating either, a 'roaring plea for possession and release, / An open verdict', or as the opening of the second stanza of 'Twin Poem' has it:

The executions become routine
But they are four hundred years too late
And in the wrong poem. (p. 17)

Sheppard's great poem, 'Internal Exile' develops this poetic further. Beginning with an epigraph from Julia Kristeva about how 'writing is impossible without some form of exile', Sheppard constructs a sense of counter-narrative and counter-form across three parts. In a series of declarative statements, the first part moves at speed 'from germ-warm subterranean wind into / Business having just been, or about to be' to the 'learned' posture of 'Holding language in suspicion' via a series of sentences, each 'a variation of the next' (pp. 28-29). The predominant use of enjambment in this first section lends a variegated texture to

---

Dialogue and Form' <http://robertsheppard.blogspot.com/search?q=host&updated-max=2016-06-13T08:00:00%2B01:00&max-results=20&start=3&by-date=false> [accessed 11 February 2019].

[27] Jean-Luc Nancy, *Being Singular Plural*, trans. by. Robert D. Richardson and Anne E. O'Byrne (Stanford, CA: Stanford University Press, 2000), p. 5.

the poem in which lexical and grammatical connections are at once connected and elided. It is a poem at home in the elsewhere.

This is a point emphasised by the one word sentence that begins the second section, 'Counterpoint', where the word fits the theme. Yet it is also emphasised by the sudden shift from lineated verse to prose, language and detail piling up into a series of statements at once connected and disconnected, until 'Counterpoint contradicted'. The poem both exposes and revels in the slide of noun and meaning from one thing to another, articulated by the sentence 'If you can see your assassin, he becomes your executioner', but dramatised more broadly by the pervasive layering of statement upon statement and the way language, on a very literal level, saturates the page and disrupts both taxonomy and nomenclature. 'What / began as art,' the third and final section states, 'was repeated years later / As a political act.' Or as the ending of the poem asks, 'Is this a model / Of the world that does not exist, straining / For a new referent?' (p. 32).

Tim Woods has suggested that 'Internal Exile' is 'a hearing of the internal dissensions within language. [Sheppard] openly exposes the manner in which language disrupts fixed social relations, and this language of disruption becomes an ethical critique.'[28] For Woods, dissension and disruption constitute the force, drive, and urgency of the poem precisely because he sees it as enacting what Sheppard terms a 'poetics of saying'. It is in the linguistic and formal 'counterpointing' that 'saying' or 'open discourse' becomes possible. Such writing is always a political act, but it is a politics of first principles and foundations. It is about how we construct the world from the ground up, or how any form of resistance or change necessitates a re-shifting of the ground before anything else. In the words of 'Internal Exile': 'Now / The writing's nearly over the work / Withdraws' (p. 32).

Such a politics of a poetics is also frequently apparent in the syntax of Sheppard's poetry. In the above three lines from 'Internal Exile' the almost-but-not-quite iambic pentameter of the middle line emblematises the ways in which the poem plays with foundational structures and rhythms. The line break between 'now' and 'the' makes the missing iamb in that middle line difficult to hear, or more to the point, it covers over that gap, at least aurally. In this respect, the poem enacts the semblance of order and the elision of gaps in order

---

[28] Tim Woods, 'Memory and Ethics in Contemporary Poetry', *English: A Journal of the English Association*, 49.194 (Summer 2000), 155-65 (p. 158).

to emphasise the precise opposite: that the ground is unstable and inconsistent, and that all systems should begin from the perspective of exile and errancy. This is a position articulated by the line break. It can be read but not heard, this inconstancy mirroring the very ethical dimension underpinning Sheppard's sense of a committed poetry.

In relation to this, there is also a formal loose connection between Sheppard's use of the line break and Rosmarie Waldrop's early work in which the object in one line becomes the subject in the subsequent line. As Waldrop puts it, in her second full-length collection, *The Road is Everywhere or, Stop this Body*, she attempts to:

> push at
>
> THE BOUNDARIES OF THE SENTENCES,
>
> sliding them together by letting the object of one sentence flip over into being the subject of the next.[29]

Waldrop achieves this by complicating the distinction between subject and object. As Waldrop puts it, 'I worked on making the object of one phrase flip over into being the subject of the next phrase without being repeated.'[30] For example:

> weightless inside a density
> about to burn
> the air
> won't take the imprint we
> talk
> doubles the frequencies
> brought up short[31]

---

[29] Rosmarie Waldrop, *Ceci n'est pas Keith, Ceci n'est pas Rosmarie* (Providence, RI: Burning Deck, 2002), p. 83. I discuss this aspect of Waldrop's writing in more detail in *Relative Strangeness: Reading Rosmarie Waldrop* (Bristol: Shearsman, 2013), pp. 83-88.

[30] Rosmarie Waldrop, 'Thinking of Follows,' *Dissonance (if you are interested)* (Tuscaloosa, AL: Alabama University Press, 2005), p. 209.

[31] Rosmarie Waldrop, *The Road is Everywhere or, Stop This Body* (Columbia, MI: Open Places, 1978), p. 13.

For Bruce Andrews, Waldrop's procedure here generates a series of displacements which chart 'a parallel between 2 senses of traffic: *the movement (of vehicles or pedestrians) through an area or along a route and the information or signals transmitted over a communication system: messages.*' As a result, Andrews continues, 'we find content doubled, folded back into the constructed spaces of the page – first, revealing and articulating an experience of motion (and of mind / heart / memory / body / dream in motion through everyday traffic): second, doing the same for an experience of speech / words / meanings / writing as this second perspective actively unfolds from a transcription and embodiment of the first.'[32] Where traditional notions of verse (derived from the Latin *versus*, 'verse' denotes a line or a row, in particular a line of writing) figure the linear form as the turning of one line into the beginning of another, Waldrop's emphasis on both the doubling and the blurring of subject and object resituates this 'turning' from a 'turning toward' to a 'turning away'.[33] In Sheppard's work this turn is perhaps most evident in the sequence of sonnets, *Warrant Error*, for the simple reason that the sequence plays on arguably the sonnet's most intrinsic formal feature, the volta. Each of these sonnets cycles and recycles around the discourse and events of the 'war on terror' but continues to insist at the same time that the world is lost and all the data 'fitful':

> You are neither inside the room nor outside. You melt
> in piny breeze from unlatched windows catching
> shadows, a hint of coffee from the cafetière
>
> Consultant to this enterprise, you de-contract from history,
> decapitated consciousness: the eyes the ears
> the brain collecting fitful data still from the world
> as it's lost.[34]

The poem, just like the rise and fall of protest and power, comes and goes, both urgent and elegiac.

---

[32] Bruce Andrews, 'The Hum of Words,' in Bruce Andrews and Charles Bernstein, eds, *The L=A=N=G=U=A=G=E Book* (Carbondale and Edwardsville, IL: Southern Illinois University Press, 1984), p. 277.

[33] The *Oxford English Dictionary* defines 'verse' as '[a] succession of words arranged according to natural or recognised rules of prosody and forming a complete metrical line; one of the lines of a poem or piece of versification'.

[34] Sheppard, *Warrant Error*, p. 47.

The aim of such a doubling form is to maintain two contradictory impulses in the poem at the same time. It manages to maintain this simultaneity largely because, while the absence of punctuation combined with the uncertainty of the syntactical relation interrupts narrative, it also at the same time propels one line into the next. In this sense, each phrase streams into the next to the extent that it is far from clear where one phrase ends and another begins. As Waldrop comments of the sequence in interview:

> [t]he object of one sentence is always also the subject of the next, so that there is no complete sentence, but each poem as a whole becomes one continuous, strangely shifting, ungrammatical sentence.[35]

It might not be pushing things too far to read 'ungrammatical' in the above quotation along the same lines as Sheppard's notion of 'unfinish'. For both Sheppard and Waldrop, the point of interplay and doubling has less to do with trying to reconstruct a specific and/or credible textual reading as it does with finding a method of writing that multiplies possible readings such that what comes into focus is both a formal and semantic ambiguity.

In Sheppard, the effect of such line breaks is two-fold: it creates a poetic often premised on speed (Sheppard's performances of his poems accentuate this idea), and, from the perspective of a poetry of saying, it complicates the relation of the pieces to the whole. For instance, the poem 'A Voice Without' appears to push towards the articulation of something concrete or definitive about the notion of 'saying' but, in that very process, constantly runs into the difficulty of stopping, standing still, finding its bearings:

> To say and not say at
> the same time, or
>
> at a different time to not
> say and yet say –
>
> eversaying, yes-
> saying, gainsaying,

[35] Joan Retallack and Rosmarie Waldrop, 'A Conversation with Rosmarie Waldrop', *Contemporary Literature*, 40.3 (Autumn 1999), 329-77 (p. 339).

truthsaying, lying,
neversaying so that it
closes into what has been
said; to say that I
am not saying, to not
say that I am not

saying, or at a
different time to say that

has been said, but *this*
will never be said (p. 94)

Here Sheppard plays on the Levinasian imperative not to enfold the saying into the said, and he does so by attempting to find a form and grammar that, in Lyn Hejinian's apposite phrase, rejects closure.[36] The poem does so by constructing a paradoxical discourse that constantly hovers, doubles back, and multiplies itself. One of the effects of the use of paradox as method, of course, is that the poem never stays still, constantly sliding into homonyms, approximations, and opposites. Yet the poem also underscores such a method through its almost total reliance on an abstracted discourse. This is a grammatical poem with an ethical aim. It wants to have 'arrived without arriving / at what has been,' to have 'left / without leaving what is known'. The problem is that, in the very attempt to articulate this proposition, the poem says as much, which is to say, it turns 'saying' into what has been said. The closing lines of the poem disappear 'into the unknown / which is left behind, as / never before, said.' The final word, the final full-stop, is the poem's unavoidable failure, the point to which it had been heading all along, a concrete example of what Wittgenstein calls 'imponderable evidence'.[37] The poetry of saying fails, but because it does so, it does not finish, but demands to be tried again. Throughout *Berlin Bursts* Sheppard repeatedly exaggerates such a failure by placing this poem in a sequence of other poems from which it can never be neatly separated.

The fact that each poem responds in kind to the others around it emphasises the incompletion of the singular lyric. Indeed, such an effect

---

[36] See Lyn Hejinian, 'The Rejection of Closure' <https://www.poetryfoundation.org/articles/69401/the-rejection-of-closure> [accessed 24 March 2018].

[37] Ludwig Wittgenstein, *Philosophical Investigations* (Oxford: Blackwell, 2009), p. 237.

is forcefully but also tragi-comically presented simply through the titles of the poems in the sequence, and their invocation of one another: 'Voices Over', 'Another Poem', 'Yet Another Poem', and 'Not Another Poem'.

At the end of *The Meaning of Form*, Sheppard writes:

> The critical function of art is born in the instant its form de-forms and re-forms in front of us, in our forming activities [...] Political formally investigative poetry will both say and not say, modified by formal resistance and interruption.[38]

In Sheppard's later poems the attempt to stage a poetry of saying becomes explicitly staged around notions of mourning, a place where resistance and elegy and the human come together. As these lines from 'Later Words on Human Unfinish' have it:

> a veiled world
> playing out singularities,
> complexities. As it
>
> darkens
> you're drained by the glow
> from the single lamp. (p. 124)

In the poem 'Gravity Be My Friend', this morphs into a state of more active defiance:

> I step
>
> from unwounded poise, as crystal light
> bursts once more in the street, printing strips
>
> that I peel from the surface of the world
> with every newly-minted tread. (p. 128)

'Fragmentary resistance to Total Society,' Sheppard writes in an essay on Adrian Clarke. 'Fragmentary guerrilla operations within language. The discourse of the state (statement) is rejected for the phrase [...] The issue is linkage, not slippage,' or what Sheppard goes on to term 'a swerved

---

[38] Sheppard, *The Meaning of Form*, p. 236.

reading.'[39]

In her important essay, 'Reflections on War,' Simone Weil wrote how:

> [o]ur great adversary remains the apparatus – the bureaucracy, the police, the military. Not the one facing us across the frontier of the battle lines, which is not so much our enemy as our brothers' enemy, but the one that calls itself our protector and makes us its slaves. No matter what the circumstances, the worst betrayal will always be to subordinate ourselves to this apparatus and to trample underfoot, in its service, all human values in ourselves and in others.[40]

Or as Hannah Arendt put it:

> [t]he greater the bureaucratization of public life, the greater will be the attraction of violence. In a fully developed bureaucracy there is nobody left with whom one could argue, to whom one could present grievances, on whom the pressures of power could be exerted. Bureaucracy is the form of government in which everybody is deprived of political freedom, of the power to act; for the rule by Nobody is not no-rule, and where all are equally powerless we have a tyranny without a tyrant.[41]

Sheppard understands and writes about the pervasive dangers of bureaucracy. And he attempts to counter it with the development of a poetics that stresses how any discourse of resistance must be at once technical, social, and ethical. In this regard, Sheppard's poetics favours rapidity over plod, the enumeration of quick gestures in a stultified age. This is not the 'empty performance' of literary experimentation for experimentalism's sake, but an attempt 'to be proximate to, to face alterity as distance, and be implored to *answer*' (p. 16). Across both his criticism and his poetry, Sheppard's writing is part jazz, part reimagining, and one of its great values is its refusal to accept things as they stand. It is a poetics of playful seriousness that wishes to remain open, unread, unfinish[ed].

---

[39] Sheppard, 'Colossal Fragments: The Work of Adrian Clarke,' in *Far Language*, pp. 47-48.

[40] Simone Weil, 'Reflections on War', *Politics* (February 1945), pp. 51-56 (p. 55).

[41] Hannah Arendt, *On Violence* (San Diego, CA: Harcourt Publishers, 1970), p. 18.

'Flashlights Around A Subjectivity': Melting Borders and Robert Sheppard's *The Flashlight Sonata*

Alison Mark

I first met Robert Sheppard in 1990, when I was studying for an MA in Modern English Literature at Birkbeck, University of London. The first module was on poetry, and one of the suggested assessment exercises was an interview with a poet. Robert was teaching at a college in Surrey with a friend of mine, and the introduction was made. It was to be a significant meeting for me, as he introduced me then to the work of Veronica Forrest-Thomson, on whose oeuvre I wrote my PhD thesis, which became the book *Veronica Forrest-Thomson and Language Poetry*. Robert subsequently came to do a very successful reading at Birkbeck, and later I wrote the article which appears here, originally a review essay on *The Flashlight Sonata*, for *First Offense* 9 (1994).

*

Published originally in 1993 as a stand-alone title, Robert Sheppard's *The Flashlight Sonata*, signalled the poetics and practice recognised back then and now as his territory.[1] Sheppard credits the title 'Flashlight Sonata' to a Kurt Schwitters collage *Der Verwundete Jäger* (The Wounded Hunter) (p. 51), and the figures who emerge from the narratives of these poems are some of the walking wounded of the twentieth century, from the soldiers and civilians in First World War Mesopotamia, through the Second World War 'Schräge Musik', and the disaffected denizens of the Blackstock Road in the 1980s to the 'deleted Utopia' of the Coda. But who is the hunter, and who the hunted? My own instantaneous associations, unarrested naturalisations – those instantaneous synaptic connections of the imagination – produced the hound of heaven and Herne the hunter; and then I recalled some lines from an earlier work by Sheppard, 'The Cannibal Club: A Novella':

---

[1] Robert Sheppard, *The Flashlight Sonata* (Exeter: Stride, 1993).

A sensualist lacking mind, in a world recoiling from the eye:
Flashlights around a subjectivity. The answers are not in heaven,
but at the tips of the fingers, when the topology of the cranium
is explored and its possessor is exposed as an Abortionist or as
a catamite. He removes his helmet and the familiar, atheistical
horns rise on his head.[2]

In his efforts to arrest the reader's process of naturalisation and
control the reception of his work he has created his own network of
connections, and my use of the word synaptic is not just metaphorical:
Sheppard's fast reading pace in performance, faster than the mind
can 'make sense of' – like that of Tom Raworth – seems designed to
institute new connections at an almost neurological level. Textually
there is also an attempt to actually shift the reader's perceptions, as
Sheppard confirmed in interview, 'to change consciousness, an aim I
share with Allen Fisher'[3] by the fragmentation and reconstitution of
that text, through the use of indeterminacy and discontinuity. What
power and possibility poetry has lies in this, that it is only through
language that we can change consciousness.

Though 'The Cannibal Club', says Sheppard in 'Poetic Sequencing
and the New' is not 'part of *Twentieth Century Blues*' – rather a 'related
text' – he also says of the larger project, of which *The Flashlight Sonata*
does form a part, 'its own borders melt'.[4] And melting borders,
fragments of perception juxtaposed and intercut with shreds of speech
and narrative are characteristic of his work, both aesthetically and
politically amounting to 'a strategic argument of forms, rather than
a rhetoric of process'.[5] The limitations of a politics of fragmentation
and uncertainty are obvious; those of a poetics rather less so, but
the fetishisation of fragmentation and indeterminacy in modernism
going-on postmodernism has accompanied an increasingly enmeshed

---

[2] Adrian Clarke and Steven Pereira, eds, *Angel Exhaust*, 7 (Summer 1987), p. 10.

[3] Alison Mark, *An Interview with Robert Sheppard* (unpublished, 1990), p. 1.

[4] Robert Sheppard, 'Poetic Sequencing and the New', in *Complete Twentieth Century Blues*, pp. 82-86 (p. 82). Although this essay was written with the (then newly published) Stride edition of *The Flashlight Sonata* to hand, for the ease of today's reader all references to Sheppard's poems are taken from the later *Complete Twentieth Century Blues* and follow quotations in the text.

[5] Barrett Watten, 'Social Formalism', in *North Dakota Quarterly* (Fall 1987), quoted in 'Poetic Sequencing and the New', p. 84.

relationship – often less a marriage than a *folie de deux* – with theory.

'The relation of theory to practice is uncertain' Sheppard claims in his introduction to his 1993 publication *net/(k)not-works(s)*; and in *The Flashlight Sonata* I see the relationship of theory to practice as less an effect of the uncertainty principle than of elements of chaos theory. I suspect that, like Allen Fisher, whose influence he has acknowledged (and to whom *net/(k)not-works(s)* is dedicated) Sheppard has more than a passing interest in the kinds of patterns generated by self-similarity – known in physics and mathematics as fractals – and their potential exploration in language. This is a predictable development from his interest in the aleatory, 'Letter from the Blackstock Road', written in November 1985, was assembled by cutting up the text of 'preformed language elements'[6] into six sheets and using a set of dice to determine the order:

> I wrote it by picking up on something Miles Davis does … He records everything from the moment he steps into the studio and then edits down. So I decided to write freely – it was all quite wonderful and frenetic – all done in a couple of weeks – and then arrange the sentences in a stochastic way whereby a random process of perception is submitted to a selection process.[7]

Jazz, blues, experimental music are clearly a powerful influence on Sheppard's work. However, unlike John Cage, who has a similar method of composition, Sheppard allowed himself to intervene in the process, including editing words, though not perceptions, to retain some of the oddities of fortuitous juxtaposition. Just as he then saw no reason to restrict himself strictly to the laws of chance, while utilising its potential for creating such juxtapositions, he clearly sees no reason why a poem – which can easily be modified in performance by the inclusion or exclusion of particular elements – should not also be mutable as a text. One of the most economical of poets, Sheppard reworks and reconfigures the different elements of his work – both verse and prose poems and theoretical statements – throughout his published material.

---

[6] Mark, *An Interview*, p. 3.

[7] Steve Pereira, 'An Interview with Robert Sheppard', *Angel Exhaust*, 7 (Summer 1987), 17-24 (p. 24).

In its original publication, *The Flashlight Sonata* formed part – though one hesitates to use such a conventional description of an element of Sheppard's project – of the works '"numbered", rather than named, *Twentieth Century Blues*' (p. 82). He 'wanted a "title" that would allow [him] to order, reorder and disorder a text or a series of strands of text in sequences, something that could be read in a number of ways'. Here he specifically mentions Fisher's *Place* as 'an inspiration', and goes on to delineate a possible index of, a possible 'reading' of *Twentieth Century Blues*, where elements of *The Flashlight Sonata* make their appearance in more than one location in the weave of the work as a whole. Some version of these proposals were later realised in *Complete Twentieth Century Blues*, which contains in a single volume all the poems Sheppard wrote 'between December 1989 and 2000' ('Introductory Note'). *The Flashlight Sonata* retains its place as part six in the original conception, but as with all the other texts assembled there its place in the sequence is disrupted by Sheppard's alternative ordering of the reading experience via multiple 'strands'. Thus, where 'Mesopotamia', the first poem in *The Flashlight Sonata*, is read in isolation from the evolving canon of Sheppard's work in its original 1993 incarnation, its inclusion in *Complete Twentieth Century Blues* brings it into structural (and potentially thematic) proximity with 'In an Unknown Tongue' from 'The End of the Twentieth Century: A Text for Readers and Writers' some three hundred pages later. This example is the book's most extreme sequential leap, certainly in the sense of the publication's linear trajectory; but the poems between them that the author has sequenced in the strand entitled 'Histories of Sensation' offer alternative routes through the text that potentially reveal yet more extreme juxtapositions and aesthetic tendencies.

Sheppard's declared programme for *Twentieth Century Blues* is that by a process of 'working on, rather than ... working out', the writing 'should constitute ... an aesthetic journey, fracturing into the new, a poetic changing by stages and confronting the changing world. There are no jumps, just swift transitions' (p. 85). However, one interesting aspect of Sheppard's resistance to the bifurcation of literature into creative text and theory is precisely his use of photographic and cinematic techniques, like the fast – or jump – cut, and montage so that the art becomes theory, rather than an exposition of it, or vice versa. This occurs most sustainedly in the interfering intercut narratives of 'Letter' (but is also clearly operating in 'Mesopotamia'). In 'Letter' there is self-consciously direct reference to such technique: 'I write for a journal that exposes the Government's secret war plans. Cut to an unused bookshelf whose stillness is supposed to be sinister' (p. 48), and 'To teach everything through one book: the façade of a house sliced away, its interior vulnerably framed for the impossible artifice of a November afternoon' (p. 51).

In 'Mesopotamia' the technique combines cinema and still photography, and as in the recuperated photographs behind Pamela Golden's paintings, 'invites the viewer to question the projection of generic and stereotypical meanings onto images'[8] by subverting within the text of the pieces the captions of the apparently quotidian snapshots from the desert war. From the specified time and location, 'Mesopotamia. Xmas 1917' with a 'click of his fingers, the suture of the sky splits in a flash-blink' (p. 18) and dissolves time and place into 'a history of sensation on the streets' (p. 19); fragmentary, heterogeneous, beautiful: 'The monochrome world flickers / At the emotive edge of our fake memories' ('The Materialization of Soap 1947') (p. 37). Fake because inevitably reconfigured for consonance with our current mentalities: the unconscious knows nothing of time; the grammar of desire is only articulated through the present tense.

And it is still with desire that Sheppard's work deals: desire, that much fetishised term – and with 'poetry as the education of desire', as he described it first in a piece of that title in 1988 (reissued in *net/ (k)not-work(s)*) and which he has since reiterated in other texts, as in the 'Afterword' to *Floating Capital*: 'Reading this work can be an education of activated desire, not its neutralisation by means of a passive recognition.'[9] The active participation by the reader in the construction of texts, particularly of linguistic experimentation, almost goes without saying. Not so this use of desire.

There are two senses in which desire is used: the first sense is the Lacanian, of desire as the very thing itself, without an object; want in an existential sense. (It is lack or desire that constitutes the subject at the time of its insertion into the order of language, and is central to a Lacanian account of subjectivity.) The second interpretation of desire that Sheppard uses is that of desire for an object: for love, for fulfilment;

---

[8] Pamela Golden, catalogue of exhibition at Gimpel Fils, London, November 1993.

[9] Adrian Clarke and Robert Sheppard, 'Afterword', in *Floating Capital: New Poets from London*, ed. by Adrian Clarke and Robert Sheppard (Elmwood, CT: Potes and Poets Press, 1991), pp. 121-25 (p. 124).

desire in its transitive sense. The problem with Sheppard's attempt to form a 'possible and necessary connection'[10] between the two senses of desire (though of course there is one, a causative rather than the connective relationship he suggests) is that it elides the important – especially for poetry – idea that the objects of want are endless metonymic replacements for the 'lost object' which is the origin of desire in the sense of lack. Desire only exists because of the primordial failure of satisfaction, which thereafter becomes an impossibility. And it is this understanding of desire, that it is by definition insatiable, that gives me problems with his avowed intention that 'reading the poem will be an education of activated desire, not a passive recognition, fulfilment or killing of desire'. Any 'fulfilment' of desire can only be a hallucinatory wish-fulfilment. Desire, either the lack, or the metonymic substitutes that are our wants, our desires for which proceed from it, is incapable of fulfilment – and only killed off by death, which is in every sense desire's end. And death, frequently violent, stalks these poems of the end of the twentieth century. (Sheppard says 'The End of the 20th Century, after Beuys' installation, is 'a rejected title for this sequencing' he now calls *Complete Twentieth Century Blues*.[11])

Poetic language – language at its outer limits – depends upon metonymic displacement. Part of the metonymic chain in 'Letter' is formed by the sense of narrative, or rather narratives, running through the poem, intertwined; references to Robin Hood and Guy Fawkes who perform a curious doppelganger act as revolutionary figures: 'Guy Fawkes doubles for Robin Hood in the slide-rule mythical poem' (p. 51), together with the stories of George and Pearl, Robyn, amongst others. But these are interrupted narratives, frustrating the reader's desire for a 'coherent' story, as there are missing elements, unexplained switches of syntax. The poem treads a narrow line between the stimulating, energising effect of the unexpected, and the ever possible negative aspect of the disjointed poem; that it just mimes informational chaos – as Sheppard himself remarked in interview, like channel hopping with a remote control device for the TV. To achieve the former without falling into the frustrating trap of the latter it is vital that the effect is not simply discontinuous, indeterminate, but that new connections must be activated, made not by the poet this time – though through his

---

[10] Sheppard, 'Re-Working the Work: Pausing for Breath', in *net/(k)not-works(s)*; also published in *First Offense* 6, pp. 55-58.

[11] Sheppard, 'Poetic Sequencing', p. 82.

provision – but by the reader.

One of his most interesting techniques to induce this is Sheppard's habit of embedding self-referential statements and poetics in the body of the poem; signpostings he says are as much for himself as for the reader, and also a part of his fusing of poetry and theory: 'You can't evaluate a perception until the process is over' (p. 38); 'the sensuous images of aesthetic liberation are not alone capable of politicising the reader' (p. 38); and most plangently: 'Why do I write the things I never say, think the things I never write?' (p. 49). As he says: 'Use of certain words makes certain philosophy' (p. 53).

This is a poem, and a collection, which looks to the future and to the future of poetry: 'This is not a letter from the basement, from the rough basement of a condemned house, etc. ... In the last analysis, it is an act of faith' (p. 50). (An element reworked with less metaphorical force in the later 'Internal Exile 3': 'She's living in the rough / Basement of a condemned house' [p. 46].) Faith is an odd sort of notion for anyone with postmodern tendencies, considering the postmodern rejection of narratives of redemption or transcendence. An act of faith from 'Utopia the F-111s taking off to defend the council house they have sold you'? (p. 59). Perhaps Sheppard's use of the expression 'act of faith' is ironic, but I don't think so – at least not entirely ironic. Ambivalence is, of course, one of the conditions of possibility of existence, let alone production, in the closing years of the twentieth century. Which brings me to the profoundly ambivalent 'Coda' to the collection:

> Utopia the memory the sensation the sonata
> Utopia the island the continent the landscape
> [...]
> Utopia the fish in the sky
> Utopia the scribbled abbreviation we always forget
> Utopia the throat microphone clammed to the wall
> Utopia the exhaustion the symbol the sign
> [...]
> Utopia the stocking-top
> Utopia the fragment the collected poems
> [...]
> Utopia the cuts Utopia the healing
> Utopia the stab of each new line
> Utopia the metaphor the box of tricks Utopia the can of worms (p. 59)

This fragmented quotation cannot do justice to the affective power of the accumulating sentences that pass sentence on the social (dis)order they describe. Sheppard's memorialisation of the 1980s deservedly has a sharper edge than those of the two 'World Wars': 'Utopia deleted Utopia' (p. 62).

To write, especially extended poems, at a time when Sheppard believes 'there really is no audience [for poetry] except the other people who are writing and occasional other people' is itself an act of faith in the future of poetry and its relevance.[12] (And of course, especially with the development and flourishing of creative writing courses at the Universities in the years since then, there have been many significant changes in that audience – too many to pursue here.) Perhaps it was Sheppard's hope that through the particulars of place and time, the Blackstock Road November 1985, Mesopotamia 1917, the dystopian end of the twentieth century displayed in this fragmented fashion we and subsequently 'all the others who will read this in time, those who lack the slender situation we have in common' (p. 49) can proceed from the particular to the universal. Like experience itself the text is left open, its fragmentary, discontinuous nature unified by the perception of the subject: writer/reader. Sheppard offers intermittent perceptions: flashlights around subjectivities, not grand narratives; a 'strategic disintegration' as Lee Harwood in the foreword quotes him as saying, rather than 'a tactical regrouping', that odd military euphemism for a retreat':

> I don't sell out to nobody. I know only how I make it. I know
> only my medium, of which I partake, to what end I know not.
> I have envisaged a new form of poetic composition. I build my
> time. (p. 56)

*

---

[12] Mark, *An Interview*, p. 7.

Coda

Very little of substance has changed in this version of the article from the original text and argument; I have no wish to be anachronistic, and this is very much of its particular time. However, I am interested – more than interested – to read Robert's epigraph to *Complete Twentieth Century Blues*, from Coetzee's *Waiting for the Barbarians*, itself a citation of Cavafy's great poem. In the spirit of this, and having lost my original final sentence of the review to contemporary relevance ('I look forward to seeing what slouches from the wreckage'), I will paraphrase from Cavafy's final couplet in multiple homage: devilish useful, these barbarians.

> Και τώρα τι θα γένουμε χωρίς βαρβάρους.
> Οι άνθρωποι αυτοί ήσαν μια κάποια λύσις

~~Mad About the Boy:~~
Robert Sheppard and ~~Orpheus~~

Christopher Madden

The association of music and poetry through the myth of Orpheus and Eurydice shows no sign of retreat, even in literary traditions in which lyric and the Orphic inheritance are placed under erasure. This applies with particular force to Robert Sheppard, who is not readily identified with the lyric tradition and whose poetry does not immediately call to mind lyricism as such. Sheppard's approach to linguistic innovation and opposition to lyric subjectivity in writing that, to all intents and purposes continues the legacies of the Movement Orthodoxy, are particularly relevant when we consider his interest in the figure of Orpheus. This 'interest' requires clarification: Sheppard is not queerly mad about the boy, if we are to take unreservedly on board the gender relations established in Noël Coward's song, to which this chapter's title alludes. In this respect, 'madness' is not so much the everyday pathology of the lover as the implication of Orpheus as the regime of desire controlling the poet's aesthetic tendencies. Crucially, the figure himself (a sort of irresistible nemesis?) stalks *The Drop* (2016), to which I will return at the end of this chapter. One line reads: 'Orpheus / Entuning the moist cavities / Of immediate lust haunting / Desire.'[1] The speaker is ambiguous about the desire in question: is 'immediate lust' generative of Orpheus' journey to recover Eurydice, or is Orpheus' song what condemns him to eternity without the object of his desire? Arguably, 'Entuning the moist cavities' links reproductive organs to the throat that sings. Neither offer release from the tormenting aporia of the Orphic condition.

The trouble with Orpheus lies with his powers of invocation. No sooner does he suggest poetry and song than he sets a metonymic trail off towards lyric and genre. This is a problem for the literary critic as much as for the poet resistant to the Orphic inheritance. Nowhere is this more forcefully evident than in relation to the singing voice as a figure for all poetry, a determination that continues to pose manifold problems for the status of lyric as a genre. For the purposes of this chapter I will address generic instability by way of Northrop Frye, a key figure in

---

[1] Robert Sheppard, *The Drop* (Hunstanton: Oystercatcher Press, 2016), unpaginated.

New Criticism, which has laboured to demonstrate ontologically the ways in which epic, drama, and lyric – and much later on novel and poem – condition reading (as a cognitive process) and interpretation (as a hermeneutic outcome). At the same time as a generic framework is established in a given text, differentiation within the speaking subject (voice is never singular) allows it to gesture towards other discursive, and indeed musical, modes. Distinctions between genre and mode are especially complicated by vague ascriptions of lyricism to texts or genres that, in the classical sense, may otherwise be defined as epic or drama. Generic classification shifts literally within and between the lines as one type of literary production manifests traits more identified with another, such that the singing or speaking voice destabilises what lyric can be taken to mean while notionally anchored in the Orphic. Robert Hampson, in 'Bill Griffiths and the Old English Lyric', highlights transitions between lyric and dramatic monologue in the fragment *Wulf and Eadwacher* as precisely the kind of destabilising feature that makes genre elusive.[2] Likewise, something is deemed lyrical even in the absence of a speaking or singing voice. It is a claim made almost to the point of banality in musical circles, where the Orphic is more obviously inaugurated by descendants of the lyre, namely when a sense of line closely resembles the human voice at it most fluent by means of instruments lacking semantic and syntactic powers in the linguistic sense. Clearly, renouncing Orpheus means to place 'song' itself in quotation marks, to undo the abiding figural relationship between song and poetry, and so ultimately to liberate line from lyre. An imposing contradiction resides within the concept of the Orphic insofar as figuring Orpheus and the implications of myth for the condition of poetry is enacted against the protagonist's dismemberment. The figure of Orpheus, in other words, rests paradoxically on irreversible disfigurement, even if the Orphic is invoked to symbolise the precise opposite.

Texts thematically and self-reflexively concerned with voice as a discursive operation provoke thoughts about the ways in which writing dynamically occupies page space. This is all the more marked – in the sense, that is, of a text bearing the formal marks or, perhaps more precisely still, the imprint of voice – with dialogically multi-voiced texts like *The Anti-Orpheus: A Notebook* (2004). The comparison thereby made with the shape and design of the poem brings us full circle to

---

[2] Robert Hampson, 'Bill Griffiths and the Old English Lyric', in *The Salt Companion to Bill Griffiths*, ed. by William Rowe (Cambridge: Salt, 2007), pp. 72-87.

lineation. If lyric is inseparable from voice, then any account of lineation cannot be separated from a poet's rejection or otherwise of the Orphic inheritance. Thus, it is to *The Anti-Orpheus*, neither poem nor narrative non-fiction but 'legally speaking' a text of poetics, that this chapter will turn in order to trace the implications of lyric for Sheppard's practice of lineation. A close reading of *The Anti-Orpheus* will be conducted by way of three theoretical interlocutors: Northrop Frye's 'Theory of Genres' from *Anatomy of Criticism* and Jacques Derrida's 'The Law of Genre' will assist this chapter's account of genre as it relates to Sheppard's poetics while Maurice Blanchot's 'The Gaze of Orpheus', which foregrounds an interpretation of 'the work' in relation to Orpheus' desire and his descent into the Underworld, will highlight which version of Orpheus threads through Sheppard's poetics precisely as a process (in the ancient sense) of making. The chapter will then move on to surveying examples of lineation across Sheppard's *oeuvre*, turning its attention to *Warrant Error* (2009), *Hymns to the God in which my Typewriter Believes* (2006), and *The Drop*. These texts have been chosen for their approaches to line and page space; crucially, they also refer to Orpheus, rejecting and distorting the inheritance in question in texts designated (legally and generically) as 'poetry'.

From a paratext on its title page we learn that *The Anti-Orpheus* was delivered in 2001 as a paper to the Edge Hill College of Higher Education Research Forum and then to the *Talks* series curated by Robert Hampson at Birkbeck College, University of London. This highlights the formal origins of the text proper, its institutional credibility, anticipated validation by the academic author's peers (not to mention the implied censor of the peer-review process), and through its dating indicates its chronological situation within an evolving corpus. Some if not all of these factors invariably influenced the formation, thematic and non-thematic scope, design, and shape of the text, which deliberately militate against conventions of linearity, continuity, and determinacy habitually enforced by academic argumentation.

While the paratext influences reading before the text proper, the epigraph offers its own distinct version of framing, as is the case with the quotation from Adrian Clarke on the text's first page: '*a speculative / art pausing for breath*' (italics original).[3] Epigraphs occupy an ambiguous relation to the text of which they are otherwise made to embody the

---

[3] Robert Sheppard, *The Anti-Orpheus: A Notebook* (Exeter: Shearsman, 2004), p. 5. Further references to this edition are given after quotations in the text.

spirit, and this is no less the case here. The reader can reasonably infer that the 'speculative art' referred to is poetics, but they are only likely to reach that conclusion if they possess knowledge of Sheppard's work as a poet-critic. Certainly, as a mode of inconclusive thought constantly in search of vindication, reaching for its bounds while exceeding limits, speculation could be characterised as a hyperventilating force. By contrast, lyricism's demand for a continuous, uninterrupted line and its tendency towards so-called sweet harmony, means it can hardly be claimed to brook the straining desperation of breathlessness. The text's oppositionality – the constitutive sense in which that 'anti' relates to the 'Orpheus' – is thereby set vividly in motion for the reader, even if any interpretation of a text that flogs continuity and linearity is unlikely to follow a steady course. Thus, the text shifts immediately from one genre to another before it has barely established itself, as in the transition from Clarke to the author quoting themselves: '"What might a poem be, elsed?' asks Pearl in the last *Empty Diary*. "To be poetry & not poetre at th same tiyme," Khalid Hakim replies' (p. 5). Hakim could equally be referring to the text in which they have been quoted: although an identifiable genre, poetics is always something other. A quotation follows from Derek Attridge (in a section entitled '*The Limits of Poetics*') and with it another generic shift and alternative route on the reader's interpretative path. This calls us to Frye's term 'radical of presentation' and his commentary on the written word as a resolutely book-bound phenomenon: 'We have to think of the *radical* of presentation if the distinctions of acted, spoken, and written word are to mean anything in the age of the printing press' (italics original).[4] Frye draws out the derivation of radical as 'root' here, which in turn indicates origin. His use of 'radical' performs more work, however, than 'root' does alone, since 'radical' cleaves origin to the sense of making substantive distinctions: thus, categorising texts and their genres is assisted once attention is paid to their mode of delivery.

The inclusion of actual poems ('Voices Within' and 'A Voice Without'[5]) in *The Anti-Orpheus* destabilises the text's genre further still and introduces an unambiguous radical of presentation at odds with what surrounds it. Moreover, 'A Voice Without' was absorbed

---

[4] Northrop Frye, 'Theory of Genres', in *The Lyric Theory Reader: A Critical Reader*, ed. by Virginia Jackson and Yopie Prins (Baltimore, MD: Johns Hopkins University Press, 2014) pp. 30-39 (p. 31).

[5] Sheppard, *The Anti-Orpheus*, p. 15 and p. 16 respectively.

into *Berlin Bursts*, where it features in a sequence of thirteen poems that address the concept of voice and of titling poems in playfully self-reflexive, even comically ironic, ways.[6] These poems' concerns around voicing and the conventions of framing enforced by titling register differently again, though, in *The Anti-Orpheus*, which creates an altogether different context for their reception. Read retrospectively as having been cut loose from the sequence into which it was absorbed at a later date, 'A Voice Without' has an independent life in *The Anti-Orpheus*, in which discontinuity encourages a method of reading influenced by shifts in genre in ways not applicable to its appearance in *Berlin Bursts*. 'The question of how we are to classify [a novel like *Heart of Darkness*] is less important than the recognition of the fact that two different radicals of presentation exist in it', Frye contends, noting how Joseph Conrad's self-reflexive employment of a narrator results in the fact that 'the genre of the written word is being assimilated to that of the spoken one'.[7] Something of Frye's commentary on the ways in which novels by the likes of Conrad is at work in the structure of Sheppard's text and the influence of its voices on the reader's conception of genre. What makes *The Anti-Orpheus* especially amenable to the kind of reading normally undertaken for a literary text is its structural organisation (its juxtaposition of genres and modes) and the range of its signifiers (from the relatively fixed language of criticism to the constitutive ambiguities of narrative and poem). The reader finds their place, however provisional, between sectional gaps by withholding the practice of continuity and determinacy afforded by much more integrated texts. '[C]aesura – punctuating the metrics with a space for thought', as *The Anti-Orpheus* states at one point. The text's asterisks are a kind of formal corollary to the page space of a poem, and it is worth noting the page-spatial characteristics of *The Anti-Orpheus* as being akin – although, it should be stressed, obviously not identical – to the layout of more experimental and creative genres. The innovative poet responds to the call for a literary-critical-resistant poetics by harnessing layout

[6] Robert Sheppard, *Berlin Bursts* (Exeter: Shearsman, 2011), p. 31. While the rationale for making connections between poems, such as I have done here, on the basis of their semantic content or form will differ from one reader to another, I am encouraged by *Complete Twentieth Century Blues* and its invitation to trace strands through the text independently of the sequence set in place by the author or publisher. Although the sequence I have established runs with the text's set order, it is not identified as a substantive section in the ways that I contend.

[7] Frye, p. 31.

to encourage a disintegrative view – both retinal and cognitive – of writerly discourse. At least two operations are held in tension here, as Adorno explains in the opening pages of *Aesthetic Theory*:

> In artworks, the criterion of success is twofold: whether they succeed in integrating thematic strata and details into their immanent law of form and in this integration at the same time maintain what resists it and the fissures that occur in the process of integration.[8]

The reader is thus charged with writerly responsibility, not only to formulate responses but to enact powers of formulation, granting some version of integration by way of interpretation. The text's oscillating rhetorical registers not only anticipate this but encourage awareness of the fissures created by non-linear motion. In *The Anti-Orpheus*, quotations from other critics are read towards and back from Sheppard's narrative fragments, which neither exclude nor include the critical entirely and vice versa. By unsettling the course of the text's genre, which Frye's central terms posits by way of its eventual delivery to its putative audience, such undecidability ironically raises the *telos of destination*, which highlights a conception of genre that cannot be fulfilled either by its originating author or even by any reader. The destination of reading is successive not terminal.

'As soon as the word *genre* is sounded,' Derrida writes in 'The Law of Genre',

> as soon as it is heard, as soon as one attempts to conceive it, a limit is drawn. And when a limit is established, norms and interdictions are not far behind: 'Do,' 'Do not,' says 'genre,' the word *genre*, the figure, the voice, or the law of genre (emphases original).[9]

The difficulty of separating the literary critic from the poet writing critically about their work is a dominant factor in identifying the

---

[8] Theodor Adorno, *Aesthetic Theory*, ed. by Gretel Adorno and Rolf Tiedemann, new trans., ed., and with a translator's introduction by Robert Hullot-Kentor (London: Bloomsbury Academic, 2013), p. 8.

[9] Jacques Derrida, 'The Law of Genre', trans. by Avital Ronell, in *Acts of Literature*, ed. by Derek Attridge (London: Routledge, 1992), pp. 221-52 (p. 224).

type of discourse 'poetics' is taken to mean in the sense given it by Linguistically Innovative Poetry. Moreover, Sheppard's key definition of 'poetics' as a 'speculative writerly discourse', highlighting as it does the movement of discourse as opposed to the application of a certain discursive manoeuvre in pursuit of an argument, crucially enables readers to distinguish between poetics and literary criticism proper. Certainly, poetics in its Sheppardian guise is troubled by the implications of poetics generally for the 'critic-function' and its claims on the practice of the poet. Speculative writerly discourse ceases to be so when the poet themselves deploy it all too readily in the service of interpretation, in the process of making auto-analytic claims on and about their own work in ways that constrain the desire of the reader. Writing in the introduction to *Atlantic Drift: An Anthology of Poetry and Poetics* (2017), Sheppard and his co-editor James Byrne agree about the risks posed by that ideological genre, the literary manifesto: 'To our minds, actual manifestoes overstep the mark and damage the speculative nature of the discourse and replace it with the "must do" of literary orthodoxies. The "how to" of creative writing manuals is another danger to its speculative freedom.'[10] This acknowledges an ineluctable fact about not only the genre of the manifesto but of genre overall, namely a link that a given piece of writing establishes between its content and form, which it then directs towards its implied reader.[11] In terms of its dynamic model of discursivity, poetics as a linguistically innovative genre seeks to retain the emergent as a condition of its identity, a kind of becoming-creative of the thinking poet's critical faculties. Speculation is methodologically apposite for the becoming-object of creative writing. 'Methodologically-speaking', in this sense, may paradoxically entail rejection of the method in question and even the linear and continuous demands normatively imposed by a discursive operation. In this context, methodologically-speaking means to speak otherwise: '[the poet] may even, ultimately, abandon the course of

---

[10] Robert Sheppard, 'Introduction', *Atlantic Drift: An Anthology of Poetry and Poetics*, ed. by James Byrne and Robert Sheppard (Todmorden and Ormskirk: Arc Publications and Edge Hill University Press, 2017), pp. 9-14 (p. 10).

[11] In the case of the literary manifesto, the implied reader is the poet; documents like Olson's 'Projective Verse', however, have equally influenced the literary critic's understanding of modern poetics as a distinct period of literary history and aesthetic development. Thus, the text's implied reader is also the critic assimilating its precepts to the 'institution of literature' as a point of critical rather than creative reference, namely in the interpretation of actual poems.

action the poetics seems to be suggesting', Sheppard warns, quoting Jerome Rothenberg, whose belief is 'that the discourse, like the poetry, must in all events resist rigidity and closure'.[12]

Such a paradigm resists formal and discursive purity, tempts a practice of genre, in other words, that is dialogically playful rather than dialectically strategic. It therefore responds to what Derrida calls 'the law of the law of genre [...] a principle of contamination, a law of impurity, a parasitical economy'.[13] Such words as 'contamination', 'impurity', and 'parasitical' lend themselves to literary traditions in which boundaries of genre and modal conventions are transgressed. Derrida's semantic field highlights discursive operations active along the spectrum of influence – from plagiarism to intertextuality – that plagues all writers with anxiety to such an extent that a version of authorial pathology could be said to spring from enforced reliance on the already said. Might Derrida offer an irrepressibly deconstructive get-out clause here? 'In the code of set theories,' he continues, 'I would speak of a sort of participation without belonging – a taking part without being part of, without having membership in a set.'[14] An author's appropriation of prior texts does not result in a claim to the work concerned. This applies equally to the adoption of genres momentarily in a text generically determined otherwise, as in the shifts between critical utterances and fictive registers in *The Anti-Orpheus*. A quotation from Attridge or Levinas does not then radically determine the text's genre; rather, the text is radically unsettled by the voices it absorbs into its elaborate tapestry, and the reader stumbles along in vain attempts to gain a foothold in an ambulatory discourse. Thus, the law of the law of genre is instrumental when approaching the genreless genre of poetics under innovative practice in the twenty-first century, which recalibrates an ancient term by mobilising numerous discursive markers without identifying itself as either literary criticism or creative non-fiction pure and simple. Derrida:

> The trait that marks membership inevitably divides, the boundary of the set comes to form, by invagination, an internal pocket larger than the whole; and the consequences of

---

[12] Jerome Rothenberg, quoted in Sheppard, 'Introduction', p. 10.

[13] Derrida, p. 227.

[14] Derrida, p. 227.

this division and of this overflowing remain as singular as they are limitless.[15]

The identification of genre becomes a major factor in the order of reading; it is the destabilising force that applies itself to those recognisable traits within the text of poetics that then retain their distinction as parts within a disconnected whole.

As we will see once our attention turns to Blanchot's essay, one facet of the work undertaken by Orpheus translates into the domain of poetics as 'making'. This foundational conception of poetics is at the root of Sheppard's career as a poet, as Robert Hampson sketches in the present volume. Sheppard's is at odds with the kind of work Blanchot outlines in view of Orpheus. The concept of work innovative poets inaugurate by their poetic system but also, as is the case with *The Anti-Orpheus*, by a text of dialogically multi-voiced poetics, would seem to place higher reliance for 'making' on the poet. This reliance shifts to the reader, however, with writerly texts in relation to which decisions about the text's genre are formed by active reading without bestowing on the reader the power of final designation. Frye's notion of the radical of presentation as highlighting genre as a practice rooted in empirical reality is particularly relevant here. The neo-Aristotelian axis of the acted, spoken, and written word – of drama, lyric, and epic respectively – foregrounds the eventness of literature, namely the time-bound and time-sensitive encounter between the text and its reader or spectator. If the time-boundedness of the literary event is a fact of its reception in the performance of a play, the oral delivery or silent reading of a poem calls us to the time-sensitiveness involved in anticipating the other. The naming of [Emmanuel] Levinas in *The Anti-Orpheus* proves the extent to which the ethical relation is axiomatic to Sheppardian poetics. This leads to a point of objection with Frye's comments on the lyric. 'The radical of presentation in the lyric is the hypothetical form of what in religion is called the "I-Thou" relationship', he writes, although what follows this invocation of the 'I-thou' relationship, which readers of Levinas will associate with the philosopher's ethical system, heralds our departure from Frye's radical of presentation: 'The poet, so to speak, turns his back on his listeners, though he may speak for them, and though they may repeat some of his words after him.'[16]

---

[15] Derrida, pp. 227-28.

[16] Frye, p. 32.

The sense of speaking for also entails speaking through, a presumption of the listener's ontology that is a step too far for the writer of *The Poetry of Saying*. Given poetry's radical of presentation in the face-to-face encounter of a live reading or performance, the poet turning their back on the listener is an odd belief for Frye to hold. The status of the word in poetry, as Frye himself was more than aware in relation to the effect of the narrator-function in Conrad, is capable of shifting between apparently opposed radicals of presentation. From collective setting to private communion, poetry demonstrates contrasting capacities for the word within signifying practice. In the final analysis, however, the dialogic constitution of the sign in Sheppard's poetry leans ever more towards the other than Frye's image of the poet turning away would have us believe.[17]

Like the poet, Orpheus does not turn away; his refusal defines him and what follows in his wake by the name of music and poetry. Contemporary lyric practice, exemplified by Claudia Rankine's *Citizen: An American Lyric*, constitutes a turning *towards*, namely by means of the second person voice as the *locus classicus* of lyric addressability.[18] 'To my

---

[17] Another essay on *The Anti-Orpheus* might trace the text's explicit and implicit fields of reference regarding alterity. Whereas in the former words like 'other', 'another', 'otherness', 'othered', 'difference', 'us', and 'we' operate unambiguously, in the case of the latter, alterity is somewhat tangentially signposted: 'Levinas', 'hospitality', 'response', 'responsibility', 'servitude', 'witness', and so on. Such linking and linkable semantics demonstrates the openness of Sheppardian poetics to experiences and categories of difference generally; or more to the point, the poet's speculative writerly discourse is able to anticipate the other through a constitutive dependency on the reader, who, as active interpretant may offer alternatives for the text's explicit and implicit fields of reference, not to mention they may also differ on what 'explicit' and 'implicit' are taken to mean as terms.

[18] *Don't Let Me Be Lonely: An American Lyric* (2004), the volume preceding *Citizen*, also explicitly signposts its genre. Neither text conforms to the recognisable image of lyric poetry: structural fragmentation and indeed the movement from poetry to prose would seem to oppose itself to the harmonious fluency expected of the genre. While it may be a stretch to identify Rankine as a avant-garde poet, the forms she adopts show a modernist inheritance that implicitly rejects lyric practice, as indeed we find with Sheppard's *The Anti-Orpheus*, another title that bears the mark of its genre: 'A Notebook.' An exposition of the meaning of the latter phrase after the colon in the text's title is beyond the scope of this chapter. Suffice to say that the noun phrase is somewhat generically indeterminate, wavering between the object in the writer's toolkit and the sense of a working document, in relation to both of which certain generic conditions are in play. It is as if Sheppard throws the cover off a work-in-progress; not so much a genre as a genreless text in search of classification, which eventually it either fulfills, rejects, or at the least destabilises. Rankine and Sheppard are therefore unlike

mind, it is impossible to consider the lyric without fully interrogating its inherent premise of universality, its coded whiteness', Sandeep Parmar writes. 'Just as the exoticised subject is flattened into a one-dimensional stereotype,' Parmar contends, 'an absence of referentiality, of the lyric "I", is likewise an enactment of violence.'[19] Sheppard's contention that subjectivity is a linguistic operation, anchored in poetic artifice, and as such opposed to the paradigm of poetic subjectivity as the source of self-expression, would appear to be a formalist privilege for poets of colour were it not for the fact that figures like Parmar and Rankine look to form in order to historicise the lyric 'I'. For Jonathan Culler, the musicality of 'I' in lyric performance is in flight from ideology and the effects of interpellation:

> The indeterminacy of meaning in poetry provides an experience of freedom and a release from the compulsion to signify. With its apparently gratuitous chiming and rhyming, its supplemental metrical organization and uses of lineation – in short its determination by a host of sensuous factors – lyric language works against instrumental reason, prosaic efficiency, and communicative transparency, quite independently of the thematic content of particular lyrics.[20]

Once lyric practice begins to take account of sexual, racial, and gender difference, terms like 'instrumental reason', 'prosaic efficiency' and 'communicative transparency' no longer refer exclusively to the bête-noirs of the Frankfurt School but instead evoke the nightmare of

Maurice Blanchot's *The Madness of Day*, the main focus of Derrida's essay, insofar as the demand by the authorities for the protagonist to provide a *récit* on the level of its presumptive 'plot' paradoxically sustains itself through 'the mentionless mention of its genre' (Derrida, 'The Law of Genre', p. 228). For an important guide on the relation between avant-garde poetics and the politics of difference, see David Marriott's critique of Language Poetry's fetishisation of the signifier against the signified in 'Signs Taken for Signifiers: Language Writing, Fetishism and Disavowal', in *Assembling Alternatives: Reading Postmodern Poetries Transnationally*, ed. by Romana Huk (Middletown, CT: Wesleyan University Press, 2003), pp. 338-46.

[19] Sandeep Parmar, with Bhanu Kapil, 'Lyric Violence, The Nomadic Subject and the Fourth Space', in Parmar, Sandeep, with Bhanu Kapil and Nisha Ramayya, *Threads* (Leeds: Clinic, 2018), pp. 7-27 (p. 10). Marriott's 'Signs Taken For Signifiers' is a key reference in Parmar's essay.

[20] Jonathan Culler, *Theory of the Lyric* (Cambridge, MA, and London: Harvard University Press, 2015), p. 304.

right-wing bigotry and its attacks on political correctness and diversity. Admittedly, Culler's focus is not on linguistically innovative poetry but on poetry generally; nor does he claim to take account of the effects of contemporary ideology on poetic discourse. It is difficult not to relate 'indeterminacy', however, and the musical and physical implications of 'sensuous factors', to linguistic innovation. Yet how far can the principle of indeterminacy go once attention is actually paid to reversing the invisibility of particular subjects in the context of a tradition, category, and practice largely formulated by a subjugating power? This prompts reflection on the constitution of 'musicality' as such, namely the conventions by which prosody has been generically realised by poets and recognised by readers. 'I was please to see the book, some papers, new poems, in Linton Kwesi Johnson's hands,' Sheppard's speaker relates in the '*Pentimento Reggae*' section of *The Anti-Orpheus*, 'as performative testimony to the *written* act amongst "a bubblin bass / a bad bad beat". …' (p. 7; emphasis original). A different music changes the shape of language, the sensuous factors of reggae disrupting the dominance of the metropole as a signifying power.

The spectre of imperialist nostalgia and structural racism, to whose recrudescence Parmar has alerted British audiences especially, threatens to throw ideological inscription back at subjects historically and presently susceptible to heteronormative white male privilege (liberal humanism's ostensible point of reference). Rankine's and Parmar's commitment to critiquing histories of imperialism and racism past and present across their poetry and criticism also entails sensitivity to the project of subjecthood as a linguistic category and discursive operation. The trope of subjectivity in poetry is somewhat supplanted by subjecthood, the lyric 'I' interpellated at the level of performative utterance. Thus, instrumental reason is exposed as the lie promulgated by 'backlash culture' and its cynical reappropriation of the so-called common ground, which seeks to undermine the 'thematic content' – namely racial, sexual, and gender addressability – of the lyric.

As I have argued elsewhere, the horizon of lyric addressability expanded after the Holocaust in the work of Paul Celan and Nelly Sachs, in attempts to bestow on the unspeakable the facility of articulation.[21] This did not result, however, in the valorisation of an integrated and unquestioning lyric practice. If Celan and Sachs somewhat tacitly

---

[21] See Christopher Madden, 'Lyric Voice and *You*: Notes on Addressability', *The Wolf*, 33 (Spring 2016), 83-95.

exposed Adorno's famous quotation, their work converges with the latter's 'On Lyric Poetry and Society' (1957), about the confrontation between an ancient genre and late modernist historical experience. In *The Anti-Orpheus*, Adorno is Orpheus recalibrated by Marxist theory, sounding the call of critique rather than singing the lyric. As critic and poet – or, to adopt his term, 'poet-critic' – Sheppard himself returns time and again to the Frankfurt School philosopher in order to address the questions on twenty-first century aesthetics he thinks still need asking. Adorno is a key reference in the *The Meaning of Form*, but it is not the 'famous quotation' we find there but a line from *Aesthetic Theory*: 'The unresolved antagonisms of reality return in artworks as immanent problems of form.'[22] Given its abstract formulation against the other's framing of an aesthetic problem in light of what Adorno would call 'empirical reality', which by definition sets itself against the aesthetic artefact, this is just as axiomatic as the line about lyric poetry after Auschwitz, possibly more so. Certainly the quotation from *Aesthetic Theory* makes itself more amenable to questioning around aesthetics without having to disentangle itself from the rhetorical corner into which each successive, not to mention decontextualised, citation has muscled it. In this regard, 'On finding a famous quotation from Adorno and realizing it was Holocaust Memorial Day', one of the text's later sections, is as short as it is pithy:

> Verse after Auschwitz? –
> Each word blackens on the page
> I don't sing: I croak. (p. 13)

These lines are terse: the mind is thinking at high velocity, poised before the prospect of ambiguity, which appears to be foreclosed by the directness of its punctuation. The question compresses an entire critical tradition generated from the most singular provocative utterance of post-Holocaust poetics, which Adorno himself later recanted, and the hyphen gestures towards this as the question that remains open, even if what follows indicates a well-rehearsed and fully assimilated response from the speaker's quarters. Yet ambiguity creeps in: the semantic richness of 'Each word blackens on the page' at first evokes the light-deprived subject of the Holocaust but also calls to mind the fact that

---

[22] Adorno, *Aesthetic Theory*, p. 7. See also Robert Sheppard, *The Meaning of Form in Contemporary Innovative Poetry* (London: Palgrave, 2016) p. 6; p. 214.

writing cannot exist as such unless white space is literally inscribed by actual (or digital) ink. Blackening on the page is an unavoidable consequence of writing: the stain indelibly marks us. The romanticist trope of nature, inverted by history and the domination of the human over the natural, resonates alongside this fact as that which we desperately wish to erase but cannot. Sheppard could be addressing Adorno directly in the last line, across the generations and the accumulated years of appropriation and misappropriation of his statement: 'I don't sing: I croak.' This rebuke seems to be articulated not merely in view of the status of lyric poetry after Auschwitz but to the entire enterprise of voicing. The openness of the hyphen is dissolved by the colon with the force of an iron door banged shut.

Mention of Orpheus is first made in *The Anti-Orpheus* in the subsection entitled 'Signature Style: an essay', which turns its attention to a letter in which is made 'a grave accusation against another' (p. 6). Citations of Orpheus' name constitute a kind of framing that paradoxically attempts to roll back on the frame in question: 'let's not name him Orpheus yet', in the writer's allusion to the one so accused; 'the one not yet known as Orpheus has claimed authorship of work that clearly belongs to another', they go on to assert in view of the named one they cannot avoid inscribing as the source of inscription itself, 'and has effaced that origin – that author – entirely' (p. 6). Roland Barthes' 'Death of the Author' essay is invoked to account for concerns around the origin of authorship and the ineluctability of plagiarism: the author cannot undo their construction as a tissue of quotations, no matter the strength of their resistance. One phrase in particular, set apart as a single sentence paragraph, appears to link the pivotal action – second, that is, to the primary action of looking back – in the myth of Orpheus to the condition of writing as plagiarism: 'The offence is, of course, in the alleged dissembling, there's no doubt about that' (p. 6). It is impossible not to relate that 'dissembling' to the terrifying denouement of the Orpheus myth. Certainly this inference makes us rethink the propositions about voice in Barthes' infamous essay and its infinitely quotable phrase, which Sheppard's speaker cites without quotation marks: 'Yet The Pseudo-Orpheus' essay *is* a tissue of quotations, but most are acknowledged' (p. 6; emphasis original).

The letter at the beginning of the essay is not only an object within narrative – simultaneously embedded in a given scene and active within the text's signifying economy – but more crucially still suggests the sense in which addressability across all genres adheres to the postal principle of deferral and delay. For this speaker, however, the hope of reply by return is comically sent up in the closing lines by way of formal address: 'Please write soon, / Yours, *etc* . . .' This is the farcical side of irony, given the statement uttered a few sentences earlier: 'I cannot reply to this anonymous text, not simply because the reply can have no address' (p. 6). The play of the signifier is a game of futility, relations between the origin and citation of utterance akin to mail stranded in the dead letter office. Yet, some six pages later, we read from two postcards that managed to avoid that bureaucratic space of lost/failed communication:

Post

cards. The first quoted Barry MacSweeney:

At Sparty Lea the trees don't want Orpheus
to invoke any magic
they dance by themselves

The second quoted Shelley:

Language is a perpetual Orphic song

and so on (p. 12)

Splitting the word 'postcards' in two and italicising 'post' in the style of a title suggests that the speaker is putting the quoted authors and their words, which have a resonance befitting their subject, historically at arm's-length, as if to imply the position of coming after; the italicised '*and so on*' undermines Shelley's authority, even if paradoxically it makes the reader yearn to know what else the postcard (and Shelley) said. MacSweeney's distancing of the Orphic is not only self-distancing but a rethinking of organicism from Romanticism onwards, Shelley included, and the privileging of human subjectivity over nature through acts of appropriative anthropomorphism. If his inference is tantamount to a speaking-on-behalf-of, this is overwritten in a good sense by an instance of non-appropriative anthropomorphism in the tercet's third line: 'they dance by themselves' remains in the orbit of the human (objectively-speaking trees move; any other verb projects a human construct upon nature), their movement self-owned (or natural to the living organism). Orpheus prompts objects to perform at the will of his controlling song, a power lost in relation to Eurydice herself, no matter how hard he keeps trying. 'He knew better than to speak for *her*,' we learn elsewhere in the text, 'ventriloquizing her lamentation, / giving voice to that which must remain unvoiced' (p. 17; emphasis original).

Three pages later we encounter another section entitled '*Post*'. At this stage the speaker of *The Anti-Orpheus* is as brutal as they are laconic: 'Writing in ancient forms shits in the mouths of the dead' (p. 15). The act of defecation suggests a view of the literary tradition by which writers – not in the service of writing as such but in the name of the ideologies for which writing is instrumentalised – have ingested what has been given them on a plate. The consequences for the work thereby enlisted by the poet's desire for new forms and forming are no less significant for being couched in the colloquial. The image of shitting as a kind of non-ecological literary recycling shifts the ground of textuality from the already said to the saying, configured through dynamic relations in literary encounters:

> The danger lies in the possible violence against the other (the past) by making it the same (present in the present as the present). There has to be responsibility towards the past, that does not violate its otherness (that's its very power
>
>   to read *us*
>
> as though *we* were other)
> (p. 9; emphases original)

A deliberate lack of flow makes us read generically otherwise, formal argumentation dissimulated by way of unconventional use of parentheses and the mid-sentence line-break. In such instances *The Anti-Orpheus* appears to argue meta-critically for the poet and poet-critic's concept of work. The pronouns 'us' and 'we' can only ever be context-specific, not a fixed entity but conditioned by their emergence. Any presumptively homogenised collectivity is problematic. How readers encounter invocations of the collective is dependent on both the strength of their ethical response to textuality and interest in the social or communal. Pronominal use extends to genres that take the collective and not the individual as their point of reference. Thus, poetry and history are not so much in opposition but read against each other's grain:

Poetry interrupts history, musicates the 'facts',
    makes the said of hegemonic (or non-hegemonic) history
            the saying of poetry,
    which will create anew; *mutually interruptive*
    a new said of non-history
                    for only the said may bear witness. (p. 8)

The lines quoted above, which appear in the same untitled section, offer a sense of Sheppard's approach to lineation and page space in *The Anti-Orpheus*, disposition of line disrupting the text's rhetorical positionality. Argumentation demands continuity and determinacy, which Sheppard displaces through the text's literary tropes. Likewise, the preponderance of critical language in *The Anti-Orpheus* militates against the lyricism that Orphic invocation threatens. Yet, if 'Poetry interrupts history, musicates the "facts"', epic and lyric no longer exist in antagonistic generic relation but rather in one of mutual animation. The text's visual properties may appear to conduct the reader's apprehension of the literary over the critical, except that what on first contact the eye detects as elements of artifice are later recognised as technique in the service of argument as opposed to expression. Faced with negotiating the text's form to such a degree relies on the speculative approach Sheppard locates in the method of poetics, itself an enhanced echo of the concept of the writerly found throughout his work as a critic and adopted as a matter of principle in the poetry as active work for the reader.

Sheppard's rejection of the reader as a passive conduit for the already said is total and unrelenting. Thus conceived, work is both labour and revelation of 'truth', expenditure of energy in the name of the process leading towards the object in question: the artwork. P. Adams Sitney, in the afterword to the Lydia Davis translation of *The Gaze of Orpheus*, highlights the influence of Heidegger's 'The Origin of the Work of Art' on Blanchot's conception of work. 'To gain access to the work,' Heidegger argues, 'it would be necessary to remove it from all relations to something other than itself, in order to let it stand on its own for itself alone.'[23] 'Blanchot puts Heidegger under a negative sign', Sitney contends, 'for him, the masterpiece is not the product of the "passageway" from "work", as Heidegger claims, but the regrettable

[23] Martin Heidegger, 'The Origin of the Work of Art', quoted in P. Adams Sitney, 'Afterword', in *The Gaze of Orpheus and other Literary Essays*, trans. by Lydia Davis (Barrytown, NY: Station Hill Press, 1981), pp. 161-97 (p. 185).

sign of the work's disappearance.'[24] Arguably the work's disappearance is the source of its renewal and reinvention, the process by which so-called masterpieces transcend their historical moment and speak beyond it to and by means of ever increasing communities of readers. Generally speaking, work is transitive, action performed on an object or something which it then transforms. Eurydice, the 'limit of what art can attain; [...] the profoundly dark point towards which art, desire, death, and the night all seem to lead',[25] represents for Orpheus both object and objective. Already, prior to his song, poetry's presumptive metaphysical content is identified by the spatial associations invoked by it. But does this cause a split between the artwork and what Heidegger calls 'the work-being of the work'?[26] Being, as a dynamic category, corresponds to the transitivity of work. However, the possibility of separating the object from the transitive act allowing it to emerge as such seems narrow.

The identity of an object known in advance of a processual act necessary for work to come into being undergoes alteration not so much because of what work bestows on it but in light of what properties of the work it assimilates to itself. The sense in which it is bound by its finitude or physical constitution means that 'artwork' and 'work of art' are relatively redundant as terms for the object we encounter during aesthetic experience. This is to do with Blanchot's melancholy recognition of the work's disappearance, but equally in play is the notion of the aesthetic object as a compromised totality. Representative rather than all-encompassing in its relation to the work, we can no more gain access to the processual than extract from the object's form categorical meaning about its content. In this way, the work's disappearance against the scene of what the object assimilates from the work is an acknowledgement of its autonomy. Thus, the concealed nature of the processual undergoes transformation by means of the writerly text's disavowal of *authoriality*, namely by delinking the aesthetic object from its presumptive origin in the writer whose authority it is the task of reading to unveil.

'Yet Orpheus' work does not consist of securing the approach of this "point" by descending into the depths. His *work* is to bring it back into the daylight and in the daylight give it form, figure and reality'

---

[24] P. Adams Sitney, 'Afterword', p. 186.

[25] Maurice Blanchot, 'The Gaze of Orpheus', in *The Gaze of Orpheus and other Literary Essays*, trans. by Lydia Davis (Barrytown, NY: Station Hill Press, 1981), pp. 99-104 (p. 99).

[26] Heidegger, quoted in Sitney, p. 186.

(emphasis original).[27] According to Blanchot, Orpheus' work cannot be fulfilled without 'the enormous experience of the depths [...] an experience in which the work is put to the test by that enormousness – is not pursued for its own sake'.[28] In Ann Smock's translation, that initial phrase is rendered as 'the measureless experience of the deep',[29] a formulation that, unwittingly or not, situates the work closer to music, a fact later underscored by reference to the 'Orphic measure'.[30] Contrasts between Davis' and Smock's translations of that key phrase, however, call to mind an evocation of space generally on the one hand against locatable space on the other: katabasis or katabatic topography. Blanchot's mythopoeic interpretation seems to bar access to the project inaugurated by Orpheus' descent into the Underworld precisely because of the failure represented by his transgression. Arguably this is one of the inevitable effects of the magnitude of his work and the realm in which he is forced to undertake it, which in turn finds expression in language that denotes magnitude generally while failing to connote anything in particular. Little wonder, then, that faced with his task Orpheus succumbs to desire, separating both from the desire motivating the work in the first place. 'But [the] forbidden act [of looking] is precisely the one Orpheus must perform in order to take the work beyond what guarantees it, and which he can perform only by forgetting the work, carried away by a desire coming out of the night as its origin.'[31] In a section Sheppard entitles '*An Orpheus for Emmanuel Levinas*', we read that 'Orpheus attempted the purest of sayings – a saying that turned the tides to the waves of his voice – to rescue Eurydice from the realm of the said' (p. 12). The dichotomy of saying and said from *The Poetry of Saying* leans heavily on these lines, in which the said of the action yet to be inflicted on Orpheus is read back onto the myth itself, the already said literally inscribed into Sheppard's mythopoiesis as a non-originating origin: narrative fiction and interpretation combined. The work of disentangling the said from the saying moves the reader closer to a post-historical origin of the work in which the institution of

---

[27] Blanchot, 'The Gaze of Orpheus', p. 99.

[28] Blanchot, 'The Gaze of Orpheus', p. 99.

[29] Maurice Blanchot, 'Orpheus' Gaze', in *The Space of Literature*, trans., with an Introduction, by Ann Smock (Lincoln, NE and London: University of Nebraska Press, 1982), pp. 171-76 (p. 171).

[30] Blanchot, 'Orpheus' Gaze', p. 173.

[31] Blanchot, 'The Gaze of Orpheus', p. 102.

literature is both confronted and refused. Moreover, the speaker's pun on 'said' for the actual katabatic realm in question is an expression of the vitality or otherwise of myth and the lurch of received utterance towards its coffin. 'The work is everything to Orpheus, everything except that desired gaze in which the work is lost, so that it is also only in the gaze that the work can go beyond itself, unite with its origin and establish itself in impossibility.'[32] Simultaneously inclusive and exclusive; transcending and reuniting with its own horizons; possible in the sense of an action nevertheless performed, which then makes its ultimately impossible: the ripeness of Blanchot's aporias for Sheppard's *telos of destination* is confirmed by the work's misalignment from the movement of its very production.

Another constitutive contradiction of *The Anti-Orpheus* is the extent to which myth refuses to recede in literary history. No writer can renounce the continuing reverberations of myth, even if, as we find with Sheppard, they strive to tame its influence on the present and future course of creation. Blanchot, in an attempt to distinguish myth from allegory and symbol, argues that '[Myth] implies an actual *presence* between the beings of fiction and their meaning, not the relationships of signs to signified' (emphasis original).[33] Any attempt to place Orpheus under erasure is frustrated by the fact that myth operates outside textuality as such. Myth endures as a result of endless dissemination in ever newer aesthetic contexts, as in the section titled '*Fiction*' in which Sheppard invokes yet another genre by one flick of the rhetorical brush: '*Once upon a time there was a sailor, and he was in love with the most beautiful woman in the world*' (p. 7; italics original). In the absence of any governing context for its reception, the text shifts between mythopoiesis and fiction without one entirely cancelling the other. Given myth is identified by a storytelling framework and not by rhetorical markers ('Once upon a time'), the fairytale ultimately inserts itself into the generic set aligned with novelistic practice. '*But, of course,*' Sheppard's fictional narrator continues, '*this was before he had become a sailor, and she was not, at that time, regarded as beautiful. So I had better begin again*' (p. 7; italics original). Another shift occurs between this sentence and the next, this stuttered beginning of the tale – a kind of origin at war with itself. By undermining itself in this way, the

---

[32] Blanchot, 'The Gaze of Orpheus', p. 102.

[33] Maurice Blanchot, 'The Language of Fiction', in *The Work of Fire*, trans. by Charlotte Mandell (Stanford, CA: Stanford University Press, 1995), pp. 74-84 (p. 78).

text seems to introduce elements of oral transmission into textuality. It also appears to deny the origin of the work while undertaking the labour necessary for its emergence. As *The Anti-Orpheus* demonstrates, the speaker of a text of poetics is as chameleonic as the speaker of a poem or narrative text proper: 'That was the dream whose very words Orpheus woke up to, with. It seemed to him an auspicious opening for the tale. But was there more he could invent? Begin again: [...]' (p. 7). The comma in the first sentence locates the minute negotiations of narration in its search for a grammar apt enough for the process of telling. Such self-reflexive concern for its rhetorical procedures recalls the reader again to the mythopoeic basis of the telling. But could it be said in view of *The Anti-Orpheus* that the work of the author, speaker, and reader is ever complete?

Arguably the temptation to link the breakdown of the lyric to a poem's design is at its strongest when the left margin is eschewed in favour of a freer disposition of line across page space. Pierre Boulez's remarks on twentieth-century music tap into the innovative poet's unconcern for hierarchical organisation: 'Time, like pitch, has three dimensions: horizontal, vertical and diagonal; distribution proceeds similarly by points, groups and groups of groups [...] Because of this morphology, local and global structures – responsible for the form – no longer obey permanent laws.'[34] Eric Mottram quotes Boulez in *Towards Design in Poetry* (1977) to relate principles of tension and relaxation in music to comparable formal approaches in modernist and postmodern poetry.[35] Postwar aesthetic developments broke the analogical stranglehold of Orpheus by way of technical comparison. It is unsurprising, then, that Boulez's language resonates with innovative poetry in the second half of the twentieth century, even if Sheppard could hardly be identified with the classical avant-garde exemplified by the French composer and conductor. Yet liberation from the left margin in poetry is certainly akin to Boulez's analysis of the spatial relations of time and pitch in music. It is also worth noting in this regard the ways in which principles of indeterminacy and discontinuity in literary practice correlate to the destabilising effects of dissonance in music. Certainly Boulez's acceptance that the deconstruction of the musical status quo

---

[34] Pierre Boulez, *Boulez on Music Today*, trans. by Susan Bradshaw and Richard Rodney Bennett (London: Faber, 1975), p. 28.

[35] See Eric Mottram, *Towards Design in Poetry* (London: Veer / Writers Forum, 2004), p. 15.

results in the composer's refusal to obey permanent laws chimes with the credo of modern poetics since Mallarmé and Pound. Sheppard's poetry continues to register not only the implications of such modernism on contemporary innovative poetry, but more particularly still the extent to which postmodernity implicates itself in aesthetic form.

Although we should wary against providing a unified perspective of an innovative poet's practice of lineation, mainly on the proviso that the form of each poem should be interpreted on its own terms, Sheppard's *oeuvre* testifies to the signifying potential that rests at the line-break rather than at the left margin, however frequently the poem is left-justified. The credibility of this argument depends on perceptions of the line – perception, that is, of what appears to the eye and what the mind apprehends: the line is retinally and rhetorically viewed as a fact of its disposition or the poem's tendency towards the sentence as a sense-making structure (emphasising the directionality of 'towards' here). It is possible to hear the sense of spatial misalignment and the freedom offered by open field poetics in the word 'disposition'. According to Marjorie Perloff, however, poets have increasingly departed from open field's ur-text, 'Projective Verse': '[W]ho would have thought that fewer than forty years after Olson celebrated the 'LINE' as the embodiment of the breath, the signifier of the heart, the line would be perceived as a boundary, a confining border, a form of packaging?'[36] In *Warrant Error*, dispositionality is a fact of skewed lineation and resistance to ideological inscription. The text's tendency to justify at the left margin does not prevent fragmentation at the line-end, a term that requires re-evaluating in light of the following poem's dislocation of measure:

Eros
rose reso-
        lved made love unsolved into lover or l-
oser, whom-
so'er Erato emboldened head to head with death.[37]

The sonnet is re*form*ulated by means of lineation and the breakdown of

[36] Marjorie Perloff, 'After Free Verse: The New Nonlinear Poetries', quoted in Anton Vander Zee, 'Introduction', Emily Rosker and Anton Vander Zee, eds, *A Broken Thing: Poets on the Line* (Iowa City, IA: University of Iowa Press, 2011), p. 19.

[37] Robert Sheppard, *Warrant Error* (Exeter: Shearsman Books, 2009), p. 37. Further references to this edition are given after quotations in the text.

single words, the discrete retinal effects of which encourage a sense of line as a thread meandering through page space. The word 'Eros' and its permutations are essential to the music of these lines, sibilance rustling across the forward momentum of its metre. The jumble of those four letters allows the reader to perceive *jouissance* at the heart of words deemed inimical to desire itself. That Eros 'rose' conveys the quality of enlivening at the origin of the pleasure principle. Yet 'reso- / lved' and 'l- / oser' tracks the movement of a negative dialectic within the short space of a few letters, the substantive principle which this poem undermines through the hyphen and line break in the anonymous term 'whom- / so'er'.

Eros and Erato recur in the 'September 12' section of *Warrant Error* to such an extent that it is justifiable to assert that the text's ostensible historico-political focus is supplanted by the mythic. In a reversal of logic from *The Anti-Orpheus*, does history musicate myth? If this sonnet sequence puts its critique of rhetoric around the so-called War on Terror roundly in the domain of the linguistic (as we know, literally right from the book's title: *Warrant Error / War on Terror*), then the tutelary spirits of poetic invocation and desire generally cannot be separated from the text's concerns with ideology. The line 'Intervene in *err* . . . history impure terror full stop' is the first in a number of instances in which the vocal punctuation of '*err*' heralds ideology or the irruption of poetic desire through the implied intransitive verb 'to lead astray'. In 'March 10', we read 'device' in '*Erratum / for Erato*: Nobody drops into the same / device twice' (p. 27) in light of the previous stanza's apostrophic invocation, which is couched in a heightened comic self-reflexivity: 'O! Muse you wing it / for shepherds sporting iambic lambs on / the platform so enthralled by Love bo- / peeping his fluttery sonnet in Venus' softest target [...]' (p. 27). Should we read 'Sheppard' in 'shepherds', the poet and his proper name dissimulated in versions of the self writing? The undecidability of the speaker by means of the second person voice means that the yearning in that apostrophe is likely to be the anthropomorphised figure of language itself.

Reference to 'ORPHIC RESONANCE' (p. 28) in another poem moves Eros and Erato closer to the occulted figure and with it meta-critically invokes the association of music and poetry precisely in order to stress its semantic and sonic characteristics. '[T]he music of a poem – no matter if metered, syllabic, or free – depends on what the syntax is doing when the line ends',[38] James Longenbach has written, a point which seems inarguable. Moreover, his preference for the term 'line end' rather than 'line break' is rooted in the observation that, 'at the point where the line ends, syntax may or may not be broken, continuing in the next line'.[39] There are no universal rules indicating to the reader that a given amount of page space amounts to a specific duration or tempo. Sheppard's minute composition of layout therefore creates variable conditions across spoken and written radicals of presentation in ways otherwise far more encoded for the musician by a score:

> Ab-
> solute dis-incarnation   redemption refutes
>
>   the one true purity is deletion   a white
>   sheet   for the lover's face   don't look into
>   those eyes   level humanity in your selves (p. 31)

Hyphenation is as much a part of signifying economy as it is the preserve of typesetting, which would likely determine a reading of the hyphen in question as, precisely, questionable, influencing the musical parameters of its delivery. Certainly 'Ab-solute' does not require a hyphen; 'dis-incarnation' does not appear in the OED along with all other words taking 'dis' as a prefix, so may in fact pass as technical use. The same applies to the phrase 'a- / symmetric war chants' in a poem a few pages later, although the hyphenation and line-break seem to typographically present the issues of balance afflicting the subject of the sentence. The use of one hyphen influences perceptions of others such that the poet's tendency to dislocate individual words appears to have been undertaken in order to grasp matters of derivation: separated from its prefix, 'solute' takes on meaning all by itself, and we read 'dis-incarnation' likewise, as if the priority of word selection is literally to stress the negative, the extent to which language structurally posits the undoing of otherwise positive terms. Much the same can claimed in view of the phrases in the concluding assemblage. These spaced-out 'clauses' are like chords, measure assisted by the eye. A general sense of flow is counteracted by the indicative mood of 'don't look into / those

[38] James Longenbach, *The Art of the Poetic Line* (Saint Paul, MN: Graywolf Press, 2008), p. xii.

[39] Longenbach, p. xii.

eyes' and 'level humanity in your selves', the first evoking the demand at the heart of Orpheus' work while the second reaches out, albeit gnomically, to the ethical intuition of the reader. Such spacing, however minimal, disrupts terms like 'line break', 'line end', and associated ways of thinking about lineation advanced by Longenbach. For Anton Vander Zee, the latter 'too often reduces the line to a holding pen for syntax, the alterations and breakages of which seem to provide a kind of pure formal pleasure'.[40] It is with left-justified verse that a tighter relation between syntax and line holds; the sense of breakage, ending, or enjambment clearer because of the spatial polarity (beginning-end logic) harnessed from one boundary to the other. Freedom from the line is exemplified by text situated page centre or distributed across page space with no adherence to the gulley, and it is not long before release from prosodic convention becomes identified with politics. Vander Zee disputes Longenbach's formalist premise that '[L]ine has a meaningful identity only when we begin to hear its relationship to other elements in the poem'.[41] As Forrest-Thomson argued (and which Sheppard has repeatedly echoed): stick to poetic artifice. '[W]e need to attend to the sound of the social that poetry, even in its most subtle formal manoeuvres, alternately reflects and refuses', Vander Zee argues, a little too ambiguously.[42] How does the social 'sound' as such if not in language and the forms in which it is given shape and design? Imposing on the actual sounds of poetry a socio-political valence even in the absence of such qualities in the signifier on the page surely tempts bad naturalisation, and worse still, bad naturalisation of form itself.

Practical problems of reading and sense-making multiply the more page space becomes part of a poem's aesthetic practice. *Hymns to the God in which my Typewriter Believes* is notable for its freer practice of spatial layout, marking a strong departure from Sheppard's left-justified tendency. Some readers are likely to identify its distributive effects as the poet's open field moment, were it not for his ambivalence towards such work.[43] In any case, all of this is not to imply, however, that lineation

---

[40] Anton Vander Zee, 'Introduction', p. 20.

[41] Longenbach, 'The Art of the Line', p. 5; quoted in Vander Zee, 'Introduction', pp. 20-21.

[42] Vander Zee, 'Introduction', p. 21.

[43] See Robert Sheppard, 'Allen Fisher's Apocalypse Then: Between *Place* and *Gravity*: Technique and Technology', in *When Bad Times Made for Good Poetry: Episodes in the History of the Poetics of Innovation* (Exeter: Shearsman, 2011), pp. 31-54 (pp. 32-35).

is at its most complex where a poem opens up the white space of the page. But the sparseness of such poems should not be read exclusively as a visual effect alone. Not least for its invocation of the Orphic inheritance, the second poem in the 'Luscious Clusters' sequence of Part Two is a case in point:

beneath the hard bark upon

his palm from her bones he'

ll build his lyre[44]

The line-break in the middle of a word is more striking in the case of a contraction, visually and grammatically so: the separation of subject and verb here function beyond a simple enough principle of layout, namely to indicate the intervention of the speaker. The indicative future tense becomes by way of graphesis much more conditional-seeming. Moreover, the line-break at the apostrophe seems to make a mockery of a recognisable beat, one formal feature jeopardising another: visuality sabotaging scansion. The formal features and stylistic distinctions that can be claimed in view of these lines lend them an air of quotation, a quality all the more emphatic once the increasing metrical fragmentation and freer disposition of line and deployment of page space of much of the rest of 'Luscious Clusters' is taken into account. Yet the gaping white space that intervenes following 'lyre' gives the impression that their antique characteristics open up the non-signifying space of poetic invocation, in response to which the wilful reader's eye is likely to drop straight down to the page bottom:

Perform the blank mirror with your incredulous life-mask. A face moulded from muddy eyefuls of self-indication[45]

Lineation similar to this featured in the clipped sentences of the first poem's prose-like paragraphs. Where the previous quotation features page centre, the two sentences above are left-justified, the first full point an interesting inclusion, especially as one is omitted from the

---

[44] Robert Sheppard, *Hymns to the God in which my Typewriter Believes* (Exeter: Stride, 2006), p. 66.

[45] Sheppard, *Hymns to the God*, p. 66.

second sentence. In the absence of the sign it is difficult to assert that unoccupied page space *can* be meaningful; instead, such poems invite the interpretation of page space in light of the fragments of text that occupy its corners or extremes. Ascribing rhythmic, metrical, or performative value in any sense to the white of the page is, as I have noted, a highly subjective matter for any interpretant, whose intuition for measure or pulse shifts according to the individual poem in question. Even multiple readings by the same interpretant will yield alternative understandings of a poem's artifice. The potential for meaning of such space would obviously be dissolved, the combined visual and linguistic effects of the poem effectively destroyed, if oral transmission read both fragments of text as if they were consecutive in the usual sense. This applies all the more forcefully when two fragments of text occupying the same page space differ formally-speaking. We infer connection of a kind, though, through their shared lexis: 'Perform' extends a field inaugurated by 'lyre', whereas 'blank mirror', 'face', and 'eyefuls' create a double allusion, a semantic field alluding to the allusion to the Orphic inheritance of the first fragment. The shift from third person to second person voice respects the void of page space separating them, as if to indicate that on the contrary, it is not so much the metaphor of a void that page space seems to carry as a gulf in which the movement from one register to another has tacitly occurred.

Preliminary judgements about the design and shape of a line cause the reader to oscillate between alternative possibilities of sense. The following example from *The Drop* is key in this respect:

> I watch
> The brimming orifice I leave
>
> Across the threshold un-
> Thinkable into the post-
>
> Human stairwell we become
> Less conscious dream
>
> Nothing short of disaster nothing
> Will do[46]

---

[46] Sheppard, *The Drop*, unpaginated.

Syntactically speaking, reports in the first person present few problems here, but the phrasal components of the passage oscillate: 'I leave / Across the threshold un- / thinkable' may run conventionally except to say that 'unthinkable' sounds almost sotto-voce, an interpolation by a subject troubled by the multiple threats posed by the threshold. Alternatively, 'I leave / Across the threshold' could stand alone, 'un- / Thinkable' running with 'into the post- / Human stairwell': both options oscillate between the unthinkability of the threshold across which the speaker leaves and the way in which it is considered unthinkable for this speaker to leave in the first place. Leaving the prefixes of 'unthinkable' and 'posthuman' hanging across the line emphasises the principle of negation working its way through the poem, as if also presenting the possibility that the drop – whatever this may be, for it is not singular – could be reversed and time itself redeemed. Similarly, 'we become / Less conscious dream' alerts us to the idea of a vacillating consciousness assisting the formation or deformation of the (morphined?) self, whilst leading towards the directive in the following 'Nothing short of disaster nothing / Will do': here, the reader is simultaneously exhorted not to engage in playful fantasy ('dream / Nothing') and to confront their ineluctable fate ('Nothing short of disaster nothing / Will do'). Whereas the repetition of 'nothing' bookends the line in the manner of a clenched fist striking a table, Sheppard plays on perhaps the most effective word in the language for an end-stopped line whilst in actual fact deploying it for the purposes of enjambment. The semantic field heavily suggests that the poem we are reading participates, if not quite belongs (Derrida again), to that distinct sub-genre of lyric practice: elegy.

Six pages later the word 'nothing' appears again in a similar regional context of 'lamentation':

Hidden in the guilt synapses each
Scoop from sleep

Fills with lamentation
Tribute towards grieving as each call

To muted voices doesn't nothing
Here except the choral

Nothing everything
Conceded to the morning[47]

The implications of 'nothing' are carried across the line but with the similar effect of finality as in the previous example. Yet 'nothing / Here except the choral / Nothing' oscillates between the tendency for needless repetition in everyday speech and the construction of the awkward-sounding noun phrase 'the choral /Nothing', a reading enforced (the imposition of dynamic relations imposed by this verb very much in play here) by the line break. Semantic sparks fly with the juxtaposition of 'Nothing everything', the line almost a non-line insofar as the ending of one abuts the beginning of another. Such reading detects a logic of simultaneity, namely that readers hear the oscillation between alternative possibilities of tracking grammar across the sinuous lines deforming sense. The concluding lines comment self-reflexively on the relationship between sound and meaning that arguably is one of the possible 'themes' that can be traced within the orbit of the Orphic, to which the text makes direct reference:

Orpheus

Entuning the moist cavities
Of immediate lust haunting

Desire the task
Of the poet is elective translation

To transmute the nothing said
Into the nothing that could

That could talk itself
Into the world [...][48]

Unusually, enjambment assists fluent syntax between the third and fourth lines: 'Of immediate lust haunting / Desire.' But as the reader accommodates the mind to the eye, they may ignore the enjambment

---

[47] Sheppard, *The Drop*, unpaginated.

[48] Sheppard, *The Drop*, unpaginated.

between 'haunting' and 'Desire' and read instead the forceful diktat of 'Desire the task / Of the poet' or even, just for a second, merely 'Desire the task'. The infinitive in line 5 decides for us, enforcing the more conventional syntactical flow of 'the task / Of the poet is elective translation', but the shape of the line makes the reader scan again as they oscillate between clashing possibilities of sense. Note also the way in which 'translation' and 'transmute', separated by line and syntax, nevertheless undergo the process connoted by the prefix both words share. 'To transmute the nothing said / Into the nothing that could / That could talk itself / Into the world': cleanly segmented syntax and the ironic charge of an implacable noun against this verb combine to reverse the illogical terms of its construction. This reversal is constrained by the thought of a further infinitive ghosting 'could' as in 'be potentially capable of': the could that could if only... If only the sense had not carried over to 'the / Shadow that casts wings between / The pillars'. Sheppard quotes an early version of these lines in the 2013 *Wolf* interview, and the contrast between the work-in-progress and the eventual publication is worthy of attention, particularly the following: 'the / shadow that casts its wings between the red / pillars that hold the whole thing up.'[49] The loss of 'red' and 'that hold the whole thing up' (even that 'its') in the 2016 first edition reveals a change of mind about the loaded significance of colour and the suggestion of a supported edifice (both architectural and non-architectural: the poem whose closing lines crumble under the edifice of what precedes it). In *The Drop*, these lines appear to have been trimmed for formalist purposes, namely to aid syntax extending much more limpidly across the line-end. 'I'm not sure that I would articulate that outside of the poem,' Sheppard relates, 'where I'm not sure what it means with any assurance.'[50] The signifying economy of mourning and melancholia raises the stakes of indeterminacy precisely where the lyric subject demands efficacy. 'Decontextualised from the previous eleven pages' refusal to mourn,' he continues, 'it is itself a kind of quotation.'[51] Clearly this relation holds between the early draft and the published text, in which self-reflexivity substitutes for, without assuming priority over, the exorbitant demands imposed by the event to which it attempts to respond.

---

[49] 'The *Wolf* Interview: Robert Sheppard', *The Wolf*, 26 (Winter 2013), 59-68 (p. 67).

[50] Ibid.

[51] Ibid.

Read alongside Sheppard's early rejection of poetic subjectivity, this unambiguous assertion of *The Drop*'s stance towards mourning puts the elegiac mode even further in doubt. The reader is forced to question the possibility of the elegiac itself against the poet's anti-lyric practice. The denial of a central and stable 'I' renders impossible the kind of direct expression characteristic of the elegy without blunting the force of mourning the poem ostensibly carries. Refusal does not amount to total disavowal, however, and the hermeneutics of nothing resonate as just this impossibility on the horizon of genre, the reader's lack of freedom from paradox constituting an alternative to the aporia of language ever fulfilling the work of mourning. Yet, as the '*Poetics and Praxis*' section of *The Anti-Orpheus* puts it: 'All this talk about the impossibility of art is impossible. (Yes, let us throw paradox back into its teeth!)' (p. 10). Orpheus 'Swinging in swingtime' is a strikingly odd image at this stage in the text and also as a key citation of the Orphic inheritance we have seen across Sheppard's work. A reference to the music of the English dance hall from the 1940s or else concerted defiance of whatever the drop and its string of negative terms are taken to mean, the phrase has a particularly sardonic resonance given the mythological figure's constant reinvention as the repository of all song and therefore of (not quite all) poetry. The swinging beat that captivates Orpheus is far from lyrical, but nor is it unmusical. Whatever, it fits uneasily with the elegiac, which cannot exist without the lyric. To confront another's death, one of poetry's eternal themes, is complicated to say the least when the 'I' refuses rather than accepts their lyric facticity in the first person and the first place. Yet *The Drop* invites the reader into an affective realm made all the more powerful by the gulf between the poem as an artefact of lamentation and the lyric self. The 'I' can withstand only so much pressure in the face of human mortality. Resistance to the Orphic inheritance in the end signals the only commensurability between life and aesthetic form available to the poet-critic.

BIBLIOGRAPHY

Adorno, Theodor W., *Aesthetic Theory*, ed. by Gretel Adorno and Rolf Tiedemann, new trans., ed., and with a translator's introduction by Robert Hullot-Kentor (London: Bloomsbury Academic, 2013)

Blanchot, Maurice, *The Gaze of Orpheus and other literary essays*, trans. by Lydia Davis, ed. with an Afterword by P. Adams Sitney (Barrytown, NY: Station Hill Press, 1981)

—— *The Space of Literature*, trans., with an Introduction, by Ann Smock (Lincoln, NE and London: University of Nebraska Press, 1982)

—— *The Work of Fire*, trans. by Charlotte Mandell (Stanford, CA: Stanford University Press, 1995)

Boulez, Pierre, *Pierre Boulez on Music Today*, trans. by Susan Bradshaw and Richard Rodney Bennett (London: Faber and Faber, 1975)

Byrne, James, and Robert Sheppard, eds, *Atlantic Drift: An Anthology of Poetry and Poetics* (Todmorden and Ormskirk: Arc Publications and Edge Hill University Press, 2017)

Clarke, Adrian, and Robert Sheppard, eds, *Floating Capital: New Poets from London* (Elmwood, CT: Potes and Poets Press, 1991)

Culler, Jonathan, *Theory of the Lyric* (Cambridge, MA and London, England: Harvard University Press, 2015)

Derrida, Jacques, 'The Law of Genre', trans. by Avital Ronell, in *Acts of Literature*, ed. by Derek Attridge (London: Routledge, 1992), pp. 221-52

Frye, Northrop, 'Theory of Genres', in *The Lyric Theory Reader: A Critical Reader*, ed. by Virginia Jackson and Yopie Prins (Baltimore, MD: Johns Hopkins University Press, 2014) pp. 30-9

Longenbach, James, *The Art of the Poetic Line* (Saint Paul, MN: Graywolf Press, 2008)

Madden, Christopher, 'Lyric Voice and *You*: Notes on Addressability', *The Wolf*, 33, pp. 83-95

Mottram, Eric, *Towards Design in Poetry* (London: Veer Books, 2004)

Parmar, Sandeep, with Bhanu Kapil and Nisha Ramayya, *Threads* (Leeds: Clinic, 2018)

Rosko, Emily, and Anton Vander Zee, eds, *A Broken Thing: Poets on the Line* (Iowa City, IA: Iowa University Press, 2001)

Sheppard, Robert, *Hymns to the God in which my Typewriter Believes* (Exeter: Stride, 2006)

—— *The Anti-Orpheus: A Notebook* (Exeter: Shearsman, 2004)

—— *The Drop* (Hunstanton: Oystercatcher Press, 2016)

—— *The Meaning of Form in Contemporary Innovative Poetry* (London: Palgrave, 2016)

—— *The Poetry of Saying: British Poetry and Its Discontents, 1950-2000* (Liverpool: Liverpool University Press, 2005)

—— *Warrant Error* (Exeter: Shearsman, 2009)

—— *When Bad Times Made for Good Poetry: Episodes in the History of the Poetics of Innovation* (Exeter: Shearsman, 2011)

Where to Begin: The 'net/(k)not – work(s)' of Robert Sheppard's 'Twentieth Century Blues'

Mark Scroggins

Beginnings

Towards the very end of "A"-12, the last section of the first half of his massive 'poem of a life' "A", Louis Zukofsky adapts the opening invocation of the *Odyssey* to address his wife Celia: 'Tell me of that man who got around / After sacred Troy fell.... / Tell us about it, my Light, / Start where you please.'[1] However much Homer's epic may be rooted in an oral tradition, the 'telling' of Odysseus' story we encounter when we pick up a copy of the poem begins not at some semi-arbitrary moment of pleasure, but at a closely calculated – and later formally codified – *in medias res*. There is nothing to stop us, as readers of long works, from beginning our readings 'where we please' (Derek Attridge suggests somewhere that neophyte readers of *Ulysses* might as well start at the beginning of Chapter 4, 'Mr Leopold Bloom ate with relish' etc.), but in the tradition of western writing both novelists and poets have expended enormous energies crafting memorable and resonant beginnings for their works: the virtuosic sixteen-line sentence opening of *Paradise Lost*, which ranges from the poem's subject ('man's first disobedience'), through the advent of Christ, the second Adam ('one greater man'), to the revelation of Torah to the 'shepherd' Moses, to a gutsy assertion of Milton's own ambition to pursue 'Things unattempted yet in prose or rhyme'; 'And then went down to the ship,'[2] the opening of Ezra Pound's *Cantos*, which as it overlays an Old English diction on a fifteenth-century Latin translation of Homer's archaic Greek, superimposes the English conjunction *and* over Homer's first syllable – '*And*ra moi enneppe, mousa, polutropon...' – and significantly hearkens back to the neutral *and* by which King James's translators chose to render the polyvalent Hebrew conjunction *waw*; 'A / round of fiddles playing Bach', the opening of Zukofsky's 'A'-1, which binds into a historical ring the 1729 Leipzig premiere of the *St. Matthew Passion* and its 1928 New York performance.

---

[1] Louis Zukofsky, *"A"* (1978; New York, NY: New Directions, 2011), p. 261.

[2] Ezra Pound, *The Cantos* (New York, NY: New Directions, 1970), p. 3.

Disseminations

Setting aside the resources of craft and cunning the poets have devoted to beginning their works, it's clear that the circumstances of publication and dissemination of many twentieth-century long poems have at times made 'starting at the beginning' problematic for the average reader. When Zukofsky received his copy of Pound's 1930 *A Draft of XXX Cantos* – a sumptuous limited edition; ordinary readers would have to wait till 1933 for a trade printing – he had only read a handful of the Cantos published thus far; he had begun his own long poem *"A"* in 1928 with little idea of the overall shape of *The Cantos*, the work to which it would later be compared, and which he would be accused of aping.[3] *"A"* itself was even more difficult of access for the average reader: the first movement to appear in print was "A"-7, published in 1931; since that movement is in part a telescoping of the themes of the first six movements, it was probably incomprehensible to most readers. The first six movements of *"A"* would only appear as a unit in the 1932 Zukofsky-edited *An "Objectivists" Anthology*, a book published in France, and which no doubt had little circulation in the United States. But just as modernist poets adapted to their own aesthetic ends the artisanal economies of the small presses and little magazines to which they were exiled by their exclusion from trade publishers and large circulation journals, by the latter half of the twentieth century poets such as Allen Fisher and Robert Duncan had begun to work principles of piecemeal dissemination into the formal structures of their serial poems.

Place / Passages

Notable in this regard are the English poet Fisher's multi-volume *Place* (1971-1980) and the American Robert Duncan's sequences *Passages* and *Structure of Rime*. Duncan began dispersing poems of his *Structure of Rime* through *The Opening of the Field* (1960), and added to it in each of his collections through the end of his life, though in later collections it was somewhat displaced by poems from the sequence *Passages*, which Duncan described as 'Passages of a poem larger than the book in which

---

[3] See December 1930 letter from Zukofsky to Pound in *Pound/Zukofsky: Selected Letters of Ezra Pound and Louis Zukofsky*, ed. by Barry Ahearn (New York, NY: New Directions, 1987), pp. 78-79.

they appear.'[4] At one point, the two sequences overlap ('An Illustration, *Passages* 20 (Structure of Rime XXVI)'; and by the middle of *Ground Work: Before the War* (1984) Duncan had left off numbering the poems of *Passages*, inviting the reader thereby to trace his or her own path among them. Similarly, in the second volume of his large topographical poem *Place, Unpolished Mirrors* (1985), Fisher proposes six different orders of reading the work; Fisher has consistently maintained 'that a reader can join the project at any point, becoming the "loci of a point on a moving sphere."'[5]

Twentieth Century Blues

Between 1989 and 2000, English poet Robert Sheppard wrote 'Twentieth Century Blues', a 75-section work – or as *Twentieth Century Blues* 14, 'Untitled', has it, a 'net/(k)not-work(s)' – that when I first encountered it was spread over four separate collections, *The Flashlight Sonata, Empty Diaries, The Lores,* and *Tin Pan Arcadia,* and a number of fugitive pamphlets and broadsides.[6] 'Twentieth Century Blues' is a searing exploration of twentieth-century history and subjectivity, and is as notable for its formal variousness – Sheppard deploys word-count and syllabic prosodies and a wide variety of stanza shapes – as for its thematic range. Equally compelling is Sheppard's thorough rethinking of the 'serial poem' form. Inspired by the multiple reading paths offered in Fisher's *Place* and by Barrett Watten's theorisation of formal refunctioning in Zukofsky's *"A"*,[7] Sheppard constructs a serial poem that invites multidirectional, recursive readings, and which is traversed by various subsidiary and overlapping shorter sequences, or

[4] Robert Duncan, Introduction to *Bending the Bow* (1968); see also *The Collected Later Poems and Plays*, ed. by Peter Quartermain (Berkeley, CA: University of California Press, 2014), p. 296.

[5] Quoted in Robert Sheppard, *Far Language: Poetics and Linguistically Innovative Poetry 1978-1997* (Exeter: Stride, 1999), p. 35. This essay, 'Poetic Sequencing and the New', is incorporated (in a heavily revised version) into *Complete Twentieth Century Blues* (Cambridge: Salt, 2008) as Section 14.

[6] Robert Sheppard, *The Flashlight Sonata* (Exeter: Stride, 1990), *Empty Diaries* (Exeter: Stride, 1998), *The Lores* (London: Reality Street, 2003), and *Tin Pan Arcadia* (Cambridge: Salt, 2004); full details of the previous publications of the poem's sections can be found in the Acknowledgements to *Complete Twentieth Century Blues* xi-xii.

[7] See Sheppard, *Far Language*, p. 38 and *Complete Twentieth Century Blues*, p. 84.

'strands.' 'We can all read the object, assemble, re-assemble it in our own way(s)', Sheppard writes. 'This will, of course, be affected by our acquired knowledge, our perceptual schema, and by the means of the texts' availability, not an irrelevant question for the non-canonical poet, relying upon fugitive small presses. We all have to start reading with what we can get...'[8]

Labyrinth; or, Maze

My own obsession, fuelled by a similar labyrinth-obsession among some of the 'high' modernists – Joyce's artist-figure is named after Daidalos, builder of the Cretan labyrinth; David Jones figures the trenches of the Western Front as labyrinths in *In Parenthesis*; Bunting writes of 'Schoenberg's maze' in *Briggflatts* – is to seize upon the labyrinth as formal analogy for *Twentieth Century Blues*. A double analogy, thanks to a happy semantic slippage: The classic *labyrinth*, as found on cathedral floors and beloved of New Age spiritualists, is a unicursal construction, guiding the viewer or walker through multiple turns to a single goal. An edifying spiritual exercise, perhaps, but of little use in containing a fierce Minotaur or preventing a prisoner from escaping. More suggestive is the common usage of 'labyrinth' as equivalent to the more modern *maze*, a construction characterised by multiple paths, choices, turnings – and occasionally, multiple entry and exit points. 'Twentieth Century Blues' hovers between the labyrinth and the maze: there is a single, unicursal path through the project, authorised by the poet, but one is simultaneously tugged away from that path by the various 'side-tracks' of the 'strands' to which many of the poems belong, and which extend beyond 'Twentieth Century Blues' itself. And even this unicursal path is characterized by maze-like repetition and recursiveness.

'Logos on Kimonos'

Let me be a bit more specific about this 'recursiveness': consider a poem from Sheppard's 1998 *Empty Diaries* entitled 'Logos on Kimonos'. One is for a moment inclined at first to read this classically, like 'Empedocles on Etna' – 'logos' as 'the Word' (cf. the Gospel According to John, first

---

[8] Sheppard, *Far Language*, p. 38.

verse), 'Kimonos' as some hitherto unrecognised Greek name – but it becomes clear that Greek-looking words in the poem are far more commonplace: here a logo is first and foremost a product emblem, a kimono a Japanese garment.

> The sky was sick metallic skin, genethetic
> meat loaf rotting over the hot city.
> Poor kids still rode the Underground. Smart
> Arses like me skated the neural Tanks,
> clipping onto Personality Composites. My latest catch
> was an Autoflesh case. My biomatic orgasm
> flushed Yen in the cybernetic maelstrom, where
> he'd picked me up on feel alone.
> Information sickness iced me, pink fuses blowing,
> melting subliminals in the cool jelly stolen
> from the Tanks. Logos on kimonos flashed
> fleshy machines. I'd MEAT and METAL lasered
> on either tit and I could clip
> ecstasy any time I liked. Flooded by
> voices, not mine, in the Tanks: nostalgia
> for human dust on the keyboard, ancient
> meat messages flattened on the screen. When
> I watch old movies I get sentimental
> over robots, strutting like pillheads from a
> bar at 5. CyberCunts fleshed on me
> by some clipwrecked pilot with a scrimshaw
> virus flutter my optic lashes to process
> the orgasm I'll use to crash his
> information-dead eyes. He's hard copy. Once
> I've jellied my button, he'll jack me
> like a deck, then roll off, a
> dead man.
>   The realisation that neither of
> us is human makes my flesh creep.[9]

This is a cyberpunk poem, almost a parody of William Gibson's 1984 genre-initiating *Neuromancer*; compare the novel's opening sentence, 'The sky above the port was the colour of television, tuned to a dead

---

[9] Sheppard, *Empty Diaries*, pp. 57-58.

channel.'[10] 'Logos on Kimonos' is sprinkled with catchphrases that evoke Gibson's techno-dystopia: the 'Tanks', 'deck', 'jack', 'personality composite'. The poem is spoken by a character that reminds one perhaps of Daryl Hannah's Pris in Ridley Scott's 1982 *Blade Runner*. Pris is a 'replicant', an artificial approximation of a human being; she has been manufactured as a 'basic pleasure model' to service the sexual needs of the offworld human military, but she is a skilled gymnast and fighter, and appears to have a homicidal streak. The world which the speaker of 'Logos on Kimonos' describes might be arresting, but the speaker's gender position within that world is of a piece with many of the collection's other poems. *Empty Diaries* presents a moving picture of the sexual and political violences of the twentieth century, told for the most part 'by a succession of female narrators, each one of whom "knows" she is narrated by a man.'[11]

Recursions

One might of course read 'Logos on Kimonos' – as I first did – in its context in the volume *Empty Diaries*, a series of poems that cover, one for each year, the years 1901 to 1990. (In that context it seems rather out of order – it is 'Empty Diary 2055', placed between 1987 and 1988.) But if one is aiming to follow the sections of 'Twentieth Century Blues' in numerical sequence, one encounters 'Logos on Kimonos' as *Twentieth Century Blues* 16. Six sections later, one will read 'Logos on Kimonos' as a section of *Empty Diaries* Part 4, which is *Twentieth Century Blues* 22; two sections after that, one reads the whole of *Empty Diaries* as *Twentieth Century Blues* 24. One has then read 'Logos in Kimonos' three times (the same is true of *Empty Diaries* 1990, which is *Twentieth Century Blues* 19, as well as part of *Twentieth Century Blues* 22 and *Twentieth Century Blues* 24). The effect, one might argue, is analogous to traversing the same pathway in a maze on successive turns, or encountering the same painting or sculpture in different passes through a large and complexly organised museum, each time noting how the piece has been recontextualised by its presentation within a larger whole.

---

[10] William Gibson, *Neuromancer* (New York, NY: Ace, 1984), p. 3.

[11] *Empty Diaries* back jacket; I assume this prose is Sheppard's.

Turnings

But the maze of 'Twentieth Century Blues' includes not merely recursive repetition, but side-paths, numbered 'strands' reappearing as subtitles throughout the poems ('Bolt Holes', 'I. M.', etc.). 'Logos on Kimonos', as well as being 'Empty Diary 2055', is 'Duocatalysis 8', 'History of Sensation 6', 'Human Dust 1', and 'Fucking Time 2'. The first 'Fucking Time' poem, a series of responses to John Wilmot, Earl of Rochester, is *Twentieth Century Blues* 15. (The title is taken from Aubrey's life of Fr. Franciscus Linus, who erected a set of exquisite but phallic sundials in his garden which were 'one night ... broken all to pieces (for they were of glass spheres) by the Earl of Rochester, Lord Brockhurst, Fleetwood Shephard, etc., coming in from their revels. "What!" said the Earl of Rochester, "doest thou stand here to – time?" Dash they set to work.'[12]) The third is *Twentieth Century Blues* 25, 'Flesh Mates on Dirty Errands'. 'Strands' such as 'Fucking Time' offer the reader other options for reading order, and emphasise the 'network'-like (or as Sheppard hazards, 'rhizomatic') structuring of the work. Such 'rhizomatic' form authorises greater readerly choice, even compositional authority. We can read 'Logos in Kimonos' in its order within 'Twentieth Century Blues' (if we are conscientious, we read it thrice); or we can turn aside from 'Twentieth Century Blues''s primary numerical ordering and follow – backwards, forwards – any of the 'strands' to which it belongs, whether 'Fucking Time', 'Duocatalysis', 'History of Sensation', or 'Human Dust'.

Shuffling / Flipping

Whichever path we choose when we reach *Twentieth Century Blues* 16, 'Logos on Kimonos', is perforce shaped by the books we have at hand. If we want to pursue the 'History of Sensation' strand, for instance, we find that 'History of Sensation' 1, 3, and 4 are contained in Sheppard's 1993 volume *The Flashlight Sonata*; when I first read 'Logos', 'History of Sensation' 2 was available only in a limited edition chapbook or broadside I had not seen; later sections were contained in *Tin Pan Arcadia*, the largest concentration of *Twentieth Century Blues* published to date. *Twentieth Century Blues* 63, 'The End of the Twentieth Century:

---

[12] Sheppard, *Complete Twentieth Century Blues*, pp. 380-81.

a text for readers and writers,' an essay in poetics that is included in every one of the approximately *fifty-five* 'strands' that traverse *Twentieth Century Blues*, had yet to appear in book form. Whichever path we take through Sheppard's 'net/(k)not-work(s)', we must do a good deal of shuffling of books and flipping of pages. Indeed, *Twentieth Century Blues* 74 is not a poem but a detailed index to the project as a whole, and Sheppard has produced as well an index to the work's 'strands'. This is a poetic sequence which, like the turnstile handout at some nightmarish Magic Kingdom, contains its own detailed and indispensable visitor's guide and map.

Tension

The conceptual, the *readerly* tension here – of which I think Sheppard is well aware – is that between the traditional linear, page-based presentation of the individual poems, and the spatial conception of the network as a whole. Can there be a *verbal* network, or a *verbal* labyrinth, given that poetry from Homer to Sheppard subsists as a pattern of sounds (phonemes) or marks (graphemes) moving forward and down the page in a single socially agreed-upon order? It is a tension analogous to that which Zukofsky identified in "A"-6: '*Can* / The design / Of the fugue / Be transferred / To poetry?'[13] Not a rhetorical question.

Presentation

The ideal presentational form for 'Twentieth Century Blues', it seems to me, is a hypertextual one, a web-based environment where a reader could click on an icon at the corner of each poem in order to be taken to the next (or previous) section of 'Twentieth Century Blues' or to the next (or previous) poem in each of the 'strands' to which the immediate poem belongs. In some ways, Salt Publishing's publication of the single-volume *Complete Twentieth Century Blues*, like Reality Street's single-volume edition of Alan Fisher's *Place*, works to foreclose the combinatory possibilities offered by a hypertextual presentation (or, as Sheppard suggests in his Note to the volume, a 'box publication' like

---

[13] Zukofsky, *"A"*, p. 38.

that of Duchamp's *Box in a Valise*[14]). Even as Sheppard is grateful to Salt for making possible a 'collection of works intended as a network, but never a Work', he notes how a 'codexical presentation' 'raises questions of organisation that the box and the hypertext evade.' 'In a sense', he writes, 'this book is another strand (as any ordering a Reader makes within it is a strand), one which I hope will make the individual blues present as apart from, as well as a part of, the network.'

Collection

As Sheppard explains in a note to Salt's *Complete Twentieth Century Blues*, this vast project is in essence a collecting and arranging of all the poems he wrote 'between December 1989 and 2000', with the addition of a number of related texts dated from 1983 to 1989 – a 'kind of Collected Poems 1989-2000, with a Selected Poems 1983-1989 interpolated into it.'[15] The typical procedure for producing a 'collected poems,' of course, is simply to string together chronologically the contents of the author's previously published volumes, though Sheppard is by no means original in deviating from that practice: Laura (Riding) Jackson's 1938 *Collected Poems*, for instance, arranges her work achronologically under various thematic headings – 'Poems of Mythical Occasion', etc. – and Marianne Moore's 1967 *Complete Poems* is not complete at all, but presents a closely culled and revised selection from her body of work. What is remarkable is how Sheppard has radically *refunctioned* his various works by arranging them within the network of 'Twentieth Century Blues', and by positioning them on the various threads that traverse and go beyond 'Twentieth Century Blues' proper.

Service

All of this is in the service of an ethics of writerly authority which Roland Barthes first theorised in his essays of the sixties, and which

---

[14] Other 'box' publications designed to be read in an order determined by the reader include B. S. Johnson's experimental novel *The Unfortunates* (1969), Robert Grenier's 1978 *Sentences* (500 poems on 5" x 8" index cards), and Anne Carson's *Float* (2016), twenty-two separate chapbooks packaged in a single plastic container.

[15] Robert Sheppard, unpublished 'Remarks on Structure and Contents', later revised to the 'Introductory Note' to *Complete Twentieth Century Blues*, p. viii.

has been much cited by the theorists of the American Language school in particular. I quote Sheppard again: 'We can all read the object, assemble, re-assemble it in our own way(s).' In earlier critical statements such as 'Propositions 1987' and 'The Education of Desire,' Sheppard argues that poetry's defamiliarising effects are crucial to the education of readerly desires, to the fostering of a politically or socially critical consciousness.[16] More recently, he has taken to reading the political ethics of his work as 'less utopian, less the text opening horizons of possibility, Marcuse's Aesthetic Dimension glittering with its prefigurations' and more openly critical and 'strategic: a denial of what we presently are...' 'The aim, however', Sheppard writes, 'has not changed: to activate the reader into participation, into relating differences, to sabotage perceptual schema, to educate desire, not to fulfil it in a merely entertaining emptying of energy. To create, above all, new continuities.'[17] Some of those continuities, some of those readerly options, are necessarily occluded in the Salt *Complete Twentieth Century Blues* (Sheppard speaks of his attempt to create 'a satisfying page-by-page read'[18]): those occlusions, I think, are outweighed by the pleasure of having this simultaneously densely woven and terminally 'frayed' work between a single set of covers.

The Force of the Codex (A Slight Return)

From one standpoint or another, every era is an era of transition. That ours seems quite vertiginously so is no doubt a function of the rapidity of technological innovation, our ever-hastening regimes of production, transportation, and communication. In no arena is such innovation so evident as in the storage and presentation of the written word. The thirty-nine volumes of the 'Library Edition' of John Ruskin (1903-1912), which took over a decade to edit, print, and assemble, glare balefully down at me from some nine linear feet of bookshelves; together they weigh more than my daughter. But they also, in literally weightless PDF form, occupy only a tiny portion of the memory on my laptop and tablet, where I can 'page' through and search them with a

---

[16] See Sheppard, *Far Language*, pp. 23-27 and pp. 28-31.

[17] Sheppard, *Far Language*, p. 37.

[18] Sheppard, 'Remarks on Structure and Contents'.

rapidity unimaginable to their first readers.

The codex – the bound collection of leaves or pages, what we call a 'book' – was itself a technological innovation that reshaped the ways readers conceived of texts. The scroll, which had to be unrolled to be read, was the standard storage device before the Common Era. (The twenty-four books of Homer's epics, it has been hypothesised, corresponded to the separate scrolls upon which portions of the poems were recorded.) By the end of the third century, however, codices were at least as common as scrolls, and by the sixth century they had displaced the scroll entirely.

It's no surprise that the book won out over the scroll in the evolution of textual storage. Codices are easier to carry about than scrolls, and certainly easier to store: shelved books are far more efficient than the series of cubby-holes one needs to store multiple scrolls. More significant to the history of reading, however, the codex facilitates a markedly different approach to the text. When you're reading a scroll, the text you've already read disappears into the rolled portion in your left hand (assuming a left-to-right script) as you unroll the new text from your right. A passage you encountered ten or fifteen minutes ago will be rolled several layers deep, accessible only through a fussy process of un- and re-rolling. With the codex, you now have the ability to flip back and forth from a later passage to an earlier, to mark a passage with a leaf, a slip of paper, or a finger – activities which were impossible – or at least far more cumbersome – with a scroll. The scroll assumed sequential, beginning-to-end reading; the codex allows you to open any page, to begin anywhere, to cross-reference and index.

The habits fostered by old technologies die hard, even as new technologies gain ascendance. Even a collection as patently heterogeneous as the Bible – sixty-odd scrolls of wildly different generic, theological, and narrative import – takes on a kind of scroll-like 'beginning-to-end' movement when assembled between a single set of covers (and received as 'scripture' by a readerly community). The Bible is a codex haunted by its origins as a collection of scrolls. But in the Christian New Testament (and even more so in the writings of the early Church Fathers) we see a codexical approach to the Hebrew Bible, a web of citation and cross-referencing, a sense that the earlier revelation is available to be flipped through (as a book) and quoted from at any point.

Twenty-five years ago, we were told from all sides that the book was dying as a form of textual storage, that we would all be reading from screens by 2018 – and that the new wave of poetry and narrative was the dispersed and multicursal network of hypertext. A decade ago, the futurists had scaled back their prophecies to predict the gradual displacement of the physical codex of by various electronic 'readers', with fewer speculations – either from the fearful mainstream or the hopeful avant-garde – about the forms of writing itself shifting in response to new technologies. Right now, the regimes of change seem to be hanging fire, if only for the nonce. The codex appears to hold its own against the electronic file, at least when it comes to the more substantial productions of the creative writerly classes.

*

Up until 2008, 'Twentieth Century Blues' named both a congeries of writings – poems and clusters of poems, prose statements and an index, published in periodicals, collected in a number of pamphlets and full-length volumes, circulated by e-mail and on the internet – and a conceptual project: the 'net/(k)not-work(s)' upon which the earlier sections of this essay meditated. In 2008, when Salt published *Complete Twentieth Century Blues*, *Twentieth Century Blues* became a codex as well.

'Twentieth Century Blues', as a conceptual project, offers a vision of free-floating poems and poetic fragments woven together in multiple intersecting strands: a kind of star-field of verse, glowing against the night sky, over which the poet has mapped a series of overlapping constellational forms. A structure, one might hazard, worthy of Case's jacked-in vision of the cyberspace in Gibson's *Neuromancer*. But the codex of *Complete Twentieth Century Blues* has a force all its own. The book is hefty, bound in black boards beneath a sober dust jacket. It is more than four hundred pages, printed on sturdy paper stock. It occupies serious real estate on the shelf. And our deeply-ingrained reading habits encourage us – or at least encourage me – to read it from front to back, from the title page to the 'Index of Strands'. Such a reading shows that Sheppard has succeeded in the goal to which he alludes in the 'Introductory Note': *Complete Twentieth Century Blues* is violent, harrowing, grim, pornographic, bewildering, and even occasionally lyrical – but it is by all means 'a satisfying page-by-page read'.[19]

The various 'strands' are still there, indicated in small print beneath each poem's title and laid out in detail in the 'Index to Strands' at

---

[19] Sheppard, *Complete Twentieth Century Blues*, p. xiii.

the end of the volume. Oddly enough, however, for this reader those alternate pathways through the labyrinth of 'Twentieth Century Blues' seem somewhat less inviting when they're offered as routes through a single codex, rather than a shuffling among piles of slim volumes and pamphlets. The glowing vision of the hypertextual constellation seems to have dimmed. Sheppard himself notes that the temporality of his collection – poems for the most part composed between 1989 and 2000, then arranged in roughly chronological order – has somehow shorted out its hypertextuality:

> Note 2007: Although I imagined it as a hypertext, the time-bound nature of the project – the year 2000 as its limit – imposed a forward trajectory on its links which it strikes me now, is alien to the multidimensionality of the hyperlink, which is why I call the work a 'pseudo-hypertext' in my 'Introductory Note'.[20]

In the end, however, the hypertext was only ever a formal analogy: a true hypertext resides among the memory, the processors, the screen of one's computer, or somehow in the unimaginable cloud of the internet; once a text is printed on paper, be it a magazine, a broadside, a pamphlet, or a book, its 'hypertextuality' can be only an analogue, a wishful formal imagining. The codexical presentation of *Complete Twentieth Century Blues* only solidifies this fact.

What then of 'Logos on Kimonos' in its latest context? It appears on pages 80 and 81 as 'Twentieth Century Blues 16,' following the bluntly lubricious 'Fucking Time', and followed by 'Poetic Sequencing and the New' ('Twentieth Century Blues 18'). The effect is jarring, in a highly effective juxtapositional sense: from the earthy, seventeenth-century sexuality of 'Fucking Time', to the phantasmagoric cybersex of 'Logos', to the cool critical prose of 'Poetic Sequencing'. This is of course the 'page-by-page' reading. If we mean relentlessly to pursue the central numbering of 'Twentieth Century Blues', we will skip ahead after 'Logos' to pages 119 through 130, 'Empty Diaries 1946-1966', which are 'Twentieth Century Blues 17'. (The whole of the collection *Empty Diaries* has been moved intact to its place as 'Twentieth Century Blues 24', though various sections appear earlier in the numbering as well. Recursiveness.) And we are invited when we read 'Logos on

---

[20] Sheppard, *Complete Twentieth Century Blues*, p. 389.

Kimonos', by the list of 'strands' under the title, to pursue five other by-ways as well.

The potentialities of these possible reading entices me, though I confess I've only explored a few of them. (Sheppard himself confesses that 'I doubt if [the strands] present interesting continua' – which means to my mind that they probably present very interesting discontinuities and juxtapositions indeed.[21]) The only thing I regret about 'Logos on Kimonos''s new home in *Complete Twentieth Century Blues* is the loss of its jarring 'original' location in *Empty Diaries*, between 'Empty Diary 1987' – a nightmarish vision of media-driven sexual desire, Duchamp crossed with Baudrillard – and 'Empty Diary 1988', a fragmentary, deeply ambivalent delineation of a post-Thatcher world in which both sexual and political freedom seemed emptied of hope. In that volume, the cyber-dominatrix voice of 'Logos on Kimonos' comes across as a trumpet of fierce self-determination in an achronological science fiction dystopia: a blast of power from the future.

There's nothing keeping me from reading 'Logos on Kimonos' in *Empty Diaries*, however; the book is on my shelf, and that particular reading option – along with its position in *Complete Twentieth Century Blues* and within the various strands that traverse and curl through that project – is always open to me. It's an aspect of the writerly freedom afforded by the codexical form itself, and underlined by all of Sheppard's gestures beyond the codex. The book as book can never achieve true hypertextuality, but in 'Twentieth Century Blues' – and even in *Complete Twentieth Century Blues* – Sheppard has created a marvellous and nightmarish textual labyrinth whose coils and complexities are inexhaustible to any single reader.

(2006-2007, Boca Raton;
revised and expanded 2018,
Montclair and New York)

---

[21] Sheppard, *Complete Twentieth Century Blues*, p. 389.

Political Rhetoric and Poetic Counterforce in Robert Sheppard's *Warrant Error*

Adam Hampton

'Our civilization is decadent and our language – so the argument runs – must inevitably share in the general collapse'
– George Orwell

The adoption of the sonnet by the linguistically innovative poet presents a potentially paradoxical state of affairs. Linguistic innovation in writers such as Robert Sheppard might seem to preclude them from embracing received forms. Yet, as Tom Jenks outlines in the present volume, contemporary innovative poets evidently regard the sonnet as a formal challenge rather than as a limitation on innovation per se, engaging it in a process of subverting, testing, and perhaps even transcending received traditions of prosody. Indeed, the sonnet has been the site of experimentation since its introduction to the English language by Thomas Wyatt, who displayed 'no consistent desire to make his lines iambic'.[1] Arguably, his diversion from metrical expectation constitutes a desire to work innovatively within its constraints, assimilating the sonnet with English traditions such as the alliterative line. Wyatt's innovations suggest that the sonnet can be a site of experimentation, where the subversion of meter, for example, acts to release the word from restraint. This is echoed by Sheppard in a 1987 interview for the magazine *Angel Exhaust*, where he addresses the notion of 'setting words free' in relation to his pamphlet *Returns* (1985).[2] Sheppard quotes William Carlos Williams, referring to 'radical mimesis' as the torqueing of the word to displace it from its signifying role in a utilitarian reality towards a creative autonomy.[3] In this sense, Williams echoes the example set by Wyatt: the frame of the sonnet enables rather than prohibits the liberation of the word in a poetic context.

Innovative poets from both sides of the Atlantic and beyond have tested the boundaries of the sonnet as to render their deviations as formal

---

[1] *Sir Thomas Wyatt: Collected Poems*, ed. by Joost Daalder (London: Oxford University Press, 1975), p. xi.

[2] Steven Pereira, 'An Interview with Robert Sheppard', in *Angel Exhaust*, 7 (summer 1987), pp. 17-24 (p. 21).

[3] Ibid.

distortions of the Shakespearean or Petrarchan varieties. The American poet Ted Berrigan's *Sonnets* (1964) consists of 88 poems collaged from repetitious phrases. Sheppard describes the pleasure of this sequence as derived from 'the wildness of collage' tensioned with the 'concentrated effect' imposed by the sonnet.[4] Winner of the New Zealand Book Award for Poetry, Michelle Leggott's third collection of poems, *DIA* (1996), contains a sequence of thirty sonnets, 'Blue Irises'. These poems subvert gender hierarchies and provide autonomy for the female voice by appropriating and collaging poetic lines from 'New Zealand women poets who Leggott believed suffered undeserved neglect'.[5] Graphic poems such as Mary Ellen Solt's 'Moon Shot Sonnet' (1964) represent a limit case in the context of formal innovation. Solt's poem offers little in the way of assimilating features to the widely available and recognisable 14-line construct. Bereft of language, the poem uses the plane of the page as a graphic space interrupted by stark black lines, in an illustrative and spatial interpretation of the sonnet form. 'Moon Shot Sonnet' was written in response to lunar photographs published in the *New York Times* in 1964. Solt appropriates the accentual markings used by scientists to demarcate the surface of the moon, placing them into shapes reminiscent of the constituent octave and sestet in the Petrarchan mould.[6] Through these digressions, Solt's work questions the very definition of the sonnet as a stable construct. Displacing historical preservation with experimental immediacy, she provides originality whilst also retaining creative agency as the 'receiver' of a predetermined formal poetic construct. Solt interrogates the devices that seek to control expression within rigid boundaries. Her dynamic writing process forefronts the author's autonomy in an examination of the dictatorial nature of meter, rhyme, and line.

Why choose the sonnet at all? What is to be gained by adopting some if not all of its distinguishing features in an examination of contemporary reality? One may find the answer in the sonneteer's inclination to sequential organisation. Sheppard himself describes the temptation towards the sonnet sequence as one motivated by both a

---

[4] Robert Sheppard, 'The Innovative Sonnet Sequence: Five of 14: The Code of the West De-coded' <http://robertsheppard.blogspot.com/2011/07/innovative-sonnet-sequence-five-of-14.html> [accessed 5 March 2018].

[5] Janet Newman, 'Listening Harder: Reticulating Poetic Tradition in Michele Leggott's "Blue Irises"', *Journal of New Zealand Literature*, 33 (2015), pp. 110-27 (p. 112).

[6] Mary Ellen Solt, 'Moon Shot Sonnet', in *The Reality Street Book of Sonnets*, ed. by Jeff Hilson (Hastings: Reality Street, 2008), p. 26.

desirable experientialism and a predilection for poetic functionality. He writes:

> This is surely the pleasure of *sequence*, if we may put it thus: the enjoyment of the variety of formed meanings encountered across the recurrences of the sonnet frame, so that dispersion and distillation are neatly balanced, that form is again the final and performed content [...] The attraction of the sonnet sequence for contemporary linguistically innovative poets is that, similarly, it provides an accessible resolution to the tension between the long poem and the lyric.[7] (italics original)

Distillation in the single poem juxtaposed with dispersion along the sequence premises a formal stability through which the sequence functions to suspend its constituent poems. The poems themselves are varied in meaning but gathered in loose assemblage – via a unifying theme, for example – across the larger chain. The reader experiences an increased intimacy with the material via a 'performative reading' of both the macroform of the larger arrangement, which functions as an area where the '*staging* of meaning and feeling' occurs, and the constituent microform of the poem (italics original).[8] There is an underlying tension between the singular energy of the poem at it runs contiguously with the linear energy of the sequence. Sheppard's reference to linguistically innovative poets who, in their varied experimentations, have applied constraint to writing, leads to the conceptualist work of poets like Christian Bök, whose *Eunoia* (2001) is comprised of univocalic poems where each of the five sections is restricted to the use of words containing one of the five vowels. Similarly, writers of the Ouvroir de Littérature Potentielle (OuLiPo or Potential Literature Workshop) apply constraint as part of the writing process. Raymond Queneau's *One Hundred Thousand Billion Poems* (1961) is a flipbook presentation of ten sonnets, where each line is printed on an individual strip and can be substituted with the corresponding line in each of the other poems. This permits variation of a restricted number of lines and generates formal diversity. Similarly, Sheppard subjects his sonnets to permutation through a predetermined structure. He throws off the shackles of meter and end-rhyme but retains

---

[7] Robert Sheppard, *The Meaning of Form in Contemporary Innovative Poetry* (London: Palgrave Macmillan, 2016), p. 50.

[8] Derek Attridge, *The Singularity of Literature* (London: Routledge, 2004), p. 109.

the fourteen-line length, divided into four stanzas, where the lines are distributed thus: 2/3/4/5. Each sonnet retains this basic structure but the stanzas themselves are dispersed differently from one poem to the next.

Warrant Error was published in 2009 in the wake of 9/11 and increasing terrorist activity across Europe and the Middle East. Sheppard formulates a response to a period of history (and its developing zeitgeist) that refuses to go away via the juxtaposition of these moments with the ill-fated land invasion of Iraq, led by US and UK forces in 2003. The language used to argue for, sustain, and legitimise that act is multiply counterpoised, placed under the microscope of Sheppard's unrelenting poetic discourse. In a poem toward the beginning of the book, he writes:

> Honour killing slaps a legal face on, when
> the evidence takes a life of its own[9]

Warrant Error appropriates and collages the language of political spin to reveal its ostensible identity as propaganda. The result is an assemblage of poems that complicates simplistic demarcations made, for example, between 'them and us' and 'good and evil', namely the kind of distorting binaries that defined the media discourse in the moment and which failed to 'allow the word "us" to be used as broadly and unthreateningly as possible'.[10] The book is a direct subversion of the quest for absolution, as it rejects binary notions in favour of polylogue. The above example of wordplay defamiliarises the invidious trope of the stereotype, working through what Sheppard calls an 'undecidability' consequent to the juxtaposition of disparate registers that otherwise destabilises their primary nomenclatural usage.[11] The result is a poetry of counterforce that functions to place in formal parity the languages of subjugation. The process emphasises the capacity of such language to be weaponised whilst exposing its impotence under the slightest of critical (and poetic) examination.

Reflecting on the consequences of discoveries in quantum physics for our understanding of reality, Allen Fisher addresses the 'role of the spectator' as participant of 'aesthetic production'.[12] Sheppard's book is

---

[9] Sheppard, *Warrant Error*, p. 21.

[10] Stephen Coleman and Karen Ross, *The Media and the Public: "Them" and "Us" in Media Discourse* (Chichester & Hoboken, NJ: Wiley-Blackwell, 2010), pp. 152-53.

[11] Sheppard, *The Meaning of Form*, p. 4.

[12] Allen Fisher, 'The Poetics of Decoherence and the Imperfect Fit', in James Byrne and Robert Sheppard, eds, *Atlantic Drift: An Anthology of Poetry and Poetics* (Todmorden

an artefact that operates to merge the poetic discourse of the writer with the interpretative faculty of the reader. As a result, *Warrant Error* explicitly stages via analogy the contributory role that we play in the production of political discourse. As it possesses this function, it would seem that *Warrant Error* in its entirety levitates above its constituent appropriated content. This is not, however, the case. The text's self-reflexivity is enhanced by frequent use of the second person voice, as if the speaker seeks to catechise itself through the principle of counter-force. Reading this book is to question not only rhetoric but also one's own collaboration in those conversations. David Orr reminds us that political language and poetic language share the common characteristic of being 'matters of verbal persuasion' and this is no more evident than in *Warrant Error*.[13] Sheppard's work is self-reflexive in relation to its own collusion, aware not only of the capacity for persuasion possessed by political and poetic discourse, but also the ease with which one may be influenced by their coercive overtures. In one line, the voice of the poem concedes 'I'll buy it', and the cost is devastatingly human: 'I pay with portions/of myself.'[14]

The text contains these moments of reflection as it moves from conceptual reportage towards a tangible physical consequence. There is an irony in placing the language that enables warfare (in its many guises) and the enduring cost side-by-side. In this examination of the word and its referent, *Warrant Error* demonstrates the tenuous process of signification undertaken between the two constituent elements of the sign, the signifier and the signified. In its analysis of language, the text induces in the reader a palpable response, and in doing so emphasises the functions and effects of rhetoric.

Writerly diligence and the kinetics of the sequence

Sheppard produces his poems out of the moment. The energy transferred from the poet to the poem is tangible in its insistence that the reader persevere. This vigour sustains the reader through each inevitable mishap as we stumble in a negotiation of intertextual references,

and Ormskirk: Arc and Edge Hill University Press, 2017), p. 76.

[13] David Orr, 'The Politics of Poetry' <https://www.poetryfoundation.org/poetrymaga zine/articles/69080/the-politics-of-poetry> [accessed 25 February 2018].

[14] Sheppard, *Warrant Error*, p. 16.

seeking to make sense of disparateness. Sheppard invites the reader to arbitrate the fashioned semantics of the press release and the newspaper headline in 'each trembling embrace' with the broken syntax of 'prime-ministerial photo-op[s]'.[15] Sheppard is known for his energetic vocal delivery in performance, defined by its 'startling velocity' as the poet delivers his poems or 'musical scores'.[16] Christopher Madden explains that 'none of [that] energy is lost when reading the poem yourself on the printed page', implying that the text retains a level of dormant energy, which, upon the engagement of a reader, has the force required to '[gesture] beyond [its own] materiality' towards an extralinguistic world removed from the confines of the book cover.[17]

Although not exclusively constituted of sonnets, the sonnet sequence provides the text's overarching formal framework. The book is presented in four sections, each containing twenty-four sonnets. There is an additional four poems, bringing the total to one hundred. The poems fluctuate between titled and untitled, and this enables an elasticity of structure that maintains the charge of kinetic dynamism across the breadth of the text. At times, the poems bleed into one another, the last line of one enjambed onto the first of the next. Across two such poems, Sheppard writes:

[...] twinkles stolen from his lustrous eyes[18]

Watch how they leave their scream-shot[19]

The effect is emphasised by the lack of punctuation and is indicative of Sheppard's destabilisation of the formal limitations of the sonnet. Language is packed into the restrictive boundaries of the form's fourteen lines until the poems function with volatility: unstable, indefinite, and irrepressible in their containment of potential energy. Sheppard writes:

---

[15] Sheppard, *Warrant Error*, p. 19.

[16] Christopher Madden, '*Berlin Bursts*: Robert Sheppard', in *The Wolf*, 26 (Spring 2012), pp. 74-79 (p. 74).

[17] Ibid.

[18] Sheppard, *Warrant Error*, p. 34.

[19] Ibid, p. 35.

Sparky the Iraqi drops to his knees, slaps his palms
in the pooled blood of the freshly slaughtered.
It is wedding day, and we bear gifts
to the party. Passengers scatter
from the windows burrow into bus seats[20]

Energy must be produced and the use of verbs is indicative. Words such as 'slaps', 'scatter' and 'burrow' are notable by their vigour. Despite 'passengers' denoting human traffic, the words 'burrow' and 'scatter' connote the animalistic, suggesting the quadrupedal creature's increased capacity for movement over the bipedal. Sheppard's presentation of vigour occurs in the confined space of the sonnet frame, producing a claustrophobia derived from the tension between the limitations of poetic form and the potency of content that revolts against compartmentalisation. The use of enjambment is an effective device in this context as it allows for the spilling over of sense from one line to the next such that reading becomes a negotiation of both content and form.[21]

The performative negotiation of *Warrant Error* evokes Charles Olson's delineation of the syllable and the line in 'Projective Verse'.[22] In reading the poems, we enter into a bodily experience where the movement from 'one perception' towards 'a further perception' is driven by linear immediacy.[23] The physicality of reading is felt keenly, particularly in the measure of the breath as it is stretched beyond the termination of the poetic line in the quest for syntactic completeness. Olson addresses the notion of the preservation of energy in the poem and its transmission to the reader during later encounters when the text is read:

[T]he line comes (I swear it) from the breath, from the breathing of the man who writes, at the moment that he writes, and thus is, it is here that, the daily work, the WORK, gets in, for only he, the man who writes, can declare, at every moment, the line its metric and its ending – where its breathing, shall come to, termination.[24] (emphasis original)

---

[20] Ibid., p. 86.

[21] Terry Eagleton, *How to Read a Poem* (Oxford: Blackwell, 2007), p. 96.

[22] Charles Olson, 'Projective Verse' <https://www.poetryfoundation.org/articles/69406/projective-verse/> [accessed 26 February 2018].

[23] Olson, 'Projective Verse'.

[24] Ibid.

The use of punctuation in the above passage exemplifies Olsonian ki-
netics and is effective in the induction of awareness; we become sensi-
tive to the measure of the breath of the author in our own recitation
of the text due to our negotiation of a series of subordinate clauses and
adjuncts. The effect is analogous to the operation of the line in Shep-
pard's poems but with one significant difference: Sheppard uses punc-
tuation scarcely. Instead, it is the syllabic quality of the chosen words,
the length of the line and where it breaks, that determine the unit of
breath. The distinct echo of the poet's own vocality is detectable when
reading the works aloud, such that a reading of the text is comparable
to standing before a work of art, intimate with the integrant strokes of
the paintbrush as once the artist was.

Madden, attesting to the performativity of Sheppard's work,
remarks that the intensity of his word sounds ring in the ear long
after reading the book. The poems carve out their sequential space
with the jagged edges of plosive phonemes, and it is at the level of the
syllable that we can detect a semblance of structure, as in the following:
'In the ballad of the blade she bites him / Obliged attack he shoots
mightily back in.'[25] The bilabial /b/ alliterates the first line with voiced
resonation and a punchiness punctuated by the slipping fricatives of
/ʃ/ and /s/. The consonant sounds are strung together with short vowel
sounds, the immediacy of the /I/ and /o/ phonemes affecting a kinetic
transmission from one consonant to the next. The second line utilises
a plosive produced in the back of the mouth. The velar /k/ phoneme
in the word-final position of 'attack' and 'back' functions as the raspy
companion of the transitory /a/ vowel sound. The navigation of these
lines impedes syllabic hesitation. The reader can only persist in the
production of Sheppard's prosodic score, its measures and cadences, as
we participate in what Derek Attridge describes as the 'forming' of the
text during a unique 'formal event'.[26] The result is an energetic recitation
and exploration of the capacities of the vocal tract, enjoying the pleasure
of experiencing the work without necessarily assimilating the form
with the content. To read *Warrant Error* in your head is unadvisable.
The sonic characteristics of the work threaten to exceed the limitations
placed upon them by received form. The poems testify to the desire
to break out of their 'pretty roome' into the world at large, to affect

---

[25] Sheppard, *Warrant Error*, p. 94.

[26] Attridge, *The Singularity of Literature*, pp. 113-14.

a full realisation of their rhythmic patterning.[27] John Donne's 'roome' in 'The Canonization', acknowledged by Sheppard in *The Meaning of Form in Contemporary Innovative Poetry* as a pun on the Italian word for stanza, is analogised with architectural precision to suggest that the continued use of 'received' form preserves the nexus of the character of the sonnet frame.[28] Sheppard's innovation with the line bears unlikely comparison with Donne's approach to the sonnet in the sixteenth and seventeenth centuries. The Renaissance poet's metrical intuitiveness and vigour of language tested the sonnet frame's capacity to communicate what T. S. Eliot describes as the poet's attempts to examine 'disparate experience' via the aesthetic of poetic form.[29] In Donne as in Sheppard, formal restriction operates to temper modes of expression and this tussle underpins the challenge set by the sonnet for those who seek to adopt it.

Warrant Error exhibits the manner of its own making. There are several self-reflexive references in the book to the poet's procedure and to the writing process generally. The text's curious sensibility is conspicuous in Sheppard's oeuvre, as the book's blurb rightly identifies when it claims that some of the poems explore the self 'with a tender and personal tone new to Sheppard's work'. The poems move through grammatical voice, the perspective changing from first to second and third point of view. The adoption of the first person pronoun 'I' lends the text a mortal cognisance, intimating through voice a proximity with the book's thematic content and reaffirming the notion that rhetoric is 'man-made' for 'man's' purpose. This implication is addressed in Sophie Collins's 'a whistle in the gloom', a poetics text written for *Atlantic Drift*, the volume of transatlantic contemporary poetry and poetics Sheppard edited with James Byrne. In it Collins reminds us that we derive our own 'autobiography' from a source 'somewhere outside' ourselves, and that the narrative 'I' 'is really anybody's, promiscuously'.[30] We cannot, of course, assume that the 'I' of the poem is the 'I' of the poet – some of the lines where the pronoun occurs are italicised, perhaps to imply appropriation – but in a text that tells in the third person of 'an affirmative thumb [that] grinds the old man's eyeball, / feeling the crack and

---

[27] John Donne, 'The Canonization' <https://www.poetryfoundation.org/poems/44097/the-canonization> [accessed 17 March 2018].

[28] Sheppard, *The Meaning of Form*, p. 48.

[29] T. S. Eliot, 'The Metaphysical Poets', *TLS*, 20 October 1921, pp. 669-70.

[30] Sophie Collins, 'a whistle in the gloom', in *Atlantic Drift*, pp. 281-91 (p. 287).

leak of its egg',[31] and in the first person 'I no longer turn up for my own recordings. / I simply send my voice along',[32] sensory disembodiment highlights a connection between human subjects to suggest an intimacy with the writer and their creative disposition. One such poem reads: 'I steal myself into the flow of writing, / tilting diagonals against rectilinear plots.'[33] The two lines describe writing as an activity *into* which the writer must enter. This space is enabling of mobility and is traversed by the writer during the creative procedure. Constructing poems is to affect obliquity upon 'rectilinear plots', altering the axis of perception to multiply apprehension in much the same way as is achieved by geometricity in the works of the Cubists. *Warrant Error* is a supremely linguistic exercise, the word is tilted, pitched, dipped into, and out of, the light. The poet focuses on the function of language by lifting it out of its original context and placing it into the augmenting realm of artifice. *Warrant Error* is a counter-manoeuvre, and this affords Sheppard's poetry the agency to appropriate as the poet *and* the politician twist language in the rhetorical act. Political language seeks subterfuge, conceals its true depths, cloaks its ideology by appealing to the interlocutor as a political being, preying upon their ideological biases. On the other hand, poetic language, in its emphasis on its own artificiality, harnesses ambiguity for readers to act autonomously.

The intensity of the poems is tempered by an affection that, when encountered, is astonishing. Sheppard dilutes the language of terror with a peculiar appreciation of the humane, moving usefully from the pensiveness of discourse towards palpable physicality. He writes: 'I put my arms around you and stop myself / Writing tales of backyard cargo cults.'[34] In the allusion to a world beyond writing, the poet suggests that creative production is meaningful only in terms of its relation to other facets of existence. By analogy, we become attentive to the human cost of political rhetoric, but also to its ceaseless presence and fundamental efficaciousness over the self. When Sheppard writes of 'the hollow of my dream / Which I want to write out', he suggests that respite can be found in writing, but also that experimentation in language may ulti-

---

[31] Sheppard, *Warrant Error*, p. 86.

[32] Ibid., p. 67.

[33] Ibid., p. 82.

[34] Ibid., p. 103.

mately lead to an invasion of the most basic of our human faculties.[35] The poet's 'eyes are full' in the presence of a world that circumscribes experience with the language it uses to construct it; somewhat paradoxically, the written word is his chosen restorative.[36]

The language of control and narrative appropriation

These poems do not 'tell' in the traditional sense – narrative defamiliarisation lurks ever close behind narrative cogency – but appropriate, blend, and subvert multiple lexical catalogues during a contradictory process that distils language to a greater concentrate. The result is a poetry comprised of language in all its colours twisting through kaleidoscopic nebula:

> Through slatted blinds you spy another
> writing a stutter scrawl of spidery infringement.
> You chisel each other into pedestal fear,
> nailed to combat mottoes, slashed
> and slotted in your mirror-script encryption[37]

Linguistic perceptivity premises his interrogation of rhetoric and is the foundation of his text's literariness; as we negotiate the poems, we become aware of the capacity of language to perform 'primary functions' via its 'staging' in the poem.[38] There are several references to one mode of transmitting language or another in the above passage: the motto, the encryption, the script, and the scrawl, which is indicative of the multifariously realised written and spoken word. Sheppard engages in the codification of these discourses, collecting and compounding disparate methods of communication, and relocating them in the sonnet frame. The semiotician Yuri Lotman describes the elevation of language from utilitarian towards artificial as the augmenting function of the poetic text.[39] The elevation is evidenced by the communicative differ-

---

[35] Ibid.

[36] Ibid.

[37] Ibid., p. 38.

[38] Attridge, *The Singularity of Literature*, p. 110.

[39] Yuri Lotman, *Analysis of the Poetic Text* (Ann Arbor, MI: Ardis, 1974), p. 32.

ences between prose and verse. In terms of expression, poetry occupies a higher plane, where language use produces a 'complexly constructed meaning' as an alternative to being wholly communicable.[40] For example, the 'mirror' of Sheppard's sonnet is a device used to suggest that language has the capacity to examine itself when placed in a poetic artefact. The fact that it is made of glass, may be hung in various rooms of a house, can feature convex or concave sections, are all irrelevant. The mirror's capacity to reflect and multiply provides the motivation for its inclusion in the poem and the reader is expected to be attentive to the fact that as an object that exists in the world the 'mirror' is inconsequential. Only in the context of the poem is the function of the word foregrounded, revealing to us a suggestion of its purpose. We may also note that the word with which it is compounded, 'script', suggests prior formulation, an indicator of stratagem and repetition. The image here is defined by the perceptibility of the poet, who presents language as constructing and deconstructing itself in a contradictory act that defers semantic cogency.

Awareness is a conduit to understanding, and the function of artifice in *Warrant Error* strikes as analogous to the function of, for example, the passive voice in the political sphere. In the essay 'Politics and the English Language', George Orwell lists six rules to fend off decadence and obscurity in the use of language: 'Never use the passive where you can use the active',[41] the fourth rule states. But why should one not use the passive voice where it is useful, as in an account of a scientific experiment? Orwell's rules are retaliatory, the 'pure wind' of political language their elected nemesis.[42] The statement George W Bush offered in response to a question about the torture of Iraqi nationals at the Abu Ghraib prison facility provides an example of the kind of passive voice that Orwell railed against: 'It's also important for the people of Iraq to know that in a democracy, everything is not perfect, that mistakes are made.'[43] The removal of the agent, the doer of the verb, suggests the cessation of responsibility. The statement is therefore incomplete, in the moment of utterance resistant to cogency of sense and understanding.

---

[40] Lotman, *Analysis of the Poetic Text*, p. 33.

[41] George Orwell, 'Politics and the English Language', in *Why I Write* (London: Penguin, 1984), pp. 102-20 (p. 119).

[42] Ibid., p. 120.

[43] *U. S. Department of State Archive*, 'Interview by Alhurra Television' <https://2001-2009.state.gov/p/nea/rls/rm/32282.htm> [accessed 15 March 2018].

The reader (or listener, in this case) can make inferences as to the agency of the verb and these may be multiple, but the use of the passive voice is motivated to obscure absolution through poly-semanticism. In this sense, political language is manufactured under controlled conditions defined by a level of attentiveness, the purpose of which is to control perception. However, Sheppard is aware that language is, ultimately, non-controllable. In the *Angel Exhaust* interview, he argues that poetic language is recalcitrant to authorial leverage due to being 'aestheticised in a dynamic imaginative zone' in which words 'have an autonomy of their own'.[44] The writer attends to the production of their work, in either poetry or political rhetoric, but cedes a part of their authority in its subsequent perception.

This is evidenced in Sheppard's repurposing of found text, where the preservation of an initial purpose is not possible. This instability is enabling of playfulness (notwithstanding solemnity in the thematic content, engaged as it is in the language of global conflict). Sheppard's appropriation intertwines various discourses in a knot of endless expansion that questions the mode of their transmission, particularly in relation to the relationship between politicians and the media:

> ... a dream of prime-ministerial photo-op:
> a fantail of microphones lays his fantastic egg, and
> blitzed martyr-bits pile up in paradise, next door[45]

The tension of semantic indeterminacy derives from the juxtaposition of syntactic structure against the application of poetic artifice. The 'and' after 'egg' indicates the presence of two syntactically independent clauses joined by the coordinating conjunction. Sheppard's preservation of a functional syntax presents the two clauses as structurally associated, but the relationship cannot be defined as causal. However, and somewhat paradoxically, the position of the line break and the enjambment operate against the expectations of syntactic coordination to imply causality. Sheppard dramatises the conjunction in the line-final position and the enjambment affects the slightest suspension in the reading, placing further the conjunction and its function into sharp focus. As a poetic device, the line break generates a hierarchical shift from which an ex-

---

[44] Pereira, 'An Interview with Robert Sheppard', p. 21.

[45] Sheppard, *Warrant Error*, p. 19.

pectation derived from a syntactic appreciation is not immune. Also, and considering the poem graphically, one of the 'independent' clauses is positioned on top of the other on the page, the poem's form acting to subvert the syntactic thrust of the constituent lines. Sheppard suggests the possibility of causality between two syntactically coherent but separate sentences via a formal sensitivity to the poetic line and the deferral of its projections.[46] The use of language is indicative. The first sentence (the second line in the example) features the pronoun 'his'. The second sentence does not feature a pronoun but does suggest an, albeit macabre, human presence in 'martyr-bits'. The possessive pronoun in the first sentence and the imbalance between the two evokes ownership. The close association is compounded by the adverbial 'next door', which suggests the kind of proximity encountered in a suburban British street rather than the monotheistic afterlife.

These imbalances are produced via the text's self-professed artificiality. The tension between cogent syntax and augmenting artifice is reminiscent of Roman Jakobson's somewhat flawed quest for parallelism as a structural foundation of the poetic text. Parallelism, Jonathan Culler explains, is the presence of the 'principle technique [...] of highly patterned language', upon which the poem is dependent if it is to elevate the language of giving information to that of artifice.[47] This is characterised by the presence of repeated items of similarity and the resultant equivalence afforded to those items. To seek out these patterns is in itself a valid pursuit, and one that features as central to many critical schemas concerned with literary studies. Jakobson demonstrates the significance of parallelism with a critical reading of one of Baudelaire's poem 'Spleen' (1857), of which Culler writes: 'In his zeal to display balanced figures, Jakobson treats grammar carelessly [and his] way of proceeding indicates the tenuousness and even irrelevance of this kind of numerical symmetry.'[48] The suggestion of irrelevance has its evidence and the claim cannot be ignored. However, Sheppard's adoption of the sonnet frame necessarily creates a group of poems that share a common, if not permutating, formal character. If parallelism exists in *Warrant Error*, it is in the very fabric of the poems' prescribed and collective form.

---

[46] Olson, 'Projective Verse'.

[47] Jonathan Culler, *Structuralist Poetics* (London: Routledge, 1975), p. 56.

[48] Culler, *Structuralist Poetics*, p. 60.

Indeed, the tension between syntactic equivalence and the subverting effect of the enjambed line in the above example both exploits and destabilises the device of parallelism by introducing the notion of hierarchy into the work. Sheppard places two parallel structures in proximity to one another, but the function is not to suggest equivalence. Rather, the subtle juxtaposition intimates the converse, a stratum of key differentiation. We cannot say that parallelism is the scaffold on which the word, the clause, and the line, are placed in equivalence, as the poems are defined by their transience, their disruption of the rules of grammar and their consequences.

Proximity and distance in the contemporary sonnet sequence

In the weblog *Pages*, Sheppard refers to poets who inspired the writing of *Warrant Error*. He writes:

> *Warrant Error* was influenced by [Ted] Berrigan [...] But I'd also written on [Tom] Raworth's sonnets by then (and on Allen Fisher's Apocalyptic Sonnets from the 1970s), Adrian [Clarke] was writing his own Skeleton Sonnets and Ken Edwards was publishing parts of his 8+6. Something was in the air.[49]

Raworth's sequence 'Sentenced to Death' was published in 1987 in the book *Visible Shivers*.[50] By contrast with Sheppard's modus operandi in *Warrant Error*, the image in Raworth's poems is conspicuous by its absence: each line appears elliptical, fragmentary, and unrealised. Clarke is also included in Hilson's anthology, which contains several extracts from the aforementioned *Skeleton Sonnets*.[51] Clarke's intertextuality is explicit, detectable across numerous references to the formal characteristics of the sonnet that have endured since the time of Wyatt.

    Warrant Error cannot be read without consideration of its intertextual relation to later experiments with the form. As well as the writers listed by Sheppard above, the poems here are reminiscent of Hilson's *In*

---

[49] Robert Sheppard, 'The Innovative Sonnet Sequence: Eight of 14: My Own Sonnets' <http://robertsheppard.blogspot.co.uk/search?q=sonnet+rooms> [accessed 15 March 2018].

[50] Tom Raworth, *Visible Shivers* (Oakland, CA: O Books, 1987).

[51] Adrian Clarke, *Skeleton Sonnets* (Bournemouth: Writers Forum, 2002).

The Assarts[52] and Geraldine Monk's *Ghost & Other Sonnets*.[53] Hilson's book contains a linguistic playfulness analogous to Sheppard's. For example, *In The Assarts* explores etymology by displacing the linguistic unit from its taxonomic class. Hilson transforms Wyatt's famous line 'Whoso list to hunt' into 'And with my 'Whoso' list', such that the nominal metamorphoses into the adjectival, the verbal into the nominal. The changes affect the function of the words in their respective contexts. Monk's collection adopts the 14-line frame of the sonnet with flexibility. Reflecting on Monk's text *Interregnum* (1994), Kat Peddie writes, '[this is] a poetic account of the Pendle Witches [that] fights back with its own language-magic'.[54] *Ghost & Other Sonnets* explores women's history through the amalgamation of appropriated discourses. The fairy tale and the ghost story intertwine with accounts of reality, the fantastical become elementary; the normative become unreal.

The suggestion advanced in these texts that language operates as the medium by which it inspects itself calls to mind Jacques Derrida's concept of the pharmakon, which in Greek can mean both 'remedy' and 'poison'. The term is derived from a reading of Plato's *Phaedrus*, where the 'function and value' of writing is discussed.[55] Derrida addresses the difficulty of definition, particularly in relation to linguistic binaries such as inside/outside and love/hate. Definition relies upon stability of meaning and this is difficult, if not impossible, to reach and maintain as meaning is derived from the difference between linguistic items and their interplay. Creative writing as a restorative for the damage wrought by political rhetoric is a paradoxical notion that fails to breach the undecidability of a single, or groups of, words. Sheppard's intertextual combination of disparate discourses, whether direct or indirect, becomes an analogy for indeterminacy: what could be called the rhetoric of poetry exhibits the enigma but does not solve it.

Despite this difficulty, in 'Word, Dialogue and Novel', Julia Kristeva states that 'any text is constructed as a mosaic of quotations; any text is the absorption and transformation of another'.[56] Likewise, *Warrant*

---

[52] Jeff Hilson, *In The Assarts* (London: Veer, 2010).

[53] Geraldine Monk, *Ghost & Other Sonnets* (Cambridge: Salt, 2009).

[54] Kat Peddie, 'Geraldine Monk' <https://blogs.kent.ac.uk/centreforcreativewriting/geraldine-monk/> [accessed 10 February 2018].

[55] Jacques Derrida, *Dissemination*, trans. by Barbara Johnson (Chicago, IL: University of Chicago Press, 1981), p. xxiv.

[56] Julia Kristeva, 'Word, Dialogue and Novel', in *The Kristeva Reader*, ed. by Toril Moi

Error is somewhat direct in its intertextual composition. At times, the sonnets enter into dialogue with other poetic works, redefining historical space for their own purposes:

> Frost-sharpened sunlight burns
> the skin. Between the staves of vapour-
> trails a sprinkle of the promised sand sings *I*
> *met a traveller from a sleeping cell*[57] (emphasis original)

Sheppard's 'I met a traveller from a sleeping cell' is an absorption and transformation of Shelley's line 'I met a traveller from an antique land' from the sonnet 'Ozymandias' (1818). There are strong thematic parallels between the two works.[58] 'Ozymandias' addresses Napoleonic advances in the Middle East and describes the satiric mocking of the Egyptian tyrant by the sculptor who unsympathetically reproduces his image. The sculpture has fallen to ruin, sat desolate in the gaping desert landscape. Similar to the sculptor's artistic interpretation of the oppressor via the appropriation of their form, Sheppard reproduces Shelley's work, submits it to augmentation, and reassigns it to another context where its purpose is to foreground both the concentration of its initial intention and the function of its renewed application. *Warrant Error* has as a central theme several purported binaries – cultural opposition between the East and the West, the tension between reality and its presentation in political language, and, as previously suggested, the difficult and complex delineation of the seemingly rudimentary notions of 'good' and 'bad', 'right' and 'wrong'. Sheppard evaluates the tenuous nature of surface simplicity via a stark revelation of narrative uncertainty. This derives from an intertextual polylogue that draws from and persists across numerous sources. In building these complex worlds, where political language, the 'gushing ruts' of 'friendless fire', is foregrounded, Sheppard exposes its shallows as well as its persistent quality of persuasiveness.

Shelley's poem opens on the word 'I', which is replaced in the latter thirteen lines by the voice of the traveller himself. Sheppard reworks

---

(New York, NY: Colombia University Press, 1986), pp. 34-61 (p. 37).

[57] Sheppard, *Warrant Error*, p. 20.

[58] Percy Bysshe Shelley, *The Complete Poetry of Percy Bysshe Shelley*, ed. by Donald H. Ryman, Neil Fraistat and Nora Cook (Baltimore, MD: University of Maryland Press), p. 326.

the line to construct a converse narrative where, instead of engaging in a dialogue, the traveller is described as 'from a sleeping cell', defined by detachment and furtiveness. The prepositional phrase introduces the notion of covert invasion, which creates a tangible distance between the traveller and the 'I' of the poem. As we have seen, Sheppard engages the rhetoric of poetry in the appropriation and reconstruction of political rhetoric. The collection assimilates the two rhetorical modes via the seizure of the cliché and the euphemism and their subsequent application in the context of the sonnet. It is difficult to describe the dynamic in moralistic terms; political language obscures sense, but so does the poetic. However, in the case of *Warrant Error*, artifice functions to explicate the initial act of subterfuge. For example, the erasure of individuality and demonisation of the other achieved by casting the 'traveller' as part of a 'sleeping cell' is exposed as the bleeding away of an indistinct 'phantasmal […] figure in the doorway' that verges on the stereotype and is indicative of scaremongering. The light that enables the perception of the scene is 'frost-sharpened', as if fashioned for its purpose. Sheppard recasts the traveller, the phantom, the figure, as imagined entities, using the language of subterfuge against itself. Where political rhetoric seeks to conceal the manner of the creation and the presence of its façade, rhetoric in poetry foregrounds the method by which its own obscurity is produced. Political stratagem is itself undermined by its rhetorical poetic counterpart.

Shelley seeks to distance himself as the poet from both the sculptor and the tyrant in the final lines of 'Ozymandias': 'Round the decay / Of that colossal wreck, boundless and bare / The lone and level sands stretch far away'.[59] Conversely, there is no sense of detachment in the Sheppard poem, where language is wrapped and squeezed by 'barbed-wire corsets' and revealed, made plain, in 'policed light that invades the portal'.[60] Sheppard's sonnet is defined by a gripping claustrophobia, the lines packed into the predetermined boundaries of the stanza. Although both poems occur across the same 14-line construct, the 'lone and level sands' of Shelley's work is expansive in contrast to the choking cilice of Sheppard's poetic space.

One of the enduring effects of reading *Warrant Error* is the recognition of the fallibility of language in its capacity to examine itself.

---

[59] Ryman et al. *The Complete Poetry of Percy Bysshe Shelley*, p. 326.

[60] Sheppard, *Warrant Error*, p. 20.

In a sense, the interrogation of political discourse by poetic discourse is at its most effective in the revelation of the linguistically concealed. Poets experimenting with form necessarily reveal the manner by which their works are constructed; reading is equally dependant on the interpretation of form as it is on content. This is not to say that the poem provides answers where the political soundbite does not. Rather, it is to state that the poem, sharing as it does the rhetorical function with political language, seeks to make transparent the method of its transmission. The objective in *Warrant Error* is not the systematic disclosure of the nature of reality, but the converse exposure of the function of political language to make opaque the mode of perception.

BIBLIOGRAPHY

Attridge, Derek, *The Singularity of Literature* (London: Routledge, 2004)

Byrne, James, and Robert Sheppard, eds, *Atlantic Drift: An Anthology of Poetry and Poetics* (Todmorden and Ormskirk: Arc Publications and Edge Hill University Press, 2017)

Clarke, Adrian, *Skeleton Sonnets* (Bournemouth: Writers Forum, 2002)

Coleman, Stephen, and Karen Ross, *The Media and the Public: "Them" and "Us" in Media Discourse* (Chichester & Hoboken, NJ: Wiley-Blackwell, 2010)

Culler, Jonathan, *Structuralist Poetics* (London: Routledge, 1975)

Derrida, Jacques, *Dissemination*, trans. by Barbara Johnson (Chicago, IL: The University of Chicago Press, 1981)

Donne, John, 'The Canonization', *Poetry Foundation* <https://www.poetryfoundation.org/poems/44097/the-canonization> [accessed 17 March 2018]

Eagleton, Terry, *How to Read a Poem* (Oxford: Blackwell, 2007)

Eliot, T. S., 'The Metaphysical Poets', in *Times Literary Supplement* < https://www.the-tls.co.uk/articles/public/archives/>

Hilson, Jeff, *In The Assarts* (London: Veer, 2010)

Kristeva, Julia, 'Word, Dialogue and Novel', in *The Kristeva Reader*, ed. by Toril Moi (New York, NY: Colombia University Press, 1986), pp. 34-61

Lotman, Yuri, *Analysis of the Poetic Text* (Ann Arbor, MI: Ardis, 1974)

Madden, Christopher, 'Berlin Bursts: Robert Sheppard', *The Wolf*, 26 (Spring 2012), pp. 74-79

Monk, Geraldine, *Ghost & Other Sonnets* (Cambridge: Salt, 2009)

Newman, Janet, "Listening Harder: Reticulating Poetic Tradition in Michele Leggott's 'Blue Irises', *Journal of New Zealand Literature*, 33 (2015), 110-127

Olson, Charles, 'Projective Verse' <https://www.poetryfoundation.org/articles/69406/projective-verse> [accessed 26 February 2018]

Orr, David, 'The Politics of Poetry' <https://www.poetryfoundation.org/poetrymagazine/articles/69080/the-politics-ofpoetry> [accessed 25 February 2018]

Orwell, George, *Why I Write* (London: Penguin, 1984)

Peddie, Kat, 'Geraldine Monk', *Creative Writing Reading Series* <https://blogs.kent.ac.uk/centreforcreativewriting/geraldine-monk/> [accessed 10 February 2018]

Pereira, Steven, 'An Interview with Robert Sheppard', *Angel Exhaust*, 7 (Summer 1987), pp. 17-24.

Raworth, Tom, *Visible Shivers* (Oakland, CA: O Books, 1987)

Shelley, Percy Bysshe, 'Ozymandias', in *The Complete Poetry of Percy Bysshe Shelley*, ed. by Donald H. Ryman, Neil Fraistat and Nora Cook (Baltimore, MD: The University of Maryland Press, 2012), p. 326

Sheppard, Robert, 'The Innovative Sonnet Sequence: Eight of 14: My Own Sonnets', *Pages* <http://robertsheppard.blogspot.co.uk/search?q=sonnet+rooms> [accessed 5 March 2018]

——— *The Meaning of Form in Contemporary Innovative Poetry* (London: Palgrave Macmillan, 2016)

———*Warrant Error* (Exeter: Shearsman Books, 2009)

Solt, Mary Ellen, 'Moon Shot Sonnet', in *The Reality Street Book of Sonnets*, ed. by Jeff Hilson (Hastings: Reality Street, 2008), p. 26

Upton, Lawrence, 'Sonnet: Cartoon Sonnet', in *The Reality Street Book of Sonnets*, ed. by Jeff Hilson (Hastings: Reality Street, 2008)

U.S. Department of State Archive, 'Interview by Alhurra Television', (2004) <https://20012009.state.gov/p/nea/rls/rm/32282.htm> [accessed 15 March 2018]

Williams, William Carlos, *Spring and All* (Paris: Contact Editions, 1923)

——— *The Embodiment of Knowledge* (New York, NY: New Directions, 1974)

'God's not too pleased with me': Robert Sheppard's Poetics of Transformative Translation

Tom Jenks

Robert Sheppard's *Petrarch 3: a derivative dérive* is a set of translations of the third poem in *Il Canzoniere*, a collection of poems by the Italian poet Francesco Petrarca (1304-'74; anglicised as 'Petrarch').[1] *Il Canzoniere* (or 'the song book'), comprises three-hundred and sixty-six poems, of which three-hundred and seventeen, including the third, are sonnets. The earliest date from 1327, when Petrarch first saw and fell in love with a young woman named Laura, in April of that year.[2] Petrarch explores his desire for Laura throughout *Il Canzoniere*, up to and beyond her death in 1348, a year in which the Black Death devastated Europe. The latter poems in *Il Canzoniere* articulate his grief and loss. *Il Canzoniere* is, as David Young notes, 'the work of a lifetime', with Petrarch adding to, editing and re-writing the poems over a period of forty-seven years, up to the year of his own death.[3] Laura's identity, like that of the 'dark lady' of Shakespeare's sonnets, has been widely debated but never conclusively confirmed.[4] Young states that answers to most questions about Laura 'must remain conjectural', but that she had 'blond hair, striking eyes, and considerable composure' and 'came from the Avignon area, most probably the village of Carpentras, where Petrarch lived in his youth'.[5] Young speculates further that 'she may well have been the Laura – the birth and death dates fit – who married into the de Sade family, a name made famous much later by the infamous Marquis'.[6]

---

[1] O.B. Hardison Jnr., Joseph G. Fucilla, and Christopher Kleinhenz, 'Petrarchism', in *The New Princeton Encyclopaedia of Poetry and Poetics*, ed. by Alex Preminger and T.V.F. Brogan (Princeton, NJ: Princeton University Press, 1993), pp. 902-04 (p. 902).

[2] Ibid., p. 902.

[3] David Young, 'Introduction', in *The Poetry of Petrarch*, ed. by David Young (London: Macmillan, 2014), pp. ix-xxiv (p. ix).

[4] Katherine Duncan-Jones, 'Introduction', in *The Arden Shakespeare: Shakespeare's Sonnets, Third Series*, ed. by Katherine Duncan-Jones (London: Thomson Learning, 1997), pp. 1–106.

[5] Ibid., p. ix.

[6] Ibid., pp. xiv-xv.

In the third poem, 'Era il giorno ch'al sol si scoloraro', Petrarch recounts seeing Laura for the first time at the church of St. Clare in Avignon, when he was twenty-two years old.[7] Petrarch, as translated by A. S. Kline, describes how 'Love discovered me all weaponless, / And opened the way to the heart through the eyes, / Which are made the passageways and doors of tears'.[8]

The act of moving a text from one language to another has generated a field of theory about the practice of translation that sometimes feels as vast and undecided as translation itself. John Ciardi states that 'translation is the art of failure'.[9] For George Henry Borrow 'translation is at best an echo'.[10] Any translation involves subjective decisions: to what extent, for example, is a translator to preserve a rhyme scheme; how might they resolve the more general tension between form and content in a language that is different from that in which the original was written? Nonetheless, the role conventionally played by the translator (in this instance Kline) is to perform a service. Kline uses his knowledge of mediaeval Italian to render Petrarch's originals into modern English and so make them more intelligible to the contemporary reader. According to Vladimir Nabokov, this is exactly what a translator should be doing. For Nabokov, the aim of translation is to get as close to the original as possible and 'the clumsiest literal translation is a thousand times more useful than the prettiest paraphrase'.[11]

Jorge Luis Borges takes a view that is typically slyer and more ludic. For Borges, the original and the translation are different texts, with the latter owing no duty of care to the former. Where a translation departs from the original, says Borges, rather than the translation betraying the source text by infidelity, 'the original is unfaithful to the translation'.[12] Harry Mathews, referenced by Sheppard in *Petrarch 3*, views translation as having its own, innate creative properties. For Mathews, translation

---

[7] Hardison Jnr., Fucilla, and Kleinhenz, 'Petrarchism', p. 902.

[8] Petrarch, *The Complete Canzoniere*, trans. by Anthony S. Kline (North Charleston, SC: Poetry in Translation, 2016), p. 20.

[9] John Ciardi, cited in Olive Classe, *Encyclopaedia of Literary Translation into English: A-L* (Abingdon: Routledge, 2000), p. 496.

[10] George Henry Borrow, *Lavengro* (London: John Murray, 1851), p. 120.

[11] Vladimir Nabokov, *Selected Letters 1940-1977* (Boston, MA: Houghton Mifflin Harcourt, 2002), p. 151.

[12] Jorge Luis Borges, cited in Efrain Kristal, *Invisible Work: Borges and Translation* (Nashville, TN: Vanderbilt University Press, 2002), p. 24.

is 'the paradigm, the exemplar of all writing. It is translation that demonstrates most vividly the yearning for transformation that underlies every act involving speech, that supremely human gift'.[13] Walter Benjamin argues that 'no poem is intended for the reader, no picture for the beholder, no symphony for the audience'.[14] The text, conceived holistically, is never just a content delivery mechanism. It is a mistake to view translation in terms of utility, with the role of the translator being simply to facilitate transmission. For Benjamin, 'any translation that intends to perform a transmitting function cannot transmit anything but communication - hence, something inessential'.[15] Translation is itself a form and 'in translation the original rises into a higher and purer linguistic air'.[16] Charles Bernstein argues that 'the translation of poetry is never more than an extension of the practice of poetry'.[17]

Recent years have seen several works of poetry that explore and develop this more tangential approach to translation. These include Philip Terry's *Dante's Inferno* (2014), Alan Halsey's *Versions of Martial* (2015) and Simon Smith's *The Books of Catullus* (2018).[18] *Bad Kid Catullus* (2017), edited by Kirsten Irving and Jon Stone, is a collection of versions of Catullus by twenty-eight writers including Vahni Capildeo, Wanda O'Connor and Claire Trévien.[19] Petrarch has also been recently translated by two other writers, Peter Hughes and Tim Atkins.[20] Sheppard dubs Hughes and Atkins 'the Petrarch boys' and cites both as inspirations for his own *Petrarch 3*.[21] Hughes' *Quite Frankly: after*

---

[13] Harry Mathews, *Country Cooking and Other Stories* (Detroit, MI: Burning Deck, 1980), p. 40.

[14] Walter Benjamin, 'The Task of the Translator', in *Selected Writings Volume 1 1913 - 1926*, ed. by Marcus Bullock and Michael Jennings (Cambridge, MA & London: The Belknap Press of Harvard University Press, 1996), pp. 253-63 (p. 253).

[15] Ibid., p. 253.

[16] Ibid., p. 257.

[17] Charles Bernstein, 'How Empty is my Bread Pudding', *Open Letter*, 12.3, (2004), pp. 66-76 (p. 66).

[18] Philip Terry, *Dante's Inferno* (Manchester: Carcanet, 2014); Alan Halsey, *Versions of Martial* (Newton-le-Willows: Knives Forks and Spoons, 2015); Simon Smith, *The Books of Catullus* (Manchester: Carcanet, 2018).

[19] *Bad Kid Catullus*, ed. by Jon Stone & Kirsten Irving (London: Sidekick Books, 2017).

[20] Peter Hughes, *Quite Frankly: After Petrarch's Sonnets* (Hastings: Reality Street, 2015); Tim Atkins, *Petrarch Collected* (London: Crater Press, 2014).

[21] Robert Sheppard, *The Meaning of Form Atkins' and Hughes' Petrarch*, Pages <http://

Petrarch's Sonnets (2015) and Atkins' *Petrarch Collected* (2014) are both larger scale undertakings than Sheppard's. Hughes produced versions of all three-hundred and seventeen sonnets in *Il Canzoniere*. Atkins went further, 'versioning' the non-sonnet poems in addition. They share with Sheppard, however, an interest in disrupting, *détourning* and deconstructing the mediaeval Italian originals by using contemporary linguistic registers and references. Hughes also gave the works of the twelfth-century Italian poet Guido Cavalcanti similar treatment.[22] Before translating Petrarch, Atkins produced versions of Horace.[23] Caroline Bergvall's versions of Chaucer, *Meddle English* (2011) and Nicholas Moore's *Spleen* (1973), a set of versions of Baudelaire, take similarly digressive translational paths.[24] Atkins offers a definition of translation that is broad and inclusive, encompassing procedural methodologies such as those used by David Cameron in *Flowers of Bad* (2007) (another set of versions of Baudelaire), bpNichol in 'Translating Translating Apollinaire' (1979) and Jackson Mac Low in *French Sonnets* (1989).[25] Cameron's translational techniques include using spellcheck software. He describes his *Flowers of Bad* versions of Baudelaire as 'false translations', being 'made without the intention of translating the literal meaning of the original'.[26] Nichol (1979) used a range of procedures and processes, including alphabetisation, re-arrangement according to word length and synonyms.[27] Mac Low's *French Sonnets* sequence is a treatment of Shakespeare's sonnets. His methods included looking up words in dictionaries and substituting them for the headword at the top of the column containing it.[28]

---

robertsheppard.blogspot.co.uk/2016/09/robert-sheppard-meaning-of-form-atkins. html> [accessed 27 February 2017].

[22] Peter Hughes, *Cavalcanty* (Manchester: Carcanet, 2017).

[23] Tim Atkins, *Horace* (New York, NY: O Books, 2007).

[24] Caroline Bergvall, *Meddle English* (New York: Nightboat Books, 2011); Nicholas Moore, *Spleen* (London: Menard Press, 1990).

[25] Tim Atkins, *Seven Types of Translation: Petrarch's Canzoniere* (unpublished doctoral thesis, Roehampton University, 2011), p. 32.

[26] David Cameron, *Flowers of Bad* (New York, NY: Unbelievable Alligator, 2007), p. 202.

[27] bp Nichol, *Translating Translating Apollinaire: A Preliminary Report* ([n.d.]) <http:// www.thing.net/~grist/l&d/bpnichol/lnichol1.htm> [accessed 1 May 2018].

[28] Jackson Mac Low and Anne Tardos, *Thing of beauty: new and selected works*, ed. by Anne Tardos (Berkeley, CA: University of California Press, 2008), pp. 178-79.

Peter Riley, in his essay 'Translation, Expanded Translation, Version, Mess' categorises Sheppard, Terry, Smith, Hughes and Atkins (together with Laurie Duggan, David Hadbawnik and Trevor Joyce) as writers who have produced 'works claiming the new tag "expanded translation"', although Sheppard disputes this, stating that 'I haven't … and I doubt if others are using it about their practice'.[29] Riley views the concept of 'expanded translation' with suspicion. For Riley, 'expanded translation doesn't just change the text, it perverts and distorts and mocks and erases it'. He is particularly hostile towards Atkins, labelled 'a modernising and recklessly erasing translator relying on bathos', implicitly ridiculing his readers 'for expecting either sense or affect'.[30] Riley is not against creative modes of translation *per se*. He approves, for instance, of Moore's *Spleen*, seeing this as transcending its ludic origins to return the self 'back to the centre of the discourse'.[31] For Riley, however, translation must retain a closer bond with the original than that demonstrated by Atkins.

Sheppard makes his own views clear in 'Translation and Trans-formation', the chapter in *The Meaning of Form in Contemporary Innovative Poetry* that deals with translation in general and with Petrarch, Atkins, and Hughes in particular. Sheppard argues that 'translation is a mode of transformation, where the formal risk of an "original" may be "translated" into a new form'. This may be through strategies 'of distance or difference, prompt or constraint, inventive re-workings or wild forms of re-imagining'.[32] As Sheppard notes, Petrarch himself 'was pretty clear that translation implied more than faithful reproduction of linguistic features', invoking apiculture to make his point: 'take care… that the nectar does not remain in you in the same state as when you gathered it; bees would have no credit unless they transformed it into something different and better'.[33] It is this 'different and better'

---

[29] Peter Riley, *Translation, Expanded Translation, Version, Mess* <http://fortnightlyreview. co.uk/2018/03/translation-expanded/> [accessed 25 April 2018]; Robert Sheppard, 'Peter Riley on my Petrarch 3 and other "expanded translations"', *Pages* <http://robertsheppard.blogspot.co.uk/2018/03/peter-riley-on-my-petrarch-3-and-other.html> [accessed 26 April 2018].

[30] Riley, *Translation, Expanded Translation, Version, Mess*.

[31] Peter Riley, 'Afterword', in *Spleen* (London: Menard Press, 1990), pp. 51–53 (p. 53).

[32] Robert Sheppard, *The Meaning of Form in Contemporary Innovative Poetry* (London: Palgrave Macmillan, 2016), p. 82.

[33] Robert Sheppard, *On Writing Petrarch 3*, unpublished.

conception of translation, where the translator is envisaged as co-creator and the taking of liberties, rather than being frowned upon, is actively encouraged, that informs Sheppard's *Petrarch 3*. In *The Poetry of Saying* (2005), Sheppard cites Rachel Blau Du Plessis' description of poetics as providing 'permission to continue'.[34] We can view the transformative methods used by Sheppard in *Petrarch 3* as providing similar permission by facilitating the production of new texts.

Unlike *Quite Frankly* and *Petrarch Collected*, Sheppard's *Petrarch 3* is not a translation of all of Petrarch's sonnets, but an iterative treatment of a single sonnet. With a nod to the characteristics of the sonnet form, Sheppard presents first a translation, and then fourteen versions of that translation. Important as Atkins and Hughes are to Sheppard's translational poetics, a more fitting analogue for *Petrarch 3* is *Spleen*, mentioned by Sheppard in the text preceding the sequence. *Spleen* comprises thirty-one versions of Baudelaire's 'Je suis comme le roi...' written under pseudonyms and entered by Moore in the 1968 Sunday Times Baudelaire translation competition. Moore's sequence, whilst being serious in its intentions, is nonetheless playful. His *noms de plume* include 'Swingsby Swingsby-Glamis-Swingsby, c/o The Wild Hart's Council, late of St. James' Square, now in with-it Piccadill', whose competition entry comes with the instruction that it is 'for the reading voice of Richard Burton'.[35] Moore states in his introduction to *Spleen* that 'one of the legitimate functions of attempted translation is to relate work translated to the contemporary world; that is to say to the world contemporary to the translator'.[36] For Moore, 'straight' translation is impossible, influenced as it inevitably must be by the translator's tastes and decisions: 'all I have against translation is that it can't be done.'[37] His recursive methodology is similar to Sheppard's. Like Moore, Sheppard assumes multiple authorial identities and utilises multiple sources, including Baudelaire.

Sheppard describes the first translation in *Petrarch 3* as a 'rough translation, shaped to the Petrarchan frame (as I call it) but lightly

---

[34] Robert Sheppard, *The Poetry of Saying: British Poetry and Its Discontents, 1950-2000* (Liverpool: Liverpool University Press, 2005), p. 194.

[35] Moore, *Spleen*, p. 40.

[36] Ibid., p. 11.

[37] Ibid., p. 13.

rhyming'.[38] Kline's translation of Petrarch's third sonnet is as follows:

> *It was on that day when the sun's ray*
> *was darkened in pity for its Maker,*
> *that I was captured, and did not defend myself,*
> *because your lovely eyes had bound me, Lady.*
>
> *It did not seem to me to be a time to guard myself*
> *against Love's blows: so I went on*
> *confident, unsuspecting; from that, my troubles*
> *started, amongst the public sorrows.*
>
> *Love discovered me all weaponless,*
> *and opened the way to the heart through the eyes,*
> *which are made the passageways and doors of tears:*
>
> *so that it seems to me it does him little honour*
> *to wound me with his arrow, in that state,*
> *he not showing his bow at all to you who are armed.* [39]

Sheppard's version reads:

> *That pitiful morning when the light of Heaven*
> *Was hidden for our mourning maker's sake,*
> *I saw you first that day, My Lady, but*
> *Was captured, disarmed, then bound to your stake.*
>
> *It didn't seem the time for shields and armour*
> *Against Love's arrows, his batters and blows;*
> *So, unsuspecting, I wept with the world,*
> *But that day my heartbreaks began, my woes.*
>
> *Love stalked me, found me, unarmed and weak,*
> *And opened my eyes, portals of tears, through which*
> *Sorrow flowed from the passage of my heart.*

---

[38] Robert Sheppard, 'Robert Sheppard on The Petrarch Boys: Peter Hughes and Tim Atkins', *Pages* <http://robertsheppard.blogspot.com/2013/12/robert-sheppard-on-petrarch-boys-peter.html> [accessed 10 June 2018].

[39] Petrarch, *Il Canzoniere*, p. 20.

> But feeble was Love's triumph to triumph
> With his arrow over one so enfeebled,
> And to not even dare to flash you his dart. [40]

Sheppard's translation mainly corresponds with Kline's. 'It was on that day when the sun's ray' becomes 'That pitiful morning when the light of Heaven'. Love discovers Kline's Petrarch 'all weaponless'.[41] Sheppard's protagonist is 'unarmed and weak'.[42] We can detect, nonetheless, in Sheppard's version, a heightening of poetic diction that we can read both as stylistic flourish and deliberate undercutting of the very notion of poetic style. The final tercet, with its flashed dart, is delivered with an eyebrow raised in an Italianate arch.[43] Sheppard states that 'in the original poem Love shows his 'bow' but 'dart' was chosen to rhyme with 'heart' in my version [...] the possessor of both bows and arrows being Cupid'.[44]

Throughout the sequence, Sheppard riffs off his own translation, referring to it thematically and also in terms of vocabulary. 'Iron Maiden', perhaps referencing Laura's speculative connection to the Marquis de Sade, fuses BDSM sexual practices and the funeral of former Conservative Prime Minister Margaret Thatcher: 'Posties brushed up their / *MaggieMaggieMaggie* chants and I cried *onions- / onions-onions*, stinging eyes fixed on your heels'. The ambiguously flashed 'dart' of the first treatment becomes here something altogether less coy: 'Would rubbery Love / through his pouch dare to flash you his horn?'[45] The Sheppardian themes of desire and submission are picked up again in 'Freeview', a poem set in 'the refrigerated hold of factory-line phone sex', which I discuss later. Other vocabularic echoes include line four of Sheppard's first treatment ('Was captured, disarmed, then bound to your stake') which is carried through into the Baudelaire-referencing 'A Florentine Vampire in Paris', who is 'holding fast the stake to my bloated heart' before flashing his fangs in the final line.[46]

[40] Robert Sheppard, *Petrarch 3: a derivative dérive* (London: Crater Press, 2016).

[41] Petrarch, *Il Canzoniere*, p. 20.

[42] Sheppard, *Petrarch 3*

[43] Ibid.

[44] Sheppard, *On Writing Petrarch 3*, p. 18.

[45] Sheppard, *Petrarch 3*.

[46] Ibid.

Positioning in *Petrarch 3* is made contingent by its physical properties. Although Crater Press publish books, Atkin's *Petrarch Collected* being one example, their output includes less traditional formats such as printed cards and poster poems. *Petrarch 3* is in one sense a poster poem in that it can be folded out to poster size. It is more akin, however, as Sheppard himself notes in a blog post accompanying the launch of *Petrarch 3*, to a map, albeit one that abets rather than aids navigation.[47] Whilst it is obvious which side to read first (the side with the title text on it) and which poem to read first (the original Italian Petrarch immediately to the right of the title text), matters quickly become more complicated. It's a logical step from Petrarch's Italian to Sheppard's largely faithful translation, which is placed just below it. Our eye is guided further by the poem panels being presented in white and the panels not containing poems being presented in muted brown, blank screens awaiting their own versions. This does not, however, help us much in deciding where to go next. Do we proceed left to right or top to bottom? Is the placement of two separate poems next to one another a random act of desktop publishing, or does it suggest a relationship? By stretching and fragmenting the poem-space, the physical format of *Petrarch 3* becomes part of the text. We are forced, quite literally, to wrestle with it to access the poems themselves. The gnomic map becomes a hypertext, encouraging multiple readings and participatory meaning making, as in *Complete Twentieth Century Blues* with its numbered subtitles delineating networks, interconnections and 'strands'.[48]

Alternative identities thread through *Petrarch 3*. Sheppard's assumption of personae in the shape of a Florentine vampire and a BDSM practitioner in a dungeon has already been noted. Elsewhere, he raids his own back catalogue to bring us poems in the voice of two of his earlier alter egos. Wayne Pratt, a deft parody of a mainstream, Larkinesque poet, appears at various times in Sheppard's work. He is the author of *The Penguin Book of British Parrots*, three poems from which appear in *History or Sleep*.[49] We find him watering a cactus in

---

[47] Robert Sheppard, 'Petrarch 3 published NOW by CRATER Press number 36', *Pages* <http://robertsheppard.blogspot.co.uk/2017/01/robert-sheppard-petrarch-3-published-by.html> [accessed 2 March 2017].

[48] Robert Sheppard, *Complete Twentieth Century Blues* (Cambridge: Salt, 2008), introductory note.

[49] Robert Sheppard, *History or Sleep* (Bristol: Shearsman, 2015), pp. 46-48.

poem sixty-two of *Complete Twentieth Century Blues*.[50] Pratt later meets his end at the hand of one Justin Sidebottom in poem sixty-seven.[51] 'VE Day 1985' is styled (or, as Sheppard terms it 'signalled') 'after Wayne Pratt' and uses Pratt's tone of parody.[52] The deliberately flat tone counterpoints the self-conscious elevation found elsewhere in the sequence. Sheppard aims another blow at mainstream poetics in 'You Know', the final poem in the *Petrarch 3* sequence, where 'It's National Poetry Day again. Duffy's / droning on the radio (again)', referring to Poet Laureate Carol Ann Duffy. Here, Petrarch is overlooked and embittered, his poetic cadences drowned out by 'your thumping Great I Ams in clumping iambics', noting ruefully that '*my* name is reduced to a rhyme-scheme you use'.[53] Also making an appearance in *Petrarch 3* is René Van Valkenborch, bilingual Flemish and Walloon poet, cracked actor of translational hauntology and the 'author' of *A Translated Man*.[54] Van Valkenborch contributes one of his trademark 'twitterodes', re-tooled here as a 'twittersonnet'. Its short lines, disrupted by slashes, give the air of a compressed, redacted text:

> dark morn
> sad god/sa
> w you/stak
> ed me/bad[55]

Self, selves and personae are also relevant to 'Empty Diary 1327'. The title, as well as alluding to the year in which Petrarch first saw Laura, also links to Sheppard's own *Empty Diary* series of poems that erupts periodically in *Complete Twentieth Century Blues* and continues to unfold in various manifestations, such as 'Wiped Weblogs', a set of eight sonnets published in online magazine *The Literateur*.[56] Sheppard

---

[50] Sheppard, *Complete Twentieth Century Blues*, p. 322.

[51] Ibid., p. 329.

[52] Robert Sheppard, 'A Petrarchan Sonnet in the Style of Wayne Pratt for Patricia Farrell', *Pages* <http://robertsheppard.blogspot.co.uk/2017/01/robert-sheppard-petrarch-3-published-by.html> [accessed 2 March 2017].

[53] Sheppard, *Petrarch 3*.

[54] Robert Sheppard, *A Translated Man* (Bristol: Shearsman, 2013).

[55] Sheppard, *Petrarch 3*.

[56] Robert Sheppard, 'Empty Diaries 2001-2008', *The Literateur* <http://literateur.com/empty-diaries-2001-2008-by-robert-sheppard/> [accessed 3 March 2017].

describes the *Empty Diary* series as 'dealing with sexual politics, generally narrated from the point of view of a woman'.[57] We can see this too in *Petrarch 3* in 'Empty Diary 1327', a dissection of the male gaze narrated from the point of view of its recipient, a woman, perhaps Laura herself, 'snarling under my wimple, / snapping this backward dilation as a trap'. The romantic Petrarchan viewpoint is undercut by references to how 'His moist balls turn to weeping eyes / for this singular event, his wordy woe' and 'Sorrow seeps from his pump'.[58] Sheppard's deliberately crude and carnal phraseology reminds us that, however abstract and courtly his formulations, Petrarch is, throughout *Il Canozoniere*, talking about and is animated by sexual desire.

Sheppard goes further in this regard in 'Freeview', where he is again 'dealing with sexual politics', although this time with a male rather than a female protagonist, a late-night channel-hopper seeking 'Relief from *Comic Relief*', 'flipping past Russia Today' to the phone sex channel Babestation Academy, where he finds 'you, Charity, shaking your shapely rump'. 'Freeview' is an uncomfortable read, the language sexualised and blunt: 'your fresh breasts not yet silicone bloaters'; 'my weak song at your tight thong'.[59] Sheppard is operating near the knuckle, but to dismiss 'Freeview' as casual misogyny or an endorsement of the male gaze would be to miss the subtlety of the piece. 'Freeview' is certainly a poem that articulates a phallocentric (or phallogocentric) worldview, but it is a poem that critiques rather than endorses it. In so doing, it foregrounds Petrarch's own objectification of Laura and his absorption of her into his taxonomy of desire. Sheppard's protagonist here, like Petrarch, is trapped in 'one way communication', in this case listening in to Charity's 'filth' over the phone or perhaps even just contemplating doing so, either way knowing that this link can be broken at any moment 'by the flick / of a switch'.[60]

In terms of potential ethical unease, however, 'Freeview' is exceeded in the Petrarch sequence by 'Now then now then then and now', written in the voice of Jimmy Savile, a disc jockey, television personality and charity fundraiser who was revered as a great British eccentric and

---

[57] Robert Sheppard, 'New poems 'Empty Diaries 2001-8' (Wiped Weblogs) in The Literateur', *Pages* <http:/lrobertsheppard.blogspot.co.uk/2016/10/robert-sheppard-new-poems-empty-diaries.html> [accessed 3 March 2017].

[58] Sheppard, *Petrarch 3*.

[59] Ibid.

[60] Ibid.

institution. On his death in 2011, as Dan Davies describes, 'his familiar face dominated the front pages of almost every Sunday newspaper in the land, while on the inside pages the great and good lined up to pay their respects'. These included a spokesperson for the Prince of Wales, who Savile 'had mentored and served as a trusted confidante'.[61] Within a year, however, the truth about Savile as a prolific sexual predator and large-scale abuser had been revealed. Savile remains one of the most poisonous figures in British culture but is here unflinchingly appropriated by Sheppard. Petrarch, in Kline's translation, describes the sun's ray being 'darkened in pity for its maker'.[62] Sheppard makes this darkness metaphysical, having Savile declare that 'God's not too pleased with me'.[63] The phrase also implies that Savile, ruthless networker and triangulator, is on speaking terms with the almighty and that even in the afterlife he remains immune from the consequences of his actions. He has not been dispatched for eternal punishment in Hell. Savile describes how he 'spun the grooves and groped the grubs / from the milk bars of Leeds to the morgue at Broadmoor', whipping 'my wet cigar out of my baby-blue trackie bottoms / quicker than it took them to smash up my tombstone'. Savile shows no more remorse in death than in life, revelling in his notoriety declaring, *pace* Adrian Henri, that 'hate is when you're feeling Top of the Pops'.[64] As with 'Freeview', we again encounter questions of legitimacy and also of cultural sensitivity. Joan Retallack, discussing 'poethics', argues that writers must be sensitive to the impact of their work and must be aware of context and interpretation.[65] 'Now then now then then and now' could certainly cause offence, even outrage, but this does not mean we should dismiss it as shock for shock's sake. We can view 'Now then now then then and now', 'Freeview' and *Petrarch 3* generally as embodying a poetics where nothing is off limits. We can also see 'Now then now then then and now' as further deconstructing the Petrarchan conceit of courtly love by questioning its moral basis. Savile, 'the rock-hard tart who pecked his way up Thatcher's snatch' was clearly an outlier and his appetites

[61] Dan Davies, *In Plain Sight: The Life and Lies of Jimmy Savile* (London: Quercus Editions, 2014), p. 322.

[62] Petrarch, *Il Canzoniere*, p. 20.

[63] Sheppard, *Petrarch 3*.

[64] Ibid.

[65] Joan Retallack, *The Poethical Wager* (Berkeley, CA: University of California Press, 2003), pp. 13-14.

monstrous.[66] However, other expressions of sexual desire in classical literature may now also cause us to baulk, such as *Romeo and Juliet*, where Juliet 'hath not seen the change of fourteen years'.[67] Sheppard raises these issues but leaves them unresolved, pushing them instead onto the reader, demonstrating once more the potential of creative translation, interrogating our notions of Savile by refracting them through a classical lens. Sheppard plays further games of identity in 'Pet', viewed from the perspective of a dog being taken 'on walkies to Seffie' (Sefton Park in Liverpool) on Black Friday. Sheppard's reference here is to how the term was used by taxi drivers to describe the frenetic last Friday before Christmas, now termed by them 'Mad Friday' to distinguish it from the late November day of consumer meltdown imported from the USA. Sheppard's usage suggests alcoholic excess and hangovers rather than extreme shopping. The term also references the Easter setting of Petrarch's sonnet. Sheppard's protagonist experiences a sexually charged episode with another animal. Again, Sheppard is artfully manipulating the Petrarchan viewpoint. In 'Now then now then then and now', these manipulations implicitly question the legitimacy of obsessive, acquisitive desire by attaching them to a morally repugnant figure. In 'Pet', Sheppard does his work through anthropomorphic comedy, with Petrarch's finely wrought erotic encounter becoming one where 'Your wet nose sniffed my arse and I growled and howled'.[68] Love has Hughes' Petrarch metaphorically 'by the balls'.[69] Sheppard's canine amorist suffers a more literal equivalent, dragged away from his beloved with his owner's 'boot in my nuts'.[70]

In 'Petrak: the first English sonnet, Good Friday 1401', Sheppard again re-tabulates Petrarch's vocabulary but to different effect. Rather than modernising, he instead moves sideways, slipping into the register of early fifteenth century English. The first line of his initial translation, 'That pitiful morning when the light of Heaven', becomes 'The morwe biganne when hevene its bemes' and the first line of the first tercet, 'Love stalked me, found me, unformed and weak' becomes 'Love cam

---

[66] Sheppard, *Petrarch 3*.

[67] William Shakespeare, *Romeo and Juliet* (Cambridge: Cambridge University Press, 2008), p. 101.

[68] Sheppard, *Petrarch 3*.

[69] Hughes, *Quite Frankly*, p. 11.

[70] Sheppard, *Petrarch 3*.

russhyng to smerte my peynes sorwe'.[71] The first English sonnets were written by Sir Thomas Wyatt and Henry Howard, Earl of Surrey in the sixteenth century, over a hundred years after this piece's declared date. The language suggests Chaucer, but Chaucer died in 1400. Sheppard explains that the title 'suggests that somebody, not Chaucer, who knew Petrarch's work, adapted it, indeed "introduced Petrarchan lyric into England over a century prior to the sonnets of Wyatt and Surrey"'. This, says Sheppard, is 'a joke at the expense of Wyatt and Surrey', both of whom are credited as the earliest adapters of the Petrarchan sonnet form into English.[72] As such, they have become important in Sheppard's own translational cosmology. This playful laying of false trails is a further layer of artifice and reminds us, in the words of François Le Lionnais in the first OuLiPo manifesto, that 'when they are the work of poets, entertainments, pranks, and hoaxes still fall within the domain of poetry'.[73] Elsewhere, Sheppard sidles into French symbolism in 'Pale', dedicated to poet Peter Manson, a tangential translator of Stéphane Mallarmé.[74]

Michael Schmidt summaries Wyatt, born 1503, as 'a courtier, soldier and gentleman', presented at the Tudor court at the age of thirteen and entering active service under Henry VIII at the age of twenty-three. He was an ambassador to France and to Rome, was Marshal of Calais for four years and was Chief Ewer at the coronation of Anne Boleyn, whose lover he was rumoured to have been.[75] Wyatt was prominent in the political class of his time and would be of historical interest regardless of his literary career. It is for his poetry, however, that Wyatt is most remembered, in particular his engagement with the work or Petrarch. Eustace Tillyard states that 'it was Petrarch whom Wyatt copied most freely. From Petrarch he derived the sonnet and certain conventional sentiments, which, once introduced into English love poetry, formed its staple subject matter, with certain interruptions and revolts, for about

---

[71] Ibid.

[72] Sheppard, *On Writing Petrarch 3*.

[73] François Le Lionnais, 'First Manifesto', in *OuLiPo: a Primer of Potential Literature*, ed. by Warren F. Motte Jnr. (Lincoln, NE: University of Nebraska Press, 1986), pp. 26-28 (p. 26).

[74] Peter Manson, *English in Mallarmé* (London: Blart Books, 2014).

[75] Michael Schmidt, *Lives of the Poets* (London: Phoenix Books, 1998), pp. 132-33.

a century and a half'.[76] Wyatt, as Atkins notes, did not regard himself
as bound by the Petrarchan originals and departed from them freely
both in terms of vocabulary and structure. Wyatt's translation of 'Poem
199' of *The Canzoniere*, for instance, is thirty lines long rather than
the standard sonnet length of fourteen and his version of 'Poem 206',
at forty-nine lines long, is ten lines shorter than Petrarch's original.[77]
This means, according to Atkins, that 'many of Wyatt's translations of
Petrarch are, in tone, focus, and form, poems that contain as much of
Wyatt as they do of Petrarch'.[78]

Surrey's versions of Petrarch are, argues Dennis Keene, 'more like
adaptations than actual translations, as Surrey's aim was to fit Petrarchan
style on to an English reality'.[79] Schmidt describes Surrey, born in
1517, as 'an exemplary linguist' who mastered Latin, Italian, French
and Spanish and who was close to 'the young Duke of Richmond,
illegitimate son of Henry VIII', a position affording him social and
political advantage. Like Wyatt, he had a career as a solider and diplomat
and was given command of Boulogne in 1545. Unlike Wyatt, he was
not able to position himself with enough skill to avoid a violent death,
beheaded in the Tower of London in January 1547. Surrey's cause was
not helped by being related to Catherine Howard, Henry's fifth wife,
who was herself beheaded in 1542.[80]

Sheppard's Wyatt and Surrey is an intriguing progression from
his Petrarch in two ways. Firstly, Sheppard's translations of Wyatt and
Surrey can be termed 'meta translations' in that they are translations
of translations, adding a further layer of distance, distortion and
ventriloquism. Secondly, Sheppard is dealing here with 'originals' that
are already in English. Wyatt and Surrey wrote in a form of English
that is now over five-hundred years old, but their work is nonetheless
more readily intelligible to the modern reader than Petrarch's mediaeval
Italian. The opening of Wyatt's version of 'Poem XIX' of *The Canzoniere*
('Son animali al mondo') reads 'There can be some fowles of sight so

---

[76] Eustace Tillyard, cited in D. G. Rees, 'Sir Thomas Wyatt's Translations from
Petrarch', *Comparative Literature*, 7.1 (1955), 15-24 (p. 15).

[77] Atkins, *Seven Types of Translation*, pp. 14-15.

[78] Ibid., p. 14.

[79] Dennis Keene, 'Notes', in *Henry Howard, Earl? of Surrey: Selected Poems*, ed. by
Dennis Keene (New York, NY: Routledge, 2003), pp. 83-91 (p. 86)

[80] Schmidt, *Lives of the* Poets, p. 139.

proud and starke, / As can behold the sunne, and neuer shrinke'.[81] Whilst the archaic spelling and terminology ('fowles' for 'birds', for instance) may slow understanding, the general meaning – that there are some birds with sight so strong that they can look directly at the sun – can be more easily drawn out. Sheppard's version of this, 'Hap 1: Som fowles there be that have so perfaict sight', part of his *Hap: Understudies of Thomas Wyatt's Petrarch* series, opens with 'I pull down the blind on the sunny train to shield my eyes / like it's 1948 and I'm some old bird from "the firm"'.[82] Sheppard's process here may more properly be referred to as 'versioning' rather than translation, a term he uses to describe, amongst other works, Terry's *Shakespeare's Sonnets* (2010). Terry subjects Shakespeare to a battery of transformational techniques, including Oulipian procedural methods. Discussing *Shakespeare's Sonnets*, Sheppard states that Shakespeare's originals 'lose form in the restless versionings of Terry's book' and that 'the new form that emerges in our encounter with the pages is actually the perceived and received difference between the original (or what is recalled of it, or what it assumed of it) and the version'.[83] Sheppard's summation could also be applied to his own 'versionings' of Wyatt. Sheppard's treatments of Wyatt's treatments of Petrarch assert their 'difference' through modernisation, both of language and in points of reference. After first re-staging the poem 'like it's 1948' and transforming Wyatt's 'sunne' to the nuclear sun of the Los Alamos atom bomb test of 1945, Sheppard switches in the second stanza to 2017. Drawing on Wyatt's background of statesmanship, Sheppard transports him to a contemporary political context, after the 2016 European Union referendum. Wyatt, once a papal ambassador, trusted by kings and intimate with queens, is now on his way 'up to town / to discuss exit strategies with the three jokers', who we can assume to be the three most prominent pro-Brexit campaigners Nigel Farage, then leader of the U.K. Independence Party (UKIP), and the Conservative politicians Boris Johnson and Michael Gove.[84]

---

[81] Sir Thomas Wyatt, cited in Patricia Thomson, *Thomas Wyatt: The Critical Heritage* (London: Routledge, 1995), p. 38.

[82] Robert Sheppard, 'from Hap: Understudies of Thomas Wyatt's Petrarch by Robert Sheppard; Hap 1: Som fowles there be that have so perfaict sight', *Poetry at Sangam* <http://poetry.sangamhouse.org/2017/07/from-hap-understudies-of-thomas-wyatt%E2%80%99s-petrarch-by-robert-sheppard> [accessed 2 May 2017].

[83] Sheppard, *The Meaning of Form*, p. 60.

[84] Sheppard, *Hap 1*.

Sheppard reconfigures Wyatt by deploying deliberately jarring and provocatively anachronistic references. He describes the Wyatt poems as weaving 'Wyatt's versions of Petrarch, Wyatt's life as an endangered servant of that first Brexiteer, Henry VIII, and a modern day civil servant of the Brexit-obsessed administration of Theresa May, together into a satirical narrative'.[85] Sheppard uses Wyatt in the way Wyatt used Petrarch: as a means of producing a new work of literature that is linked to, but not bound by, the original. Sheppard notes that, at the time of writing *Petrarch 3*, that he had no 'presentiment' that he would subsequently enter into a discourse with the work of Wyatt and that of the Surrey.[86] His evolving versions of Surrey, *Surrey with a Fringe of Top*, are similar to his versions of Wyatt in that they operate by updating the originals. Sheppard's 'Direct Rule: In Peace with Foul Desire' is, in his words, 'a translation into Contemporary Politics' of Surrey's sonnet 'Th'Assyrian king, in peace, with foul desire'. Sheppard transposes Surrey's 'Assyrian king', with his 'filthy lusts that stain'd his regal heart' to modern day North America and the Presidency of Donald Trump. Surrey's poem ends with the king, made decadent by lust, taking his own life 'to shew some manful deed', Sheppard's with the President poised over the nuclear button, ready to 'whoosh us all to show some "manful" deed'.[87] Sheppard's remark that the poem is a translation of Surrey into contemporary politics is illuminating. The poems in the Surrey sequence do this more directly than those in the Wyatt sequence. 'Direct Rule: In Peace with Foul Desire', which is not one of Surrey's Petrarch poems, appears online in the *International Times* with Surrey's original above it, inviting the reader to make connections and comparisons. Discussing the Surrey poems, Sheppard states that, unlike those of Petrarch and Wyatt which are well known, they are 'obscure (but shouldn't be, and weren't in the past)', prompting Sheppard to 'experiment' with parallel presentation.[88] Sheppard here expands further the boundaries of translation, the transposition of historical

---

[85] Sheppard, *On Writing Petrarch 3*.

[86] Ibid.

[87] Robert Sheppard, 'Direct Rule: In Peace with Foul Desire', *International Times* <http://internationaltimes.it/direct-rule-in-peace-with-foul-desire/> [accessed 10 May 2018].

[88] Robert Sheppard, 'Poem by Earl of Surrey with my intralingual translation in International Times', *Pages* <http://robertsheppard.blogspot.co.uk/2018/03/normal-0-false-false-false.html> [accessed 10 May 2018].

events to contemporary circumstances being not just incidental to the translation process, but an act of translation itself.

As well as his versions of Wyatt and Surrey Sheppard has, since publishing *Petrarch 3*, produced versions of Charlotte Smith and Elizabeth Barrett Browning and 'overdubs' of Milton.[89] From the small samples available, Sheppard's Milton 'overdubs' appear to be of a different character to his versions of Wyatt and Surrey. Despite Milton's reputation as a political poet, Sheppard's treatments are more personal in nature. Sheppard's version of Milton's sonnet XIX 'When I consider how my light is spent', about his blindness, sees Sheppard using the idea of blindness to express personal darkness, as his 'shadow sweat pure light in ill-lit rooms'.[90] Whereas Sheppard uses Wyatt and Surrey as templates to overlay and interpret contemporary events, his relationship with Milton's originals appears to be more as foundational spark, with the 'versioning' mode as response rather than transformation.

Returning to *Petrarch 3* and to more procedural methods, we find the most extended exercise in translational technique in the sequence, 'Semantic Poetry Translation with Semiotic Fringe', which Sheppard dedicates to Stefan Themerson (1910-1988) and his theory of semantic poetry, where words are substituted for their definitions to produce an extended, exploded text. Themerson was a Polish-born poet, novelist, composer, filmmaker, visual artist and publisher who moved to Britain in the 1940s. The Semantic Poetry (SP) process, according to Themerson, gives words 'the flesh of exact definition; instead of allowing them to evoke the clichés stored in your mind, you may try to find the true reality to which every word points'.[91] The term 'semantic poetry' first appeared in Themerson's novel *Bayamus* (1945) which, with its three-legged protagonist, was approvingly described by philosopher Bertrand Russell, a friend of and long-time correspondent with Themerson, as 'nearly as mad as the world'.[92] *Bayamus* develops the idea that, just as a musical score can be read in a number of ways

[89] Robert Sheppard, 'Some Overdubs of John Milton's sonnets published by Stride and others', *Pages* <http://robertsheppard.blogspot.co.uk/2018/03/robert-sheppard-home-page-overdub-of.html> [accessed 8 May 2018].

[90] Robert Sheppard, 'Overdubs', *Stride* <http://stridemagazine.blogspot.co.uk/2018/04/overdubs.html> [accessed 8 May 2018].

[91] Stefan Themerson, *On Semantic Poetry* (London: Gaberbocchus, 1975), p. 27.

[92] Bertrand Russell, cited in Nick Wadley, *Reading Stefan Themerson* <http://www.dalkeyarchive.com/reading-stefan-themerson/> [accessed 2 May 2018].

(horizontally, vertically, following the melodic line, according to the chord structure, and so on) and produce different realisations, so too can a poem. Sheppard's poem weighs in at one-hundred and two lines and sprawls across four panels of the map format publication. At some points, Sheppard appears to be taking Themerson on face value, inserting rafts of alternative definitions: 'who was wanting strength / or mental / or moral / or artistic / force.'[93] At others, his reference to Themerson is more structural, adopting Themerson's characteristically indented lineation. In keeping with the sequence, Sheppard's approach to technique here is non-dogmatic: procedure as permission rather than proscription. Themerson himself did not employ his own methodology rigidly and neither does Sheppard.

It is this absence of rigidity that characterises Sheppard's poetics of translation. In *Petrarch 3*, he deploys a range of approaches: procedural methods in 'Semantic Poetry Translation with Semiotic Fringe', formal constraints and compressions in 'twittersonnet'; modernisation in 'Freeview'; and the adoption of multiple voices and personae in 'Iron Maiden' and 'Now then now then then and now'. Particularly in 'Freeview' and 'Now then now then then and now', we find Sheppard unafraid to use creative translational methods to tackle difficult topics, such as sexual politics. In his versions of Wyatt and Surrey, Sheppard is more explicitly translating events as well as language, rebooting the Tudor originals by relocating them to post-Brexit Britain and Trump's USA. In this, Sheppard is in accord with Moore, one of the writers (along with Atkins, Hughes and Mathews) to whom *Petrarch 3* is dedicated, and his assertion that 'one of the legitimate functions of attempted translation is to relate work translated to the contemporary world'.[94] Sheppard's poetics of translation can be aligned with those of Borges, Benjamin, and Bernstein, who all regard translation as something more than a functional service to the reader. This view of translation admits a constellation of methods, strategies, tactics, and techniques disallowed by more conventional approaches. Sheppard posits, both in theory and in practice, a translational mode that is open, fluid, permissive, voracious and, above all, creative.

---

[93] Sheppard, *Petrarch 3*.

[94] Moore, *Spleen*, p. 1.

BIBLIOGRAPHY

Atkins, Tim, *Horace* (New York, NY: O Books, 2007)

—— *Petrarch Collected* (London: Crater Press, 2014)

—— *Seven Types of Translation: Petrarch's Canzoniere* (unpublished doctoral thesis, Roehampton University, 2011)

Benjamin, Walter, 'The Task of the Translator', in *Selected Writings Volume 1 1913-1926*, ed. by Marcus Bullock and Michael Jennings (Cambridge, MA & London: The Belknap Press of Harvard University Press, 1996), pp. 253-63

Bergvall, Caroline, *Meddle English* (New York: Nightboat Books, 2011); Nicholas Moore, *Spleen* (London: Menard Press, 1990)

Bernstein, Charles, 'How Empty is my Bread Pudding', *Open Letter*, 12.3 (2004), 66-76

Borrow, George Henry, *Lavengro* (London: John Murray, 1851)

Cameron, David, *Flowers of Bad* (New York: Unbelievable Alligator, 2007)

Ciardi, John, cited in Olive Classe, *Encyclopaedia of Literary Translation into English: A-L* (Abingdon, Oxon: Routledge, 2000)

Davies, Dan, *In Plain Sight: The Life and Lies of Jimmy Savile* (London: Quercus Editions, 2014)

Duncan-Jones, Katherine, 'Introduction', in *The Arden Shakespeare: Shakespeare's Sonnets, Third Series*, ed. by Katherine Duncan-Jones (London: Thomson Learning, 1997), pp. 1-106

Halsey, Alan, *Versions of Martial* (Newton-le-Willows: Knives Forks and Spoons, 2015)

Hardison Jnr., O. B., Joseph G. Fucilla and Christopher Kleinhenz, 'Petrarchism', in *The New Princeton Encyclopaedia of Poetry and Poetics*, ed. by Alex Preminger and T. V. F. Brogan (Princeton, NJ: Princeton University Press, 1993), pp. 902-04

Hughes, Peter, *Quite Frankly: After Petrarch's Sonnets* (Hastings: Reality Street, 2015)

—— *Cavalcanty* (Manchester: Carcanet, 2017)

Keene, Dennis, 'Notes', in *Henry Howard, Early of Surrey: Selected Poems*, ed. by Dennis Keene (New York, NY: Routledge, 2003), pp. 83-91

Kristal, Efrain, *Invisible Work: Borges and Translation* (Nashville, TN: Vanderbilt University Press, 2002)

Le Lionnais, François, 'First Manifesto', in *Oulipo: a Primer of Potential Literature*, ed. by Warren F. Motte Jnr. (Lincoln, NE: University of Nebraska Press, 1986), pp. 26-8

MacLow, Jackson and Tardos, Anne, *Thing of beauty: New and Selected Works*, ed. by Anne Tardos (Berkeley, CA: University of California Press, 2008)

Manson, Peter, *English in Mallarmé* (London: Blart Books, 2014)

Mathews, Harry, *Country Cooking and Other Stories* (Detroit: Burning Deck, 1980)

Moore, Nicholas, *Spleen* (London: Menard Press, 1990)

Nabokov, Vladimir, *Selected Letters 1940-1977* (Boston, MA: Houghton Mifflin Harcourt, 2002)

Nichol, bp, *Translating Translating Apollinaire: A Preliminary Report* ([n.d.]) <http://www.thing.net/~grist/l&d/bpnichol/lnichol1.htm> [accessed 1 May 2018]

Petrarch, *The Complete Canzoniere*, trans. by Anthony S. Kline (North Charleston, SC: Poetry in Translation, 2016)

Rees, D. G., 'Sir Thomas Wyatt's Translations from Petrarch', *Comparative Literature*, 7.1 (1955), 15-24

Retallack, Joan, *The Poethical Wager* (Berkeley, CA: University of California Press, 2003)

Riley, Peter, 'Afterword', in *Spleen* (London: Menard Press, 1990), pp. 51-3

—— *Translation, Expanded Translation, Version, Mess* <http://fortnightlyreview.co.uk/2018/03/translation-expanded/> [accessed 25 April 2018]

Schmidt, Michael, *Lives of the Poets* (London: Phoenix Books, 1998), pp. 132-33

Shakespeare, William, *Romeo and Juliet* (Cambridge: Cambridge University Press, 2008)

Sheppard, Robert, 'A Petrarchan Sonnet in the Style of Wayne Pratt for Patricia Farrell', *Pages* <http://robertsheppard.blogspot.co.uk/2017/01/robert-sheppard-petrarch-3-published-by.html> [accessed 2 March 2017]

—— *A Translated Man* (Bristol: Shearsman Books, 2013)

—— *Complete Twentieth Century Blues* (Cambridge: Salt, 2008)

—— 'Direct Rule: In Peace with Foul Desire', *International Times* <http://internationaltimes.it/direct-rule-in-peace-with-foul-desire/> [accessed 10 May 2018]

—— 'Empty Diaries 2001-2008', *The Literateur* <http://literateur.com/empty-diaries-2001-2008-by-robert-sheppard/> [accessed 3 March 2017]

—— 'from Hap: Understudies of Thomas Wyatt's Petrarch by Robert Sheppard: Hap 1: Som fowles there be that have so perfaict sight', *Poetry at Sangam* <http://poetry.sangamhouse.org/2017/07/from-hap-understudies-of-thomas-wyatt%E2%80%99s-petrarch-by-robert-sheppard> [accessed 2 May 2017]

—— *History or Sleep* (Bristol: Shearsman Books, 2015)

—— 'New poems "Empty Diaries 2001-8" (Wiped Weblogs) in The Literateur', *Pages* <http://robertsheppard.blogspot.co.uk/2016/10/robert-sheppard-new-poems-empty-diaries.html> [accessed 3 March 2017]

—— *On Writing Petrarch 3*, unpublished

—— 'Overdubs', *Stride* <http://stridemagazine.blogspot.co.uk/2018/04/overdubs.html> [accessed 8 May 2018]

—— 'Peter Riley on my Petrarch 3 and other "expanded translations"', *Pages* <http://robertsheppard.blogspot.co.uk/2018/03/peter-riley-on-my-petrarch-3-and-other.html> [accessed 26 April 2018]

—— *Petrarch 3: a derivative dérive* (London: Crater Press, 2016)

—— 'Petrarch 3 published NOW by CRATER Press number 36', *Pages* <http://robertsheppard.blogspot.co.uk/2017/01/robert-sheppard-petrarch-3-published-by.html> [accessed 2 March 2017]

—— 'Poem by Earl of Surrey with my intralingual translation in International Times', *Pages* <http://robertsheppard.blogspot.co.uk/2018/03/normal-0-false-false-false.html> [accessed 10 May 2018]

—— 'Robert Sheppard on The Petrarch Boys: Peter Hughes and Tim Atkins', *Pages*<http://robertsheppard.blogspot.com/2013/12/robert-sheppard-on-petrarch-boys-peter.html> [accessed 10 June 2018]

—— 'Some Overdubs of John Milton's sonnets published by Stride and others', *Pages* <http://robertsheppard.blogspot.co.uk/2018/03/robert-sheppard-home-page-overdub-of.html> [accessed 8 May 2018]

—— 'The Meaning of Form Atkins' and Hughes' Petrarch', *Pages* <http://robertsheppard.blogspot.co.uk/2016/09/robert-sheppard-meaning-of-form-atkins.html> [accessed 27 February 2017]

—— *The Meaning of Form in Contemporary Innovative Poetry* (London: Palgrave Macmillan, 2016)

—— *The Necessity of Poetics* <http://www.pores.bbk.ac.uk/1/Robert%20Sheppard,%20'The%20Necessity%20of%20Poetics'.htm> [accessed 10 June 2018]

—— *The Poetry of Saying: British Poetry and Its Discontents, 1950-2000* (Liverpool: Liverpool University Press, 2005)

Smith, Simon, *The Books of Catullus* (Manchester: Carcanet Press, 2018)

Stone, Jon and Kirsten Irving, eds, *Bad Kid Catullus* (London, Sidekick Books, 2017)

Terry, Philip, *Dante's Inferno* (Manchester: Carcanet, 2014)

Themerson, Stefan, *On Semantic Poetry* (London: Gaberbocchus, 1975)

Wadley, Nick, *Reading Stefan Themerson* <http://www.dalkeyarchive.com/reading-stefan-themerson/> [accessed 2 May 2018]

Wyatt, Sir Thomas, cited in Thomson, Patricia, *Thomas Wyatt: The Critical Heritage* (London: Routledge, 1995), p. 38

Young, David, 'Introduction', in *The Poetry of Petrarch*, ed. by David Young (London: Macmillan, 2014), pp. ix-xxiv

European Fictions

Zoë Skoulding

Robert Sheppard's *A Translated Man* (2013)[1] and the collaboratively-written European Union of Imaginary Authors project, collected in *Twitters for a Lark* (2017), are the first two works in his planned trilogy by fictional poets.[2] The use of heteronyms is often a high-risk enterprise, breaking the conventions of authorial guarantee and shifting the habitual grounds of reading. The creation of fictional authors in a European context has taken on resonances since the 2016 referendum on leaving the European Union that were unforeseen by most in 2013. The nationalist fantasies that sustained the vote for Brexit were a far more dangerous fiction, a simplification of identity that obliterated the multiple and complex intercultural relationships on which a functioning society depends. The very real anxieties generated by this situation have put Sheppard's playful inventions under a pressure that did not exist when the project began. However, since play, in its sense of free movement, is exactly what is at stake, this work offers forms of resistance to reductive thinking, articulating the pluralities of British poetry as well as its relationships with European identity. If the field of contemporary innovative poetry to which Sheppard's work belongs tends to be identified with a transatlantic, anglophone space, the emphasis on bilingualism in *A Translated Man,* and imaginary translation in *Twitters for a Lark,* references a more varied linguistic context, one that reveals the European and multilingual influence already present in this tradition while opening it to future cross-currents.

Chris Daniels, the English translator of perhaps the most famous inventor of heteronyms, Fernando Pessoa, describes the device like this:

> Imagine a vast novel about a coterie of writers in a very particular time and place. All the writers have different styles and concerns and social backgrounds and they write all different kinds of things [...]. The novel includes all of their writings. Excise the narrative trappings of a traditional novel and leave only the

---

[1] Robert Sheppard, *A Translated Man* (Bristol: Shearsman Books, 2013).

[2] Robert Sheppard et al., *Twitters for a Lark* (Bristol: Shearsman Books, 2017).

writings of the fictional characters. That's the easiest way to understand heteronymy.[3]

Daniels points out that heteronymy need not necessarily create multiplicity, because a heteronym could be the author of a single conventional novel, but that the structure invites proliferation of identities. This is true in the case of Sheppard's heteronymy, which is elaborate and multi-layered. Furthermore, its novelistic trappings are retained to some extent through the supporting documentation of introductions, biographical notes and even diary entries that build a narrative, if one that is fractured and highly unreliable. René Van Valckenborch, the fictional Belgian at the heart of the project, is mediated into English by two fictional translators, Annemie Dupuis from Quebec and Martin Krol from South Africa. The bilingual French-Flemish context of Belgium is thereby brought into juxtaposition with two bilingual contexts that encompass English, allowing an almost convincing context for Sheppard's heteronymic poems as well as a double layer of fictional insulation between author and text. The European Union of Imaginary Authors is supposedly an invention of Van Valckenborch, first appearing in the Flemish-English 'translations' of Martin Krol in *A Translated Man*, and then expanded through a series of collaborations in *Twitters for a Lark*.

The heteronym can be a means of moving into a different world of references and a geographical relocation. The Dupuis translations of Van Valckenborch begin with a sequence from *thingly*, referencing the French poet Francis Ponge in their forensic description of objects like the scissors whose 'limbs of flexing steel leap in / frozen cuts of light'.[4] Dupuis' diary quotes Van Valckenborch quoting Ponge: 'Objects, landscapes, events, people, give me much pleasure,' as well as his additional comment: 'I am composed of their variety, which would allow me to exist even in silence.'[5] This variety does not settle into anything like imitation of Ponge, but radiates into other connections, such as the surrealist films of Czech director Jan Švankmajer, whose world of things is equally strange and tangible. There may be references to mussels and Jacques Brel, but the poems are not on the whole defined by a Belgian

---

[3] Chris Daniels, 'Translator's Notes', in Fernando Pessoa, *The Collected Poems of Alberto Caeiro* (Exeter: Shearsman Books, 2007), p. 197.

[4] Sheppard, *A Translated Man*, p. 15.

[5] Sheppard, *A Translated Man*, p. 123.

locale. The lens of the heteronym is complicated by Dupuis' Canadian perspective; she quotes Nicole Brossard's *Mauve Desert* in her diary: 'Have you never thought that my body would disintegrate if ever it entered the twisted stuff of words?'[6] Here, the heteronym is a constraint that navigates between a possible body and its disintegration in language, between a non-French francophone identity and its relations to the literatures of France and other francophone countries. The spatial concerns of the Krol translations dramatise the repositioning enabled by the poem, for example in 'Ode to Zip': 'The crane framed below a bridge (with man on it gull above it) is less transformed than simply formed. Ex-form the boat its oar furred with snow. Through the room through the next flat against the wall Van Gogh's ear for music.'[7] Van Valckenborch's Flemish identity connects him here to Amsterdam, an imagined language opening up a set of spatial connections that are not a given but a process of forming and transformation. In relationship to novelisation, there is an effort here to inhabit a cultural and historical perspective, to construct a 'world' in a way that linguistically innovative poetry often resists, but the world is textual and linguistic, formed of writerly connections rather than national boundaries.

Sheppard's invention may be compared with Erín Moure's construction of the Galician poet Elisa Sampedrin, who lives a more rural, elemental existence than her Montréal-based creator.[8] One is likely to read this work in the context of Moure's translations of the real Galician writer Chus Pato, and of her free translations of Fernando Pessoa's heteronym Alberto Caeiro in her collection *Sheep's Vigil by a Fervent Person*.[9] As Sheppard points out in his discussion of her work in *The Meaning of Form*, Moure's term 'transelation', used first of this book, is applicable to 'acts of homage and celebratory excess' elsewhere in her work.[10] The borders between heteronym and author, translation and 'original' are destabilised by an interest in 'letting yourself be foreigned by language as you work'.[11] Heteronymic invention draws on reading

---

[6] Sheppard, *A Translated Man*, p. 124.

[7] Sheppard, *A Translated Man*, p. 15.

[8] Erín Moure, *Little Theatres* (Toronto: Anansi, 2005).

[9] Erín Moure, *Sheep's Vigil by a Fervent Person* (Toronto: Anansi, 2001).

[10] Robert Sheppard, *The Meaning of Form in Contemporary Innovative Poetry* (London: Palgrave Macmillan, 2016) p. 92.

[11] Angela Carr, Robert Majzels, and Erin Mouré, *Translating Translating Montreal*

from several different sources; rather than a translation, which can only ever be a partial response to a single source, it draws on a more complex intertextual encounter.

> There is a sense in which every reading of a text by an individual is a translation, because ink and paper, or pixelated light and darkness, are 'read' through a body, an individual apparatus impossible to replicate in terms of its cells and experiences and the ways in which that experience has affected its neural maps and capacities. This body may not even know its own filters and how they act when it 'reads'.[12]

Moure's description reveals the act of reading as individual, transformational and therefore productive of multiplicity. Far from being a false construction, the use of heteronyms may more truthfully describe the plurality of the writer formed by reading.

Heteronymy is, nevertheless, haunted by controversy, most famously in the case of Ern Malley, Australia's most famous invented poet. Malley was created in 1943 to expose the gullibility of a magazine editor, Max Harris, who was initially humiliated when the poems he published turned out to have been written by James McAuley and Harold Stewart as a parody of modernism, but went on to stand by his initial admiration of the poems. The later reclamation of Malley, particularly by the New York School, points to the strength of the aleatory techniques they used. This reception against the grain of the authors' intentions turns the joke on them, casting their autonomy into doubt by recognising the intertextual, generative potential of language. In 1976 John Ashbery invited his students at Brooklyn College to compare Malley's 'Sweet William' with one of Geoffrey Hill's 'Mercian Hymns'.[13] Ashbery's point, David Lehman observes, is that 'genuineness in literature may not depend on authorial sincerity'.[14] Like most of the poems in *Twitters for a Lark*, the sixteen poems constituting the oeuvre of Ern Malley were written collaboratively, a mode of working that tends to lift the

---

(Montreal: Press Dust, 2007), p. 41.

[12] Sophie Collins, ed., *Currently and Emotion: Translations* (London: Test Centre, 2016), p. 29.

[13] David Lehman, 'The Ern Malley Poetry Hoax: An Introduction' <http://jacketmagazine.com/17/ern-dl.html> [accessed 8 July 2018]

[14] Ibid.

pressure of expectation and invite playfulness. Even when created by one writer, a heteronym has an element of this freedom, just as a mask liberates an actor into becoming someone else. Sheppard's 'The Ern Malley Suite', which is written under his own name, concludes *Twitters for a Lark* with a reference point that underscores both the mischief and irony of the project.[15]

The presence of René Van Valckenborch (listed as such on the poster but performed by Sheppard) at the North Wales International Poetry Festival in 2013 brought two different worlds into collision. One was Sheppard's fictional heteronymic universe, and the other was a group of visiting European poets and a collection of arts organisations based in Wales whose work had focused for several years on developing links between 'real' writers across Europe. Despite the warm response to Sheppard's characteristically energetic reading, it was a potentially awkward combination, and one for which I was responsible as organiser. In conversation after the event, an audience member took exception to the perceived colonialism of a project that would invent poets of other languages rather than allowing those languages to be heard. This was a fair comment, since the occasion was focused on the voicing of different languages and the physical presence of writers presenting their work. Heteronymic play does not replace the need to attend to the genuinely distinct perspectives that are offered by translation, but in a live event where time was limited it may have seemed that such a replacement was being made. Furthermore, the careful fictional layering of the project is less obvious in a live context, where humour can diminish nuance at the same time as engaging an audience. For this reason I would disagree with Billy Mills' comment in a review that *Twitters for a Lark* is a conceptual work that 'does its work without being read at all, the idea of what it is, what it stands for, takes precedence over the contents.' It is conceptual and it certainly does do some work without being read, but closer attention reveals how distant it is from the kind of caricature in which the project could have resulted in different hands. Mills acknowledges as much, noting its dense interweaving of references from the classical world to contemporary politics and stating that 'what it stands for [...] is resistance to the nonsense idea that the UK is, or can be, anything other than European.'[16]

---

[15] Sheppard et al., *Twitters for a Lark*, pp. 96-99.

[16] Billy Mills, 'Poetry after Brexit; some recent reading' <https://elliptical movements. wordpress.com/2018/05/13/poetry-after-brexit-some-recent-reading/> [accessed 8 July 2018]

In bilingual countries like Wales, translation is a live and sometimes painful daily practicality that does not always feel open to play. If Wales is a country in which public life is officially bilingual, this is a result of decades of struggle, protest and sometimes imprisonment on the part of those who have fought for equal status for the Welsh language. On the other hand, the meeting at the festival of the real poets Sheppard and Eiríkur Örn Norðdahl enabled further inventions – the appendix of *Twitters for a Lark* takes us into the fictional history of Frisland (not to be confused with Friesland), a 'phantom island' for which the lower end of Greenland was once mistaken. The fragments of the *Tale of Queen Brenda* have been recovered, we learn, from scraps of hide sewn into shoes or bedclothes, 'brittle-boned Brenda and her Berserkers' contesting the reverence with which the past is held as a guarantee of national identity. The fragments interrupt themselves, as here, where they incorporate future imaginary mistranslation:

> …'Song is but wind!' scoffed the foolish Frislandian,
> 'Music a fart through a sawn-off boar's tusk!'
> 'Insult not the boar or the bear!' she snarled, bearing teeth.
> 'I didn't say "bear". I don't know what a "bear" is. But I do know…'[17]

At the same festival in Bangor, a round table discussion on poetic practice focused on the question 'What do you break?' Örn Norðdahl's response was that he breaks traditions, and that it is necessary to do so in order for them to regrow and to create a living culture. This is a controversial position to assert in bilingual north Wales, but he insisted that it was a necessary one precisely because of and not despite Icelandic having only 358,000 native speakers. *Queen Brenda* may be seen, therefore, as both a rupturing and a continuation of the inventive proliferations of legend.

Despite their imaginary engagements with other languages, both *A Translated Man* and *Twitters for a Lark* are shaped by Sheppard's anglophone context and the backdrop of the British Poetry Revival. Yet although this strand of UK poetry tends to be viewed in relation to America as a continuation of earlier modernisms, it also draws on a history of plurilingual influence in the modernist tradition, from first-generation English speakers like Charles Reznikoff, Louis Zukofsky or William Carlos Williams, not to mention Pound's pursuit of

---

[17] Sheppard, *Twitters for a Lark*, p. 101.

internationalism and deployment of translation as a creative strategy. In the 1960s, Lee Harwood's early meeting with and translation of Tristan Tzara channelled Dada influence into English, while Bob Cobbing's concrete poetry and emphasis on performance related him more closely to Henri Chopin or Pierre Garnier than precedents in British poetry. During Eric Mottram's editorship of *Poetry Review* from 1971, it was poets from this radical background who took control of the conservative Poetry Society, opening it to avant-garde and international perspectives. Sheppard, who discusses this moment in *When Bad Times Made for Good Poetry*, notes that during this period *Poetry Information*, a magazine published by the Society in parallel with *Poetry Review*, was 'open to reviews of translations and of foreign poetry' including not only Bataille and Blanchot but also 'lesser-known younger writers such as Anne-Marie Albiach and Jacques Roubaud'. Writing of the 1976 Poetry Society manifesto, a document that was both politically and aesthetically radical, he comments that 'this ethos [...] strengthened the manifesto's conviction "that poets are not exclusively concerned with their native tongue"'.[18] As Peter Barry's *The Poetry Wars* suggests, this sensibility might subsequently have led to a more plural landscape in British poetry had most of the radical poets not resigned (with the exception of Harwood) in a heated confrontation with the Arts Council. Since the foremost UK poetry institution was handed back to a reactionary leadership in an atmosphere of extreme hostility, the public visibility of experimental poetry was abruptly diminished, and with it the canonical status that would make it available to translators abroad.

Because of this history, innovative poetry in the UK has not been as fully represented internationally as the mainstream, particularly in the poetry festivals that link communities of writers. This has changed in recent years, partly through the efforts of organisers like Steven Fowler, whose collaborative *Camarades* and *Enemies* events have enabled many of Sheppard's collaborations, but comparatively few UK poets from more innovative backgrounds are involved in the kinds of exchange and translation that shape poetic practice in elsewhere in Europe. Given this situation, it is important to consider whether Sheppard's heteronymic project enables cross-cultural understanding or unintentionally reinforces a monolingual viewpoint by offering an ironic substitute for translation. The paradoxical propositions of Derrida's *Monolingualism*

---

[18] Robert Sheppard, *When Bad Times Made for Good Poetry* (Exeter: Shearsman, 2011) p. 23.

of the Other suggest what might be at stake: '1. We only ever speak one language. 2. We never speak only one language.'[19] The invented translation takes a position that points to the outside of English, revealing its relational and hybrid status. Derrida writes, 'a language can only speak itself of itself. One cannot speak of a language except in that language. Even if to place it outside itself.'[20] Yet, at the same time, the very impossibility of a metalanguage 'already introduce into it some translation and some objectification in progress,' so that we have a glimpse of 'the mirage of another language'.[21] The heteronym creates an elsewhere beyond English, not just estranging it but pushing it into dialogue with other contexts.

This happens frequently in the EUOIA poems, for example in the poems of Mirela Nemoianu from Romania, by Sheppard and Robert Hampson, signalled as Romanian by the title 'strofa' or stanza for each one. No. 75 begins:

I wanted to go to a place
that did not know who I was

I was wrapped in silence
so deep and long that

I cannot unpack myself in words
when I speak[22]

The foreignness of the framing leads into a text that accords with Derrida's observation, 'I have only one language; it is not mine'. The poem is dedicated to the Romanian-born German writer Herta Müller and echoes her themes of dispossession and linguistic unease; like many of the poems it may not be a real translation but it creates a network of references linking English with other languages. Dedications to real writers and artists are one of the ways in which this imagined community shifts towards a real one. The collaborations often come

---

[19] Jacques Derrida, *Monolingualism of the Other, Or, the Prosthesis of Origin* (Stanford, CA: Stanford University Press, 1998), p. 8.

[20] Ibid., p. 22.

[21] Ibid.

[22] Sheppard et al., *Twitters for a Lark*, p. 81.

out of a depth of previous reading and translation, for example the Oulipian constraint used in Belgian Paul Coppens's poems by Sheppard and Philip Terry, Raymond Queneau's *lipolepse* or 'quennet'.[23] While a series of Van Valckenborch's quennets appears in *A Translated Man*, the form has been developed in English through Terry's translation of Queneau's 1975 *Elementary Morality*,[24] and Terry's own *Quennets*.[25]

The structure of the heteronym pushes towards a plurality of thinking, destabilising simplified constructs of national belonging. If there sometimes seems to be a particularly British sense of irony at work, it is because any categorisation is fraught with irony, as Denise Riley's work so deftly explains.[26] If some of the poets of EUOIA occasionally seem recognisable, familiar from poetry festivals, or indeed the European Poetry Academy, which folded just before EUOIA came into existence, this may be because of real-life structures that are equally fictional in their suggestion that a writer can represent a particular territory. Frances Kruk and Robert Sheppard's contribution for Germany is a blank page, the bio note summing up the project: 'Karla Schäfer does not exist. If she were to exist, Germany might too.' The conditional framing of this comment invites consideration of the collective fictions of nationhood. In a literal sense, Germany as the entity it is today has not existed as such for half the lives of many of its inhabitants, but the existence of countries is often far from evident or uncontested, Britain (from a Welsh perspective, for example) being a case in point.

Writing Europe, a 2003 essay collection that followed a symposium on the same theme, was a publication to which some of EUOIA's members might have contributed, had they been real. Brought together on the cusp of the EU's expansion eastwards in 2004, the writers reflect on literature and identity, laying out their hopes for Europe as a cultural space and exploring the histories of conflict that lay behind them.[27] Fifteen years on, the optimism of that moment has been replaced by a more fraught political landscape, but looking back at

---

[23] Sheppard et al., *Twitters for a Lark*, p. 17.

[24] Raymond Queneau, *Elementary Morality*, trans. by Philip Terry (Manchester: Carcanet, 2007).

[25] Philip Terry, *Quennets* (Manchester: Carcanet, 2016).

[26] Denise Riley, *The Words of Selves: Identification, Solidarity, Irony* (Stanford, CA: Stanford University Press, 2000).

[27] Ursula Keller and Ilma Rakusa, eds, *Writing Europe* (Budapest: Central European University Press, 2004).

essays like Croatian novelist Dubravka Ugreši's is instructive as well as nostalgic. Likening the national frames of literary representation to the Eurovision Song Contest, she explores the motivations for oversimplified national identifications, suggesting that they are both critically and commercially driven as the quickest route from the periphery to the centre: 'for many people an identity tag is, at the same time, the only way to communicate, not only locally, but also globally, to be accepted and recognised as a *Bosnian* writer, as a *Slovene* writer, as a *Bulgarian* writer.'[28] However, she notes the way in which this model of cultural exchange undermines Europe's declared multiculturalism by focusing on a structure that underscores differences, particularly in the case of non-European cultures. To counter this tendency, she argues for greater recognition for what she calls 'dysfunctions', or situations in which writers 'outstrip the conceptual apparatus' that would contain them in particular categories:

> What are the Dutch to do with me? I live in Amsterdam, but do not write in Dutch. What are the Croats to do with me? I do write in Croatian, but I don't live there. What are the Serbs and Bosnians to do with me? The language I write in is BCS (Bosnian-Serbian-Croatian, the neat abbreviation dreamed up by translators at the Hague Tribunal). What are the Dutch to do with a Moroccan writer, who, instead of writing profitable prose about the cultural differences between the Moroccans and the Dutch, which everyone would understand, has undertaken to recreate the beauty of the Dutch language of the nineteenth century, which present-day Dutch writers have forgotten[?][29]

What, indeed, do national discourses 'do' with writers other than press them into moulds that fit dominant discourses? This 'conceptual apparatus' is limiting and distorting, yet its enforcement remains pervasive. The humour that surfaces in *Twitters for a Lark*, for example in the voluminous biographical note for Luxembourgish Georg Bleinstein (1965-2046) is often directed at just these expectations, a performance of an imaginary identity that foregrounds its own construction. Bleinstein, we read, is 'estimated to have been responsible

---

[28] Keller and Rakusa, *Writing Europe*, p. 331.

[29] Ibid., p. 333.

for as much as 33% of Luxembourgish poetry since 1995', including the work of the indisputably real and widely translated poet and novelist Jean Portante.[30] Portante, however, as an Italian born in Luxembourg, who writes in French, lives in Paris and has a substantial reputation in Latin America, is an example of the many real writers who expose literary nationhood itself as a fiction.[31] The Europe imagined through Sheppard's heteronyms is one that, through the ironic disruption of national frames, encourages more complex forms of understanding.

The poems in *Twitters for a Lark* tend to emphasise the distance between a UK context and the invented writer's locale, multiplying viewpoints translocally, for example in Cristòfol Subira's Catalan poem, by Sheppard and the Welsh writer Alys Conran. 'Performance Between Two Points', which references places in Barcelona such as the Columbus Monument and Carrer d'En Gignàs, reflects the invented poet's experience as a street performer, beginning: 'Balance / is a tenuous line to grip / with your toes.'[32] As the poem progresses the focus shifts to a linguistic balancing act in play in lines like: 'dance your way through these mirrored / alphabets where, / in the basement bar, vowels blast open a black tobacco way.'[33] The dance through language and space, or the sense of language inhabiting particular locations, emphasises the bilingual sensibility that also makes Subira write in both Spanish and Catalan. By making a connection between the bilingual Welsh-English (and Catalan-speaking) writer Conran and a city in which she has previously lived, it also links Barcelona with north Wales and its related, though different, linguistic complexities.

Carte Vitale, the French poet invented by Sheppard with Sandeep Parmar, is named after the French health insurance card and takes the position of an immigrant to France. This allows the poem to explore an outsider's view through the lens of race as Europe is presented through its historical exclusions. Some of the reference points are perhaps obvious ones – German occupation, Pierre Laval's wartime collaboration, a bust of Napoleon. There is a suggestion of Camus as well as contemporary refugees in the 'body of an arab' that 'rocks at high tide / at the foot

---

[30] Sheppard et al., *Twitters for a Lark*, p. 108.

[31] Jean Portante, *In Reality: Selected Poems*, trans. by Zoë Skoulding (Bridgend: Seren, 2013).

[32] Sheppard et al., *Twitters for a Lark,* p. 90.

[33] Ibid.

of the white cliff'.[34] Following the 2016 referendum and its ensuing sensitivities there is a risk that details like these might be read as a stereotyping of France and its political past. However, the poem is more accurately read as interrogating, from within, the racial exclusions that run through all European identities, an issue often explored in Parmar's poetry and criticism in relation to the UK and USA. The word 'white' echoes through the text as a reminder that being European, from the point of view of most of the world, carries with it a history of race privilege that Europeans of all backgrounds must confront. The splintered narrative leaves race and gender identity in flux, circling round topographical references to Paris, such as the Boulevard de Magenta and 'sensitive urban zones'. Like the imagined migrant poet, the poem is located in relation to France but has an unstable point of view that shifts between interior and exterior perspectives. This play of movement allows a complex, multidimensional view of Europe to emerge.

The effort of inventing a plausible context for each invented writer might be seen as expanding the reach of the poem's references, broadening its imaginative sphere to encompass an unfamiliar culture, but only if it is accepted that there is to begin with a proper perspective and a certain area within which a poem is expected to range in its associations. This is manifestly not the case for Sheppard or his collaborators. Jahan Ramazani, arguing for a 'transnational poetics', makes the case for poetry as a form that, above others, travels imaginatively, in parallel with Edward Said's 'travelling theory' and James Clifford's 'travelling cultures'.[35] He acknowledges the risks of this approach, pointing to Pound as one of several examples: 'Does Pound's syncretic verse too easily appropriate Chinese, Greek and Spanish locales and myths and place names for his self-elegiac purposes? Surely the risk [...] is there [...] But such criticisms may assume a too-rigid model of identity.'[36] For Ramazani, such risks, although they must be considered carefully, are outweighed by poetry's potential to create new spaces of intercultural discourse. To be too quick to condemn cross-cultural reference is:

---

[34] Sheppard et al., *Twitters for a Lark*, p. 45.

[35] Jahan Ramazani, *A Transnational Poetics* (Chicago, IL: University of Chicago Press, 2015), p. 51.

[36] Ibid., p. 59.

to presuppose the discreteness and stability of each cultural unit, when each culture is always already thoroughly enmeshed in a multitude of others. It is to impose an ethical and quasi-legal notion of cultural ownership that is inimical to poetry's radial connections, imaginative leaps, and boundary-crossing ventures. And it is to box creative expression within identitarian preconceptions resisted by poetry's hybridising, associative force.[37]

The poems of *A Translated Man* and the collaborations in *Twitters for a Lark* are speculative, conjectural unsettlings of identity that resist damaging simplification. They imagine unknowable viewpoints and explore imagined frames of reference, but they also lay claim to a shared European vision that has shifted, since the first poems were written, towards something that can less easily be taken for granted. By playing with Europeanness and its contradictory tensions they keep its potential open, recognising a shared history, performing a collective identity and imagining a future, despite current difficulties, of relationships to come.

---

[37] Ramazani, *A Transnational Poetics,* p. 60.

The Expressive Tension Between Text and Painting in the Collaborative Work of Robert Sheppard and Pete Clarke

PATRICIA FARRELL

This chapter will consider the collaborative works by Robert Sheppard and Pete Clarke[1] – shown as the exhibition, 'Manifest', in the Arts Centre at Edge Hill University (April 2013) – in terms of a problematics of reading that these pieces potentially present. I argue that there is a way of reading that problematises the works and is problematised by them, that they exemplify in a very particular way an expressive tension between text and painting that reading is forced to encounter. There may be possible ways of mediating the simultaneous presence of text and the visual elements of painting and collage that allow for a less problematic model for reading but, although these might be more congenial and comfortable, I would contend that they are less productive, aesthetically and ethically, in terms of sensible affect and consequent behaviour.[2]

How might reading find it itself traversing the problematic field of the work, what are the effects upon it, and how might it respond? My proviso will be that, for this question to work – for it to be an aesthetically and ethically good question – there should not be anything approaching a definitive solution to it. Each encounter with a piece, each instance of reading is what Gilles Deleuze would call a 'local solution', which is a moment of realisation of how this question persists.[3]

Clarke, as a visual artist, talks specifically about paintings as works which are read, as well as looked at, and a piece by him is intended as

---

[1] Many of Robert Sheppard's and Pete Clarke's collaborative works can be accessed at <http://robertsheppard.blogspot.co.uk/search?q=pete+clarke>. See, for example, the posts for 13 July 2016, 23 June 2015, 11 April 2013, and 9 April 2013.

[2] How responding to the work resonates in how we question our habitual behaviours and attitudes and the habitualisation of thinking they produce.

[3] The concept of the 'local solution' is created by Deleuze in *Difference and Repetition* (London: Continuum, 2001) – itself an essay in the creation of concepts – to substantiate how difference is brought into the terrain of *poiesis*, turning the problematic field into a version of itself, acting as a 'local [rather than universally definitive] solution'. Each version has its own poetic imperative, leading to further versions; local solutions are not points of arrival, but informative points of departure.

an event, to quote the artist, of 'fractured speech, discordant sounds, noisy colours, mute gestures and scratchy surfaces, a sensed alphabet of structural devices and pictorial conventions [...] an attempt at a "modern" vocabulary of public, private and remembered spaces, a sensed alphabet of structural devices and pictorial conventions'.[4] Questions will possibly be raised in a reader's mind about the level of metaphor being employed in Clarke's statement. (This reader would want to keep the literal of painting at a distance from the interpretative of language: painting to speak on its own terms, not analogously or metaphorically in relation to language.) However, I would argue, that an ontological, as opposed to analogical, attitude to reading both Clarke's works and his intentions for them, in terms of his literal placing of Sheppard's text in the visual field – the congruence of visual mark-making and elements of linguistically innovative poetry – rather than assimilating text as an additional analogical device, foregrounds the effect of text in its difference of kind, rather than degree of readability, creating the tension within reading which is, in itself, literally productive of sense ('making a difference', as Deleuze would put it) for reading.

We enter uncertainly here into the dialogue of text-places and paint-places: into the dialogue of language and painting: into an interrogation of the words' relation to colour and the manipulation of materials. As Sheppard would point out in the classroom to his writing students, we read text in a particular way, top left to bottom right, that does not apply to painting. There is a dissonance here not only between physical spaces but between cognitive spaces. This problematic tension is potentially productive insofar as it is difficult to come to terms with.

Clarke, the visual artist, has in some cases, found and selected but, in all cases, situated the language of Sheppard, the poet. Sheppard, in effect, opens his work up to a reading by Clarke who expressively responds to moments in the poems, translating them into a different context, a context of difference. Sheppard in allowing his reader to reconfigure the poem in this way enacts the linguistically innovative poet's commitment to the poem as the site of the production, rather than the donation, of meaning.

In topographical terms, Clarke says, text is intended to work in his paintings as a screen, as an articulator of space. In this respect, it is

---

[4] Pete Clarke interviewed by Gabriel Gee in *Looking Back: Facing Forward: Mistakes and Metaphors: Paintings and Drawings by Pete Clarke* (Liverpool: Victoria Gallery and Museum, University of Liverpool, 2009), p. 40.

what it does. As a linguistic presence – a body of words taking place on the painting – it would also signify (as Wittgenstein argues) by being what it does, as placed here in another place. In the transposition of text into the visual work, Clarke is dislocating the work and relocating the words, opening a conduit to something potentially new in expression. All the elements having found their places, the title of the piece is then, he says, 'in' the work, not on the label. The work becomes in effect, he suggests, a form of palimpsest: a complicated dissensus of time and space which finds its descriptive moment as *this* local solution to the simultaneity of text and painting.

The collaboration between Sheppard and Clarke shown in the 'Manifest' exhibition can be said to start in 2010 with the three prints 'Ode to Forme', 'Lyric' and 'Manifest',[5] produced for the 'Poetry Beyond Text' project, which involved a range of collaborations between poets and other practitioners and which was initially displayed in the Arts Centre in Dundee before moving to the Scottish Poetry Library and the Scottish Academy in Edinburgh.[6] The catalogue for 'Get Back', an exhibition of Clarke's graphic works in Cologne which includes these collaborative pieces, states that:

> Each of these prints contains poetic text on various scales, some resembling 'headlines' or titles, others reading as frag- mented and repeated 'body' text. There is a visual assembly of these component elements that is suggestive of Russian Constructivist prints, combining abstract colour shapes, blocks of text, and oblique angles and these historical visual influences interact with a 'poetic of increased indeterminacy and discontinuity, the uses of techniques of disruption and of creative linkage', to apply Sheppard's own description of the 'Linguistically Innovative Poetry' movement in which he has played a notable part.

Sheppard gave three poems to Clarke, who then treated them according to his own poetic principles as a visual artist. The presentation of pre- existing poetry in a visual field was an experiment that Clarke had

---

[5] The three originating poems were published in Robert Sheppard, *A Translated Man* (Bristol: Shearsman, 2013), as purportedly written by the fictional Belgian poet René Van Valckenborch.

[6] For these images, see <http://www.poetrybeyondtext.org/clarke-sheppard.html>.

already been conducting for some time, for example in an extensive series of works that make use of a damaged and annotated copy of T. S. Eliot's *The Waste Land and Other Poems* that he found by chance in a library. However, there is a set of variables in how he uses Sheppard's work that, I would argue, produces a particular range of effects.

'Ode to Forme' is a poem whose subject is printing, influenced particularly by Sheppard's visit to the museum in Antwerp which houses examples of the presses and publications of the sixteenth-century printers Christophe Plantin and Jan Moretus. We see Sheppard's complete text against a visual background using a colour scheme that Sheppard commented to Clarke was redolent of pieces from the latter's Eliot project. We need to get close to the piece to read the text and in so doing we realise the complexity and subtlety of this visual background, particularly the shifting spatialisation of its surface. Nevertheless, there is a sense that the text as a physical and aesthetic entity is set against rather than involved in the a-linguistic treatment; also, that there are two distinct reading positions for this piece: one for the image and one for the poem.

This changes with 'Lyric' and 'Manifest' where a direct dialogic dynamic is set up between the text and the visual elements – 'Lyric' works with the shape of the poem on the page, 'Manifest' works against and across the grid pattern of the text. This dynamic dialogue, in which text and the non-textual inform and animate each other, without ever resolving into each other, having been established, is developed further in subsequent works.

The 2011 series *This Is Not Guilt*, from which numbers two and three were in the exhibition, demonstrates this. Of this and the following series *Tangled Scree*, Clarke says:

> The *This is Not Guilt* and *Tangled Scree* series are a combination of silkscreen print with traditional letterpress. They attempt to create a visual equivalent for Robert's poems, thinking about visual tension in terms of compositional structure and frag-mented surfaces. I collect letter type and the works use various fonts to try to replicate and or dislocate the patterns of speech. I am interested in the relationship between looking and reading, with the images and surfaces creating interference, a dialectical sense of images held somewhere between construction and falling apart.

The text for *This Is Not Guilt* is the opening of section two of the poem 'Reading the Reader', Sheppard's response to Bernhard Schlink's novel, *The Reader*, from the collection *Hymns to the God in which my Typewriter Believes*.[7] This book is a portable repository of poetic language from which Clarke – without requiring Sheppard's specific authorisation – can pick out and relocate words and passages, allowing them to establish a set of different behaviours in his visual fields. This technique of spontaneous inventive finding inevitably influences the production of the prints in different ways from the more directly collaborative process of Sheppard, either contributing existing poems, or writing poems for the occasion of a print series: taking language out of its context rather than translating the context of the textual piece. The work finds, and has found for it, things that it incorporates to become its own thing.

The visual mark-making interferes with the message whilst drawing attention to the physical contours of the typography – coloured edges 'haunt' as well as highlight words. The different versions of the print emphasise the affective responses reading makes to colour. The more vibrant version – the more immediately engaging for a readerly response – is the more interfering of the form and content of the text. We are alerted to the effects of matters of 'quantity', as well as quality, in the production of a visual work – the correlation of scale and colour intensity. Clarke's use of these quantitative effects and the graphic activity of the printed marks foregrounds the materiality of language – language as physical mark. We may still be inclined to perform a textual version of reading, top left to bottom right but these are 'Visible words', as the critic Johanna Drucker would term them:[8] language as an entity, simultaneously organising and disrupting the field of reading – foregrounding poetry as a material practice – the manipulation of things ('stuff') that makes something happen: that makes a difference, brings something into presence.

Tangled Scree,[9] in its three very distinct versions, letterpress on paper, silkscreen and letterpress on paper and letterpress and wood

---

[7] Robert Sheppard, *Hymns to the God in which my Typewriter Believes* (Exeter: Stride, 2006), pp. 43-62.

[8] See Johanna Drucker, *The Visible Word: Experimental Typography and Modern Art, 1909-1923* (Chicago, IL: University of Chicago Press, 1994).

[9] Robert Sheppard, 'Quennet for the Artist Pete Clarke' <http://poetry.sangamhouse. org/2017/07/quennet-for-the-artist-pete-clarke-by-robert-sheppard/> [accessed 8 July 2018].

relief on paper (this last version being shortlisted for the Adrian Henri prize in 2013) is the most evidently collaborative of the works Sheppard and Clarke have produced so far. Its text is a quennet – a poetic form invented by Raymond Queneau, one of the founders of OuLiPo, a literary movement that investigates the unpredictable potential of formal constraints – written by Sheppard from photographs taken by Clarke of derelict sites in Liverpool.

Writing from photographic images is a technique that Sheppard frequently uses to generate texts. To quote Sheppard from a talk written for the Open Eye photography gallery in Liverpool, on ekphrasis and creative linking:

> [M]y practice seems to have been blithely to take a lot of details from lots of photographs from both selected and random sources, and to use them in literary collages that are analogues for the photomontages these scraps might have made, in acts of what I call 'creative linkage'. [...] My daily practice of writing – it either gathers notes for poems or remain as exercises in keeping 'writing fit' – usually uses photographs, and to simplify, one source has been returned to regularly, the German artist, Hans-Peter Feldmann's book *Voyeur*, a collection of all kinds of photographs, indeed, all the types I've habitually used elsewhere: from art photography to vernacular snapshots, from pornography to advertising.[10]

Other works cited in Sheppard's talk include his 'Empty Diaries' series – 'one poem for each year of the twentieth century, and which was a creative linkage using (amongst many other stretches of language) [...] photographs of all kinds, from photojournalism to art photography, related to the appropriate year' – and 'Shutters' – 'which I wrote for the dancer Jo Blowers, which used the ectoplasmic mist of early photographs, Lady Hawarden's well-known images of her daughters in diaphanous interiors'. Several of the collaborative works published by Sheppard and Farrell under 'Ship of Fools' also use specific photographic materials as a source for both poet and visual artist.[11]

---

[10] See 'Robert Sheppard: Talk for the Open Eye Gallery on Poetry and Photography December 2016' <http://robertsheppard.blogspot.com/2017/01/robert-sheppard-talk-for-open-eye.html> [accessed 8 July 2018]

[11] See, for example, *Mesopotamia* (1987), *The Cannibal Club* (1990), *The Blickensderfer*

However, in the case of *Tangled Scree*, the text, rather than the photographs he took of Liverpool, is the material that Clarke has then worked with to produce the three versions of the print.

Clarke's final pieces are a presentation of the city as a serial event of form and expression rather than a representation. We are particularly aware of how each different version as presented makes its own difference in terms of a range of effects for reading: in the comparatively sparse letterpress version – which foregrounds the aesthetic effects of different typefaces, the affective response to its red lettering and the way in which this makes the grey paper paradoxically resonate – as much as the more colourful and painterly silk-screen version and the graphically dynamic wood relief version. This last version provides an example of how the contours of type work with and against the contours of visual elements to produce rhythmic and a-rhythmic effects which provoke a sensible response not limited to the eye's reading of visual rhythms. We are presented with a set of problematic fields for reading that operate simultaneously as, what Charles Bernstein would term, absorptive and anti-absorptive surfaces, consecutively engaging and dislocating our aesthetic response:[12] effects of depth, manipulations of space which become haptic as well visual. And this sensible reading experience is involved in reading's engagement with the problematic intelligibility of the works. As well as being a screen which inflects a spatial reading of the surface, language performs what we could call its customary role as a filter – conceptualising and naming percepts – the descriptive adjective-noun pairings that make up the body of the quennet. The co-terminous presence of the sensible and the intelligible – not-language and language – enacts a passage from a perceptual encounter to a potential conceptualisation that does not fully arrive or resolve, unless we lose our nerve and start shutting down parts of the reading experience. As time goes on, we notice more and more; the passage of reading persists. The problematic field, across which reading is attempting a determined excursion with no fixed set of directions, insists. The potential, the inherent power, of the piece to excite the eye and the mind in their embodied involvement persists, insists.

The linguistic and a-linguistic are not in opposition; they do not contradict (express directly against one another) but also do not present a continuum; they express simultaneously but differently, forming what

Punch (2002) and *Looking Thru' a Hole in the Wall* (2010).

[12] See Charles Bernstein, 'The Artifice of Absorption' in *A Poetics* (Cambridge, MA: Harvard University Press, 1992)

Deleuze would call a 'discordant harmony',[13] which is, he argues, the optimum milieu for the productive provocation of thinking and the genesis and evolution of unpredictable moments of reading that make a material difference, that present something unforeseen rather than merely representing something already experienced, something that has both aesthetic and ethical consequences. Jean-Francois Lyotard, in considering the productive, rather than the merely representational aspects of the work, remarks 'It speaks to you? It sets us in motion'.[14] Perhaps we could say that, in their productive potential, these pieces simultaneously speak and set in motion.

There is always an ongoing interplay between the sensible and the intelligible in our experience of language but it is foregrounded here: language as haptic, as well as language for the eye, the mind and, of course, the ear. Even in our silent reading, we trace the contours on the picture plane, as we trace the sound contours of the language – 'ruinous steps – urinous stairwells'. We may begin to haptically sense the virtual – but nevertheless real – sonority of the purely visual elements of the presentation. These involved responses both inform and disrupt each other, allowing the potential of the pieces to aesthetically and ethically excite reading to persist, insist.

'Moving through the conventions' is another example of Clarke's inventive discovery of Sheppard's language, with words taken from a piece called 'Venus and Adonis', from the prose collection, *Unfinish*. The full sentence is: 'I can see her moving through the conventions, solving crimes with the bristles that grow out of her chins.'[15] The found materials repeat but don't imitate something in the world: repetition as the productive alternative of representation. The topological play of the printed surface, which maps and folds and turns in front of the eye, challenges reading. Its dynamism is infectious: how does it make you behave? Behavioural response from one viewer to another will differ. And as is often the case in Clarke's work there is no authoritative focal point to anchor habitual ways of reading a visual field. The calligraphic lacunae that sit adjacent to the text, the enhanced physical presence of the words and their visual texture contribute to this versioning of readerly responses. We can sense the sensible/intelligible interplay of

[13] See Gilles Deleuze, *Difference and Repetition*, p. 146.

[14] Jean-François Lyotard, *Libidinal Economy*, trans. by Iain Hamilton Smith (London: Athlone Press, 1993), p. 51

[15] Robert Sheppard, *Unfinish* (London: Veer, 2015), pp. 10-11.

the decision about the placing of 'the conventions' outside the worked surface of the wood relief – and perceptibly sensing it is more productive aesthetically and ethically than explaining or interpreting it. The moves and expressions of the piece translate into moves and expressions on the part of reading. The experience is contingent, particular, subjective – and this is, as such, productive, so long as the meaning of the piece remains unfixed – a percept perpetually becoming a becoming-concept. And the piece makes it happily difficult to fix; ideally, it makes it impossible.

Reading receives another set of challenges in Sheppard's and Clarke's recent series, in the haptic complex of the mixed media and collage pieces, 'In mid seas stands a tower',[16] 'Dead as a door step,'[17] 'Walled in a lost city'.[18] Again, the words are picked at random from *Hymns to the God*; Clarke grabbing quantities of language but making spontaneous qualitative, aesthetically and ethically evaluative choices that allow things to emerge, to begin to happen. There is an immensity in these pieces just in terms of the number of techniques and their consequent effects – the painterly, the photographic, the iconographic, the abstract, clearly demarcated blocks of colour and diaphanous washes, the shifts in perspective – as well as the presence of typography that partakes of and becomes implicated in these tactics of visual poetics. They make you stand back, come up close and wonder where to stand. Each foray into reading produces a nexus of objects of attention, unfolding a field that is sequentially coming into different events of coherence, such that each individual piece is an event of coherence that is forever moving towards its horizon. Strange things can happen.

Where the text is concerned the pieces will not prevent left/right, top/bottom reading entirely, but this is dislocated: not subverted but perverted, in Deleuze's sense, that is, persistently turned aside by the non-linguistic. However, the simultaneity-without-correspondence of text and non-text also foregrounds the correlation-without-identification between the pictorial and non-pictorial. The eloquently affective blue and purple blocks, whose reading is further problematised by the presence of language.

There are also echoes of other pieces in this series, which are not however direct references to each other – or if we force them to be

---

[16] See 'Yoghurt: Sephardic Transformations' in Sheppard, *Hymns to the God*, pp. 72-75.

[17] See 'A Liverpool Poem' in Sheppard, *Hymns to the God*, p. 37.

[18] See 'National Security, Huyton 1940' in Sheppard, *Hymns to the God*, pp. 88-89.

direct references they lose their effect. The blue and purple blocks, have their versions in the earlier painting 'Invisible Cities'.[19] They are not symbolic but, in their particular scale and colour intensity, they are expressive and by virtue of this become structural devices for reading, carrying ways of reading between pieces.

In 'Dead as a door step', we have Sheppard's word 'step' and a picture of steps. But Sheppard's step is not these steps, and these steps are not the same as the textual steps in 'Tangled Scree' or the iconographic steps in 'Manifest'. 'Steps' and 'steps' are not mimetic, although like any ongoing process this 'project' accretes a history: something repeats in the instances. Rather than the chance encounter of an umbrella and a sewing machine on an operating table there is the encounter between 'steps' and simultaneously 'steps'. Less extravagant than Lautréamont's, more mundane, this encounter is subtly more expressive and effective. Not opposites and not mediatable towards identity, textual and non-textual elements simultaneously clarify and obscure, ground and unground each other. We as readers find ourselves – with two possible readings of the phrase 'find ourselves' – choreographing and being choreographed by the tension between words and marks or visual passages: co-constituting a surface, how do we find they make the surface behave? They inform each other but never resolve, constituting in the intimacy of their discordant harmony, what Deleuze calls incompossibility in 'the same world'[20], a dynamic irresolvability that sustains its paradoxical coherence by an imperative of persistent invention and discovery on the part of both expression and reading.

---

[19] A reference to Italo Calvino's 1972 novel *Le città invisibili*.

[20] Deleuze constructs this concept of incompossibility 'in the same world' through his critical reading of Leibniz. The necessary maintenance of the optimum reality that Leibniz believes to be the actual and best of possible worlds relies upon an order of maximum convergence, of perfect compossibility. Points that instigate the divergence of series of genesis and evolution, would initiate other, incompossible, worlds, which fail to resemble the real world. Deleuze argues that Leibniz does, however, leave in play for thinking that which he methodologically excludes: that is the points that bring into being the divergence of series that generate states of incompossibility, and consequently there is a potential in Leibniz's argument to see 'that divergence was itself an object of affirmation, or that the incompossibles belonged to the same world' (*Difference and Repetition*, p. 51), and 'we can see why the notion of incompossibility in no way reduces to contradiction and does not even imply real opposition: it implies only divergence' (*Difference and Repetition*, p. 48).

A Response to Vitality in Robert Sheppard's *Empty Diaries* and 'Wiped Weblogs'

Joanne Ashcroft

I attended my very first poetry reading in the Rose Theatre at Edge Hill in 2005. Robert Sheppard read and introduced other readers comprising members of what I came to know as the Poetry and Poetics Research Group, which he then convened and which I now organise. Sheppard's performance style was visually and sonically striking, involving movement of the body and the projection of a voice distinguishable from the regular speaking one with which he introduced his poems. For me, it was revelatory, introducing possibilities for language and rhythm in poetic form that would influence my life as a poet and researcher in poetics.

As well as a certain vitality in performance, Sheppard's work exhibits an energy on the page. We might read Sheppard through Peter de Bolla's term of the 'optic', the poem as energy print, suffused with activity and intensity both on the page which is also tangible in performance.[1] This chapter will give a reading of vitality in Sheppard's work focused on four poems: 'Empty Diary 1902' and 'Empty Diary 1905' from *History or Sleep: Selected Poems* (2015), '2001: Zoe the Dial-up Camwhore' from 'Wiped Weblog', and 'Empty Diary 2015', recent additions to *Empty Diaries*, one of Sheppard's collections and key sequences of poems that were revised and expanded after publication of the original book. Through musicality and movement in the language and structure, I consider how music and the diary as a form contribute to a sense of human activity, community, and care for the other in Sheppard's work. I will then examine fluidity and indeterminacy in the lyric subjectivity, images, and sexual politics in Sheppard's 'Empty Diary' poems through a perspective of sexuality and the female body.

The Stride edition of *Empty Diaries* is in four sections with poems numbered from 1901 to 1990. Our first impression of the book, moving from poem to poem, is that it is visually striking in the variety of shifting forms and structures. Measurements relating to number and time are important to the dynamic system of structuring at work in these poems. Sheppard's note to the text explains:

---

[1] Peter de Bolla, *Art Matters* (London: Harvard University Press, 2003), p. 21.

The twelves, twenty-fours and thousands of its numbering relate to the measures both within and between texts in this work. The measures relate to mechanical measurements of human time. Word count (by line, poem, sequence, part) follows this numerical rule closely. Parts one, three and four are each a thousand words long. Part two (the first to be composed) escapes this organisation, since some texts are organised by syllables, and there is no overall word count for it.[2]

If we look more closely at the poems in section one, we see that a pattern emerges regarding the number of words per line. Seven of the 'Empty Diary 1901-1912' poems have seven words on each line. As a 'mechanical measure of human time' the number seven can, of course, be related to the number of days in a week. However this pattern changes in each of the other five poems. 'Empty Diary 1902' has four words per line, whereas 'Empty Diary 1903' has three words on each line and 'Empty Diary 1911' has six words per line. The pattern shifts again in 'Empty Diary 1908' which has alternate lines of four and three words per line. The most remarkable, because most intricately structured, is 'Empty Diary 1907' which repeats a one, five, three, one, five, three, three structure in all of its three stanzas. Here is the first stanza of the poem:

> voluptuous
> watched the fat pulp of
> his neck bulging
> rodent
> fingers still collars rebelling against
> iron furnace conversations
> a buoyant hysteria

The complex and varied ordering of 'mechanical human' time in *Empty Diaries* is applied inside a tight compression of time, that is, a calendar year. Diaries are generally daily records of events and experiences, and a conscientious diarist would make three hundred and sixty five entries for each year. Well acquainted with the form, Sheppard has his own diary keeping habits. In a blog post titled 'Diary entries. Poems about the Belvedere pub Liverpool', which draws on the contents of his unpublished diary activity, he writes: 'I've always said my diary was trenchantly non-

---

[2] Robert Sheppard, *Empty Diaries* (Exeter: Stride, 1998), p. 62.

literary.'[3] Another blog post, 'Basho's Famous Haiku and Three Variations', reveals how Sheppard's diary entries can work with his poetry writing practice: 'These poems come from a diary I kept between January and April 2018.'[4] In *Empty Diaries*, there is a single diary 'entry', a single poem, for each year. The poems are not long, varying in line length, from twelve lines to twenty four. Each poem contains a flurry of activity as if condensing a year in its compact field of space and time on the page. The effect is that time bends and folds while moving us rapidly through the century from its beginning, 1901, to the last decade, 1990, before a new millennium. Here is 'Empty Diary 1902' in full:

> Tumble into this myth
> from his bed water
> jug trembling in the
> words of his story
> not mine as the
> uitlanders charge through photographers'
> ash checks for stolen
> diamonds tubes rupture kaffirs'
> anuses ripping a splinter
> of my soul accordant
> with their 'passion' veil
> snows my visage cruel
> beauty freezing service as
> meal time canes crack
> on prettiest knees aching
> at cold fire-places
> sweating girls dusty enemies
> slanted portraits gold panned
> from excrement my hand
> on her thin shoulder
> 'Make the bitch perform

---

[3] Robert Sheppard, 'Robert Sheppard: Diary entries. Poems about the Belvedere pub Liverpool' <http://robertsheppard.blogspot.com/2017/05/robert-sheppard-diary-entries-poems.html> [accessed 8 August 2018].

[4] Robert Sheppard, 'Robert Sheppard: Basho's Famous Haiku and three variations' <http://robertsheppard.blogspot.com/2018/06/robert-sheppard-bashos-famous-haiku-and.html> [accessed 8 August 2018].

There is a concentration of activity in the rapid succession of images, each of which depict or involve movement. From the first word, 'tumble', there is a sense of being carried along by a current of language. The poem is peppered with highly active verbs ('charge' and 'ripping'). This is a world of activity in which even domestic objects, the water in the jug is 'trembling'. Verbs used as adjectives create images of 'freezing service', 'sweating girls', and 'slanted portraits'. Although not actions themselves, the words 'stolen' and 'dusty' used as adjectives both imply that activities have taken place in order to achieve those states. There are violent actions, 'rupture' and 'crack', inflicted on the body. Charles Altieri identifies a move from the confessional to a 'becoming articulate about the conditions within which the process of imagining enriches the possibilities of fully investing in the specific life one is leading'.[5] Characteristic of Sheppard's work, the tumultuous series of events and experiences depicted in 'Empty Diary 1902' resist the idea of linearity or any integration of autobiographical detail. Beginning in a domestic scene, 'his bed' very soon become images, 'as uitlanders charge', 'kaffirs', 'dusty enemies' and 'gold panned', which are not confined to the self and a circle of family and friends. In this poem we are drawn to notice a flood of human activity, a history, which both includes, and has a consciousness beyond, the domestic.

'Empty Diary 1905' begins with what seems the promise of a more intimate personal record of a Jane Austen-style romance. We even find ourselves in the romantic capital, Paris. However, images are soon defamiliarised, becoming surreal. Here is the poem in full:

> She falls for him, conventional longing well
> tutored, no pose held, broken but breathing,
> yet she keeps a finger in a
> page of last year's tightly scribbled diary:
> the ranked delights of the Paris corsetière,
> the dummies' impersonal whorish display of lace
> and china flesh, a flat-buttoned pressing
> of chamber-maids' etiquette; can't bear his:
> 'I sleep, I wake, I never dream'

[5] Charles Altieri, 'What Is Living and What Is Dead in American Post-modernism: Establishing the Contemporaneity of South American Poetry' in *The Lyric Theory Reader: A Critical Anthology*, ed. by Virginia Jackson and Yopie Prins (Baltimore, MD: The Johns Hopkins University Press, 2014) pp. 477-86 (p. 477).

; wants to slit his throat, to hoist
him dripping from his penis; her story
stalled, veins in her bare neck pleading

The 'whorish display of lace' and 'pressing / of chamber-maid's etiquette' turn any notions of courtly romance on their head. Even the speaker in the poem identifies this as a romance turned sour, 'can't bear his: / "I sleep, I wake, I never dream"'. The semi-colon on the next line suggests a whole list of grievances could follow but the poem cuts to 'wants to slit his throat'. However, beyond the frenetic activity, 'slit' and 'hoist', these violent images and jump cut narrative fragments are structured to do more than disrupt the idea of a diary as an outlet for sensitive contemplations of life. Taking the line, 'the dummies' impersonal whorish display of lace' as a unit, just as time bends and folds, word associations shift and bend. The structure of the line is a determiner and plural possessive noun, 'the dummies', then a string of adjectives with the strange combination of 'impersonal whorish'. How we respond to the word choices and to their possible combinations and classes, is left open by the minimal grammar and punctuation, which usually acts as a guide. Speaking of Frank O' Hara and Robert Creeley, Altieri writes, 'poetry becomes direct habitation, a directly instrumental rather than contemplative use of language'.[6] The same applies, but with much more considerable force, to Sheppard. Meanings bend and fold by association, images are pushed beyond the familiar, the everyday. Nathaniel Mackey, in an essay on black music and the poetry of Amiri Baraka, argues:

> Poems seek to circumvent stasis, to be true to the mobility of thought, perception and the play of unconscious forces. Their 'tendency towards obliquity' is a gesture that pushes the limits of what we can take to be meaningful.[7]

From the title alone, *Complete Twentieth Century Blues* gives Sheppard away as a 'blues' man. The blues can be defined as:

> (1) A 12-bar form built on the I, IV, and V chords; (2) a scale with a flatted third, fifth, and perhaps a seventh; (3) a poetic form;

---

[6] Ibid., p. 477.

[7] Nathaniel Mackey, *Discrepant Engagement: Dissonance, Cross-Culturality, and Experimental Writing* (Cambridge: Cambridge University Press, 1993), p. 40.

(4) a way of articulating tones; (5) a set of verbal sentiments similar to those used in folk blues songs; (6) a vaguely defined, mythic 'feeling' that some say is basic to all jazz.[8]

The reference to a twelve-bar sequence adds to the number system at work in *Empty Diaries*. Seven of the twelve poems in the first section have twelve lines. 'Twelve' also relates to calendrical time, twelve months in a year, reminding us of the temporality imposed on the diary writer. 'Empty Diary 1902' has twenty-four short lines. In these poems, Sheppard takes the twelve-bar sequence as a numerical theme and allows his own complex variations on the form. We receive the image of a 'blues' mind moving, that is moving in the patterns of another logic, a free association which links to improvisation in music, particularly jazz and blues. 'Empty Diary 1902' begins:

> Tumble into this myth
> from his bed water
> jug trembling in the
> words of his story

The images in these poems similarly make the kind of 'spiraling, dreaming movement of associations, spurts of energetic pursuit of melody and motifs, and driftings away' that Mackey finds in Baraka's poetry.[9] Of course, just as the number system is varied and complex, so are Sheppard's musical tastes, which are certainly not confined to blues and jazz. Thus, reference made to the Noël Coward song in the title of *Complete Twentieth Century Blues* introduces an altogether different musical tradition, one rooted in camp irony as opposed to the authenticity of blues and jazz.[10] By further contrast, Sheppard has noted that 'Empty Diary 2015' 'has a touch of the bossa nova about it',[11] a Brazilian jazz music 'usually played quietly, with minimal percussion'.[12] Yet: 'I've got the

---

[8] 'Jazz Glossary: Blues', Centre for Jazz Studies, Columbia University <http://ccnmtl.columbia.edu/projects/jazzglossary/b/blues.html> [accessed 8 August 2018].

[9] Mackey, p. 38.

[10] Robert Sheppard, *Complete Twentieth Century Blues* (Cambridge: Salt, 2008), p. 331.

[11] Robert Sheppard, 'Robert Sheppard: Empty Diary 2016 published in the 50th edition of Erbacce' <http://robertsheppard.blogspot.co.uk/2017/09/robert-sheppard-empty-diary-2016.html> [accessed 8 August 2018].

[12] 'Jazz Glossary: Bossa Nova', Centre for Jazz Studies, Columbia University <http://

blues like George Herbert got God, like Ted Hughes got Crow, like Bill Griffiths got prison, like Malcolm Lowry got drink, like Iain Sinclair got fancy walking shoes', Sheppard comments in interview, 'like Otis Spann got pianistics, like Tom Jenks got Twitter-sculpting, like David Miller got soul, like Rosmarie Waldrop got the splice of life ... As content.'[13]

For Mackey, the blues lends an 'aurality [...] and increased orality [...] with its attendant redefinition of poetic measure and line' with attention to rhythm, pitch, timbre and melody.[14] In poetry, we experience the movement of language as a combination of sound, rhythm, and semantic meaning.[15] In 'Empty Diary 1902' syllables rattle across the short lines. The monosyllabic words and distribution of voiced consonants create a shaken sense of movement, as heard and felt in these lines:

> uitlanders charge through photographers'
> ash checks for stolen
> diamonds tubes rupture kaffirs'
> anuses ripping a splinter
> of my soul accordant

Even the polysyllabic words 'uitlanders' and 'photographers' do not stem the rhythm here. The lines have a texture in which sound and sense move, improvised in broken time, across the lines. At the point of enjambment we are propelled by the semantic flow across to the next line. However, the strangeness and uncertainty of the juxtapositions still bend and slide our perceptions from one line to another in a fevered flow.

A dynamic combination of syllables is found in 'Empty Diary 1905'. The lines are composed of an artillery of syllables:

> She falls for him, conventional longing well
> tutored, no pose held, broken but breathing,
> yet she keeps a finger in a
> page of last year's tightly scribbled diary:

ccnmtl.columbia.edu/projects/jazzglossary/b/bossa_nova.html> [accessed 8 August 2018].

[13] '*The Wolf* Interview: Robert Sheppard', *The Wolf*, 29 (Winter 2013), 59-68 (p. 65).

[14] Mackey, pp. 31-2.

[15] See Derek Attridge, *Poetic Rhythm: An Introduction* (Cambridge: Cambridge University Press, 2008).

Although the sound moves like a cannonry, the meaning flows more easily from one line to the next than it did in 'Empty Diary 1902'. 'Schräge Musik' is both the name of a type of gunfire and derives from the German for shaky, off-tune music: literally slanting or jazz music.[16] The sound patterning in these poems attempts a mimesis of automatic firing adding another layer of history, that of a century of warfares, to the backdrop of these poems.[17]

The phrase 'read as domestic journal, or read as plan of war', appears more than once in *Complete Twentieth Century Blues*. There are references to different kinds of conflict, including domestic, social, and political, in the poems. In particular 'war' captures a type of combative energy, a back and forth movement I perceive between the genders 'at war' in the lyric subjectivity of these poems. *Empty Diaries* is aware that 'history' is gendered male. In 'Empty Diary 1902', the female speaker tells us that these are 'the words of his story not mine'. Further, without a proper name to identify 'her', she could only 'tumble into this myth'. 'Empty Diary 1905' begins, 'she falls'. The verbs 'tumble' and 'falls' both refer to passive unintentional actions. However, it is not a case of the male overpowering the female in these poems. These 'empty' diaries have at least one entry. Referring to the domestic and the foreign, we have seen that history in *Empty Diaries* is both individual and collective. Here history, and the narrative in the poems, is also gendered, not just 'his story' of 'Empty Diary 1902' but 'her story too' of 'Empty Diary 1905'.

In 'Empty Diaries 1901-1999' the shifting pronouns he / she and indeterminate 'I', the ''we', 'you', and 'they', for me, demonstrate a kind of dialogic movement between the male and female identities in those poems. This fluidity and ambiguity also effects a dynamic questioning of the subject writing and the subject written about. In 'Empty Diary 1902' the pronominal ellipsis, 'tumble into this myth', leaves us guessing the gender of the speaker in the poem and we are naturally led, or culturally conditioned, to assume that this is an opposition of male and female. From a speaker who asserts this is 'his story not mine' we deduce that we are being addressed by a female. Through this series of oppositions, lyric subjectivity in the 'Empty Diary' poems undergoes a con-

---

[16] 207 Squadron Royal Air Force History, 'Schräge Musik & The Wesseling Raid 21/22 June 1944: A New Weapon for a New Tactic – Schräge Musik' <http://www.207squadron. rafinfo.org.uk/wesseling/wesseling_schrage_musik.htm> [accessed 8 August 2018].

[17] For one account of the influences of jazz music in post-WWI Germany, see Cornelius Partsch, 'That Weimar Jazz', *New England Review*, 23.4 (2002), 179–94.

tinuous process of dissolving and recombination. This is enacted by back and forth movements, a combative energy in the shifts of pronouns.

In 'Empty Diary 1905', shifts in possession of narrative extend to possession of the body in the alternating 'his penis', 'his throat', and 'her bare neck'. In Petrarch's sonnets Laura was only fragments of a body. The tables turn here so that the treatment works both ways and these poems become a counterpoised territory for male and female bodies. The combat in these poems works as an offensive / defensive (language) game of possession. In 'Empty Diary 1905' this applies to the ownership of speech and writing, which fall into opposition. We find that 'she keeps a finger in a page of last year's tightly scribbled diary', while the reported speech, 'I sleep, I wake, I never dream' seems to belong to 'him'. I read this opposition as a move by Sheppard to give us a reintegrated gender-shifting body as a vision of a lyric subjectivity that brings both genders together to regard, and come into discourse with, each other. Through this lens Sheppard offers an alternative vision of female subjectivity, one which offers women another way of being seen and, more importantly, of *seeing*.

The climax in 'Empty Diary 1902' is striking:

> from excrement my hand
> on her thin shoulder
> 'Make the bitch perform

On the surface the final utterance ends the poem on a misogynistic note. However, this utterance is reported speech, made by a speaker outside the poem. The speech marks open but are left unclosed. The poem ends on this imperative but the action is not followed up on as no one does in fact make 'her' perform. Speech is left hanging, unfinished. The juxtaposition of the pitiable image of 'her thin shoulder' makes the final line all the harsher. We are meant to feel the impact of the language in this final image. In discussing the opposition of the expressive and the reflective, Mackey writes that the point is 'to unthink the perversions of thought endemic to an unjust social order'.[18] Interestingly, 'Empty Diary 1905' concludes with time stopped: 'her story stalled, veins in her bare neck pleading.' At this point in the poem, speech fails 'her'. It is the body, the female body, that finally speaks.

---

[18] Mackey, p. 42.

The ways in which bodies speak is vividly at work two recent poems in Sheppard's sequence that also heralds the twenty-first century: 'Empty Diary 2001: Zoë the Dial-up Camwhore' and 'Empty Diary 2015'. In *The History of Sexuality*, Michel Foucault argues that a focus on taboo and sex as power acts as a smokescreen to what might be seen as freedom. For Foucault, it is in sexuality that power and vitality lie.[19] Within this context, I see Sheppard's awareness of the power of sexuality in the female figures narrated in 'Empty Diaries', of which the female voice of the 'Wiped Weblogs' is also aware. It is, in part, a knowledge of the power of sexuality that drives these female-centred versions of history in the twentieth century and pushes them onward. The 'Wiped Weblogs,' written between 2001 and 2008, are described by Sheppard as:

> a sequence dealing with sexual politics, generally narrated from the point of view of a woman. These recent ones use a lot of internet flarf and detritus, combined with references to the first recorded uses of various technologies (and their jargons, like 'selfies') and first uses of various sexual practices (and their jargons, e.g., 'pegging'). I see them as a sort of egregious Tom and Jerry sequence with several characters (like Fuckeye and Stonehead) running through them. (The cat Gruntcakes and the dog Gruffnuts never made it into the final mix.) Everything gets excessive, even the line-lengths. They are continuations of the 'Empty Diary' strand that ran through Twentieth Century Blues, 1901-2000).[20]

These 'Weblog' poems now have an extra dimension to their titles: '2001: Zoë the Dial-up Camwhore' and '2002: The Icel Sock Puppet Texts Herself to Virginity'. There is also a shift to a narrative 'I' by the female subject of the Weblog poems. Here is 'Empty Diary 2001: Zoë the Dial-up Camwhore' in full:

> Zoë puts me up for it to accept that consensual sex once
> means that any future sex act is with the man's consent

---

[19] See Michel Foucault, *The Will to Knowledge: The History of Sexuality: Volume 1*, trans. by Robert Hurley (London: Penguin, 1998), pp. 103-14.

[20] Robert Sheppard, 'Robert Sheppard: More Wiped Weblogs (Empty Diaries) in *Blackbox Manifold* 17' <http://robertsheppard.blogspot.com/2017/01/robert-sheppard-more-wiped-weblogs.html> [accessed 8 August 2018].

I misread the signs (as ever) Plunderhead's boys
are hooked up to drips under spotlights if only I'd known
that on my first occasion feeling critical pulses against
my tongue watching the pegging vid now I know
what to do with them chained drugged sperm donors

so what does that make the rest of us for a good wipe
as I watch Chloë's lips slurping round Fuckeye
perhaps they'll tell me the truth just what they feel
about our black ops our attempts to hack reality
in the enslaved language of restless digital natives
with their flesh heaving love for puppet pricks I'm
the top of a head bobbing in the background (again)[21]

There is a sense of immediacy in this use of first person ('I misread,'
'I watch'), as well as a new sense of control, of power, and of intimacy
with the speaker. Our understanding of the speaker in the poem being
female comes from 'Zoë' in the title. There is an intriguing dynamic of
innocence and knowing moving between 'I misread the signs (as ever)'
and 'if only I'd known' to 'now I know what to do'. There is comedy in
the sexual images which is not so much explicit as 'flesh heaving love
for puppet pricks' and implied by 'the top of a head bobbing in the
background (again)'. '[W]riting is: the science of the various blisses of
language, its karma sutra', Roland Barthes writes.[22] The lines here are
pulses of syllables arranged in phrases which drive across the longer
lines of this poem: 'Zoë puts me up for it to accept that consensual sex
once / means.' The word 'means' pulls us into the second line where
it then effects a pause, before 'that any future sex act is with the man's
consent' picks up the flow and propels us across the line again. Carol
Bellard-Thomson concludes from her reading of Rabelais, whose *Gar-
gantua and Pantagruel* (c.1532-c.1564) contains explicit sexual images
of the female body, that 'female modesty', far from being a basic trait, is
an imposition required by a society unwilling to accept female sexuali-
ty.[23] Further, Sheppard's text enacts a linguistic jouissance, a journeying

[21] Robert Sheppard, 'Empty Diaries 2001-2008' <http://literateur.com/empty-diaries-
2001-2008-by-robert-sheppard/> [accessed 8 August 2018].

[22] Roland Barthes, *The Pleasure of the Text*, trans. by Richard Miller (New York, NY: Hill
and Wang, 1975), p. 6.

[23] Carol Bellard-Thomson, 'Rabelais and Obscenity: A Woman's View', in *The Body and*

out into pleasure. This is also evident in 'Empty Diary 2016':

> Her blink traps all   a cry caught
> In her throat curtains the ruins
> Behind her imperfect beauty her mind
> Perfectly balanced tracks your movements
>
> She loves silver waterfalls dropping into steely pools
> Smog-free air ringing with well-being
> She drops a social class or two in perfect pitch
> A wall of cloud and tipping metal topples
>
> Close up she's just dust a fusty form or
> Anti-form skimpiness raised to the power
> Of unlaced plumage it rustles on her head
> She smiles abstractly at whatever distracts from
>
> Her power of display her gown hangs lose
> As supposition enfleshes her shoulder[24]

It is notable that the music influence of the bossa nova I mentioned earlier makes for a different rhythm and a particular sensuality in this poem. In contrast to the possession of narrative in 'Empty Diary 2001: Zoë the Dial-up Camwhore', the third person pronoun 'her' makes this a female who is narrated. There is also passivity in the way of her being regarded as a sensual body. The soft 's'-sounds slink through the poem in images of 'silver waterfalls', 'steely pools', 'skimpiness' and 'unlaced plumage'. As Barthes asks, 'is not the most erotic portion of a body where the garment gapes?'[25] There is a move to fourteen lines of the sonnet form in both poems. This female may be narrated by a man, but 'she' is aware of the fascination that she holds for him, 'her power of display', and this makes her quite capable of returning his stare.

the Text: Hélène Cixous, Reading and Teaching, ed. by Helen Wilcox, Keith McWatters, Ann Thompson, and Linda Williams (Hemel Hempstead: Harvester Wheatsheaf, 1990), pp. 164-74 (p. 174).

[24] Sheppard, 'Robert Sheppard: Empty Diary 2016 published in the 50th edition of *Erbacce*'.

[25] Barthes, p. 9.

Vitality is an energy print which also suffuses the depiction of lyric subjectivity in Sheppard's 'Empty Diary' poems. The energy print in Sheppard's writing unleashes a sense of aliveness that in turn presents an image of human activity and community beyond a single conscious- ness. This energy is productively at work in the texts and equally is passed on both to the reader of the printed page and the listener during live performance. Studying and more recently working and collaborat- ing with Sheppard, this vitality continues to impress me – it's catchy and catching in a way that feeds my own enthusiasm and desire for knowledge and it drives me to push on in my own work as a poet.

BIBLIOGRAPHY

207 Squadron Royal Air Force History, 'Schräge Musik & The Wesseling Raid 21/22 June 1944: A New Weapon for a New Tactic – Schräge Musik' <http://www.207squadron.rafinfo.org.uk/wesseling/wesseling_schrage_ musik.htm> [accessed 8 August 2018]

Altieri, Charles, 'What is Living and What is Dead in American Postmodern- ism: Establishing the Contemporaneity of Some American Poetry' in *The Lyric Theory Reader: A Critical Anthology*, ed. by Virginia Jackson and Yopie Prins (Baltimore, MD: Johns Hopkins University Press, 2014), pp. 477-86

Barthes, Roland, *The Pleasure of the Text*, trans. by Richard Miller (New York, NY: Hill and Wang, 1975)

Bellard-Thomson, Carol, 'Rabelais and Obscenity: A Woman's View', in *The Body and the Text: Hélène Cixous, Reading and Teaching*, ed. by Helen Wilcox, Keith McWatters, Ann Thompson, and Linda Williams (Hemel Hempstead: Harvester Wheatsheaf, 1990), pp.167-74

De Bolla, Peter, *Art Matters* (Cambridge, MA, and London: Harvard Univer- sity Press, 2001)

Foucault, Michel, *The Will to Knowledge: The History of Sexuality: Volume 1*, trans. by Robert Hurley (London: Penguin, 1998)

Mackey, Nathaniel, *Discrepant Engagement: Dissonance, Cross-Culturality, and Experimental Writing* (Cambridge: Cambridge University Press, 1993)

Sheppard, Robert, *Complete Twentieth Century Blues* (Cambridge: Salt Pub- lishing, 2008)

——*Empty Diaries* (Exeter: Stride, 1998)

——'Empty Diaries 2001-2008' <http://literateur.com/empty-diaries-2001- 2008-by-robert-sheppard/> [accessed 8 August 2018]

—— *History or Sleep: Selected Poems* (Bristol: Shearsman Books, 2015)

—— 'Robert Sheppard: Basho's Famous Haiku and three variations' <http://robertsheppard.blogspot.com/2018/06/robert-sheppard-bashos-famous-haiku-and.html> [accessed 8 August 2018]

—— 'Robert Sheppard: Diary entries. Poems about the Belvedere pub Liverpool' <http://robertsheppard.blogspot.com/2017/05/robert-sheppard-diary-entries-poems.html> [accessed 8 August 2018]

—— 'Robert Sheppard: Empty Diary 2016 published in the 50th edition of Erbacce' <http://robertsheppard.blogspot.co.uk/2017/09/robert-sheppard-empty-diary-2016.html> [accessed 8 August 2018]

—— 'Robert Sheppard: More Wiped Weblogs (Empty Diaries) in Blackbox Manifold 17'
<http://robertsheppard.blogspot.com/2017/01/robert-sheppard-more-wiped-weblogs.html> [accessed 8 August 2018]

—— '*The Wolf* Interview: Robert Sheppard', *The Wolf*, 29 (Winter 2013), 59-68

But What of the Real Robert Sheppard?

Ailsa Cox

Introduction

When I started at Edge Hill University there were two of us. Robert and me. Poetry and prose. I had an MA in Creative Writing from Lancaster, while his was from the University of East Anglia. I had recently brought out a 'Writers and Their Work' book on Alice Munro (2003), while his was to be on Iain Sinclair (2010). I was BA Programme Leader, and he led the MA. Of course we weren't entirely left to our own devices. There was a number of dedicated part timers, and several colleagues from the department – English and Film Studies – pitched in, especially with the MA. But essentially we were a two-man band. Thirteen years later, at the time of Robert's retirement, there were seven full-timers in the Creative Writing team. The BA Creative Writing had grown from a joint or minor subject to a single honours, and we were now within a department that had added Creative Writing to its title, alongside English and History (losing Film along the way, but that's another story). These developments, and the distinctive way in which Creative Writing is still taught at Edge Hill, are largely down to Robert.

In the second part of this chapter I will discuss Robert's approach to Creative Writing pedagogy, but before I do so it seems important to conjure those aspects of his practice that come to mind when I think of his work at Edge Hill. (He will remain 'Robert' throughout, since my account is entirely subjective – tempting though it is to throw in a pun on the pastoral connotations of the surname.) One of the many axioms of Creative Writing teaching is the interdependency of research (i.e. writing) and teaching. For many of us, our brains crowded with the multiple demands made by our institutions, this is an idealistic stance. Judging by his prodigious output, Robert has kept the balance between the two more successfully than most – and never at the expense of his students.

Robert is not one of those small number of luminaries who grace their institutions like patron saints, materialising now and then to dispense their wisdom on their journey round the international literary circuit. Nor is he one of those Creative Writing teachers who secretly

believe themselves to be the Robin Williams character in *Dead Poets'
Society*, equating inspirational teaching with the cult of personality. And
yet it seems important, before I discuss Robert's thinking, to give you the
measure of him, some version at least of the flesh-and-blood person. The
years since we began working together have seen the exponential growth
of pedagogical jargon, along with a drive to calculate the aims, methods,
and results of every session according to a set of fixed criteria. And yet
in practice, so much of what goes on in the classroom is conditioned by
unpredictable factors, including the strange chemistry of any particular
year group, and including the style of the teacher.

So what can I say about the 'real' Robert Sheppard? Devilry and
mischief – sometimes overt, sometimes lurking behind an outward
impassivity. The quick flare of wit, the sudden whip crack of laughter.
All of these add something dangerous and impromptu to a curriculum
and teaching methods that are carefully considered and intellectually
challenging. A couple of winters ago, there were sudden power cuts at
Edge Hill, transforming the whole campus into an eerie underworld.
These were nearly always on MA nights; on one of those nights, he'd
just come in to teach the session, even though he'd been unwell. You
could just make him out in the gloom, a figure in a dark cap and
overcoat, looking something like a spy or a fictional detective with his
cane and his briefcase stuffed with manuscripts. (Robert is very fond of
the Swedish TV version of *Wallander*.)

But what of the not-so-real? The cult of non-personality? Or of
multiple identities? Robert's interrogation of authorship and identity
seem to me to have informed his contributions to Creative Writing
pedagogy in important ways. Part I of this chapter focuses on this
aspect of his work through some of his prose writing, while Part II looks
more closely at his work on secondary discourse and his contribution to
pedagogy at Edge Hill and beyond.

Part I

Robert has been fascinated by invented writers, several times donning
the mask of René Van Valckenborch, author of *A Translated Man*
(Shearsman, 2013), and founder of the 'European Union of Imaginary
Authors'. As the (fake) Lithuanian 'Jurgita Zujūtė' notes in the foreword
to *Twitters for a Lark* (Sheppard and others, 2017), 'Robert Sheppard'

himself is included as the UK contributor to the European Union of Imaginary Authors (EUOIA) anthology with 'The Ern Malley Suite'. In March 2018 he celebrated the mock centenary of Ern Malley's birth in the supposed city of his birth, Liverpool.[1] Both Robert and his co-conspirators in the Ern Malley Orchestra played it straight, fooling at least one of my Edge Hill colleagues (or so Professor Victor Merriman claims, though I only have Victor's own word for his credulity). As 'Zujūtė' concludes: 'the conducting and co-creating presence of Robert Sheppard […] is constantly guiding progress with his poetics of what he rather mysteriously calls "multiform unfinish."'[2] This playfulness with fictional personae is partly a riposte to those old Creative Writing chestnuts – 'find your voice', 'write what you know'. None of us speak, let alone write, with just one voice. Authoring a text is itself a type of performance, a concept explored in Derek Attridge's *The Singularity of Literature* (2004), which became essential reading on the MA.

One writer who most definitely did exist, and whose after-life has been the focus of some of Robert's work, and of mine, is Malcolm Lowry (1909-1957), the Wirral-born author of *Under the Volcano* (1947). Both Robert and I contributed creative texts to *Malcolm Lowry: From the Mersey to the World,* edited by Bryan Biggs and Helen Tookey, in conjunction with a festival and exhibition celebrating Lowry's centenary at the Bluecoat, an arts centre based in Liverpool. Robert's essay is far from the sum total of his Lowry-inspired work, which includes poems performed at the annual 'Lowry Lounge' event at the Bluecoat.

As Robert says in his essay, 'Malcolm Lowry's Land', 'people either "get" Lowry or they don't. It's a matter of recognition, attunement to an existential rhythm'.[3] Lowry's prose is free-ranging, intense, vivid, swerving back and forth between thought, sensation, memory – the myriad impressions assailing his characters, notably his drunken alter ego, the Consul, in *Under the Volcano*, his best-known novel. In

---

[1] 'Ern Malley 1918-1943' was held at the Handyman, a micro-brewery and performance space on Smithdown Road in south Liverpool. Robert profiled the event on *Pages*: 'Ern Malley 1918-1943: Celebrating the centenary in his place of birth Liverpool (set list)' <http://robertsheppard.blogspot.com/2018/03/ern-malley-1918-1943-celebrating_14.html> [accessed 13 August 2018]

[2] Robert Sheppard and others, *Twitters for a Lark* (Bristol: Shearsman, 2017), p. 8.

[3] Robert Sheppard, 'Malcolm Lowry's Land', in *Malcolm Lowry: From the Mersey to the World*, ed. by Bryan Biggs and Helen Tookey (Liverpool: Liverpool University Press, 2009), pp. 133-37 (p. 136). Further references to this edition are given after quotations in the text.

composing his own text, Robert resists romanticising the biographical figure of Lowry as the addled genius, the hero-outsider, 'but know I continue to see my own selves there, much as Lowry did, assuming his various guises, however doubtfully' (p. 136). Lowry stands, as clearly as any invented writer, for the figure of an author who is generated by his own texts, and cannot be fully retrieved through biographical data. In Lowry's case, the texts themselves exist in multiple versions, or, like *In Ballast to the White Sea*, have been lost and found.

'Malcolm Lowry's Land' consists of two sections. The first reconstructs a pilgrimage to Lowry's grave in Sussex, made by a youthful Robert, armed with notebook and camera. The second describes an attempt to return, thirty years to the day. It is a collage of notebook jottings, quotations from Lowry, newspaper clippings, railway announcements and so forth, very much in the spirit of Lowry's multiple voices. The physical return to Lowry's grave is thwarted, not least by even greater deficiencies in public transport than in 1979. Thanks to the Internet, the older Robert is able to make the journey virtually, and to discover the cottage where Lowry lived and died, a place he was unable to find on the first excursion. Returning to Liverpool, he concludes that the act of writing itself brings the 'image of time' that he seeks 'the human elsewhen that enfolds the present, multiple genealogies of belatedness' (p. 137).

The 1979 trip is narrated in the second person, highlighting the division between the narrator and the narrated self. The boundary between the two is blurred in the line 'You don't remember the black girl in dungarees at Lewes station, don't remember how you discovered that there were no buses to Ripe on Sundays' (p. 133). At which point in time does this 'you' stand? What is his relation to the 'I' who wonders whether either of the two policemen who help with directions in 1979 might have been on duty at the time of Lowry's sudden and, in some ways, mysterious, death?

Negation is also used in 'The Given' (first published 2010), included in the 2015 collection, *Words out of Time*, subtitled *Autrebiographies and Unwritings*: 'I don't remember going to the Grenada Portland Road, Hove, don't recall the film on show, and don't remember, on the same day, seeing a play, or its plot, or its title.'[4] Most conventional autobiography, even while acknowledging the fallibility of memory,

---

[4] Robert Sheppard, *Words out of Time* (Newton-le-Willows: The Knives Forks and Spoons Press, 2015), p. 11. Further references to this edition are given after quotations in the text.

ultimately stages its victory over time. The relentlessly repeated sentence pattern 'I don't remember' throughout Section I of 'The Given', with a couple of significant later variations, 'I disremember [...] I do not remember' (p. 18) parodies conventional autobiographies, refusing the discourse of nostalgia.[5] Section II is patterned as a sequence of unanswerable questions: 'Why does he *not* think the Third World War is coming, as the RAF rehearses in the East Anglian skies?' (p. 21' emphasis original); 'Why doesn't he bring up Billy Cotton and Uncle Bert?' (p. 27); and, close to the end of the section:

> How can he be sure, listening to his poems on the radio, that he'll never experience himself as an object again, examining his wordy slime, even as you read of him now, walking on Alderley Edge, while he recalls the thick socky atmosphere of the holiday caravan in Inverness in 1968, the weaving of dreams around things? (p. 32)

The radio image recalls the short poem that prefaces 'The Given', beginning 'I remember I re / Member' (p. 9), before referring to radio interference, caused by passing cars, an image of disruption but also of recurrence. The use of third person once again draws attention to the gaps between the narrating and narrated self and between the narrator, the implied author and the real author. As in 'Malcolm Lowry's Land' (referenced in *Words out of Time*), Robert is working through old journals, notes, and drafts, manipulating these ephemera into a non-linear prose structure that is driven by rhythmic energy and narrative compression.

Section III and IV retain the third person narration of Section II, accelerating the pace by fragmentation, often removing the subject from the sentence: 'Thinks of radio voices, disembodied, fluxing and fading, wavebands drifting, whistles and thunderclaps. Realises the reader must be the hero' (p. 35). Robert's account of writing 'The Given' on his blogzine, *Pages*, yields more insights than I have space to paraphrase.[6]

---

[5] The 'I don't remember' litany deliberately echoes Joe Brainard's anaphoric *I Remember*, first published in 1975 and now available through Granary Books. Brainard's text consists of very short, mostly single-sentence, paragraphs, each beginning 'I remember', the seeming randomness of these fragments evoking, paradoxically, the irretrievability of the past.

[6] Robert Sheppard, 'Robert Sheppard: Writing the Given: Materials and Procedure' <http://robertsheppard.blogspot.com/2010/07/robert-sheppard-writing-given.html> [accessed 9 August 2018]

His discussion of his stochastic methods for composing these later sections, including the focus on diary entries from the month of May in Section IV comments specifically on the resistance to self-analysis: 'The text is allowed to make its own history, to become the biography of a practice of writing rather than my autobiography.'[7]

These examples of Robert's prose explore what Gérard Genette calls 'transtextuality', the complex and sometimes barely discernible interplay of diverse texts within one another.[8] The poem written on the occasion of the 1979 pilgrimage to Lowry's grave remains, to the best of my knowledge, unpublished; it has been subsumed by its own palimpsest, the original notes, whose traces have themselves been reconfigured in the published essay. The emphasis on process, multiplicity, and the protean nature of words on the page, which also distinguishes his work in poetry, is key to his pedagogical practice.

Part II

To Robert, it is crucial to remind students that those who teach Creative Writing are active practitioners, something he has achieved by sharing current projects and pre-occupations. He has also been extremely generous about including students and former students in readings, collaborations, and publications, including the series of twenty-five Edge Hill poets featured on his blogzine *Pages,* in celebration of twenty-five years of Creative Writing teaching at the university.[9] The belief in the provisionality of texts and the instability of authorial identities evidenced in his own practice translates into a pedagogical emphasis on writing as process rather than product. Michelene Wandor's challenge to what she calls the 'Romantic/therapy axis' addresses a tension in the Creative Writing workshop between objective close reading of the work-in-progress and supporting self-development.[10] These tensions

---

[7] Ibid.

[8] Gérard Genette, *Palimpsests: Literature in the Second Degree,* trans. by Channa Newman and Claude Doubinsky (Lincoln, NE: University of Nebraska Press, 1997), p. 1.

[9] Robert Sheppard 'Twenty Five Years of Creative Writing at Edge Hill University: 25 Poets an introduction' <http://robertsheppard.blogspot.com/2014/09/twenty-five-years-of-creative-writing.html> [accessed 9 August 2018].

[10] Michelene Wandor, *The Author is Not Dead, Merely Somewhere Else: Creative Writing Reconceived* (Basingstoke, Palgrave Macmillan, 2008), p. 131.

are unlikely to ever be fully resolved, but a playful approach to the generation of the text as something other than the effusion of a single and essential subjectivity helps liberate both teacher and student. A chapter aimed at undergraduates, co-authored with Scott Thurston, highlights the common misapprehension that:

> Poetry must be always personal, the exposure of some traumatic emotional wound or of the ecstasies of love, for example. [...] Either you will be horrified at the thought of having to commit continual acts of literary self-revelation, or you will revel in it, seeking to shock or impress your audience. Neither is fair; neither is productive. Let's try something else.[11]

That final sentence gives the chapter its title, 'Trying Something Else'. Others will be able to provide a fuller account of Robert's teaching of poetry, but those three words will serve as a motto, as I move on to provide a wider background to his work at Edge Hill and the development of his ideas on supplementary discourse.

The Creative Writing MA began in 1989, ahead of the massive expansion of UK provision that took place towards the end of one century and the beginning of another. It was founded by Mike Hughes and subsequently taught by Jenny Newman and Pam Jackson. Robert took over from 1996, at a time when the nature of Creative Writing as a definable discipline, with its own research methods and pedagogical strategies was being articulated and interrogated. The (then) English Department at Edge Hill was fortunate in having a Head of Department, Gill Davies, who appreciated the nature of Creative Writing as pedagogy and research method. There was never the 'us and them' mentality that some creative writers have experienced in English departments elsewhere.

Just before I arrived at Edge Hill, Robert led a research project into 'Supplementary Discourses in Creative Writing Teaching' (2003) on behalf of the Higher Education Authority and the English Subject Centre. Assisted by Scott Thurston, Robert set up a series of questionnaires and interviews, involving both staff and students. A painstaking investigation into the varieties of 'commentary', 'reflection', 'self-assessment',

---

[11] Robert Sheppard and Scott Thurston, 'Try Something Else: Poetry Writing', in *The Road to Somewhere: A Creative Writing Companion*, ed. by Heather Leach, Helen Newall, Julie Armstrong, Robert Graham, and John Singleton (Basingstoke: Palgrave Macmillan 2005), pp. 207-16 (p. 208).

etc., that typically accompanied creative assignments across all university levels was conducted. The report's key findings affirm the importance of 'supplementary discourses which encourage students to reflect critically on their creative work at the level of individual piece of coursework, module or programme', noting both a commonality and a heterogeneity in the approaches used across all levels in a variety of institutions.[12]

The report acknowledges the balance to be struck between maintaining flexibility and a drive towards some degree of commonality in the defence of Creative Writing as its own subject area, distinguished from yet also sometimes incorporating other disciplines. Another important point is the need for students to reflect on their ongoing process, rather than the final product. It is noted that 'student writers are sometimes expected to read their own work as though they were reading the work from the outside, or they were ordinary readers rather than its unique originator' (p. 35). During this research period, the concept of 'reading as a writer' had been adopted by most institutions, as a means of avoiding this type of response to both published texts and those produced by the students themselves. The report draws attention to the need to clarify the term and to find ways to teach it.

Amongst the formal recommendations is one suggesting 'that centres consider adopting formal criteria and the separate awarding of a clearly defined mark to substantial supplementary discourses, so students will be more aware of their function in assessment processes' (p. 39). Another is that at Ph.D level forms of supplementary discourse should be publishable in their own right, not limited to a purely descriptive commentary, an explanation, or an appendix. Fifteen years later, these two points seem especially significant to the consolidation and development of the new discipline.

Robert's pamphlet, *The Necessity of Poetics*, draws on the work of American poets, including Charles Bernstein, Jerome Rothenberg, and Rachel Blau DuPlessis, to argue for the centrality of a type of discourse that might supersede mechanical or post-event iterations of the Creative Writing exegesis. The document was given its first outing in the

---

[12] Robert Sheppard and Scott Thurston, 'Final Report: Supplementary Discourses in Creative Writing Teaching at Higher Education Level' (Higher Education Academy/ English Subject Centre, 2003). Available at <http://english.heacademy.ac.uk/2015/10/ 26/supplementary-discourses-in-creative-writing-teaching-edge-hill/> [accessed 9 August 2018]. The full report is downloadable from this site; subsequent quotations are taken from this document.

Proceedings of a Creative Writing Conference at Sheffield which took place in 1999; its present incarnation, complementing the 'Supplementary Discourses' project, dates from 2011. *The Necessity of Poetics* offers a clear definition of poetics as 'the products of the process of reflection upon writings, and upon the act of writing, gathering from the past and from others, speculatively casting into the future'.[13] It is 'a way of letting writers question what they think they know' (p. 2). A series of epigrams offer fractured, sometimes gnomic, definitions of a practice that is fundamentally dynamic and multifaceted: 'to talk of theoretical poetics is not accurate; to talk of practical poetics is no less accurate' (p. 2).

'Poetics' is a term that still frightens some students whose school or college education has trained them to provide set answers to a limited number of questions. As Robert observes in his inaugural lecture[14], the freewheeling nature of poetics is also a corrective to the notion of 'craft', promulgated by some Creative Writing handbooks. Nothing could be further from the discourse of the 'how-to' manual, with its handy tips and unbreakable rules ('show not tell', 'write what you know', etc.). Though the word 'poetics' may be unfamiliar to most, *The Necessity of Poetics* points to historical examples:

> from Aristotle, through Horace, into (in English anyway) Sidney, Puttenham, Campion, Dryden and Pope (both in verse), onto Wordsworth's 'Preface', Coleridge's *Biographia*, the assertions of Shelley's *Defence*, some of Keats' letters. Onto: Henry James' essays and *Prefaces*, and D.H. Lawrence's spirited defences of both free verse poetry and the modern novel. (p. 9)

Above all, it is something that must be useful to the student in developing their autonomy as a writer, and is as relevant to prose and to script as it is to poetry.

The ideas in the 'Supplementary Discourses' project and in *The Necessity of Poetics* fed into the 2008 Creative Writing Benchmark Statements from the National Association of Writers in Education (NAWE) which provided precise yet flexible definitions of the discipline and its research methodologies. As a member of NAWE's Higher Education Committee, Robert was one of several people

---

[13] Robert Sheppard, 'The Necessity of Poetics' (Liverpool: Ship of Fools, 2003), p. 2. Further references to this edition are given after quotations in the text.

[14] Delivered in 2007, the lecture was published on *Pages* in 2017.

responsible for this affirmation of subject specificity in both teaching and research: 'Creative Writing is research in its own right. All Creative Writing involves research in Creative Writing whereby experience is transmuted into language (and some of that experience may concern language itself).'[15] This precise wording has disappeared from the 2018 'Creative Writing Research Benchmark Statement', though it is echoed in Section 3:1, on methodology: 'The actions of Creative Writing research inherently include investigations and explorations both in and of creative practice, whereby experience is transmuted into language; some of that experience may concern language itself.'[16] Perhaps the rewording reflects a greater confidence in the acceptance of practice as a legitimate research methodology in the academy at large.

Much has happened between those two benchmarking statements, as Paul Munden's 2013 report, 'Beyond the Benchmark: Creative Writing in Higher Education', demonstrates. Amongst other developments, Munden notes the tightening grip of the employability agenda on the undergraduate curriculum. A Faustian bargain has been made available to those advocating the study of Creative Writing on the grounds of the high financial turnover of the creative industries, including film, TV, gaming, and 'Harry Potter theme parks' – all of them ultimately dependent on the wordsmith. Arguments are also made for the transferable skills of the majority of graduates, who will not become published writers.

Munden cites testimony given to a House of Commons Select Committee by Josie Barnard. Barnard, a Senior Lecturer at Middlesex University, gives some example of how skills learnt on her courses may be utilised in a business career:

> A manager who studied with me described how she gained a new understanding of structure through Creative Writing that helped her take macro company targets, break them down, and apply them locally on a micro-level. A television producer from a mid-sized firm who studied with me detailed how his fresh understanding of the best way to develop a narrative

---

[15] NAWE Higher Education Committee, 'A Subject Benchmark for Creative Writing' (York: NAWE, 2008), p. 13.

[16] Derek Neale, 'Creative Writing Research Statement' <https://www.nawe.co.uk/writing-in-education/writing-at-university/research.html> [accessed 26 November 2018]

thread improved his spoken presentations and led directly to an increased number of contracts.[17]

Just before the publication of Munden's report, in conversation with Rupert Loydell, Robert observed 'the friction mounting between supposed vocational orientations in the subject and art's claims to operate as a critique of society (often by developing forms that directly contest what that legitimising society holds dear).'[18] Some of the anonymous university teachers quoted in *Beyond the Benchmark* echo Robert's concerns, such as this warning against 'the encroachment of "Cultural Industries" and the sense that we should deliver deliverables that can be weighed on a scale of economic or cultural interest. That betrays a lack of confidence in educational process.'[19]

There's no avoiding the discourse of 'employability' in today's educational climate. We even have a module on the MA, designed by Robert, entitled 'Cultural Industries'. But we interpret such concepts in relation to an independent and self-sustaining literary practice. According to a preliminary survey in research carried out by the Authors' Licensing and Collecting Society (ALCS), writers' earnings have in fact been falling despite a recent growth in publishers' profits and the increasing significance of the cultural sector.[20] On both the Edge Hill BA and the MA, we give systematic advice on the practicalities of getting published, maintain links with agents, publishers, and theatres, etc., and offer internships. But none of this counts for anything without a self-motivated artistic identity, or the ability to keep a space for writing in your life despite inevitable economic pressures.

In the early stages of developing the BA Single Honours, we kept returning to the phrase 'cultural citizens'. I think it was Robert who

---

[17] Josie Barnard, 'Support for the creative economy' (Culture, Media and Sport, 2013). Available at: <http://www.publications.parliament.uk/pa/cm201213/cmselect/cmcumeds/writev/suppcrec/m088.htm> [accessed 9 August 2018].

[18] Rupert Loydell, 'Even the Bad Times are Good: Rupert Loydell & Robert Sheppard' <http://www.stridebooks.co.uk/Stride%20mag%202012/Jan%202012/rupertand robertint.htm> [accessed 9 August 2018].

[19] Paul Munden, 'Beyond the Benchmark: Creative Writing in Higher Education' (York: Higher Education Academy, 2013), p. 36. It's not impossible that the speaker is Robert himself, since the team at Edge Hill contributed their comments.

[20] ALCS, '2018 Authors' Earnings: A Survey of UK Writers' (London: ALCS, 2018) <https://wp.alcs.co.uk/app/uploads/2018/06/ALCS-Authors-earnings-2018.pdf> [accessed 9 August 2018].

coined that phrase, but his ideas were also shared by a third addition to the Creative Writing team, Swiss-born poet and translator Daniele Pantano. We situated Creative Writing within a multi-disciplinary context. Students needed to be open to the influence of other contemporary forms, for instance the visual arts, and as part of their first year course they visited Tate Liverpool and produced a 'cultural artefact' alongside their written texts. That module was called 'Reading the World' because it was precisely what we were training writers to do – to observe and to process reality, in the widest sense of that word, both as it was observed directly and as it was transmitted through artistic expression. We wanted students to think of themselves as artists, each developing their own autonomous practice, informed by curiosity and linguistic experiment. Some details of that particular module, along with all the others first delivered in 2011, have been modified along the way; but all of our programmes are infused by this philosophy, which Robert has done so much to advocate. In his 2007 inaugural lecture he confessed his initial scepticism towards Creative Writing, 'because it seemed antithetical to the kinds of explorative poetry and poetics I was writing and writing about, in favour of what is known in the US as the "workshop poem", a neat formulaic and formalist lozenge of experience, lightly spiced with epiphany or leavened with moral.'[21] (He might also have been describing the consolatory patterns of the 'workshop story'.) We have Robert to thank for the rewards of such scepticism, and for a faith in linguistic innovation that liberates his students.

---

[21] Robert Sheppard, 'Inaugural Lecture Part 1: Poetics as Conjecture and Provocation' <http://robertsheppard.blogspot.com/2017/03/robert-sheppard-inaugural-lecture-part.html> [accessed 9 August 2018]

BIBLIOGRAPHY

ALCS, '2018 Authors' Earnings: A Survey of UK Writers' (London: ALCS, 2018) <https://wp.alcs.co.uk/app/uploads/2018/06/ALCS-Authors-earnings-2018.pdf> [accessed 9 August 2018]

Barnard, Josie, 'Support for the creative economy' (Culture, Media and Sport, 2013) <http://www.publications.parliament.uk/pa/cm201213/cmselect/cmcumeds/writev/suppcrec/m088.htm> [accessed 9 August 2018]

Brainard, Joe, *I Remember* (New York, NY: Granary Books, 2001)

Genette, Gérard, *Palimpsests: Literature in the Second Degree,* trans. by Channa Newman and Claude Doubinsky (Lincoln, NE: University of Nebraska Press, 1997)

NAWE Higher Education Committee, 'A Subject Benchmark for Creative Writing' (York: NAWE, 2008)

Neale, Derek, 'Creative Writing Research Statement' (York: NAWE, 2018)

Sheppard, Robert, *A Translated Man* (Bristol: Shearsman Books, 2013)

—— 'Inaugural Lecture Part 1: Poetics as Conjecture and Provocation' <http://robertsheppard.blogspot.com/2017/03/robert-sheppard-inaugural-lecture-part.html> [accessed 9 August 2018]

—— 'Malcolm Lowry's Land', in *Malcolm Lowry: From the Mersey to the World*, ed. by Bryan Biggs and Helen Tookey (Liverpool: Liverpool University Press, 2009), pp. 133-37

—— 'The Necessity of Poetics' (Liverpool: Ship of Fools, 2011)

—— 'Twenty Five Years of Creative Writing at Edge Hill University: 25 Poets An Introduction' <http://robertsheppard.blogspot.com/2014/09/twenty-five-years-of-creative-writing.html> [accessed 9 August 2018]

—— *Words out of Time* (Newton-le-Willows: The Knives Forks and Spoons Press, 2015)

—— 'Writing the Given' <http://robertsheppard.blogspot.com/2010/07/robert-sheppard-writing-given.html> [accessed 9 August 2018]

Sheppard, Robert, and others, *Twitters for a Lark* (Bristol: Shearsman, 2017)

Sheppard, Robert, and Scott Thurston, 'Final Report: Supplementary Discourses in Creative Writing Teaching at Higher Education Level' (Higher Education Academy/English Subject Centre, 2003). Available at: http://english.heacademy.ac.uk/2015/10/26/supplementary-discourses-in-creative-writing-teaching-edge-hill/ [accessed 9 August 2018]

Sheppard, Robert, and Scott Thurston, 'Try Something Else: Poetry Writing', in *The Road to Somewhere: A Creative Writing Companion*, ed. by Heather Leach, Helen Newall, Julie Armstrong, Robert Graham, and John Singleton (Basingstoke: Palgrave Macmillan 2005), pp. 207-16

Wandor, Michelene, *The Author is Not Dead, Merely Somewhere Else: Creative Writing Reconceived* (Basingstoke, Palgrave Macmillan, 2008)

Who is Robert Sheppard?

Allen Fisher

This chapter includes a bundle of extracts from Robert Sheppard's *The Meaning of Form in Contemporary Innovative Poetry* (2016) with alerts of similarity to, and difference from, Samuel Beckett, Jacques Derrida, Emmanuel Levinas, Friederike Mayröcker, and Jacques Rancière. I aim to consider the concepts of damage and disruption in modernist practice and in the process of doing so implicate a further dimension: a critique of the concept of the self. They are terms that reiterate inside the work of Robert Sheppard, sometimes referred to as 'the Bluesman', and against the work of many of his lyrical contemporaries. The idea of deliberate disruption promotes what I would call the imperfect fit, the aesthetic necessity. There is a brazen disruption that can be read as a knowing damage, a positive turn. This articulation of damage and disruption undermines that artefact of human existence, the idea of the self. We can only provide an informed guess regarding who Robert Sheppard is.

There is a focus on establishing and disrupting a self that challenges traditional concepts of identity. This constitution and disruption of a self through remembering, or through the facture of a relationship to other selves, produces a possible imaginary rowing boat, an example of autography, of 'writing the self', as texts concerned with identity and the impossibility of establishing a stable self and of representing an individual's life through language. Robert's writing the self is a search for language beyond representation which explores the relationship between the self and the other body, between internal thought and cognition of the world; as such it is a challenge to autobiography and biography, a large proportion of which is a disruption of the subject.

Robert Shepherd has been involved in the future of more than one conscious self, an unusual expectation and one that he fulfils. We are suspended between our desire to experience the poem and the memories that compete for awareness, in this process we become conscious of ourselves. It is the special task of the poet to facture the poem and provide the potential for the pattern of connectedness between the spacetime of past place and time and immediacy, a pattern which might provide meaning to the emergence of self-consciousness. Angelika Rauch identifies the alienation of self from self in passages written by

Novalis where the poet formulates what Rimbaud was to follow with, 'Je est un autre' ('I is somebody else').[1] Robert Sheppard, like Novalis and Rimbaud, has an openness to an experience of that self-doubt which gives him the potential for everyday ethical expertise, the experience of profound vulnerability to the other, that is by the disruptive experience of self-questioning that leads to moral maturity. Emmanuel Levinas leads to an elaboration of this in his lecture 'Substitution' from 1967:[2]

> What is the relation between the 'oneself' and the *for self* of representation? Is the 'oneself' a recurrence of the same type as consciousness, knowledge, and representation, all of which would be sublimated in consciousness conceived as Mind? Is the 'oneself' consciousness in its turn, or is it not a quite distinct event, one which would justify the use of separate terms: Self, I, Ego, soul?[3]

Robert begins *The Meaning of Form*: 'Poetry is the investigation of complex contemporary realities through the means (meanings) of form.'[4] In his first chapter reading Terry Eagleton's *How to Read a Poem*, he notes that Eagleton differentiates Yuri Lotman's theory[5] from New Critical formalist analysis[6], where formal elements must blend to confirm perceptions, but it also differs from Veronica Forrest-Thomson's will toward coherence and her need for thematic synthesis. Eagleton writes: 'Each system deviates from or "disrupts" the others.'[7]

---

[1] Angelika Rauch, 'The Hieroglyph of Tradition, Freud, Benjamin, Gadamer, Novalis, Kant', *Criticism*, 43.3 (Summer 2001), 352-55. The quotation from Rimbaud appears in his 'Letter to Georges Izambard', May 13th, 1871.

[2] The 1967 lecture became the text 'Substitution' in 1968. I understand that this forms a pivot for Levinas' subsequent *Otherwise and Being* in 1974. I am obliged to James Byrne who suggested the affinity to Levinas in the Robert Sheppard Symposium.

[3] Emmanuel Levinas, *En découvrant l'existence avec Husserl et Heidegger*, 2nd ed. (Paris: Vrin, 1967), pp. 217-233. ['Language and Proximity', in Levinas, *Collected Philosophical Papers*, trans. by Alphonso Lingis (The Hague: Martinus Nijhoff, 1987), pp. 109-15]. There is too much elaboration in the published text to provide here in quotation. I have put some examples from Levinas' section two in Appendix 1.

[4] Sheppard, *The Meaning of Form*, p. 1.

[5] Yuri Lotman, *Analysis of the Poetic Text* (Ann Arbor, MI: Ardis, 1976).

[6] See Peter Barry, *English in Practice* (London: Arnold, 2003).

[7] Terry Eagleton, *How to Read a Poem* (Oxford: Blackwell, 2007), p. 53.

Robert notes:

> However, Eagleton is more skeptical when it comes to
> questions of value. If, in Lotman's view, 'good poems are those
> in which there is a satisfying interplay between the predictable
> and the disruptive' and bad poems are, informationally
> speaking, simply 'those which are either excessively predictable
> or excessively normal [...] how would so-called automatic or
> aleatory writing, or the unconscious flow of a Dadaist poem,
> fare on this account', let alone the formally investigative and
> linguistically innovative poetries examined in this study?[8]

'A present formal action [...] is disrupting the valency of past
significations, even if they are drawn again into the poem.'[9]

One of the foci for Robert, discussing work by Erín Moure, is
that 'the mood [...] is clear despite the formal disruption of linguistic
and syntactic codes'.[10] Commenting on the recognisable chorus in a
poem by Moure, Robert notes that it 'begins coherently enough', but
that 'pointers maintain the poem in a state of formal unfinish; it is
choral-like in its repetition, but curiously foregrounding its material
presence in a way disruptive of choral calm and decorum'.[11] And later,
he notes that we are aware of 'Moure's confessed disruption of archival
conventions, her own annarchival play'.[12]

'It is a sleight of hand and mind,' notes Robert on Rosmarie
Waldrop's work, 'to conjure narrativity from propositional language,
and one productive of a discursive but formally disruptive prose', which
he then footnotes: 'The calm and poise of the spoken voice, particularly
the hurt feelings of the rejected "I", slightly unsettles Waldrop's assertion
about the movement.'[13] Later he notes her 'Oulipo-like clinamen that
deliberately disrupts the scheme'.[14]

---

[8] Sheppard, *The Meaning of Form*, p. 37; and Eagleton, *How to Read a Poem*, p. 54.

[9] Sheppard, *The Meaning of Form*, p. 55.

[10] Ibid., p. 96.

[11] Ibid., p. 97.

[12] Ibid., p. 98.

[13] Ibid., p. 124 and n. 6.

[14] Ibid., p. 125.

In discussing the work of Vanessa Place, Robert looks to work by Kenneth Goldsmith. He writes:

> The reference numbers that dot this and other passages of *Statement of Facts*[15] operate to deautomatise our responses by interrupting the narrative that clearly does not just 'draw you in' as Goldsmith reports. The paragraph (the work generally) does do that, but it does more, through operations of form, to disable the reader or listener, and draw him or her into a disruptive formal world of substantiated statements in distanciated sentences.[16]

Robert quotes from an interview with Jacques Rancière: 'The dream of a suitable political work of art [...] is in fact the dream of disrupting the relationship between the visible, the sayable and thinkable' – the three essential regimes of his thinking – 'without having to use the terms of a message as a vehicle'. Instead, producing 'meanings in the form of a rupture with the very logic of meaningful situations.'[17] Robert, reading through Rancière, notes:

> Dissensus (rather than consensus, both socially and artistically, in relation to heteronomy as well as autonomy) produces the manifold and broadly translational devices of formally investigative poetry (including that poetry now called linguistically innovative), but varieties of montage and de-montage emphasising disruption, interruption, imperfect fit, and unfinish, as well as transformation and transposition – creative linkage in other words – put disorder at the heart of art's order, while simultaneously putting order at the heart of its disruptive practices.[18]

Rancière's work continues to inform Robert in *The Meaning of Form*:

---

[15] Vanessa Place, 'Statement of Facts', in *Against Expression: An Anthology of Conceptual Writing*, ed. by Craig Dworkin and Kenneth Goldsmith (Evanston, IL: Northwestern University Press, 2011), pp. 489-95.

[16] Sheppard, *The Meaning of Form*, p. 144.

[17] Jacques Rancière, *The Politics of Aesthetics*, ed. and trans. by Gabriel Rockhill (London: Continuum, 2004), p. 63.

[18] Sheppard, *The Meaning of Form*, p. 236.

How can the notion of 'aesthetics' as a specific experience lead at once to the idea of a pure world of art and of the self-suppression of art in life, to the tradition of avant-garde radicalism and to aestheticisation of common existence? [...] At the end of the fifteenth [of his *Letters on the Aesthetic Education of Mankind*], [Friedrich Schiller] places himself and his readers in front of a specimen of 'free appearance', a Greek statue known as the 'Juno Ludovisi'. The statue is 'self-contained', and 'dwells in itself', as befits the traits of the divinity: 'idleness', her distance from any care or duty, from any purpose or volition. [...] The 'self-containment' of the Greek statue turns out to be the 'self-sufficiency' of a collective life that does not rend itself into separate spheres of activities, of a community where art and life, art and politics, life and politics are not severed one from another. Such is supposed to have been the Greek people whose autonomy of life is expressed in the self-containment of the statue. [...] At first autonomy was tied to the 'unavailability' of the object of aesthetic experience. Then it turns out to be the autonomy of a life in which art has no separate existence – in which its productions are in fact self-expressions of life. [...] The plot of a 'free play', suspending the power of active form over passive matter and promising a still unheard-of state of equality, becomes another plot, in which form subjugates matter, and the self-education of mankind is its emancipation from materiality, as it transforms the world into its own sensorium.[19]

All the interlocutors are figments of internal thought and cognition and as such are unstable and interchangeable. These are appropriations of the voices of others, altered into emanations of a shifting self. The material taken from other texts enters altered, muddled, thrown into disorder. They are deliberate demonstrations of damage and alliteration, breakage and repair.

'Damage' is a feature of Robert, the Bluesman's work, but a smaller theme in *The Meaning of Form*. Referring to Moure's work, he notes that she 'never lets us forget that she is approaching partial and damaged texts on occasion: 'This folio much deteriorated, and it is clear that the copyist did not know the language', a textual 'note' marked by

---

[19] Jacques Rancière, 'The Aesthetic Revolution and Its Outcomes', *Log*, 22 (Spring/ Summer 2011), 16-21 (p. 19).

an asterisk 'explains' at the bottom of a poem.[20] However, the lack of any matching asterisk in the text signals that the isolated note is false or fictional (the 'afterword' tells us that the attributions and scholarly archival numbers are often false, provided in translational excess).' Alerted to John Wilkinson's discussion of Barry MacSweeney's work, the Bluesman notes: 'For Wilkinson, the violence of "Liz Hard" and "Jury Vet" curdled as personal resentment, but for a brief period the Iron Lady helped to reinscribe MacSweeney's personal demons in an idiom tellingly connected with social damage.'[21]

Texts are stripped of their original meaning, the other now speaks on behalf of the signifier of the other for the purpose of reading it and reading its own self in a pool of sticky silver from a molten mirror. The impossibility to grasp a self, to establish a stable self and to assert an identity persist. It is a trans-European crash box that narrates an autobiographical reading of itself with a ploy to prevent any closure and solidification. The Bluesman's texts describe the self and its others, but only within language. In this respect they are examples of giving faces to absence and makes those faces visible and readable. They are also acts of defacement, made visible in language and not the face itself. The face remains invisible, outside of language, absent. The Bluesman splits into a multitude of selves and others, a dialogical overflow alienated from himself.

Friederike Mayröcker writes: 'I am removed from my self, unfathomable, I have moved away from my self [...] I live at a distance from my self, I regard my self as a person who is close to me, with whom I am, however, not identical.'[22] Jacques Derrida argues: 'it is the ear of the other that signs. The ear of the other says me to me and constitutes the autos of my autobiography.'[23]

The Bluesman represents the unrepresentable essence of the self as non-essence. The attempt at undoing the self fails in the sense that there is always something that remains: the final void and silence cannot be

[20] Erín Moure, *O Cadoiro* (Toronto: House of Anansi, 2007), p. 76.

[21] John Wilkinson, 'The Iron Lady and the Pearl: Male Panic in Barry MacSweeney's "Jury Vet"', in *Reading Barry MacSweeney*, ed. by Paul Batchelor (Newcastle: Bloodaxe Books, 2013), pp. 87-106 (p. 105).

[22] Friederike Mayröcker, 'Lection', in *Gesammelte Prosa IV 1991-1995*, ed. by Klaus Reichert (Frankfurt: Suhrkamp, 2001), p. 373. Translated by Hanne Schweiger (2004).

[23] Jacques Derrida, *The Ear of the Other: Otobiography, Transference, Translation*, ed. by Christie MacDonald (Lincoln, NE & London: University of Nebraska Press, 1985), p. 51.

achieved. If the 'deconstructed body in [Samuel Beckett's] *Worstward Ho* is indicative of the fragmentation and distortion of the self' and if 'one frequently encounters a distorted body in Mayröcker's texts, making the fragmentation of the self visible', for the Bluesman the complex is multiplied. 'Both in *Still Life* and in *Worstward Ho* [...] the body and self are reduced to their utmost minimum at the end of the text, when the movement of language that generated the text comes to a standstill'.[24] The Bluesman's text moves to counter this direction; the Bluesman has many names and for that reason unnameable. We call him 'Robert Sheppard'.

Referring to Rosmarie Waldrop, Robert writes:

> [Denise] Levertov is clear that there is such a thing as 'the poetry of linguistic impulse' involving an 'awareness of the world of multiple meaning revealed in sound, word, syntax', which would seem to describe an absorption into poetic artifice (and Waldrop's work, in fact), even if for Levertov this involves the exceptionalism of the 'apparent distortion of experience in such a poem for the sake of verbal effects'.[25]

Any representation of a single self becomes impossible through its constant deferral and the constant rewritings of the selves and others.

The memories which the voice comes upon narrates a state of *decoherence*.[26] In Beckett's *Proust*, the self can never integrate where it has been into where it is, can never make sense of where it has been, because the self is in constant flux. The self of today is different from the self of yesterday, and since where it has been has altered the self, the self is never the same, is never at one with itself but lacks a centre and an essence.

---

[24] Hannes Schweiger, 'Samuel Beckett and Friederike Mayröcker: Attempts at Writing the Self', *Samuel Beckett Today /Aujourd'hui*, 14 (2004), 147-60. Samuel Beckett, *Worstward Ho* (London: John Calder, 1983). Friedericke Mayröcker, *Stilleben* (Frankfurt: Suhrkamp, 1995).

[25] Denise Levertov, 'Some Notes on Organic Form' <https://www.poetryfoundation.org/articles/69392/some-notes-on-organic-form-56d249032078f> [accessed 14 July 2018]

[26] I have elaborated on this term in *Imperfect Fit: Aesthetic Function, Facture and Perception in Art and Writing since 1950* (Tuscaloosa, AL: The University of Alabama Press, 2016).

It will be impossible to prepare the hundreds of masks that rightly belong to the objects of even his most disinterested scrutiny. [...] The individual is the seat of a constant process of decantation, decantation from the vessel containing the fluid of future time, sluggish, pale and monochrome, to the vessel containing the fluid of past time, agitated and multicoloured by the phenomena of its hours.[27]

Beckett's later texts become more and more self-enclosed and minimalistic, he reduces the descriptive content of his text and moves towards silence. The Bluesman works in a different set of directions: the outcome is a spread of languages and the moves are in stresses of knowledge and incomprehension.

Robert writes:

Leaving aside considerations of the relationship between beauty and truth in post-Romantic thought which culminates in Pater's purist awareness that [in Angela Leighton's words] 'form [...] shuts in beauty and shuts out truth', Leighton draws out the ambiguities of Clive Bell's and Roger Fry's Modernist mantra of 'significant form', which is usually taken as a plea for the autonomy of the artwork but more accurately 'registers the contrary pressure of significance, and therefore the stress of incompatibles being brought together', content and form.[28]

The consistent and unfortunate feature of modernist poetry is the insistence on the idea of the 'self'. In *The Meaning of Form*, Robert directly refers to the concept ninety-one times. This is not here a question of who is Robert Sheppard, or who the poets are in *Twitters for a Lark*. It is a question of poets and their prevalent recurrences. Reading Susan Wolfson,[29] Robert notes that,

while her quasi-deconstructive reading of work by Samuel

---

[27] Samuel Beckett, *Proust & 3 Dialogues with Georges Duthuit* (London: John Calder, 1965), pp. 12-15.

[28] Sheppard, *The Meaning of Form*, pp. 16-17; Angela Leighton, *On Form: Poetry, Aestheticism, and the Legacy of a Word* (Oxford: Oxford University Press, 2007), p. 10 and p. 13.

[29] Susan J. Wolfson, *Formal Charges* (Stanford, CA: University of Stanford Press, 1997).

Taylor Coleridge centres upon his tropic play and indeterm-
inacy, particularly with regards to his use of simile that his
formalist poetics overtly devalues, the genetic approach to the
work of William Wordsworth shows how revisionary stages of
The Prelude articulate and self-interrogate a dynamic process of
unfinished forming,[30] announcing with Muriel Rukeyser that
in the position of the reader of poetry as a witness we are 'about
to change [and] that work is being done on the self'.[31]

Discussing the work of Vanessa Place, Robert recalls Roland Barthes:

The Author, when believed in, is always conceived of as the
past of his own book: book and author stand automatically
on a single line divided into a *before* and an *after*. The Author
is thought to *nourish* the book, which is to say that he exists
before it, thinks, suffers, lives for it.[32] (emphases original)

However, for Robert:

The author matters, but not quite in the way his or her stoutest
traditional defenders imagine. It is a functioning principle of
the text, authoredness rather than authority, signature rather
than person, which exists as much as for the most conceptual,
anonymous, or impersonal, as for the most expressive, self-
declaring, or confessional writings.[33]

Later, in a discussion of John Seed's *Pictures from Mayhew II*,[34] he writes:

Sincerity of witness balances the technique of performance.
The resistance to our drive to authenticity matches the tension
between the recuperative historian and the distanciating poet
in Seed himself, though he is not a 'mouthpiece' or passive

[30] Sheppard, *The Meaning of Form*, p. 9.

[31] Muriel Rukeyser, *A Muriel Rukeyser Reader*, ed. by Jan Heller Levi (New York, NY: W.W. Norton, 1994), p. 166.

[32] Roland Barthes, 'The Death of the Author', in *Image Music Text*, trans. by Stephen Heath (Glasgow: Fontana/Collins, 1977), pp. 142-48 (p. 145).

[33] Sheppard, *The Meaning of Form*, p. 140.

[34] John Seed, *Pictures from Mayhew II* (Exeter: Shearsman Books, 2007).

conduit, but an agent of significance in his ghostly authoredness. The poetic – to remember the origins of the word as 'making' – pulls the non-poetic into its dynamic formal force-field.[35]

Robert looks back to Adorno who suggests how form mediates its critical function, 'by operating on the world through itself, by turning onto, or back to, itself: 'Form converges with critique. It is that through which artworks prove *self-critical* (the emphasis is Robert's).[36] As Robert later confirms:

> Autonomy, announced with a clarion call by Marcuse, becomes the necessary condition of art as critique. Under monopoly capitalism, in Adorno's subtle thinking, artistic autonomy operates equivocally, as [Simon] Jarvis puts it: 'On the one hand, it heightens the illusion of art's independence; yet on the other, it is this illusory being-in-itself', the critical self-reflectiveness [examined earlier], 'which makes possible the thought of real freedom from naked coercion, total dependence'.[37]

Autonomy, as an historical and ontological state for the art object, nevertheless 'depends on a heteronomous moment for its very possibility'.[38] 'This is a relationship of critical re-cognition not of monadic (or monastic) negation. Autonomy, like a variety of freedom, is always autonomy from.'[39] Robert subsequently notes that:

> Rancière realises the subtlety of Adorno's use of the terms when he comments: 'The autonomy of [Arnold] Schönberg's music, as conceptualised by Adorno, is a double heteronomy: in order to denounce the capitalist division of labour and the adornments of commodification, it has to take that division of labour yet further, to be still more technical, more "inhuman" than the products of capitalist mass production. But this inhumanity,

---

[35] Sheppard, *The Meaning of Form*, pp. 151-52.

[36] Theodor Adorno, *Aesthetic Theory*, ed. by. Gretel Adorno and Ralph Tiedemann, trans. by R. Hullot-Kentor (London: Continuum, 2002), p. 144.

[37] Simon Jarvis, *Adorno: A Critical Introduction* (Cambridge: Polity Press, 1998), p. 117.

[38] Ibid., p. 123.

[39] Sheppard, *The Meaning of Form*, pp. 217-18.

in turn, makes the stain of what has been repressed appear and disappear and disrupt the work's perfect technical arrangement'.[40] 'This is a complex example of the self-interrogation of art works and demonstrates how form has a vital function to play in these manoeuvres or out-manoeuvres.[41]

To repeat Robert, using Schiller's assertion in *On the Aesthetic Education of Man* (1795), 'Man [...] is only wholly Man when he is playing and he shall play only with Beauty'.[42] Robert writes: 'The shaping of beauty can only be facilitated by the "play impulse" but the "object of the form impulse" is "shape [...] a concept which includes all formal qualities of things and all their relations to the intellectual faculties".'[43]

Hello Robert Sheppard, we know who you are.

Appendix 1.

'Does not everything take place as if the disclosure of self to self came to be added to the identity of the object, an identity originating in the idealising identification that thematising thought bestows kerygmatically on adumbrations?[44] What is the relation between the "oneself" and the *for self* of representation? Is the "oneself" a recurrence of the same type as consciousness, knowledge, and representation, all of which would be sublimated in consciousness conceived as Mind? Is the "oneself'" consciousness in its turn, or is it not a quite distinct event, one which would justify the use of separate terms: Self, I, Ego, soul?

---

[40] Jacques Rancière, *Dissensus: On Politics and Aesthetics*, ed. and trans. by Steven Corcoran (London: Continuum, 2010), p. 129.

[41] Sheppard, *The Meaning of Form*, pp. 236-37 n. 2.

[42] Friedrich Schiller, *On the Aesthetic Education of Man*, trans. by Reginald Snell (Mineola, NY: Dover Publications, 2004), p. 80.

[43] Sheppard, *The Meaning of Form*, p. 219, quoting Schiller, *On the Aesthetic Education of Man*, p. 76.

[44] Emmanuel Levinas, *En découvrant l'existence avec Husserl et Heidegger*, 2nd ed. (Paris: Vrin, 1967), pp. 217-33. ['Language and Proximity,' Levinas. *Collected Philosophical Papers*, trans. by A. Lingis (The Hague: Martinus Nijhoff, 1987), pp. 109-15].

Philosophers have for the most part described the identity of the oneself in terms of the return to self of consciousness. For Sartre, like Hegel, the *oneself* is posited as a *for itself*.[45] The identity of the I would thus be reducible to a turning back of *essence* upon itself, a return to itself of essence as both subject and condition of the identification of the Same. The sovereignty of the "oneself," positing itself as one being among others, or as a central being, would only be abstraction referring back to the concrete process of Truth where this return is accomplished; referring back, consequently, to the exposition of being – lost and rediscovered – to the expatiation and stretching out of time, referring back to the logos. This approach must be placed in question.'[46]

'The oneself which lives (we are almost tempted to say, without metaphor, which palpitates) alongside the movements of consciousness or intentionality, which are said to constitute it, does not bear its identity as do identical beings, themes, or parts of discourse, where they show themselves and where it is necessary that they remain identical; that is to say, they say themselves without being unsaid. The identity of ipseity is to be distinguished from the identity which allows a being to enter into discourse, to be thematised, and to appear to consciousness.

To be sure, reflection upon the self is possible, but this reflection does not *constitute* the living *recurrence* of subjectivity, a recurrence without duality, but a unity without rest, whose un-rest is due neither to dispersion of exterior givens nor to the flux of time biting into the future while conserving a past. The living identity of oneself is not distinguished from the self and does not lend itself to either a synthetic activity or recollection or anticipation [...].'[47]

---

[45] Jean Paul Sartre, *L'être et le néant*, pp. 37-84; *Being and Nothingness*, trans. by Hazel E. Barnes (London: Routledge Classics, 2003), pp. 119-58. Georg Wilhelm Friedrich Hegel, *Wissenschaft der Logik*, Gesammelte Werke 21 (Hamburg: Felix Meiner, 1985), pp. 144-51; *Science of Logic*, trans. by A. V. Miller (London: George Allen & Unwin, 1969), pp. 157-64.

[46] Emmanuel Levinas, *Basic Philosophical Writings*, ed. by Adriaan T. Peperzak, Simon Critchley, and Robert Bernasconi (Bloomington and Indianapolis, IN: Indiana University Press, 1996), pp. 83-84.

[47] Levinas, *Basic Philosophical Writings*, p. 84.

The Robert Sheppard Roundtable

This 'Roundtable' occurred between 4th April and 1st August 2018. Three questions were sent to the following participants by email: Gilbert Adair, Adrian Clarke, Alan Halsey, Chris McCabe, Geraldine Monk and Sandeep Parmar.

What was your first point of contact with Robert Sheppard's poetry, poetics and/or criticism?

Gilbert Adair: Looking over various of Robert's writings lately, lines from 'Internal Exile 3'—'Fulfil desire; / *KILL IT*'—evoked a striking audio-visual memory of the relish with which he leant into belting out this paradox (I heard it more than once in the late 80s). I'd first heard him reading at King's [College London] 6 or 7 years earlier. It was interesting—I may have an entirely false memory of it involving at one point some speaker in a cellar; and I can't remember if we spoke afterwards. We didn't become friends until he moved down to London and started attending & soon reading at SubVoicive. There was always a pleasingly daft quality to him (from what else could issue a crack like 'Pretentious?—*moi?*'), even as he kept his eyes—and his ears—open, and his intelligence sharp (from what else lines like 'We are statues of ourselves, stiffened eulogies / in the arthritic history of imperial endeavour' ['Empty Diary 1954']?).

That meant I was reading early versions of the poems that years later would accumulate into *Complete Twentieth Century Blues* (2008): 'Letter from the Blackstock Road', then the turn to history with 'Mesopotamia' and 'Schräge Musik', fully if obliquely embraced in the mostly short, always surprising concentrates of the 'Empty Diaries' sequence. The whole thing presents the kind of verbal palpability that I love in long poems such as *The Faerie Queene, Paradise Lost,* and *Jerusalem,* born of diction (often recalcitrant and/or intricate phrasings), sonic push-pull, vivid references to physical matters, and (a 20th-century contribution) a variety of formal approaches that as we read, thickly scaffold each other. And a coda on those 'vivid references to physical matters', deployed with a novelist's eye for detail if not within novelistic framings: 'Empty Diary 1927' and '1951' sculpt precise renderings of the invisible membranes wrapping what the former poem calls '[t]hese tyrannical objects', commodity fetishes in all their ideologised glory,

that it's grimly bracing to get a localised handle on at work in post-
WW2 social relations:

> You trip up slippery
> steps to appointment you shake his confident
> fist: smile at his unscheduled rubber horns (*CTCB* 124).

Adrian Clarke: I first encountered Robert at Gilbert Adair's Sub-
Voicive reading series in 1983 and subsequently at events Bob Cobbing
organised at the London Musicians' Collective. I was struck by his
energy and sometimes irreverent humour, but, struggling at that
time to sound like a pre-War Western European poet in translation,
the first examples of his work I encountered, which evidenced some
contemporary English sources, did not prepare me for what was to
come. That began with 'Letter from the Blackstock Road', from which,
prior to its publication by Oasis in 1988, I heard Robert read with
immediate excitement at the speed of its disorienting of the familiar
in abruptly spliced discursive fragments, their brief sentences' syntax
struggling to keep up. I faintly recognise something of the impression
that work left in the second section of my 'Spectral Investments'
(Writers Forum, 1991).

   In this period – in which we co-edited *Floating Capital: new
poets from London* (Potes & Poets Press, 1991) – we were both regular
attenders at Bob's Writers Forum Workshop where Robert suffered
continued exposure to my sequences of 'neo-Formalist' four-words-per-
liners, which may eventually have provoked him to go a word shorter
in 'Seven' (1992) and, most notably, *Free Fists*, originally published by
Writers Forum with appropriately striking facing page illustrations by
Patricia Farrell in 1995. These, in turn, led me to strip down to two
words a line and something approaching Robert's violent enjambments
in 'Millennial Shades' (Writers Forum, 1998) in an attempt to respond
to the 1997 election campaign and its aftermath.

Alan Halsey: An exchange of letters in the late 1970s. I forget how
this came about; perhaps he'd responded to one of my booklists and it
took off from there. The exchanges became quite dense and detailed,
revolving around the then-emergent 'language poetry' and also in
response to Veronica Forrest-Thomson's *Poetic Artifice*. This was the
first correspondence I'd had with a poet who seemed to have reached a

similar crux in his work as I felt in mine. As I remember we disagreed about many things but this made the exchanges more fluid – I think we both changed sides more than once. It must have led to Robert's featuring in the first issue of *Rock Drill* poems from my *Sections Drawn across the Vortex* which in some part derived from our correspondence: an attempt to shift focus on the high modernist poetry I'd been taking as given.

Chris McCabe: Reading *Complete Twentieth Century Blues* when it was released in its entirety by Salt. I was massively impressed by the scope, scale, and ambitions of this epic project – epic as defined by Pound, as a long poem containing history.

Geraldine Monk: 'I don't remember…' begins the riff in the first section of Robert Sheppard's *The Given* (The Knives Forks and Spoons Press, 2010) and I don't remember when I first encountered the writings of Robert Sheppard but in his bibliographical entry on his *Pages* blogzine he has a list of magazines in which his work has appeared down the decades. He begins with these four, *Platform, Doris, Alembic, Palantir*, and then goes on to mention about a hundred more. This incantation of mainly small press magazines, together with a few establishment publications thrown in the mix, is not only familiar to me but it echoes my own decades of poetry navigations as my writings have also appeared in the majority of the magazines he mentions.

Between them these magazines will have published contributions from thousands of poets but many of those aspiring poets will have fallen by the wayside years ago and dwindled into dimly remembered names if indeed they are remembered at all. The *don't remember poets*. Others are what I call *the incurable poets* as I often use this term to describe my own condition. We are the poets who roamed and still roam the small mag scene like spectral wolves. We inhabit their spaces and then move on to inhabit other spaces or, if the publication was enduring (many of them weren't enduring and would only last for a few issues before folding), we'd return to the same space and enjoy the familiarity of an old haunt.

All poetry magazines have their own unique approach to editorial selection and presentation and many names that appeared in these publications, *the incurable poets* would develop into a core of poets whose names would become commonplace and eventually they become a kind of poetic family. It would be through this channel of small magazines that I would initially meet most of the poets who would later become my colleagues and in many cases my real friends. Robert Sheppard was one such name who I first encountered in the pages of small press magazines and who would eventually become one of my treasured poetry colleagues and dear friends.

Sandeep Parmar: I first found Robert's book *The Poetry of Saying* when I was desperately trying to make sense of the British innovative poetry scene. That was probably about ten years ago and I've read it profitably since. Robert's critical work has hugely informed my thinking about both recent literary history (mostly 1960s onwards) and poetics. It's an antidote to the Movement and post-Movement doldrums. And I found clarity there, ways of shaping a sense of connectedness between poets where there were gaps obscured by the mainstream—all of this was invaluable as I was writing my essay 'Not a British Subject'. I later discovered his poetry, first in *Complete Twentieth Century Blues* and later, online, *The Anti-Orpheus: A Notebook*.

Are there any specific works of his that make you want to write, or have changed your thinking or practice about poetry, poetics?

GA: His editorial in the January 1988 edition of *Pages*, which noted that 'the loss of an effective power base' (for publishing, work-sharing, readings, on-the-spot creation and collaboration, camaraderie, and promotion of an international cast of practitioners) following the 1977 ouster of members of the British Poetry Revival from the Poetry Society, found younger poets emerging in London obliged to work 'in [social] fragmentation and incoherence'. Additionally, he found among these poets an aesthetic moving away from the open field poetics prominent in the Revival toward a questioning of 'the dominant reality principle' via techniques of linguistic indeterminacy and discontinuity. The need was urgent, then, for these younger poets, Robert included, to better recognise their aesthetic kinship and to document and debate their working poetics.

My response to this editorial, published with others in the March *Pages*, began: 'Linguistically innovative poetry (for which we haven't yet a satisfactory name)…' I sounded a caution against validating parataxis

in and of itself—'[a]dvertisements are ample in discontinuities'—
and added a corollary cited approvingly by Robert in *The Poetry of
Saying* (2005): 'Cutting across formations categorised as discrete,
"discontinuity" *is* so only if it makes *other* relations; or else it is mimesis
of actual informational chaos' (p. 194).

'Linguistically innovative poetry', then, that Maggie O'Sullivan
would harvest for her 1996 anthology *out of everywhere: linguistically
innovative poetry by women in North America & the UK*, began as no
more than a stop-gap reference to, shorthand (if it weren't so infernally
clunky) for something still lacking 'a satisfactory name'. But Robert's
editorial was the direct cause of my articulating a summary of thoughts
and impressions I'd been mulling over for some years, which in turn
yielded a term that could be taken up or dropped as communal needs
were felt.[1] Chapter 6 in *The Poetry of Saying*, 'Linguistically Innovative
Poetry 1975–2000', has a remit extending well beyond the London-
based poets of the original editorial; and lacks a colon in its title.

AC: I am nervous of the term 'influence', with its origin in the Greek
phluein – to flow abundantly. Discounting the Bloomian anxiety with
its source in Freud, what is at issue – beyond adolescent possession by a
single poet, *pace* Eliot – seems, rather, to be a trickle, or, perhaps more
accurately, a nudge. There is evidence Robert has provided many of those
beyond the ones I described earlier, while his poetry is too generously
various to have drowned many adolescents. He has consistently resisted
the demand of commercial publishing to develop an identifiable
'voice', rather subjecting it to the kind of 'radical disorder' in and across
sequences that he finds in Tom Raworth's 'sonnets', and has, at the
same time, resourcefully met the challenge of doing otherwise, both
aesthetically and in terms of finding an audience.

AH: It's that correspondence which I mentioned earlier, rather than
specific works by Robert. He went on to publish his *Complete Twentieth
Century Blues*, I turned away from longer poems or overarching
projects. Perhaps it's coincidence that in later work we've both created

---

[1] 'It's probably correct that it was first used in *Pages*. I appropriated it – after it had been
bandied about quite a bit – for OOE [*out of everywhere*], or the blurb surrounding it.
There had been so many other terms – 'avant-garde', 'language-centred', etc., none of
which were satisfactory. I don't think 'linguistically innovative' totally worked either...'
[from Ken Edwards in a letter to Maggie O'Sullivan (16.7.2018)]

fictitious poet-personae and interested ourselves in the unremembered (I particularly enjoy his *Words Out of Time*) or perhaps there's a sub-conscious connection going back to those letters.

CM: As a writer of prose (like Sheppard) I was very excited by Sheppard's autrebiographies (*Words Out of Time*) which extend his invented auter personas into fictional prose. This chimed with my own fictional writing which also explores invented poetic terrains of the imagination, an approach which I've also drawn from Roberto Bolaño.

I've recently been reading Sheppard's *The Meaning of Form in Contemporary Innovative Poetry* and this has had a big impact on my thinking about the form of poetry as the meaning itself, an argument that I've enjoyed from the perspective of Veronica Forrest-Thompson. Re-reading some of the key poets behind my work, such as Barry MacSweeney, have been illuminated by Sheppard's challenging of the traditional idea of form being merely an extension of sense meaning.

SP: *The Anti-Orpheus* really focused my thinking around form and the lyric subject, of course developed also throughout *The Poetry of Saying*. My distrust of coherent and closed lyric strategies was shaped by Sheppard's writing in both these texts. For my own attempts at not lyric disengagement but lyricism in process, always contingent, I think *The Anti-Orpheus* is a guiding text. When Sheppard writes that 'Poetry interrupts history, musicates the 'facts', / makes the said of hegemonic (or non-hegemonic) history / the saying of poetry, / which will create anew; mutually interruptive / a new said of non-history' this is hugely liberating and, inevitably, true for anyone climbing down from themselves, their histories learned or imposed upon them.

How do you think Sheppard's work has contributed to shaping an aesthetic for British poetry and poetics today?

AC: His activities have significantly furthered the alternative poetries in various ways, not least in demonstrating that theory with a strong political focus can shape a poetry fleshed with vividly realised detail, but no less notably through his contributions to poetics, and criticism informed by considered ethical concerns. To these achievements should be added his activities as organiser, educator, and provider of information and valuable links through his excellent *Pages* website. While some of its context has changed, taking full account of that he has done as much as anyone to fill the gap left by Cobbing and Eric Mottram.

AH: One example of many: the serial mimeo issues of *Pages* during the 80s and early 90s were one of the key periodicals giving a home to the more adventurous poetry which was being sidelined by slick and depressingly conformable product. Some long-established small presses were going out of business and the newer generation such as Salt and Shearsman belonged to an unforeseen future; a lot of good work might have been left in desk drawers or never written. A serial mimeo with an editor as dedicated as Robert ensured continuity and sustained a sense of community, as vital in its time as its American predecessors a decade before. In some respects ephemeral but with a materiality I miss in blogs and webzines.

CM: Through activation of ideas into action, demonstrating a dynamic praxis that gathers momentum from the history of the avant-garde and collaboration with his contemporaries. The diversity of Sheppard's aesthetic is fundamental here, a generative approach bringing in sound poetry (collaborations with Cobbing, etc) as well as a concern with 'fact', historiography, and documentary which has kinship with L=A=N=G=U=A=G=E poetry and the psychogeography of Iain Sinclair. Everything is up for grabs in Sheppard's work, each sequence or poem is an experiment towards what might be possible in (and through) the form.

GM: Although I think of him as first and foremost a poet he is much more and his output across a broad spectrum is prodigious. I am amazed at where he finds the time and energy. Apart from his former academic work as Programme Leader of the M.A. course at Edge Hill University he is a shrewd critic, not just on the writings of poets and poetics but on a wide range of artistic disciplines, and is just at home writing about music and the visual arts especially of the more innovative or non-mainstream varieties. His reference points in his poetry and criticism shows the mind of a true polymath and he certainly introduced me to the extraordinary work of Berlin artist Charlotte Salomon in his *Hymns to the God in which my Typewriter Believes*. For that alone I am indebted to him.

Being part of a group sometimes known as 'linguistically innovative poetry', his poetry skews language to take on big themes and his writing can be seen as a comprehensive poetic chronicling of our times on an epic scale culminating in his *Complete Twentieth Century Blues*. Sheppard's writing is rough, rude, quirky, serious, learned, and never afraid to be humorous. In short it is as irreverent as it is relevant. Finally, his generosity in writing about and promoting the work of others has been unstinting and invaluable, especially in a country which largely chooses to ignore its innovative poets. For the record, Robert Sheppard has put it all on the record.

SP: Sheppard wears many hats, all suit him: teacher, editor, translator, publisher, critic and of course poet. To be the sort of thinker who can mediate all these things with discipline and generosity is really rather remarkable. His work as a critic, his integration of the material history of British poetry from the 1960s onwards with the underlying aesthetic questions drawn from poetics and philosophy, is what I value perhaps most of all these. Here I think Sheppard finds the most dialogic of his roles—in reading beyond the artifice of poetry that appears to develop a mimetic social relation. Here he has become a crucial steer for where we may find ourselves, and how we come to think about the nature of language.

The Wolf Interview: Robert Sheppard

CHRISTOPHER MADDEN: In the Proem to your recent collection of 'unwritings' in *The Given*, mention of electrical interference in valve radios from passing cars is framed as 'This heartless / Irritation this re- / Iteration of the pure prosaic'. Thinking about the quotidian in the context of poetry, one of the conventional aspects of which seeks to transmogrify what is perceived and experienced, how do you view the relationship, if at all, between 'unwriting' and the idea of *undoing*?

ROBERT SHEPPARD: The prosaic is 'pure' here, remember (possibly because ennobled by the passage of time), and yet the writing is 'lyric'. 'Unwriting' I use in a rather technical sense (and have since I first adopted the term in 1985 or whenever) of involving the taking of a piece of my own earlier writing and treating it, either systematically or intuitively, to see what it might have to say (to me, to others) in an altered state. It is undoing, certainly, but it's also making something new, transforming it as well. But that's not to deny the quotidian. I like quiddity. I like that electrical interference and isolate it in that piece, but what I don't do is float it into an anecdote (this is my grandfather's wireless too close to the traffic of Old Shoreham Road in Portslade). I suppose I hope I'm one of Christopher Middleton's 'artificer poets' in that respect, whom he contrasts to the purveyors of anecdotage, as I isolate the tokens of 'the pure prosaic'.

CM: Unwriting enacts some sort of defamiliarisation of the self. In *The Poetry of Saying: British Poetry and Its Discontents, 1950-2000*, you make the distinction between a poetry '*embedded in* its artifice' and one 'that has as its chief dimension *mimesis of* a recognisable social world'. Given Modernism's reformulation of mimesis, which certainly neither jettisoned artifice nor alienated itself from representing the external world, I am wondering whether contemporary poetics can ultimately deny the force of mimesis. It remains problematic, but it remains (with us) nevertheless. Whither the relation, then, between that which is familiar and that thing being defamiliarised?

RS: We could never encounter the completely other (so says Derek Attridge): defamiliarisation must involve some necessary recognition of the object treated, estranged, distanced, transformed. It's not about the insertion of noise into communicative transparency. I think the contemporary interest in the everyday (seen in lots of writers from cris cheek to the conceptualiasts, via the situationists of course) is probably a practical answer to that question. 'Mimesis' is not the central problem of the poetry of the said; it's an issue about the kind of mimesis, I suspect, where it becomes its 'chief dimension', its raison d'être. In the social perspectives of the Movement Orthodoxy, mimesis seemed tied up with self-expression as though the self was a thing to be represented rather than used as a transformative principle.

CM: In *Warrant Error* the sonnet seems to be deployed as a transformative principle. Your subject here is not so much the self as the propaganda around and mediascape of the war on terror, which is reworked (or remade) under the microscope of the form. I liked the epigraph from Bill Griffiths: 'What better disguise for evil than sonnets?' I suspect this might have something to do with rhetoric...

RS: I have a pun on 'sonnetize' and 'sanitize' somewhere in that book, though I don't think sonnets necessarily *disguise* evil! There are puns throughout from title to the hundredth poem but it's most pronounced in sections where I'm trying to shove the language of the War on Terror up itself, or transform it, I suppose. So 'terror' begat 'error'. I had pages of terms I could play around with in that way. I'd done something similar in 'Killing Boxes' during the First Gulf War, and it's obviously a reaction to 'rhetoric' in its debased sense.

I am also trying to take the frame of the sonnet and allow other structures (not least my line counting in verselets of 2/3/4/5 lines) to inhabit it, or re-form it, to create a new space for thinking and feeling. Most surprising to me are the more traditional poems (love poems, for example) that break out at various points, as though both the unrelenting dogma of neo-con and fundamentalist alike forced me to consider the 'human convenant' and 'human unfinish' quite directly, even personally, at the level of content. On the other hand the transformations of the sonnet embody a formal kind of unfinish. This expands, in one way, into the 'Six Poems Against Death' in *Berlin Bursts* and, in another, towards the prose works of an unpublished manuscript called (unsurprisingly!) 'Unfinish'; it's prose poetry, poets' prose, poetics, even narrative, all in one. This is a long way from rhetoric; 'unfinish' has turned into an ethical-formal amalgam – and the sonnet is at the heart of it in *Warrant Error*, with its rich history, but also with its sheer visible qualities. You can have all kinds of 'visual' sonnets based on its line-conventions (Jeff Hilson's *Reality Street Book of Sonnets* demonstrates the love-hate potentialities of its framing) and they seem to evoke that history and repudiate it at once. Having your cake and eating it comes to mind, I think! Maybe finishing your cake and unfinishing it might be a better analogy.

CM: Indeed, the history of the sonnet is rich in formal innovation, yet the sonnet's status as an object is unquestionable. While its conventions vary, the process of manipulating the reader's mind through rhetoric remains intact. Referring to Tom Raworth's 'Eternal Sections', however, you claim that 'if they are "sonnets", [...] then they exhibit a volta – a turn – in nearly every line, and the power of this ensures that estranging disorder is put back into montage'. The images in *Warrant Error* have an accelerated perspicacity that corresponds to the turning movement of the volta. This unsettles the sonnet-as-object, reformulating it as what you have called an 'event'.

RS: I'm worried a bit by the way you're jumping from my critical work to my poetry here. I know there is a relationship but I wonder if I am the best person to address the transfer of concepts from one to the other. One reason for the conjectural discourse of poetics is to allow writers to dialogue with their practice and while it might pick up the odd literary critical term along the way, particularly if the poet juggling his poetics is a poet-critic, those terms might function in different ways in poetics, as speculative instruments not as analytic concepts. 'Putting disorder back into montage' is a phrase of Rancière's and I'm a great magpie of useful terms for poetics – and that one is useful for suggesting that disruptive techniques may have been not nearly as disruptive as they should have been.

CM: Perhaps we should talk about another kind of transfer, then, which is not unrelated to the one you mention: namely from page to performance and vice versa. I remember hearing you read from *Berlin Bursts* in Liverpool and was struck by the velocity of your performance style; afterwards I discovered this is conveyed on the page too. As a reader/listener I am 'thrown', as it were, into poetics: I am simultaneously the text's receiver and co-implicated in its production. Velocity somehow calls to mind Olson's talk of breath and field composition in his essay 'Projective Verse'. To what extent does the breath feature in your work, and do you view it as another disruptive technique, perhaps?

RS: Olson has always seemed too literal to me, and like most prosody, his looks less clear the more you look at it. But I do think this is a prosodic issue, but more a question of poetics than theory, speculative in other words, and I'm speaking for myself alone. I was much taken by the 'Swift Nudes' paintings by Duchamp in the mid-80s, and they seemed apposite analogies to this vectoral poetics. Flashes of thing across the image. I'm glad you see it as related to the page. I suppose crudely one might identify unpunctuated (asyntactical or not) shorter lines as requiring or suggesting a pretty sharp pulse, whereas punctuated (whether syntactical or not) longer lines require or suggest (perhaps even demand) a slower pulse, nearer to that of speech. It's now a matter of feel for me. I don't theorise it. I also take the performance of a poem pretty seriously. It is after all an act of forming the poem itself for the audience (and me); it's not strictly secondary. And it must form itself in the right way, with the page suggesting the form of that re-forming in performance.

However, although I'm speaking for myself, there are clear precedents. The father of the shoot from the hip school of reading is, of course, Tom Raworth (who I suspect developed his sense of speed from Olson) and I've always thought that what he was trying to do was put into action something he talks about in poems of the 1960s a lot, that of evading the intellect and knowing in favour of intuition and being. I've always wondered whether he's trying to bypass the intellect and get the poem straight in somehow. The poem is thereby doing something rather than saying anything. I'm not signing up to that as my method, but certainly a performance might convince before full understanding is possible. (That has to be true with complex language in some ways.) Disruption is not the term for this; rupture might be. Interruption even, given that 'interruption is one of the fundamental devices of all structuring', as Walter Benjamin has it. In Raworth the volta in every line is also a pulse, so interruption is a prosodic feature as well as a disruptive one; it is structuring the poem. It's on the page: it's in the performance.

There is a communal aspect to this too. Among some London poets there seems to be a vectoral imperative: Ulli Freer, Adrian Clarke, Jeff

Hilson all read fast; Miles Champion used to read too fast to actually hear any of the words! Scott Thurston has early poems that work best fast, though he's now a more meditative writer and the performance forms have followed that.

CM: Pausing is related to disruption insofar as what feels like an effect of pulse and pacing in effect installs a structural gap. I'm not sure what fills this gap, and perhaps that cannot – nor shouldn't – be anticipated as it is likely to be different every time. My own instinct as a reader towards the paragraph blocks of *The Flashlight Sonata*, for instance, is precisely to pause, and the resulting momentary silence exerts something on my reading. This is complicated by the heterogeneous form of the sequence, in which blocks of text (some small, tempting intervallic silence; some breathlessly edifice-like running for pages) feature alongside sharp lines and what could be called, to adapt your phrasing, shot-from-the-hip enjambment. Your reference to Benjamin put me in mind of constellations. Would 'constellation' describe your approach to, perhaps even feel for, structure? And where might the pause feature in all of this?

RS: Variable caesurae. Variable intervallic pulses (non-pulses, silences). All those terms evoke the restless different-every-time rhythm of the poetry (and prose to a certain extent) I hope. 'Constellations' suggests to me Adorno's block prose arrangement of argument by juxtaposition which I don't think I've adopted, as well as the spatial practices of Mallarmé and the later concrete poetry of Eugen Gomringer.

However, my latest book *A Translated Man*, being the double oeuvre of the fictional Belgian poet René Van Valckenborch, was partly constructed by bifurcating my practice (a little as I described it above) and inventing some new (alien) metrical tricks. His Walloon poems are all in 'roll and tumbling tercets', the enjambments a development of the abrupt line breaks of *Berlin Bursts* in fact, a 'vectoral poetics' as the fictional translator comments, speaking to René himself: 'Your cognitive prosody: the pleasure of speed against *la petite mort* of each line break.' That is a way of stressing (pun intended) the complex multi-systemic nature of lineation and sense in that (unpunctuated) flow. That technique may be cognitive is something I've been struggling with; it's not just creative writing 'craft'. On the other, Flemish, side he writes with a much more constelled artifice. His interest in space is not just geographical and geometrical but is metrical and page-spatial, in that the poems feature, again quoting the fictional translator's diary: 'your principle of interruption, your spatial poetics'. I found those poems more difficult to finish, which was partly the idea, of course. To extend my range (to adopt a suitably spatial metaphor).

CM: Spatial poetics, unpunctuated flow: it's little wonder you were drawn to Van Valckenborch. Veronica Forrest-Thomson's analysis of the semi-colon in 'In a Station of the Metro' questions why it exists at all, why Pound couldn't have used a dash or even a comma. Modern poetics privileges unpunctuated flow for spatial reasons: all components of prosody are then tracked by the eye, fall under the scopic regime of the visual. Punctuation is an inconvenience, it's like litter. In your work orthographic cues feel embedded in, or are implied by, lineation and spatial arrangement but also the propulsive energy of certain words. Would you agree?

RS: Not entirely. I agree there are all sorts of visual prosodies that have hardly been tracked and tackled critically, but I also think that there are plenty of opportunities for complex syntactic play with punctuation that can't quite work without it. You also discover and invent various mixed practices, as and when, or when the material suggests. I have prose paragraphs conventionally punctuated but for the last (missing) full stop (I stole that from Roy Fisher). Open parentheses in 'Empty Diaries' (that's from Olson.) Some of the unpunctuated poems have capital letters at the start of each line which is a non-syntactic punctuation device to slow down the pace of reading (not the velocity of performance, or not that only, but the speed of eye-reading). Richard Bradford's book *The Look of It* only scratches the surface.

CM: The page is a score; a system of notation for various settings and agents of the text. Your collection of writings spanning December 1989 and 2000, *Complete Twentieth Century Blues*, alludes to your abiding interest in live music performance and that most powerful of musical genres. Could you elaborate on the ways in which the blues feature in this collection and your work generally?

RS: As content. As mythology. *Blues, why do you kerb-crawl, you been following me all night?* As alternative career? As alter ego: Little Albert

Fly. 1990. My guitar-genius friend Tony Parsons' children still think that's my name. *Motherless Child Blues.* Go see his band The Blind Lemons.

And now, with the new guitar admonishing me every moment I don't pick it up, since Patricia bought it last year, silently replete with riffs borrowed from Rice Miller, McKinley Morganfield, Peter Green, Duster Bennett. Though now I'm more likely to pluck out a Tony Joe White, strum a Leonard Cohen, cry-thrash a P.J. Harvey or camp up a Kinks number, on my return to the world of aching fingerpads, breath-sentences, sustained notes. Strictly private. Strictly entertainment.

Joe Turneresque. Belting it out. *If your ma-an gets per-son-al.* The first time I sang un-amplified that Robert Johnson blues in a Brighton pub: I'll never forget the sudden drop in conversation, the silent listening. *Why don' you have your fun?* 1977. *Give Albert a harp – something to do with his hands when he's not singing.*

I've got the blues like George Herbert got God, like Ted Hughes got Crow, like Bill Griffiths got prison, like Malcolm Lowry got drink, like Iain Sinclair got fancy walking shoes, like Otis Spann got pianistics, like Tom Jenks got Twitter-sculpting, like David Miller got soul, like Rosmarie Waldrop got the splice of life…

As content.

As form? More difficult to say. Though now, I see the versioning, the sampling, the 'strands' of the preposterous indexing of *Twentieth Century Blues* as analogous to the constant re-functioning and re-forming of songs and parts of song caught in the blues tradition: the borrowed lines, the stolen riffs, the ripped-off cadences, the quotes, the appropriation. It's more assimilative than Conceptual Writing. Ventriloquial eternity. Lemon Jefferson *inexpressive as the wine-dark riverside.*

CM: You're quoting from 'Freeze It', a poem in the same strand as 'Smokestack Lightning: A Mythology of the Blues', in which a number of muses from the blues tradition are 'repurposed' or reanimated, brush up against each other in a kaleidoscopic portrait. Yet as the title indicates, you're problematising history here, which likely accounts for the paradox at the heart of *Complete Twentieth Century Blues* and its rhizomatic structure. Given the collection's fin-de-siècle suggestiveness, was it ever your overarching intention to argue for alternative models of history?

RS: Yes and no. Perhaps 'argues for' makes it seem more like historiography, as does the word 'models'. It was historical in that it was a 'time-based' piece of work, expiring at the millennium, but also with a strand like 'Empty Diaries' stretching from 1901 to 2000, it was weaving petite histoires through the meganarratives of Twentieth Century History. Its deliberately complicated 'strands' of multiple titles are meant to contribute to that, rhizomatic as you say, to describe how we might read through it, but possibly also a 'constellation' of meaning-forms to come back to an earlier metaphor. 'The Lores' is the core of the poem, consisting of numerically-ordered and hugely impacted poems traversing history, Thatcherism, philosophical ideas, plus the texture of the contemporary streets. With a lot of loose ends because it was everything written in those years. I feel quite distant from it now, but pleased and alarmed still by its monstrosity. It's grim stuff, the blackest impaction of societal depression, with flashes on utopian parkways desperately trying to compensate. I remember first reading Nate Dorward's review of *Tin Pan Arcadia* and he quotes that line from *1984* about a foot stamping on a face forever, and says that's the effect of reading the book. I put *The Gig* down and switched on the radio. It was July 7th 2005. Bombs had gone off all over London, it seemed, at the time. I made notes. I wrote 'Byron James Is Okay', the last poem in *Warrant Error* with that criticism ringing in my ears and thinking, yes, this is the world, but also grasping for more positive human values (not that they are *not* there in *Twentieth Century Blues*, I hope. At least the blues ring out true.)

CM: The irony is that history might have made an elegy of the last poem of *Warrant Error*. Thankfully it was otherwise. Tellingly, *Berlin Bursts* followed with a focus on art from other disciplines (relating in some ways to the 'text and commentary' approach to be found in *Hymns to the God in which my Typewriter Believes*). You comment that 'Six Poems Against Death', at the heart of *Berlin Bursts*, gesture back to the six sonnets towards the end of *Warrant Error* entitled 'Out of Nowhere'. What role does your interest in the history of art have in relation to such resistance to elegy or rather turn to more positive human values?

RS: A lot of my things allude, use, praise, and re-function art works of various kinds throughout my work, and I'm not sure how I relate them to human values. I'm slightly nervous to articulate a 'philosophy' outside of art works themselves. I did risk it in the second of those six poems. It's almost completely quotations (Doreen Massey through to Philip Roth) and I affirm 'reasons for living happily out of nowhere and now and then on to multitopia bearing the stories so far whose passions read as co-eval becomings geographies of affect in capital Isness where human unfinish is all about…'. I quote it deliberately as prose to show how it doesn't (quite) work as discursive prose and of course it unfinishes in 14 lines. Writers with philosophies (rather than poetics) tend to be rather tedious and I try to keep the philosophy as prompts for poetic action. I have a series of quotations on the wall here ('Eight Theses' that are part of *Unfinish*). One is a quote from Badiou: 'His judgement was always anchored in poetry, or in the very subtle thinking that surrounds it.' (He was describing Mandelstam.) That's a kind of axiomatic meta-prompt for me. So perhaps that may explain the turn to art works, that they might speak more eloquently, because silently, of those values. Or am I just making that up and really have no idea why I am drawn to one thing rather than another? I can dress it up as 'multiform unfinish'.

The relation of resistance to elegy to human values seems a clearer question this afternoon, because this morning I spent time revising a pair of elegiac poems for my father, one short, one long. The short one (unpunctuated but with retarding capitals at the start of each line) ends: 'Elegy lost in action on the outskirts of an event', which is less negative than it first seems; the second is subtitled (for the moment, but perhaps permanently) 'A Kind of Elegy', in which I have these lines (punctuated with sharp enjambments for thrust and interruption):

> The task
> of the poet is elective translation,
> to transmute the nothing that is said
> into the nothing that could
> talk itself into the world: the
> shadow that casts its wings between the red
> pillars that hold the whole thing up.

I'm not sure that I would articulate that outside of the poem, where I'm not sure I know what it means with any assurance. Decontextualised from the previous eleven pages' refusal to mourn it is itself a kind of quotation.

CM: The word 'unfinish' has featured prominently in our discussion, and now there's 'multiform unfinish', a particularly resonant phrase in the context of *A Translated Man*, in which you edit the double oeuvre of René Van Valckenborch. How did you begin to organise the work of this enigmatic, elusive writer?

RS: In my inaugural lecture I told my audience, 'Writers do not often sit down and inscribe "Poetics" at the top of a sheet of paper and then enumerate an orderly blueprint for writing a particular named text.' But that's exactly what I did, in the way I described earlier, the bifurcatory poetics. Van Valckenborch didn't arrive as a fiction, like Tropp in my short story 'Tropp', with any particular traits, physical or mental. In fact, partly due to his bilingual near-impossibility, he is an enigma, as you say, to those who 'edit' and 'translate' him, though those characters may have made him up. And he's an enigma to me. The translator Annemie Dupuis seems the most real to me because she has the luxury of her diary at the end of the book. Van Valckenborch is not an autobiographical poet, by the looks of it. I wanted him to be defined (if that's the right word) by his indistinctness; his ontological status is as unstable as that of fictional poems in any situation, say in a novel. One of the problems of persona poems, even Pessoa's, is that they *demonstrate* a poetic personality. I wanted the poems to be real ones, but in an imaginary collection. They 'developed' along two parallel trajectories until he 'disappears' as demonstrated by his ridiculous Magritte-inspired 'Cow' poems in Walloon, his Flemish experiment in creating his own fictional translations (one for each EU country, though there are only 5 in the book), and in the ever-wilder imaginings of Dupuis in her diary. I wrote the early poems (supposedly from the year 2000) and then developed his poetics (plural) towards the 2010 vanishing point. I seem to remember some of the diary entries were written *ahead* of the dates they carry, which left me a little uneasy. But the material came quickly. I wrote *only* Van Valckenborch poems for about a year.

CM: It seems Van Valckenborch wore a number of masks in his life: the sense of this is carried in a modernist-inspired sequence as part of the Walloon oeuvre (from *masks and other masks*, 2002). For me, he continues a distinct poetic inheritance: Poe-Baudelaire-Breton. The taut psychogeography of those 'Twitterodes' (from the Flemish oeuvre) surely make him the man of the (Web 2.0) crowd. Did this come to mind during your year-long traversal?

RS: He owes more to Ponge as a Walloon and to the OuLiPo as a Fleming (I didn't know anything about the Belgian Formales group of poets until after I'd finished). Clearly he is a psychogeographer in his Henri Lefebvre inspired sense of the production of space. I was deliberately feeding that in to the Twitter stream – and he's restlessly investigating page-space as well as actual space. Breton (of *Nadja*) may be there. But Breton's polar opposite Queneau is too. Baudelaire is probably always there, but I wanted to steer away from those influences. Your question is unusually complex in this case because there's what I've contrived to be Van Valckenborch's influences and what are the actual ones on me. And I might keep quiet about those, even if I'm certain (or even correct) about what they are. I wanted to have some fun with this fictional situation. And fun pushing myself into unusual writerly positions with the 'Twitterodes' and writing about film (he's the buff) and so on. I could allow myself to be influenced by him, too! After all, in one version of his European Union of Imaginary Authors the UK poet he invents is me!

CM: What would you ask Van Valckenborch if you had the chance?

RS: I'd be more worried what he'd ask me! That Sinclair suspicion that the creatures you make up will find you out. Or more precisely, that it would turn out like the plot of Peter Carey's *My Life as a Fake*, which is a cross between the Ern Malley affair and *Frankenstein*!

Signature & Ethics:
Robert Sheppard interviewed by Edmund Hardy[1]

EDMUND HARDY: To begin with a relationship between artifice and artifice in the writing of poetry, I'm interested in your poems apparently written from photographs, most noticeably in the *Empty Diaries*, though elsewhere too.

ROBERT SHEPPARD: Your question catches me at an interesting moment. The other day I went to Tate Liverpool to see the exhibition *Making History: Art and Documentary in Britain*. One of my ex-students works there as a guide. I asked her if she'd been doing any writing. She said she thought she might have had with all this art around her, but hadn't. I recommended the documentary photographs – Bill Brandt, Roger Mayne, originators of images I have used, Mass Observation – rather than the paintings in the exhibition, not because their realities are not filched and filtered, but because, if we use them judiciously and deceitfully, we can imagine that they are not artificial just long enough to achieve artifice ourselves.

For that reason, I tend not to work with whole photographs, but to look at them askance, to squint at them, as it were, to see if they are showing something they didn't mean to show, or start to narrate a history that seems to be unwilled, as in *Empty Diaries*. Or to see if some figural element will make me say what I didn't want to say. (Christopher Middleton: 'Poems have become experiences that did not exist before the poem.') Once used, they are discarded. As I say to students, as I take away the images they have been working from, much to their annoyance, 'It's turned into words now.' Often, I feel no need to identify the sources, because they are so unsystematically processed and unrecognisable. I'd hate readers to be able to say 'That poem describes a Humphrey Spender.' At the moment I am using notes I made from a small book of photographs gathered by the artist Hans-Peter Feldmann, *Voyeur*, so that I am making texts at two removes from his arrangement of found images.

---

[1] Interview edited from an email exchange between Edmund Hardy and Robert Sheppard which began on 17th April 2006 and continued for four weeks. [Eds: The interview was originally published on 'Intercapilliary Space', where it can still be accessed: <http://intercapillaryspace.blogspot.com/2006/06/signature-ethics.html>]

Curiously, I have very few poems set before the invention of photography. *Fucking Time*, using Rochester materials, does use visuals, but they are deeply implicated in the collaborative processes I've undertaken with Patricia Farrell. Perhaps the history of photography has dictated the temporal scope of my imagination, I don't know, but I hope not.

Patricia's books of early photos were always lying around the place; she'd be sketching from them. I've read my Roland Barthes, I haunt photo galleries, and I even take the odd photo (though only once for creative purposes, in preparing *Looking North*), but I am interested in a far too dilettante way. I am fascinated by the slightly out of focus quality you get in the earliest photographs, as though the world is emerging from an ectoplasmic fog, and this strange window that opens on what we assume was another world. My poem 'Shutters' was a response to the photographs of Lady Hawarden, her daughters draping the furniture in front of this foggy light beyond the open shutters. Theorising the erotics of the male gaze in this is beyond me.

I'm drawn to the richness of the materials: access to the Spanish Civil War in *The Lores*, or I'm playing more distant games, such as in the strand of poems through *Twentieth Century Blues* called 'Impositions', which (imaginatively) superimposes two images and responds to the results. (I once saw a group of paintings by Art and Language at the ICA that literally did this.) The freedom you suspect the techniques and materials grant me is that the 'thing' is non-verbal and so can be transformed into various linguistic patterns of response, either brutally close to the materials or at some considerable aesthetic distance. The nearest I get to the *ekphrastic* is my performance 'Sudley House' which is an (anti-)guide to one of Merseyside's most intimate, domestic art collections, but even there I mix imagery from contiguous paintings, although (since the text is performed to an audience in front of certain paintings, three Turners, a Bonington, a Corot, for example) I speak to them, almost literally. But that's a contextually determined exception, a site-specific piece.

More recently, and particularly in *Hymns to the God in which my Typewriter Believes* I am using verbal materials more. But your question suggests that I haven't finished with such images yet, and never will.

EH: This attraction to elements which 'will make me say what I didn't want to say' seems to recur in your work, now more playfully than before in the 'texts and commentaries' of *Hymns*?

RS: I took the bull by the horns, not only playfully, but wilfully, in *Hymns*, to immerse myself in materials that seemed alien to the Robert Sheppard whose name may not be unpeeled from the surface of my other books. The book is very European in scope; I attempt 'translations' from languages I don't know. The artists saluted are often female, or from traditions alien to my own (such as Anne Sexton), and I was working consciously against the use of images, though playing with page-space in ways I hadn't hitherto. I like the feeling of dislocation that I get when I look at the poems, the feeling that I didn't write them.

As soon as I declare a conscious proscription I am unconsciously working to unravel it (which can be a risky enterprise for a poet-critic). This morning, before approaching your question, I drafted a poem beginning with full rhyme and continuing a two-beat accentual dropped line:

> *Dawnlight streaks*
> > *the ice-capped peaks*
> Guitars sleep
> > on their backs and snore

Someone in the control tower is signalling me not to do that. This poem is formally similar to the 'text and commentary' on the Sephardic song you mention, although in that poem you can see how the Sheppardic variations unfold, in an almost Oulipean way, as riffs on the speculative metaphors of the 'original': '*If* the sea was made of milk…' The poem was one possible *THEN*…

The 'text and commentary' on Schlink's novel *The Reader* is structurally modelled on that book (one paragraph per chapter), which is not a technique I employ throughout, but it works here; isn't that what jazz musicians call a contrafact? I'm exploring my reading response ('It made me shake!') as well as responding to the unlikely choice of material, in the very responses as I make them, building another text, with its network of associations and metaphor as I do, that takes the reader (I hope) a long way from my originary shaking. In that case it is lifting itself beyond unease, but it's also exploring the fresh unease I felt increasingly during the writing process (hence my quotations from Celan and Perec in each part as counter words, especially the latter's 'The literature of the concentration camp does not get attacked'), not least of all when I was faced with the narrator's own unconsidered attack on 'experimental writing', which implicates my practices (and Schlink's) in an ethics beyond the ethics of literacy which is the novel's subject.

Simpler answers to your question would suggest the necessity of my finding new avenues after *Twentieth Century Blues*, to keep going; and another has to do with age, of not feeling I *have* to make particular aesthetic moves because I'm following the party line. Such a formulation is contrary to the function of poetics, as I now conceive it.

EH: When you mention, 'The artists saluted are often female', as a new departure in *Hymns*, are you particularly aware of responding more to male artists in the past?

RS: Yes. Although at the same time significant artistic collaborators have been women. In writing *Hymns* it wasn't programmatic: it just happened in looking for different materials. There's also Jiří Kolář or Hugo Dachinger.

EH: I want to ask a few questions about *The Poetry of Saying*, your recent critical book subtitled 'British Poetry and its Discontents, 1950-2000'. Though utilising Bakhtin and to a certain extent Vološinov, you choose a different site in developing, from the concepts of Levinas, a poetics which will always come back to an ethical interpretation.

RS: I appropriated my central concepts, the opposition between the saying and the said, a sense of face-to-face encounter with otherness, substitution, responsibility, and others I have forgotten, largely after becoming very excited by the implications of Levinas's suggestive remark in an interview: 'Man can give himself in saying to the point of poetry - or he can withdraw into the non-saying of lies. Language as *saying* is an ethical openness to the other; as that which is *said* – reduced to a fixed identity or synchronised presence – it is an ontological closure of the other.' That set me off onto the development of an ethical – but I don't think metaphysical – level for my theory, to match the technical and the socio-linguistic levels. I was immensely helped by Robert Eaglestone's *Ethical Criticism, Reading After Levinas* (Edinburgh: Edinburgh University Press, 1997), although I think that it was also from that source that I derived the less than accurate notion that Levinas himself divorced his theological writings from his philosophy. Levinas's own response to the massacres in the Sabra and Shatila camps suggests he was not able to particularise what he finds so easy to universalise. He seems to be selective about Otherness in a way that denies the commonalities of biological humanity. What saves his philosophy (even from himself) is that it is concerned to show the grounds of ethicality in relationship, not in the diktats of moralism. It is very suggestive for the development of a poetics.

EH: In the Raworth chapter you write of Raworth's 'apprehension of velocity', perhaps the speed of intuition which is the speed of practise (and performance), or going so fast that, in 'Catacoustics', 'artifice swallows itself'. Speed instead of 'connectives'. Can you say more about a social comprehension of this high speed form, in Raworth and in your own practise, your speeded-up collage where the connectives have 'melted'?

RS: Velopoetics! Part of my apprehension (rather than comprehension) of speed has to do with intense experiences of *listening* to performances of poetry during the late 1980s. A tape of Raworth reading *Eternal Sections*. The experience of hearing Maggie O'Sullivan live at Sub Voicive. Both of these – the tape played over and over, the reading experienced only once – induced experiences that approach what I later equated with the openness of 'saying'. Language particles seemed to detach themselves not just from reference, but from syntax, a deterritorialised experience of language that re-territorialised as a *ritornello*, in Guattari's formulation, an existential refrain that sustains the self and yet melts it into forces of intersubjectivation. That's how he would put it anyway. In Raworth's case this was to do with speed of delivery (in O'Sullivan's case to do with neologism and rhythm). I don't remember whether the fact I was trying to write in similar forms made me more receptive to this, but I was also aware of making effects through a speedy delivery, of writing in ways that create fleet performances, like Duchamp's 'swift nudes' that fizz and whistle across his surfaces. A celerity of mind, part immediacy, and sustained by references to its own processes. I thought – as I do not now – that what a poem does is more important than what it says. Looking back, it seems less tied to the practice of the language poets than it appeared at the time – I'm talking about the 1980s, works like 'Daylight Robbery' and 'Swift Nudes'.

What I notice now – having checked out the CD of Raworth reading *Writing* – is that Raworth's work is full of interferences to the flow, jump-cuts, interruptions, that both attest to the celerity and yet break it, and this strikes me as Levinasian too, as Tim Woods and others have pointed out also. This is the necessary rupture that erupts the quality of saying into the said. The 14 line poems that Raworth 'juggled' into final assemblage seem to balance those demands absolutely.

How this translates into my own work I'm not sure. I read some of my texts at a pace, if they seem to demand it, or demanded it during their construction or creation, and I am aware of an 'accelerated collage' at work in my jumps and swings, though I am much less addicted to such procedures these days. Notational high-speed *writing* is perhaps an illusion (this is something I am discussing with Cliff Yates at the moment, for his PhD), an artifice that initiates liberation in the reader; Pound intuited that 'images' produced just this sort of ritornello, so it's nothing new. Of course I am not validating speed alone (the logic of Velopolis we live within); mental celerity must equate with more foundational notions of the aesthetic and the imagination, or even ethical action, rather than pure technical proficiency. I am intensely aesthetic rather than technical.

EH: In your chapter on Maggie O'Sullivan you write about the 'spectral saying on the saidness of the material page' which is reading, and quote Christopher Middleton on the voices of a text which, launched by the poet's, are 'a kind of *endophone*'. So reading involves an inner speaking and an inner ear, voices imaginary and unmistakable. You seem to have a level of faith in *reading* as the other of a text? 'To read is to be proximate to, to face alterity as distance, and be implored to *answer*, as Bakhtin would say'.

RS: That last remark is a description of this interview, isn't it, but maybe of all textual dialogue?

Despite what I say about the effectiveness of O'Sullivan reading above, or perhaps because of it, really… You are quoting from a caveat right at the end of the book about the *limits* of performance, which is pretty much an unquestioned valorised term in the poetics I've been associated with – and, of course, I've done my bit as a performer and I'm proud of it! Middleton – a marvellous writer of poetics as a speculative discourse and a poet of major significance, it seems to me; I am currently re-reading him – argues that the sonic patternings of language are too complex to be perceived in oral performance alone.

His conjectures suggest an important limitation upon performance, or rather, they displace actual performance onto a more complex performative relationship with the eye and brain, which is just as bodily in its way: 'The reader imaginatively somatizes the vocality of the text, for it has aroused in him various other sense-traces, which may be hard to fix.' It's a slightly different point, but my reading of O'Sullivan's poem 'Naming' in *The Poetry of Saying* is a slow motion tracking of semantics and etymology, sonics and page-spatiality, through the text. It necessarily interrupts performance in a narrow sense.

There's a broader point here, I think, which links my long-held faith in the reader with more recent questions of form. I noticed, at the *Partly Writing* conversations I attended at Bury in 2005, some contributors really wanted to get text moving, quite literally, morphing and diving on screen, which is, of course, a form of performance. (In fact, florid-faced lecturers are already bouncing textual fragments across their multi-coloured Powerpoint screens in quite an alarming way.) What they seemed to be forgetting was that the movement of the reading eye across the printed page already performs that kind of spatial dancing, a little like Middleton's sonic eye. If you're not careful, the performative in the hands of some performers – not Raworth and O'Sullivan, of course – *does our reading for us.* People are shouting at me! That text is morphing before my eyes, beyond my control or recall! These are experienced as alienating, endless streams of saying, not at all like the experience of reading and re-reading Raworth, but as something un-anchored to the said, the necessary materiality I talk about in my book, that stops the saying and the said becoming merely a tired binary. (Certain concrete poems get very pedantic in their iconicity, though never the great ones, which are concerned with the nature of signification itself.) Only a kind of restedness can allow us to appreciate the irreducible otherness of the work, from which it derives its power, it seems to me. To borrow a formulation of Derek Attridge, literary works must be allowed to stage their own meaning(s), which is what Raworth and O'Sullivan can do.

EH: You mention that you've written a few short stories recently. What's going on there?

RS: For ten years I've taught creative writing and worked with fiction writers as well as poets at Edge Hill. In a very ordinary sense, the skills of editing I have learned about fiction made me decide simply: it's time to have a go, and stage my own meanings! Actually, this is a return to work I was doing years ago, and there's always been a touch of fictionality and narrativity in my poetry anyway. But the forms that are coming out are quite interesting to me. They are works of poetics – that other discourse to which I willingly owe allegiance: a 'text and commentary' on Breton's *Nadja* set in Liverpool, called *Thelma*, or stories about writers which chew over issues at the heart of writing. (The first part of *Thelma* will appear in *Tears in the Fence* soon.) Having written a book on Iain Sinclair probably has something to do with it too. The fiction obsesses over the ethics of writing, sometimes parodying my actual poetic work to test its limits. But it's too early to see where this will lead, or even how much I will attempt to publish. Oddly, the stories rise unbidden into consciousness, like false memories, and demand to be written, quite unlike the poetry. I think the experience is quite a profound one because it seems to be changing the way I'm working, the ways I think about my poetry, in a fashion that is not conclusive enough to express yet.

This has also got something to do with the experience of reading Christopher Middleton again (though that is my current pre-occupation): his sense of the poem as artefact mediating the world of things and language, his feeling for the liminal and the demonic, his conjecture that poetry comes out of 'a sudden swerve of language crystallising in some daring, voiced image, which somehow alerts the whole nervous system', as he puts it in his Shearsman book *Palavers*. They are both provocations to my habitual ways of thinking and working, I suppose. And that, at the greatest level of generality, is what poetics does to you, for you, if you are receptive as a writer.

I have a sense of wanting to move towards a writing that is both complex and lucid, that avoids my most obvious 'avant-garde' strategies. I also feel that I no longer belong to a grouping of writers, a fructifying feeling I certainly had in the decade from 1985 in London (which I even allow myself to trace in *The Poetry of Saying* - and can be found on my *Pages* blogzine as the serialised 'A History of the Other'). At a certain age I suppose poetics becomes more individualised. In fact, I just found myself saying all of these things in a footnote to an article on Krszyztof Ziarek recently, quite unbidden.

EH: Can you say something about your new 'September 12' poem?

RS: One of the impulses behind writing fiction was to swerve away from this sequence of near-sonnets because I felt that it was the best thing I'd ever written. Its poetics are probably embodied in a piece entitled 'Rattling the Bones (for Adrian Clarke)' which appears on Softblow and which will hopefully stand at the head of a volume. It's pretty clear what happened *before* September 12, of course. It's about the aftermath of that – which sounds like an inadequate summary. I'm currently working on another sequence of 24 to supplement it, at the moment called 'September 10', the ones that I mentioned earlier, that use my notes from Feldmann, and the little quote from the opening lines of a poem comes from that too. I hope you will forgive me if I decline to say much more about it - the fear of talking it away, or of falsely influencing it, and all that. Instead, here's the one I wrote yesterday, still in draft form, the ninth of the series. It can also stand as an unpolished example of my use of multiple photographic images:

Giving Up Whatever Ghost

He slouches in the front row of the stalls
adjusting opera glasses at his nose. While he
inspects the safety curtain you scrutinise his nape,
scrubbed, beneath his slicked-back denial of hair

The curtain rises; his glasses descend. Democracy
breaks out, caught in its own crossfire:

Teargas hits the centre of the crowd; it fans out
cursing and gasping. One hand reaches
for the bread; three mouths moisten in this:

The soprano's dress slips down her frame.
The ringlets of her wiry wig cascade
as crescendo beckons; her throat tightens.
Her shoulders struggle free into the perfect air
of purest song; embrace wordless blackout.

EH: Is Guattari's *Chaosmosis* an important book for you? When you speak about Guattari you seem to get closest to a politics of writing.

RS: Do I? I use a small part of *Chaosmosis* in *The Poetry of Saying* – one of the bits I could understand, I am no exegete of this material - as part of an argument about autopoiesis in the work of Maggie O'Sullivan – her becoming embodied in her poems - that is actually lifted by Guattari from early Bakhtin. There was a time when everybody read Deleuze and Guattari but now they only read Deleuze. (At this moment Patricia is working downstairs on her PhD on Deleuze (and Lyotard).) Guattari's relegated in that reassessment despite the contribution he made to Deleuze's thought, to the development of *concepts* (which, they both agreed, was the purpose of philosophy).

I was much taken by a 1987 micro-text of Guattari published in Poetics Journal 8 called 'Text for the Russians', which was an address to writers in which he talks about making 'virulent fragments of partial enunciation work by virtue of shifts in subjectivity', making ritornelli, and also states: 'The poetic function is more than ever called upon to recompose artificially rarefied and resingularised universes of subjectivity' and he praises poetry's 'capacity to promote active, procedural ruptures at the core of significatory tissues and semiotic denotatives, from which to set new worlds of reference to work.' (It's what we all want to hear and my 'Empty Diary 1987' pays homage to, and quotes from, this brief and suggestive statement.) I might then have been more interested in those linguistic 'tissues' than the 'worlds of reference' – but it gave me a different way in than the language poets, maybe, to begin thinking about *Twentieth Century Blues*. Some of this returns in Guattari's *Chaosmosis* which – Patricia tells me – is regarded by the continental philosophy community as incoherent.

Over the last year or so I've been reading Guattari's historically prescient late essay of 1992, *The Three Ecologies*, which argues for the inter-dependence of the psyche, the socius and the environment. *Thelma* launches off on this one: Just for once a book, opened at random, has an answer. It says I am 'a montage of drives haunting the socius'.

Following on from the ethical turn in my thinking – *The Poetry of Saying* and also my poetics piece *The Anti-Orpheus* I find myself approaching an aesthetic turn – there's a real turn here (at last) in the culture, represented by a book like Derek Attridge's *The Singularity of Literature*. All of which takes me back somewhat – it's not a homecoming but a new discovery – to Adorno and Marcuse, and thus back to the political as embodied in the estrangements of form. (The latter is the 'unnamed thinker' in the fourth of my *Berlin Bursts* on Shadow Train.

Most recently I have been considering Krzysztof Ziarek's *The Force of Art* (2004), which tries to make an anti-aesthetics of out of both Adorno and Heidegger.

Ziarek conceives of the work of art as a force field. It is not an object but an event, inhering in neither form nor content, and this eventness makes the artwork a forcework, in his central neologism.

In the work of art, forces are no longer tethered by the dominant social reality. In a redefinition of the concept of the autonomy of the artwork, as that is theorised by Adorno, Ziarek insists not only that artworks transform and re-work their forces, but that they transform the ordinary relations of social power, and the receivers of the artwork can carry this non-violent, power-free relationality into social praxis. All this sounds very promising, politically speaking. However, Ziarek's dissolving of the artwork as an object in order to maintain its forcework, means that artistic *making* (and poetics as formulations of that), artistic *materiality* and *medium* (and aesthetics that account for the negotiation of these) are ruled out of court, so that formal innovation as a factor in contemporary artistic and literary practice is undervalued. In short, it's a book that doesn't (yet) speak to me as a poet, so it will have to await its moment. I'm not very scholarly or philosophical about all this – and ever more aware of this as Patricia's work progresses - but I hope that I don't produce what Marjorie Perloff witheringly calls 'theory buzz'.

EH: In *The Anti-Orpheus* the letter there ('Signature Style') speaks of the act of signature. What are the implications of that act?

RS: You sign the frame because you are responsible for the artefact you produce and you should say so afterwards. Robert (or whatever your author-function is) made this. It is not to say that the 'me' that makes the text is the 'I' that might (or might not) appear in it. Neither is this 'signature' in the metaphorical sense of a significant stylistically identifiable set of traits or procedures that seems to unify an author's work – and Perloff has written recently of signature as such an 'identifying mark' in the work of the language poets, a group of writers who have been vociferous against the effects of 'voice' in poetry, which is, of course, the most common metaphor for this.

But there is another rôle for 'authoredness', as Derek Attridge calls it in *The Singularity of Literature*. 'A full response to the otherness of the literary work includes an awareness of, a respect for, and in a certain sense … a taking of responsibility for, the creativity of its author.' We acknowledge the poem, or whatever, has been 'written' he says, is 'a writing' which requires a *reading*, in the fullest sense.

While Perloff is not advocating a simple return to 'voice', neither is Attridge advocating a simple return to author's intentionality. Both an ethics of signature and an awareness of authoredness belong to the *reading* of a work. This doesn't mean this won't have implications for (or in) the act of creativity, if only this is holding such formulations in your mind as you write. Perhaps this is partly what Roy Fisher was enacting, making his mark, when he wrote, in *Wonders of Obligation*,

> The things we make up out of language
> turn into common property.
> To feel responsible
> I put my poor footprint back in.

EH: In your interview with Tim Allen for the Salt book *Don't Start Me Talking* you mention, in passing, a poetics of strands (almost to be found) in Yeats as he returns to particular places and themes. In your *Twentieth Century Blues* the strands are named and numbered. How does this idea of strands relate to the cubo-seriality identified by Charles Bernstein or other ideas of stretched (if broken) composition?

RS: The idea of strands was very distantly suggested by Yeats – those Coole Park poems – and also by Robert Duncan's 'The Structure of Rime' sequence that cuts across his books, between poems, and then I wondered what would happen if you permitted yourself to link not just one sequence but several and then allow them to interrelate and interrupt one another. Very early into the project I described the method as I saw it developing (in the article 'Poetic Sequencing and the New'). Certainly I was thinking about Zukofsky, filtered through Barrett Watten's writing on him, quoted in that piece, and about Allen Fisher's multiple-reading routes through *Place* (rendered slightly redundant by the recent book presentation of that work). I probably had more anti-models than models, more examples of what I didn't want it to be. It's actually a set of hyperlinks, although that example was unknown to most of us when I began in 1989.

In this question about my work I find it is impossible for me to present a reading or contextualisation of it, because I believe deeply that that is the freedom of the reader and critic. I can talk about poetics, of course. But I can never read my own work: in fact, I passionately believe that that is the reason for the existence of poetics as a specific discourse, to allow writers to have dialogue with their processes without imposing interpretations upon their products.

EH: What was the atmosphere like at Writers Forum over the time that you attended? Can you remember the first time you went?

RS: No, I can't remember the first time, but it was only in the 1990s, although I had known Bob since 1973: the first poet I'd met, by the way. The atmosphere was described in my piece for Bob's 75th birthday, rather well, I think: the mixture of rapture, drunkenness, exuberance and concentration. It had the structure of a Quaker meeting; anybody who got the call could stand up and give forth. Anything goes was the aesthetic rule but there were subtle controls, Bob's eyes mainly. He had these deep-set penetrating eyes that could look through you. And so: you would get the regulars like Lawrence Upton, Adrian Clarke, Betty Radin, Johan de Wit, Patrick Fetherston and Patricia and myself, always with something new to offer, and a number of them (not me) performed sound poetry with Bob. Jennifer Cobbing (Pike) would drop in to dance now and then, all in the upstairs room of a pub with a pool table in the centre, covered with Writers Forum booklets. Then he'd have extraordinary guests: major concrete poets like Arrigo Lora-Totino or Pierre Garnier, the Russian sound poet Dimitri Prigov. Steve MacCaffery and Karen Mac Cormack dropped by to see us all once. I'm in danger of leaving names out... I wish I'd kept better records....

In short it was the least directed and most focussed workshop I've ever attended, whose atmosphere I greatly miss, but sadly believe I would never be able to approximate, as a workshop facilitator, either inside or outside the academy. It was also a venue for visiting writers, as I've said, and it was the slipway for launching every Writers Forum booklet. It was also a place of friendship, and occasionally a bit of fighting.

EH: Might we see a follow-up to *The Poetry of Saying*, another large critical project?

RS: *The Poetry of Saying* took 25 years to finally get done. My little book on Sinclair took a couple. So I'm getting quicker! I have plans to write a book on the discourse of poetics within formally innovative poetries, but apart from a general piece defining poetics – and a couple of articles – one on Allen Fisher and Charles Bernstein, another on Maggie O'Sullivan – nothing has been written yet, other than a proposal. But the more I think of what I 'should' do as a critic makes me feel slightly desperate to get back to writing poetry.

Robert Sheppard

from The English Strain

Direct Rule: Huge Power and Sinful Sleep
for Charles Bernstein

Like a policeman on leave in Liverpool, this poem can't shake
off its look: it's partly another poem (the one on which
I rest my writing pad so I can't read it anymore): the poem
with Alexander the Great no less. It alludes to Wyatt's *Psalms.*

But I'm pointing (look!) to Wyatt's *Penitential Sonnets,*
the ones I did, relating Wyatt's concupiscence and peccability.
The students gravely grind these poems into notes, while Wyatt *dies*
in his mistress's arms again, punning away like a Tudorbethan jokebook.

Even putting it on Twitter won't get Bo and Go or Fox and Dox
to RT it or DM me. Trump's bitter fruit hangs like fake outsider art
on the wailing wall of his mirrored pout. Some of these bastards
are going to need a footnote (if we're lucky) like Darius and Uriah.

They weren't lucky. Click *here* to access Sheppard's 'aesthetic justice'.
Then act it out all over the show like it's a metaphor for real justice.

July 2017

Direct Rule: While Life did Last that League was Tender

Mary Shelton in Wyatt's acrostic tripped down the margins
of a masterly pastime, played by Master Clere in her plackets.
He was your dogging dog, my lord, on hand with his hand.
His victories of Boleyn and Boulogne conflate in your bad spelling.

Was it a wheeze to watch Kelso flaming, huddled close as
twenty villages and hamlets and crops were scorched?
At Landrecy you were saluted by enemy fire, reprimanded by Bo.
At Montreuil, with four hundred starved French before,

and six hundred slaughtered after, you left a thousand
glorious English corpses curated for your Brexit show.
You ordered the captains forward. *Clere* saved your life…

Remember when you were both students at Cambridge?
You booted that beggar, burnt a £20 note in front of his hooter.
You're having a last laugh alone, in your last, lost, sonnet.

                                                    3rd August 2017

Thou hast thy calling to some palace-floor

Rush off, behind shades, tinted windscreens,
honing the rhymes of your prize-dick limerick.
Behind your hunch, palace functionaries hand-toss
at rumours of my fecundity, and wink.

This stage is too poor for your puffy part: daily,
you needs must announce a cross-channel bridge
or a new shining complex manured on dark bodies.
Here behind the latch I count your gold.

The roof of our love-nest hosts noisome finches;
it's infested with mice scratching at your cricket bat.
On Sky News you applaud the Shithole President.

You think you are the thinking woman's idiot
with your phallocratic notches. A voice within chants:
It's me, calling you back, alone, the Wimpole resident.

And wilt thou have me fashion into speech

Flicked on the President's Club skirt and bustier –
without a word, bore a candle to your Euro-sceptic table.
Big Tease, a blonde wave of black-tie lust huffing
genital generosity, you blew it roughly out.

After you auctioned a walk-on part in your poems,
I blew you, charitably, on my knees, in luxury seclusion –
but held you at arm's length for months: missed calls,
smutty voicemails, stained tie. 'Til I rolled over, speechless.

Here I am on my back, a part in your risible poems,
Brazilian Sonnets. One is 'wooed, but unwon', 'tough as
election promises', 'heartless by the' alliterative 'hearth'.

I'm here just to rip my briefs off. But that fantasy bridge
and the NHS windfall were my ideas! So is tying you up
with your filthy tie for real grief from real party whips.

26th January 2018

from **The Accordion Book**

1
after David Ter-Oganyan

Form becomes reform on this stretch
of paintbox limbs. Destruction is con-
structivist shivering, a black box with
unruly wires, splats! on grids. We

lean over our futures: white on black,
we silhouette our capering. One of us
faces the tank (we've learnt this pose from
YouTube footage) as they pounce to the beat.

A red wipe-out. The tank invades its own
negative space, a burst of nothing as it
trundles into screen-wipe. The map
becomes trajectories as lines take their walks

across neat crosses to the presidential brick.
Black wedges in white, the mass demo is
all the obscurations of the anti-state merging
in disaffected interference to the message:

the neat squares with their incredible names,
the lazy boulevards with their rational numbering,
the individuals with their spheroid beauties, all conspire
against collective horizons. Containers spill

an immigrant breeze. Dark boats in charcoal
stalk the coastline, a blat! of fire as a chopper
dives, muted explosions out to sea. Swirling
vectors loop through leaping fists. Banners

enfold their slogans. Faces are daubed on the iPad.
A statue topples, pose maintained. Military hardware
sprays your eyes until you're bent over, vomiting spice
in the metro, cut and pasted from several schools of art.

Ink flows to draw this knife, though you implore the car
to give you a lift to Trëkhpudny Lane. Is that a burger
or a bomb in your hand? you joke. We join
the passive menace of female artists pussy-rioting,

weeping in summer dresses, hoisting vodka bottles
to enflamed eyes. Our tired slogans from Adorno
prove art's autonomy while *Fuck Off* sounds life-
affirming as a wind-up onion detonates tears.

Blacks on greys mime several revolutionary scenarios
but the drawing of a man lighting a woman's cigarette
will not endanger your health. She twists over, nude,
puffing. Letters dance above her nicotined back.

She places her mind into my vacancy and I enfold it.
Political resistance as total simulacrum:
fists of blue cloud rough up the sky,
post images through slits in her forehead,

a firebomb delivery of terror silhouettes, triumphal
architecture transfigured by searchlit graffiti. She stands
boldly framed in her window, hiding stars beneath the sill,
pulling on an e-cigarette. Close up, her tensed lips break

into scribbles as though she is disintegrating, limbs
of light thrashing her darkness. Green ovals eye her.
Her question arises before its hammer is struck,
trellised on beams of matter of fact

unpeeling themselves while the fruit of knowledge
is fixed in her tiny fingers by the lithography
of the moment. A parabola pisses a man
into a ditch. Darkness congregates, up to no good.

She scores the sky with expletives. Maps
show vectors of thought traversing continents
but closing down the arguments, pointing one way only
to her mausoleum of poses and swoons.

2

Purposive before the broken units
in freefall, merely a moment sliced
from a roll of overscaled disaster,
breathless between gobbles of voice,

you jump to the beats in the DIY heat,
though earwigging the girl in a trilby
who drones on about the John Cage score
that's tattooed to your sweaty arm.

Nothing doing, just the words,
taking their places in sentences on
the screen in place of things, clippings
randomised by the program.

The artists can chew their brushes to bits.
Nobody claims to have authored this;
nobody will claim to read it. Bad photos
of everything you do become the things

you do. Two girls in leather shorts
carrying leather satchels
watch a grunting man in theatre-scrubs
drowning under a cracked skein of germs.

The ideological centre is a towering twist,
creaking above you, magnetic pulse. At
the margins, a search engine is literally
a scrabble through decades-old book dust.

You're out-competed by your own jokes;
as curation stalks creation, a locked cell laughs off
its key. Its wall of vinyl singles puts afflatus
on hold, a thumbscrew niche for muted critique.

Out on the beribboned plaza
or on a tabletop spread with a Lego map

of Europe, the depersonalised aggregate tells you
it's the only game in town to project your throat,

eyeballs in whirlwinds. The margin
is a waving figure on a sinking mud-flat.
Centrist commonsense bricks itself,
in its shuttered sauna of theremin tortures.

It's the talk of the town, plunging
into nightpools of unreflective moons,
the touch of your lips, even the taste of tears,
photoshopped onto your swaddled body.

A man holds his head between loose collars.
Out of its mouth trickles conventionally
progressivist constructions, blindfolded women
dancing in a sealed hall of swooping gulls,

waiting for their own shadows to arrive at
their feet, a disappointing allegory like a
game of chess or adolescent Nietzscheans
posing for uncropped photos in a Berlin brothel,

though their testicles, soft as moth wings,
flutter in the palms of their entranced guardians,
with their expectations of Lego empires
and fasting Kultural Kommandos who spout Latin.

Bovine masks float like afflatus before
the faces of topophobic geographers
slipping into the folds and creases
of their contour maps. You may kiss my red lips

but a necrotic landscape – Perspex
stairways to an Alpine intention –
is pasted across our embrace.
Machinegunrattles about the dignity

of labour waste my exchangeable
hysteria. Four books on stylish shelves,
their spines contrasting primary colours,
begin a bare-knuckle fight between

differing accounts of the latest war. A bridge
between the eyes of the peacock shield
and *glocal* competition lifts us towards lists of prices.
The piano is shaved of value. You simply breathe.

3

The portraits on the wall have dimmed themselves
like photo-sensitive glass. A mask on the melt,
these features feature in your feature: the human
extract coiled into cold affirmation, a road movie,

a biopic: *25 musky spunkers* present
a fabricated dream of a fabricated body.
She confesses: *I built this cloud architecture,*
a burlesque structured & sutured by desire,

with teams of stickmen scribbled into the plans.
I curve like deliverance through thingy time,
unmentionable vices mingling like sexual
fluids in secret rooms under the floorboards,

with history. With piggy-squeals, like all fictional entities,
he eternally re-enacts the primal scene of his making.
Nobody promised art would be good for you; like him,
you pass from narcissism to universal blank. And back

to the old dream: *the bones of my corset moan*
straps stretch down the backs of my thighs. She
clutches her ears like a drag-queen; sex words
snuggle up gently to her garter's line-break.

She wishes she had only one name of one syllable,
a bullet to patent her steely becoming, to throw
her backbone into the petrified splash, not the fleapit
where generations of underlings spat blood.

She cleaves her black tongue; it hangs from a tree.
The clues are written on the inside of her body,
fleshly cavern, inky with implication, like the roof of
a mouth, blue words blur from months of surveillance:

she invites multiple donors to empty their tubes
into the gripped tufts of her coiffure, entertains
a gush of adolescents, tickling one another's testes
with their girly fingers, as she bobbles out of her corset,

tightened chords of artifice *my report reports,*
buzzwords buzzing along the rush of our vision,
moving through a crowd of whatnesses: ex-pop
star serial killers in the dock, spilling beans and brains.

All puppets slip the bonds of the actual, even 'Stickman'
sprayed on a wall amid superheroes with their multi-
coloured tight-chested neuroses: *Stickman sticks*
to his story I stick to his flypaper flesh uncoiling.

Fizzles smoke like curls of hair,
twisting beyond category, report and
portrait, over the fiction, as she dabs on
lip-gloss for the ooze-monkey. Her ring

finger dallies over this raid on bandit art;
a soldier taking a selfie next to a corpse
mirrors an imagining and a dance frozen on a tablet
& I ooze & I'm turned & turned again inside out as

the judge edges into the microphone. It catches
his breath. He turns toward her, and runs through
the indictment once more. His breathing, his listening,
his understanding, sharpen. She's beginning to be believed.

4

These are your executioners not your anointers
beached on your back like a barbershop chorus
in one of these stories. A flesh-flash
in a tunnel opens upon electric lines netting the sky

over the stretching chimneys of crouched buildings. These
levels of attention bring you lofty penthouses or squat sheds
where old men practise scrimshaw. A print-shop prints
on the morning. Glasshouses shouldn't throw shadows,

like belief or grief reproducing themselves.
Too many beliefs among so few facts test
the tense curves of the bridge's girders. You're tossed from
its concrete edge by sheer knowledge of the absolute.

Good people, like the mother who brushes her boy's
hair, find the largest stones to finish you off. Bones
crack in instant judgement, immediate justice.
Deep in the desert the explosions are buried.

They're warped in innocence, quite unprotected.
A changing-room musk seeps through this carnival.
A terrorist stretches pantyhose over an artificial arm.
A gun is a thought, a passionate embrace of mind

and flesh. Everybody laughs like their neighbours,
nudging hysteria in the belly. The next moment's sliced
from a roll of fun: somebody flips, but the vodka stays
in his glass. Vast clippings, a future archive of atrocity,

is piled for pulp, hydraulic mouths fanning woodchip.
The accordion book is silent, folding away the multiple
stories: behind glass, they exhibit themselves, assemblages
of spare parts, configured as though before time had started,

when the woman in the blue dress, juggling with knives,
aware of before and after, of how she came to be

and of how she came to be staring up at a free blade
frozen by a camera, evolved at some edge

of her mind to make her mind her mind, with the
feathery tickle of her tongue stud, her closing,
intimate knees. She makes the call from the bed,
succulently lipped. He registers resistance to a gaze,

not his, somebody else's shadowy cleaving to spill
himself into. Centipede eye-lashes lash his repulsion,
feelers for rags tattering over a teasing plunge. His tangle
of cloying yearning drops to the floor. He meets himself.

Stamping at the drama of becoming yesterday,
she thinks with the bad things that exist,
chewing on the metal strip
in bank notes, to make money *feel*, softening

its affect with saliva. Her hand is a medium,
sheeny with finish. He watched her face, once,
rolling off her leaking form. She scribbles the world
into action minutes for the mind in her arm that pulls

the hair that pushes her into reality. Relate
the shape of this fact as it spreads on placards of itself,
hoisted aloft amid a public rhetoric of evidence
and engagement that will only be defeated by laughter.

A memory stick tails from her bunch
of keys. The air is full of grit; dust on
the screen furs her body, a foxy form
slinking through funhouse loops, giddy with motility.

All the books are shelved, spines to the wall, next
to the training manual. Leather straps hang thick from
the ceiling, like forest creepers. Flesh streaks
down one wall; blood smears the window.

Make your own palace of pallets by looking hard.
Drapes drape over the phials of birdsong. She belts
the frock of engagement tight; she's so obviously
the centre of this atmosphere that she needs to do

something to shift it, a mote's breath, but there are
too many forms and not enough things here. The news
breaks, rushes by signage, brick and steel strewn with
smashed letters, naked wires. The breached plumbing festers...

2014-2015

Robert Sheppard: A Bibliography

The main purpose of this Bibliography is to serve as a comprehensive record of Robert Sheppard's work, enabling readers to pursue avenues opened up by the content of this book. Given this poet-critic's prolific output frequently turns its attention to the writing of others, the Bibliography also exists as a valuable resource for scholars researching the British Poetry Revival, Linguistically Innovative Poetry, and poetry in the late twentieth and early twenty-first centuries generally, particularly although by no means exclusively in the context of the UK.

As is customary for bibliographies of this nature, entries are listed in chronological order. The process of surveying the span of an author's work is assisted better by date organisation than by alphabetical or even genre classification, both of which would result in the scholar getting caught up in the multicursal thickets of a maze, however alluring this might be to the author and readers of the constellatory *Complete Twentieth Century Blues*.

The author's category divisions and their titles have been retained as a matter of principle while following as much as possible (though inevitably with some stylistic variation) the MHRA guidelines adopted by this book for individual entries. One section especially, however, presents potentially vertiginous problems, both for its author and for any archivist: 'Magazines containing poetry, creative prose, and fiction (1972-2018)', though bibliographically idiosyncratic, is an instance of where the author's archival methodology should be respected rather than deleted outright because of the omission of poem titles and pages numbers, and so on. To do so would entail the loss of a key distinguishing feature of the author's *oeuvre*. Despite these omissions, this section – or perhaps, in today's technological parlance, the resulting 'word cloud' – is in actual fact an accurate representation of the range and scope of the author's poetry publishing across the span of forty-six years. It is possible to discern from it the changing but recognisable shape of the *socius* in which the author is a major figure and of the evolution of little magazine poetry publishing in the UK. The author, in a post on his weblog *Pages* written during the production of this book, explains the rationale behind detailing all appearances of his poems in little magazines: 'It is incomplete, of course, because I have stopped it. While I think that the list of my reviews and articles informs, this list will be perhaps of interest to other poets who published in these years. What I'm going to do is simply list the magazines in order of my appearance in them, one appearance each.'[1] Hence the section included here. The task of detailing to the nth degree according to the usual bibliographical rules is tempting, but the inevitability of threads left untied militates against the process (and frustrates the totalising will of the bibliographer). The editors

---

[1] Robert Sheppard, 'Updated My Website and added a full bibliography', *Pages* <http://robertsheppard.blogspot.com/2018/09/updated-my-website-and-added-full.html> [accessed 1 October 2018].

therefore follow the author's sensible decision to offer an impression rather than a comprehensive record.

The sections 'Pamphlets and Shorter Publications' and 'Ship of Fools' Pamphlets and Artists' Books' reflect the fact that the publishing culture of Linguistically Innovative Poetry is a diverse field, embracing DIY publishing and more conventional formats by established outfits. The Ship of Fools imprint is an especially vital acknowledgement of Sheppard's collaborative practice and indeed his ethic, repeatedly affirmed to generations of students and of course a major feature of the British Poetry Revival onwards, to seize the means of production. Rather than integrating such titles within the broader category of 'Pamphlets and Shorter Publications', Ship of Fools has rightly been given its own section to stress the DIY aesthetic as a discrete but distinct category.

Another stylistic variation within the MHRA guidelines is made necessary by the status of the magazine as a genre and publication within Linguistically Innovative Poetry. A marked tendency for issues of little magazines to be collated within volume numbers is a recognisable convention of academic journals, something which is underlined by the corresponding dedication with which articles, reviews, and manifesto-type utterances are assigned as a significant feature of a publication's intellectual culture. This situates little magazines outside even the category of the literary periodical, and so the rules for pagination adopted in this Bibliography adhere to those advised for journals. Sheppard's little magazine *Pages* may on the face of it appear to exclude itself from this rule. 'At the level of the page,' Sheppard explains about producing the magazine, 'I decided that I would number the pages sequentially across issues (rather than have issue numbers) to suggest that this was a process as much as a monthly product.'[2] Certainly it is tempting to view the inclusion of page numbers alongside the title as an anticipatory nod to its future home in some archive. And as can be expected from this source, the reader has work to do even locating each page number, since there are no page markers within each title, only in the title itself. Two referencing options are available in light of this: accepting that page references have been placed alongside the title as if part of it, likewise italicising those numbers (e.g. *Pages 1-8*); or following the rule for formatting issue numbers, i.e. placed after the italicised title but before the comma in Roman type (e.g. *Pages* 1-8). While each option has its relative merits, the Editors have opted for the first. Such considerations bear scrutiny here as part and parcel of the wayward and haphazard operations of small press publishing and poetics at the vanguard. And if all of this belies the informal ethos with which little magazines were (and continue to be) funded, produced, distributed, and subscribed to, this

---

[2] 'On *Pages*: An interview between Robert Sheppard and Joey Francis', *Jacket2* <https://jacket2.org/commentary/pages> [accessed 1 October 2018].

is because their content demonstrates the ways in which innovative poetics straddles contrasting (perhaps even agonistic) worlds of cultural production. The relative independence of little magazines, for instance, has enabled them to eschew the prestige of well-known publications while offering content that arguably transcends their editorial constraints. The title (and term) 'magazine', therefore, is neither an exact fit nor entirely inaccurate; re-setting the terms of aesthetic agendas changes the rules of the bibliographic game.

Titles or author names enclosed in square brackets in sections of reviews by the author and on his work serve to assist readers in pinpointing the precise subject matter reviewed, something which remains unhelpfully ambiguous by the provision of review titles alone. In the section 'Articles' under 'Criticism on Robert Sheppard', page numbers have been omitted from titles in which the frequency of passing mention of the author is too high to justify locating chapters as a Robert Sheppard-focussed entity or even localised passages discussing his work. Entries followed by an asterisk indicate where it is has not been possible to find the details omitted; an entry is followed by 'nla' when the URL concerned is no longer available.

The Editors are indebted to the author for the exhaustive labour of initially compiling this Bibliography and for allowing them to trawl through his private library in order to bring it to its current form.

Full-Length Poetry and Creative Prose Collections

Daylight Robbery (Exeter: Stride, 1990)
The Flashlight Sonata (Exeter: Stride, 1993)
Empty Diaries (Exeter: Stride, 1998)
The Lores (London: Reality Street, 2003)
Tin Pan Arcadia (Cambridge: Salt Publishing, 2004)
Hymns to the God in which my Typewriter Believes (Exeter: Stride, 2006)
Complete Twentieth Century Blues (Cambridge: Salt Publishing, 2008)
Warrant Error (Exeter: Shearsman Books, 2009)
Berlin Bursts (Exeter: Shearsman Books, 2011)
A Translated Man (Exeter: Shearsman Books, 2013)
Words Out of Time (Newton-le-Willows: Knives, Forks and Spoons, 2015)
History or Sleep: Selected Poems (Bristol: Shearsman Books, 2015)
Unfinish (London: Veer Publications, 2016)
Twitters for a Lark: Poetry of the European Union of Imaginary Authors (with Others) (Bristol: Shearsman Books, 2017)

Short Fiction

The Only Life (Newton-le-Willows: Knives Forks and Spoons, 2011)

Pamphlets and Shorter Publications

Feeble Days and Weak Ends: Autobiography (Filey: Fiasco Publications, 1974)
Poems from the Waiting Room (Southwick: 14 Great Grandchildren Press/
    Supranormal Press, 1974)
Triptych (Southwick: 14 Great Grandchildren Press/Supranormal Press, 1976)
Lecture Notes (Southwick: 14 Great Grandchildren Press/Supranormal Press,
    1978)
Dedicated to you but you weren't listening (London: Writers Forum, 1979)
The Frightened Summer (Durham, Pig Press, 1981)
The Factory Island Poems (Norwich: Supranormal/Rock Drill Press, 1981)
Of Appearances (Manchester: Supranormal/Rock Drill Press, 1983)
Returns (Southsea: Textures, 1985)
Private Number (London: Northern Lights Publishers, 1986)
Letter from the Blackstock Road (London: Oasis Books, 1988)
Internal Exile (Southampton: Torque Press, 1988)
Codes and Diodes (with Bob Cobbing) (London: Writers Forum, 1991)
Invite! and Incite! RWC Extra July 1994 (poetics)
Fox Spotlights (Cheltenham: The Short Run Press, 1995)
Free Fists (with Patricia Farrell) (London: Writers Forum, 1996)
Neutral Drums (with Patricia Farrell) (London: Writers Forum, 1999)
Blatent Blather/Virulent Whoops (with Bob Cobbing) (London: Writers Forum,
    2001)
The Anti-Orpheus: A Notebook (Exeter: Shearsman Books 2004)
Risk Assessment (with Rupert Loydell) (no location: Damaged Goods, 2006)
The Given (Newton-le-Willows: Knives Forks and Spoons, 2010)
The Drop (Hunstanton: Oystercatcher Press, 2016)
Petrarch 3: a derivative dérive (Crater 36, 2017)
The Working Week (Devoran: Smallminded Books, 2017)
Hap: Understudies of Thomas Wyatt's Petrarch (Newton-le-Willows: Knives,
    Forks and Spoons, 2018)

Ship of Fools Pamphlets and Artist's Books

Mesopotamia (with images by Patricia Farrell) (London: Ship of Fools, 1987)
Looking North (with images by Patricia Farrell) (London: Ship of Fools, 1987)
The Education of Desire (London: Ship of Fools, 1988)

The Cannibal Club (with Patricia Farrell) (London: Ship of Fools, 1990)
Killing Boxes (London: Ship of Fools, London, 1992)
Wayne Pratt: Watering the Cactus – the deathbed edition (1999 Ship of Fools, London, 1992, revised 1999)
Logos on Kimonos (with images by Patricia Farrell) (London: Ship of Fools, 1992 revised ed. 1998)
Seven (with images by Patricia Farrell) (London: Ship of Fools, 1992)
Icarus - Having Fallen (with Patricia Farrell) (London: Ship of Fools, 1992)
Transit Depots/Empty Diaries (with John Seed [text] and Patricia Farrell [images]) (London: Ship of Fools, 1993)
net/(k)not/-work(s) (London: Ship of Fools, 1993) (poetics)
Fucking Time (with images by Patricia Farrell) (London: Ship of Fools, 1994)
Jungle Nights in Pimlico (with images by Patricia Farrell) (London: Ship of Fools, 1995)
The Book of British Soil (with Patricia Farrell) (London: Ship of Fools, 1995)
Soleà for Lorca (Liverpool: Ship of Fools, 1998)
Birthday Boy, A Present for Lee Harwood, ed. with Patricia Farrell, anthology containing poetry by John Ashbery, art by Andrzej Jackowski, and others, 1999
Depleted Uranium (Liverpool: Ship of Fools, 2001)
31st April or The Age of Irony (Liverpool: Ship of Fools, 2001)
The End of the Twentieth Century (Liverpool: Ship of Fools, 2002)
The Necessity of Poetics (Liverpool: Ship of Fools, 2002)
The Blickensderfer Punch (with Patricia Farrell) (Liverpool: Ship of Fools, 2002)
Turns (with Scott Thurston) (Liverpool: Ship of Fools/The Radiator, 2003)
Where Treads of Death: five books of Iain Sinclair reviewed (Liverpool: Ship of Fools, 2004)
Looking Thru' A Hole in the Wall (with Patricia Farrell) (Liverpool: Ship of Fools, 2010)
The Necessity of Poetics (revised edition) (Liverpool: Ship of Fools, 2011, reprinted 2012-2016)
Liverpool Hugs and Kisses (with Robert Hampson) (Liverpool: Ship of Fools/ Pushtika Press, 2015)
Fandango Loops (with Patricia Farrell) (Liverpool: Ship of Fools, 2015)

Note: Ship of Fools was set up in the mid 1980s by Robert Sheppard and Patricia Farrell for the purpose of publishing their art and text collaborations, though it has been used for other purposes on occasions, sometimes unrecorded here.

Anthology and other gatherings: poetry, creative prose, and fiction

'Discord', in *Kent and Sussex Poetry Society Folio*, 1973

'The Blickling Hall Poem', in *Anthology 1980: Royal Sheffield Institute for the Blind*, 1981

[from 'Letter from the Blackstock Road'], in *The New British Poetry*, ed. by Gillian Allnutt, Fred D'Aguiar, Ken Edwards, and Eric Mottram (London: Paladin, 1988), pp. 336-39

Floating Capital: New Poets from London, ed. by Adrian Clarke and Robert Sheppard (Elmwood, Connecticut: Potes and Poets Press, USA, 1991)

[from 'Killing Boxes'], in *A Purge of / Dissidence*, ed. by Robert Hampson, 1991, unpaginated

'Thirteen', in *Wasted Years*, ed. by Robert Hampson, 1992, unpaginated

'The Micro-pathology of the Sign', 'Verse and Perverse', 'The Magnetic Letter', 'Codes and Diodes are Both Odes', in *Verbi Visi Voco: a performance of poetry*, ed. by Bill Griffiths and Bob Cobbing (London: Writers Forum, 1992), pp. 225-29

'A halo flares', in *Programme for Woodwork Festival* (Vauxhall Pleasure Gardens, May 1993)

'The Overseas Blues', in *Horace Whom I Hated So*, ed. by Harry Gilonis (London: Five Eyes of Wiwaxia, 1993), unpaginated

'Strange Meetings with Justin Sidebottom', in *Short Attention Span*, ed. by Kelvin Corcoran (Cheltenham: A Between Meetings Publication, 1994), unpaginated

'Jungle Nights in Pimlico', in *Motley for Mottram*, ed. by Bob Cobbing and Bill Griffiths (London: Amra/Writers Forum, 1994), unpaginated

'Two Poems for the Festival', in *Smallest Poetry Festival in the World* programme, December 1994, unpaginated

[from *The Lores*], 'New British and Irish Writing', *West Coat Line Number 17*, (29/2) ed. by Peter Quartermain, 1995, pp. 85-87

'The Lores Book Ten', in *Talisman* 'A Selection of New UK Poetry', ed. by Richard Caddel and Peter Middleton (New Jersey: Talisman Press, 1996), pp. 167-69

'Variation and Themes', in *My Kind of Angel* (for William Burroughs), ed. by Rupert Loydell (Exeter: Stride, 1998), pp. 142-44

[from *History or Sleep*], in *Poems for Kosovo*, ed. by Rupert Loydell (Exeter: Stride, 1999), pp. 76-77

[from *Empty Diaries* and *Twentieth Century Blues* 24] 'Empty Diaries 1905', 'Empty Diaries 1936', 'Empty Diaries 1944', 'Empty Diaries 1954', 'Empty Diaries 1968', 'Empty Diaries 1987', and 'Empty Diaries 1990', in *Other: British and Irish Poetry Since 1970*, ed. by Richard Caddel and Peter Quartermain (Hanover, NH: Wesleyan University Press, 1999), pp. 238-42

'The Materialization of Soap 1947', and 'Internal Exile 1', in *Anthology of Twentieth-Century British and Irish Poetry*, ed. by Keith Tuma (Oxford and New York: Oxford University Press, 2001), pp. 866-69

Babylon Burning: 9/11 five years on, ed. by Todd Swift, *Nth Position* (web)

'National Security, Huyton 1940', and 'A Liverpool Poem', in *Eight Days a Week: Liverpool-Köln Exchange*, Liverpool, 2006

'The Novel', in *The Flash*, ed. by Peter Wild (Manchester: Social Diseases, 2007), pp. 154-55

Performance website, ed. by Joe Stretch (January 2007)

'Small Voice', in *Don't Start Me Talking*, ed. by Tim Allen and Andrew Duncan (Cambridge: Salt, 2007), p. 355

'Angel at the Junkbox', in *Sinatra, but Buddy I'm a Kind of Poem*, ed. by Gilbert L. Gigliotti (Washington D.C.: Entasis Press, 2008), pp. 84-85

'The Lebanon', 'Liverpool July 2nd 2007', 'Afghanistan', 'London', 'Iran', and 'The Netherlands', in *Liverpool Poets*, ed. by Alan Corkish (Liverpool: Erbacce Press, 2008)

'The English Poems', in *The Reality Street Book of Sonnets*, ed. by Jeff Hilson (Reality Street: Hastings, 2008), pp. 226-28

'Burnt Journal 1949', in *Salamanders and Mandrakes: Alan Halsey and Gavin Selerie at Sixty*, ed. by David Annwn (Wakefield: IS Press, 2009), unpaginated

'July 2nd 2007', in *Uplift: A Samizdat for Lee Harwood from his friends*, ed. by Patricia Scanlon (Portslade, Artery Editions, 2009), unpaginated

'Malcolm Lowry's Land', in *From the Mersey to the World*, ed. by Bryan Biggs and Helen Tookey (Liverpool: Liverpool University Press, 2009), pp. 133-37

'A Voice Without', and 'Not Another Poem', in *Troubles Swapped for Something Fresh: Manifestos and Unmanifestos*, ed. by Rupert Loydell (Salt: Cambridge, 2009), pp. 101-02

'Roosting Thought', and 'Yet Another Poem', in *The Other Room*, ed. by Scott Thurston, Tom Jenks, and James Davies (Manchester, The Other Room, 2009), unpaginated

'From Hepworth's Garden Out', in *From Hepworth's Garden Out*, ed. by Rupert Loydell (Exeter: Shearsman Books, 2010), pp. 9-12

'Tentatives', in *An Unofficial Roy Fisher*, ed. by Peter Robinson (Exeter: Shearsman, 2010), pp. 71-72

[from 'Manifest', 'Ode to Forme', and 'Lyric'], in *Poetry Beyond Text: Vision, Text and Cognition* (with Pete Clarke), Poetry Beyond Text, University of Dundee, 2011, p. 22 [Ode to Forme p. 43]

'The Given, Part One', in *The Alchemist's Mind*, ed. by David Miller (Reality Street: Hastings, 2012), pp. 75-80

'Spook Hill 1952', in *Gathered Here Today: Celebrating Geraldine Monk at Sixty*, ed. by Scott Thurston (Newton-le-Willows: Knives, Forks and Spoons, 2012), p. 46

'Empty Diary 1955', in *The Dark Would* (various media), ed. by Philip
   Davenport (Manchester: Apple Pie Editions, 2013), unpaginated
'In Unadopted Space', in *Sculpted*, ed. by Lindsey Holland and Angela
   Topping (Aughton: North West Poets, 2013), pp. 107-11
'The Li Shay-yin Suite', in *News from Afar: Ezra Pound and Some
   Contemporary British Poetries*, ed. by Richard Parker (Bristol: Shearsman,
   2014), pp. 268-72
[from EOUIA Translations], in *The Other Room* 6, ed. by Scott Thurston,
   Tom Jenks, James Davies (Manchester: The Other Room, 2014), pp.
   68-69
'The Hippest Man to Walk the Planet' (pp. 12-13), 'Angel at the Junkbox'
   (pp. 24-26), 'Spectres of Breath' (pp. 74-75), 'Improvisation upon
   a Remark of Gil Evans' (p. 81), and 'Round Midnight' (p. 99), in
   Yesterday's Music Today, ed. by Loydell and Ferguson (Newton-le-
   Willows: Knives Forks and Spoons, 2015)
'Book One, Poem Three' (Sophie Poppmeier), in *Festschrift for Tony Frazer*,
   ed. by Aidan Semmens <http://tonyfrazer.weebly.com/robert-sheppard.
   html> [accessed 7 September 2018]
'Arrivals', in *Best British Short Stories 2016*, ed. by Nicholas Royle (Cromer:
   Salt, 2016), pp. 14-17
'The Book of Names, or Late at the Tate', in *Face Down in the Book of
   Revelations: for Peter Hughes*, ed. by Lynne Hughes (Hunstanton:
   Oystercatcher/Sea Pie, 2016), unpaginated
'breaking point', in *Badge of Shame: Purge 5*, ed. by Robert Hampson
   (Guildford: Pushtika, 2017), unpaginated
'Hap Hazard', in *For Robert [Hampson]: An Anthology*, ed. by Redell Olsen
   (London: Royal Holloway University of London Poetics Research
   Centre/Crinoline Editions, 2017), p. 33
'Beefore or Never', in *Click Clack: produced on the occasion of the Captain
   Beefheart Weekend, Liverpool*, JARG (November 2017), unpaginated

Magazines containing poetry, creative prose, and fiction (1972-2018)

*Platform, Doris, Alembic, Palantir, Great Works, Words Worth, Oasis, Figs,
Kudos , Angel Exhaust, Molly Bloom, Reality Studios, The Artful Reporter,
Rock Drill, PN Review, New Statesman, Ninth Decade, Reality Studios, Staple
Diet, Slow Dancer, Archeus, First Offense, Raddle Moon, RWC, Fragmente,
Responses, Critical Quarterly, Memes, Scratch, A4 Anonymous, :that:, Ramraid
Extraordinaire, Grille, Object Permanence, Talus 8, AND, West Coast Line,
Blue Cage, Mirage #4/Periodi(ical)#47, Talisman, Tears in the Fence, Boxkite,
A.bacus, Vertical Images, Stride, The Gig, Counter-Hegemony, Shearsman, Lynx,
Jacket, Terrible Work, Fire, Emergency Rations, cul de qui, Neon Highway, Pores,*

Call, Citizen 32, Poetry Salzburg Review, Softblow, Shadowtrain, Intercapillary Space, Exultations and Difficulties, Free Verse, The David Jones Journal, Pages, Popularity Contest, Skald, Agenda, Stimulus-Respond, New Writing, Veer Off, Parameter, Short Fiction, Litter, Signals, English, Poetry Wales, Erbacce, Paraxis, Adirondack Review, Ekleksographia, Onedit, Eyewear, Sunfish, Roundyhouse, VLAK, Form and Fontanelles, Stand, The Claudius App, Damn the Caesars, The Wolf, Sugar Mule, Blackbox Manifold, Otoliths, International Times, Blazevox, Card Alpha, Noon, The Literateur, 3am Magazine, Poetry at Sangam, Adjacent Pineapple, A Restricted View from Under the Hedge, The Guardian, Cumulus

Mixed Media

Postcard in pack: *In their Own Words* (with Jeffrey Baker), Bank Street Arts, Sheffield: 2009
Avant Garters – zimzalla avant object no. 35 A pair of garters with monostitchs, wrapped in gold, sealed in wax, 2016

Exhibitions

'Post Sound Art? Intermedia', Triskel Arts Centre, Cork, Ireland, 8-27 November 1993
'Different Alphabets' (with Patricia Farrell), Bury Art Gallery, Text Festival, 17 September-27 November 2005
'In their Own Words' (with Jeffrey Baker), Bank Street Arts, Sheffield, 5 November-5 December 2009
Text for Bryan Eccleshall's celebration of the 1911 theft of the Mona Lisa, Bank Street Arts, Sheffield, 2011
'Poetry into Text' (with Pete Clarke), University of Dundee (Centre for Contemporary Art), March 2011, Scottish Poetry Library, Scottish Royal Academy Edinburgh, November-December 2011
'Adrian Henri Prize' (with Pete Clarke), 20-20 Gallery, Much Wenlock, 2013
'Manifest: Collaborations with Robert Sheppard' (with Pete Clarke), The Arts Centre (Edge Hill University), Ormskirk, 11-26 April 2013
'Deep Black' (with Pete Clarke), Krakow Print Biennial, Poland, September 2015
'Am Ende ist es Poesie: an Exhibition of Art Relating to Poetry' (with Pete Clarke), Betonbox, Düsseldorf, Germany, June 2016
'Ship of Fools Exhibition' (with Patricia Farrell), The Arts Centre (Edge Hill University), 1-31 March 2017
'dwarf planet (pluto)' ['twittersonnet'], 'Knives Forks and Spoons Illuminations', Blackpool, September-October 2018

Audio Recordings

1983, 3, (cassette), 1975
Archive of the Now <https://www.archiveofthenow.org/authors/?i=87>
    [accessed 7 September 2018]
Points of Reference, (CD), Edge Hill Poetry And Poetics Group, 2007
Ekleksographia Wave Two (sound file), ed. Philip Davenport, ahadadabooks,
    2010
The Claudius App, 2012

Broadcasts

Friday Looking Sideways, BBC1, 11 June 1976
Poetry Now, BBC Radio 3, 2 September 1983
Poetry Now, BBC Radio 3, 7 October 1983
The Most Curious Specimen, BBC Radio 3, 25 October 1985
'Robert Sheppard', *Clearspot*, Resonance FM, 5 November 2003
Interview, BBC Radio Merseyside, April 2007

Edited Books

Floating Capital: New Poets from London, with Adrian Clarke (Elmwood,
    Connecticut: Potes and Poets, 1991)
News for the Ear: A Homage to Roy Fisher, with Peter Robinson (Exeter:
    Stride, 2000)
The Salt Companion to Lee Harwood (Cambridge: Salt, 2007)
The Door at Taldir: The Selected Poems of Paul Evans (Exeter: Shearsman,
    2009)
Atlantic Drift: An Anthology of Poetry and Poetics, with James Byrne
    (Todmorden and Ormskirk: Arc and Edge Hill University Press, 2017)

Journals and Magazines Edited

1983 (with Tony Parsons and John Purdy), 1-3, 1974-77 (cassettes)
Rock Drill (with Penelope Bailey), 1-5, 1980-85
Pages, 1-400+. Series One: 1987-1990. Series Two: April 1994-May 1998.
    Series Three and Four as a blogzine: 2005-ongoing.
Journal of British and Irish Innovative Poetry, with Scott Thurston, 2009-2014

Criticism by Robert Sheppard

Books

Far Language: Poetics and Linguistically Innovative Poetry 1978-1997 (Exeter: Stride Research Documents, 1999; second printing 2002)

The Poetry of Saying: British Poetry and its Discontents, 1950-2000 (Liverpool: Liverpool University Press, 2005)

Iain Sinclair (Plymouth: Northcote House, 2007)

When Bad Times Made for Good Poetry: Episodes in the History of the Poetics of Innovation (Exeter: Shearsman, 2011)

The Meaning of Form in Contemporary Innovative Poetry (London: Palgrave, 2016)

Articles and Book Chapters

'The Bathwater and the Baby: A Formalist-Humanism', *Reality Studios*, 3.3 (1981), 53-55

'Working the Work: Notes Towards and Beyond *Internal Exile*', *First Offense*, 3 (1988), 46-49

'Theoretical Practice', *Pages 65-72*, 1988, 65-66

'Re-working the Work', *First Offense*, 6 (1990)*

'New British Poetry in the 1980s', *Tyuonyi*, 6-7 (August 1990); reprinted in *Poesie Europe* (Frankfurt), December 1994, pp. 130-31

'Recognition and Discovery in the Eighties', *Fragmente*, 2 (Autumn 1990), 208-10

'Afterword' (with Adrian Clarke), *Floating Capital: New Poets from London*, ed. by Robert Sheppard and Adrian Clarke (Elmwood, Connecticut: Potes and Poets, 1991), pp. 121-25

'The Poet as the Letter C' (Cobbing), *Fragmente*, 4 (February 1992), 88-91

'The Necessary Business of Allen Fisher' (Introduction), in *Future Exiles*, ed. by Allen Fisher, Brian Catling, and Bill Griffiths (London; Paladin, 1992), pp. 11-17

'British Poetry and its Discontents', in *Cultural Revolution: The Challenge of the Arts in the 1960s*, ed. by John Seed and Bart Moore-Gilbert (London and New York: Routledge, 1992), pp. 160-80

'De-Anglicising the Midlands: The European Context of Roy Fisher's *City*', *English*, 41.169 (Spring 1992), 49-70

'The Work of Paul Evans', in *The Empty Hill: Memories and Praises of Paul Evans (1945-1991)*, ed. by Lee Harwood and Paul Bailey (Hove: Skylark Press, 1992), pp. 72-78

'Lee Harwood and the Poetics of the Open Work', in *The New British Poetries: The Scope of the Possible*, ed. by Robert Hampson and Peter Barry (Manchester: Manchester University Press, 1993), pp. 216-33

'Poetic Sequencing and the New: Twentieth Century Blues', *Jacket 9*, October 1999, <http://jacketmagazine.com/09/shep-shep.html> [accessed 7 September 2018]

'A Gap at the Heart of Things: The Poetics of David Miller', in *At the Heart of Things: The Poetry and Prose of David Miller*, ed. by Rupert Loydell (Exeter: Stride, 1994), pp. 16-20

'Artifice and the Everyday World: Poetry in the 1970s', in *The Arts in the 1970s: Cultural Closure?*, ed. by Bart Moore-Gilbert (London and New York, Routledge, 1994), pp. 129-51

'Bob Cobbing: Sights and Soundings', *AND*, 9 (July 1995), 87-92; republished on *Jacket 9* <http://jacketmagazine.com/09/shep-cobb.html> [accessed 13 August 2018]; partly reprinted in *Bob Pub*, to accompany the exhibition *Bob Cobbing: Bill Jubobe*, CHELSEA space, London, 2014

'Adhesive Hymns: Creative Linkage in the Work of Ulli Freer', *Pages 362-380* (January 1996), 363-67; republished on *Jacket 9* <http://jacketmagazine.com/09/shep-freer.html> [accessed 13 August 2018]

'Linking the Unlinkable', *Pages 362-380* (January 1996), 379-80; reprinted in *Generator*, 7, vol. 2 (April 1996), 52

'Tune Me Gold: Notes on the Total Technique of Maggie O'Sullivan, *First Offense*, 10 (April 1996)*

'Biblioklast! Bob Cobbing: Text: Book: Performance, in *The Artist's Book Yearbook 1996-97* (Stanmore: Magpie Press, 1996), 65-70

'Negative Definitions: Talk for the Subvoicive Colloquium, London 1997', *Sulfur*, 42 (May 1998), 180-85

'Performance: Trackings and Projections', *AND*, 10 (September 1998), 61

'Elsewhere and Everywhere: Other New (British) Poetries', *Critical Survey*, 10.1 (1998), 17-32

'A thing or two upon the page', in *Word Score Utterance Choreography*, ed. by Bob Cobbing and Lawrence Upton (London: Writers Forum, 1998), unpaginated

'The Poetics of Writing; The Writing of Poetics', *Creative Writing Conference 1999, Proceedings* (Sheffield Hallam University, 1999), pp. 99-109

'The Poetics of Poetics: Charles Bernstein and Allen Fisher and the Poetic Thinking That Results', *Symbiosis*, 3.1 (April 1999), 77-92

'Making Forms with Remarks', in *The Thing About Roy Fisher: Critical Studies*, ed. by John Kerrigan and Peter Robinson (Liverpool: Liverpool University Press, 2000), pp. 128-48

'Freedom Forms', in *News for the Ear*, pp. 84-85, by Robert Sheppard and Peter Robinson (Exeter: Stride, 2000)

'A Bloated Bubble A: Cobbing's Third *ABC*', in *For Bob Cobbing: A Celebration*, ed. by Lawrence Upton (London: Mainstream, 2000), unpaginated

'The Necessity of Poetics', *Pores*, 2001 <http://www.pores.bbk.ac.uk/1/ Robert%20Sheppard,%20%27The%20Necessity%20of%20Poetics%27. htm> [accessed 13 August 2018]

'The Performing and the Performed', *How 2*, 2002*

'Poetry and Ethics: The Saying and the Said in the Linguistically Innovative Poetry of Tom Raworth', *Critical Survey*, 14.2 (2002), 75-88

'Whose Lives Does the Government Affect?: Looking Back at *West Wind*', in *Removed for Further Study: The Poetry of Tom Raworth*, ed. by Nate Dorward (Willowdale, Ont., The Gig, 2003), pp. 192-203

'Beyond Anxiety: Legacy or Miscegenation', *Boxkite: A Journal of Writing and Poetics*, 3-4 (2003-4), 283-88

'Try Something Different' (with Scott Thurston), in *The Road to Somewhere: A Creative Writing Companion*, ed. by Robert Graham and others (Basingstoke, Palgrave, 2005); 2nd edn, pp. 194-203

'When Bad Times Made for Good Poetry: Iain Sinclair's Autistic Poses', in *Eseje o Wspolczesnej Poezji Brytyskiej i Irlandzkiej*, ed. by David Malcolm (Gdansk: Wydawnictwo Uiwesytetu Gadanskiego, 2005), pp. 104-18

'A Carafe, a Blue Guitar, Beyonding Art: Krzysztof Ziarek and the Avant-Garde', in *Avant-Post: The Avant-Garde Under "Post-" Conditions*, ed. by Louis Armand (Prague: Litteraria Pragensia, 2006), pp. 264-80

'Everything Connects: The Cultural Poetics', in *City Visions: The Work of Iain Sinclair*, ed. by Robert Bond and Jenny Bavidge (Newcastle upon Tyne, Cambridge Scholars Press, 2007), pp. 32-43

'Public Poetics: The Manifesto of the Poetry Society', in *Poetry and Public Language*, ed. by Tony Lopez and Anthony Calechu (Exeter: Shearsman Books, 2007), pp. 231-43

'Introduction', in *The Salt Companion to Lee Harwood*, ed. by Robert Sheppard (Cambridge: Salt, 2007), pp. 1-7

'It's a Long Road', in *The Salt Companion to Lee Harwood*, ed. by Robert Sheppard (Cambridge: Salt, 2007), pp. 18-34

'Poetics as Conjecture and Provocation: An Inaugural Lecture Delivered on 13 March 2007 at Edge Hill University', *New Writing: The International Journal for the Practice and Theory of Creative Writing*, 5.1 (2008), 3-26

'Critical Tuning: Radio Interference and Interruption as a Poetics for Writing', *VLAK*, 1.1 (2010), 62-5

'Experiment in Practice and Speculation in Poetics', eds. Peter Middleton and Nicky Marsh, *Teaching Modernist Poetry* (Basingstoke: Palgrave Macmillan, 2010), pp. 158-69

'The Colony at the Heart of the Empire: Bob Cobbing and Mid-1980s London', in *Hidden Agendas: Unreported Poetics*, ed. by Louis Armand (Prague: Litteria Pragensia, 2010), pp. 29-47

'Talk: The Poetics of Maggie O'Sullivan', in *The Salt Companion to Maggie O'Sullivan*, ed. by Chris Hamilton-Emery (Salt: Cambridge, 2011), pp. 154-78

'Stefan Themerson and the Theatre of Semantic Poetry', in *Eseje o Wspólczesnej Poezji Brytyjskiej i Irlandzkiej*, ed. by Blaim, Ludmiły Gruszewskiej, and David Malcolm (Gdańsk: Wydawnictwo Uniwersytetu Gdańskiego, Ludmi, 2011), pp. 245-63

'Linguistically Wounded: The Poetical Scholarship of Veronica Forrest-Thomson', in *The Writer in the Academy: Creative Interfrictions*, ed. by Richard Marggraf Turley (Cambridge: Boydell and Brewer, 2011), pp. 133-55

'Reflections on Reflection: Supplementary Discourses in Creative Writing Teaching in the UK', in *Teaching Creative Writing*, ed. by Heather Beck (Basingstoke: Palgrave, 2012), pp. 111-15

'Poetics and the Manifesto: On Pierre Joris and Adrian Clarke', *Jacket2*, August 2014 <https://jacket2.org/article/poetics-and-manifesto> [accessed 13 August 2018]

'A Voice Smears Across a Screen: Material Engagement with Form, Forms, and Forming', in *Torque 1: Mind. Language. Technology.*, ed. by Nathan Jones and Sam Skinner (London and Liverpool: Torque Editions, 2014), pp. 166-70. Available at: <http://torquetorque.net/wp-content/uploads/Torque1MindLanguageAndTechnology.pdf> [accessed 13 August 2018]

'Artifice and Artificers: The Meaning of Form in the Work of Christopher Middleton', *The Wolf*, 31 (Winter 2014), 87-94

'An Alphabet of Effects: Introduction', Bob Cobbing, *ABC in Sound*, 5th edn (London: Veer, 2015), unpaginated; partly reprinted in *Boooook: The Life and Work of Bob Cobbing*, ed. by William Cobbing and Rosie Cooper (London: Occasional Papers, 2015), p. 46

'Took Chances in London Traffic', in *Clasp: Late Modernist Poetry in London in the 1970s*, ed. by Robert Hampson and Ken Edwards (Bristol: Shearsman, 2016), pp. 115-18

'Taking Form: Experimental and Avant Garde Forms', in *The Portable Poetry Workshop*, ed. by Nigel McLoughlin (Basingstoke: Palgrave Macmillan, 2017), pp. 76-84

'John Seed's Poetics of the Punctum: From Manchester to the "Mayhew Project"', in *Poetics and Praxis 'After' Objectivism*, ed. by W. Scott Howard and Broc Rossell (Iowa City: University of Iowa Press, 2018), pp. 82-98

'"*Era il giorno ch'al sol si scoloraro*": A derivative dérive into/out of Petrarch's Sonnet 3', in *Translating Petrarch's Poetry: L'Aura del Petrarca from the Quattrocento to the 21st Century*, ed. by Carole Birkan-Berz, Guillaume Coatalen, and Thomas Vuong (Oxford: Legenda, forthcoming 2019)

Selected Reviews and Miscellaneous Pieces

'Jeremy Spencer's Albatross/Bognor' (with Peter Guild), *New Musical Express*, 11 January 1975, p. 35

'Peter Redgrove's *Sons of My Skin / Selected Poems 1954-1974*', *Poetry Information*, 14 (1975), 36-37

'Ezra Pound Reads His Cantos: The World's Great Poets, Vol II' and 'Adrian Henri' (LP recordings), *Poetry Survey*, 2 (1977), 5-6

'Reading Prynne and Others' [Prynne, Forrest-Thomson, and Ackroyd], *Reality Studios*, 2.2 (1979), 25-27

'Review of Iain Sinclair's *Suicide Bridge* "A Boom of the Furies"', *Iron*, 29 (1980), 23-24; republished as 'Afterword', in Iain Sinclair, *Suicide Bridge* (Cheltenham: Skylight Press, 2013) pp. 199-202

'Tom Pickard's *Hero Dust*', *Chock*, 5 (1980), unpaginated

'The Thing About Roy Fisher', *Kudos*, 6 (1980)*

'Roy Fisher's *Poems 1955-1980*', *Rock Drill*, 2 (1981), pp. 18 and 20

'Far Language: Barry MacSweeney's *Odes*', *Reality Studios*, 3.2 (January-March 1981), 30-32

'Paul Evans' *The Manual for the Organization of Perfect Tourneys*', *Iron*, 34 (1982)*

'Nothing: or Ourselves' [Carolyn Forché's *The Country Between Us*], *PN Review* 35, 10.3 (January-February 1984), 75-76

'The Other Tradition' [Marjorie Perloff's *The Poetics of Indeterminacy*], *PN Review* 32, 9.6 (July-August 1983), 63

'Anglo-American Poetry: The Work of Paul Evans', *Ninth Decade*, 1 (June 1983)*

'The Unknowable Symphony' [John Ash's *The Goodbyes*], *PN Review* 37, 10.5 (March-April 1984), 54-55

'Taking and Grafting' [Edwin Morgan's *Grafts/Takes*], *PN Review* 37, 10.5 (March-April 1984), 52

'Humanism, Holy Terror and Sympathy' (John Freeman), *The Many Review*, 2 April 1984*

'Quoof Reading' [Paul Muldoon's *Quoof*], *PN Review* 41, 11.3 (September-November 1985), 69

'The Probity of Language' [Asa Benveniste's *Throw Out the Life Line, Lay Out the Corse: Poems 1965-1985* and Anthony Howell's *Notions of a Mirror*], *PN Review* 42, 11.4 (March-April 1985), 60-61

'Discovering The British Dissonance' [Kingsley Weatherhead's *The British Dissonance*]', *PN Review* 44, 11.6 (July-August 1985), 65

'Not Venturing Abroad' [various], *New Statesman*, 31 May 1985, pp. 29-30

'Sudden Entries' [Robert Creeley's *Memories* and *Mirrors* and John Welch's *Out Walking*], *PN Review* 45, 12.1 (September-October 1985), 81

'Growing Up' [Hugo Williams' *Writing Home*), *New Statesman*, 11 October 1985, p. 36

'DIY' [Peter Finch's *How to Publish your Poetry* and *Getting your Poetry Published*, and *Ken Edwards and Reality Studios*, ed. by P. Bailey), *PN Review* 49, 12.5 (May-June 1986), 51-52

'Timeless Identities' [Roy Fisher's *A Furnace*], *Times Literary Supplement*, 20 June 1986, p. 677

'Metaphysical Humanism' [*Not Comforts//But Vision: Essays on the Poetry of George Oppen*], *PN Review* 50, 12.6 (July-August 1986), 53-54

'Irregular Actions' [Allen Fisher's *Unpolished Mirrors, Brixton Fractals*, and *Spanner 25: Allen Fisher Necessary Business*], *PN Review* 53, 13.3 (January-February 1987), 95-96

[Lee Harwood: *Monster Masks* and *Dream Quilt*], *Reality Studios*, 8 (1986), 90-92

'The Micropathology of the Sign', in Bob Cobbing, *Processual* (London: Writers Forum, 1986), unpaginated

'The Alternative Voice' [Henri, McGough, Angels of Fire, Pickard, MacSweeney], *Times Literary Supplement*, 23 January 1987, p. 92

'They Fuck You Up' [post-Movement poets], *New Statesman*, 21 August 1987, p. 22

'Fast Verse Outlets' [Lasdun, Duffy, Jamie, Craig, and Burnett], *New Statesman*, 29 January 1988, pp. 31-32

'Beyond Revival', *Pages 49-56* (January 1988), 49-51

'Poets from the Front Line' [Ken Smith, Reading, Murray, Reynolds, and Duncan], *New Statesman*, 13 May 1988, pp. 31-32

'Gravity-haunted Logos', *New Statesman/New Society*, 15 July 1988, pp. 41-42

'Flesh, blood and family', *New Statesman and Society*, 23 December 1988, p. 36

'Utopia Revisited' [John Ash's *Disbelief*], *PN Review* 63, 15.1 (September-October 1988), 57-58

Three entries: John Ash, Christopher Middleton, Tom Raworth, in *The Cambridge Guide to Literature in English*, ed. by Ian Ousby (Cambridge: Cambridge University Press, 1988)

'Need for Responsible Criticism of Poetry', Letter to *The Independent*, 10 November 1988; republished in *Pages 129-136* (1988), 129*

'Commitment to Openness' [Raworth, Fisher, and Harwood], *Times Literary Supplement*, 10 March 1989, p. 257

'Imperfect Knowledge: Introduction', *Association of Little Presses Catalogue 1990-91* (1990), unpaginated

'This is, I suppose…' *Responses*, 2 (Robert Sheppard edition; February 1991), unpaginated

'The title…' *Responses*, 6 (Maggie O'Sullivan edition; October 1991), unpaginated

'Positioned Responses', *Angel Exhaust*, 8 (December 1992), 113-17

'General Editorial', *Pages 219-238* (April 1994), 219-20

'Spanner in the Scanner' and 'The Masked Poet and the Blindfold Test', *A4 Assemblage, Reponses*, 20 (September 1994), unpaginated

'Recording and Informing a Generation' (Eric Mottram obituary), *Pages 280-281*, 1995, 280-81

'*The Art of Practice: 45 Contemporary Poets*', and '*A Curious Architecture*', *Stride*, 37 (1995)*

'A Thumbnail', *West Coast Line,* number 17 (29/2) (Fall 1995), p. 112

'Letter to Ken Edwards', *Pages 381-396* (February 1996), 393-94

'Re-tooling for the Alternatives' [report from *An International Poetry Conference/Festival, The New England Center, Durham, New Hampshire, 29 August–2 September 1996*], *PN Review* 114, 23.4 (March-April 1997), 12-14

'Afterword to *Pages*, Second Series', *Pages 421-445* (May 1998), 421

'Poetic Risk', *Gare du Nord*, 2.2 (June 1999)*

'Dear Lee…', Introduction to *Birthday Boy: A Present for Lee Harwood* (Liverpool: Ship of Fools, 1999), unpaginated

'Invitation' (with Peter Robinson), in *News for the Ear*, ed. by Robert Sheppard and Peter Robinson (Exeter: Stride, 2000), p. 7

Three entries: Bob Cobbing, Iain Sinclair, Tom Raworth, *Contemporary Poets* (London: St Martin's Press, 2001)

'New Connections', *Stride*, 2002*

'Guessed Disappearance' [Iain Sinclair and Rachel Lichtenstein, *Rodinsky's Room*, and Iain Sinclair, *Sorry Meniscus: Excursions to the Millennium Dome*], *Stride*, 2002 <https://www.stridemagazine.co.uk/2002/august/sinclair.htm> [accessed 11 September 2018]

'Bob Cobbing', *Guardian*, 7 October 2002, p. 20

'Disobedient Versions' [Sinclair], *Terrible Work*, December 2002, nla

'Fugueurs in a Landscape' [Iain Sinclair's *London Orbital*], *PN Review* 149, 29.3 (January 2003), 86

'Supplementary Discourses in Creative Writing Teaching' [with Scott Thurston], English Subject Centre, 2003 <http://english.heacademy.ac.uk/2015/10/26/supplementary-discourses-in-creative-writing-teaching-edge-hill/> [accessed 11 September 2018]

'DRACULA plc' [Iain Sinclair's *White Goods*], *Poetry Salzburg Review*, 5 (Autumn 2003), 43-48

'Where Threads of Death', [Iain Sinclair], *Pores*, 2004*

'Coincidences and Contraries: Two extracts for Douglas Oliver', *Intercapillary Space*, 2006 <http://intercapillaryspace.blogspot.com/2006/07/coincidence-and-contraries-two.html> [accessed 11 September 2018]

'Poets Behaving Badly' [Peter Barry's *Poetry Wars: British Poetry of the 1970s and the Battle of Earls Court*], *Jacket*, 31, October 2006 <http://jacketmagazine.com/31/sheppard-barry.html> [accessed 21 September 2018]

[review] *Ideas of Space in Contemporary Poetry* by Iain Davidson, *English*,
    56.216 (2007), 377-80
'Write Everything Down; i.m. Lisa Ratcliffe', *Black Market Review*, 2009, nla
Robert Sheppard and Scott Thurston, 'Editorial', *Journal of British and Irish
    Innovative Poetry*, 1.1 (2009), 3-9
[review] *Meaning Performance* by Tony Lopez, *Journal of British and Irish
    Innovative Poetry*, 1.1 (2009), 103-7
'On "Stops and Stations": from a Tribute to Roy Fisher', *Eyewear*, October
    2010 <http://toddswift.blogspot.com/2010/11/sheppard-on-fisher.
    html> [accessed 11 September 2018]
'Angela Leighton's *On Form: Poetry, Aestheticism, and the Legacy of a Word*,
    Journal of British and Irish Innovative Poetry, 3.1 (March 2011), 63-66
'Caroline Bergvall/Carol Watts', *Poetry Wales*, 47.2 (2011), 62-64
'Mimeo Memes' [*Mimeo Mimeo*], *Journal of British and Irish Innovative
    Poetry*, 4.1 (March 2012), 106-08
'Evading the Canon' [*The Andrew Crozier Reader*], *Stride*, April 2012
    <http://stridemagazine.co.uk/Stride%20mag%202012/April%202012/
    Andrew%20Crozier.shepp.htm> [accessed 11 September 2018]
'Voices' [CDs by Julie Tippetts and Juxtavoices], *Stride*, August 2013
    <https://www.stridemagazine.co.uk/Stride%20mag%202013/
    August2013/Tippetts.sheppard.htm> [accessed 11 September 2018]
'Ceaseless Curiosity' [Allen Fisher's *The Marvels of Lambeth*], *Stride*,
    August 2013 <http://stridemagazine.co.uk/Stride%20mag%202013/
    August2013/sheppard.fisher.htm> [accessed 11 September 2018]
'A slow game' (Harwood), *Stride*, 2014 <https://www.stridemagazine.co.uk/
    Stride%20mag%202014/december2014/The%20Orchid%20Boat.htm>
    [accessed 11 September 2018]
'Glancing Off' [Raworth], *Poetry Salzburg Review*, 28 (Autumn 2015), 46-53
'Rosmarie Waldrop's *Gap Gardening*', *The Wolf*, 34 (Winter 2016), 62-67

Interviews Conducted

'Stories: Being an Information: An Interview,' in *Robert Creeley: The Poet's
    Workshop*, ed. by Carroll F. Terrell (Orono, Maine: The National Poetry
    Foundation, 1984), pp. 35-56
With Roy Fisher: *Turning the Prism* (Toad's Damp Press, 1985); partly re-
    printed in *Interviews Through Time and Selected Prose*, ed. by Tony Frazer
    (Kentisbeare: Shearsman Books, 2000), pp. 76-89
'So It Shifts: An Interview with Lee Harwood', in *The Salt Companion to Lee
    Harwood*, ed. by Robert Sheppard (Cambridge: Salt, 2007), pp. 8-17

Internet Resources

Personal website: robertsheppard.weebly.com
Website of the European Union of Imaginary Authors <euioa.weebly.com>
Blog: *Pages* <robertsheppard.blogspot.com> (*Pages* contains over 750 posts, featuring poetry, poetics, criticism, comment, and links. It is archived by the British Library.)
'*Pages, 1987–1990*, (ed. by Robert Sheppard)', *Reissues, Jacket2* <https://jacket2.org/reissues/pages> [accessed 17 August 2018]

Criticism on Robert Sheppard

Books

Alison Mark, *Veronica Forrest-Thomson and Language Poetry* (Plymouth: Writers and their Works, Northcote House, 2001)
Andrew Duncan, *The Failure of Conservatism in British Poetry* (Cambridge: Salt, 2004)
Peter Barry, *Poetry Wars: British Poetry of the 1970s and the Battle of Earls Court* (Cambridge: Salt, 2006)
Charles Bernstein, 'Fraud's Phantoms: A Brief Yet Unreliable Account of Fighting Fraud with Fraud', in *Attack of the Difficult Poems* (Chicago: Chicago University Press, 2011), pp. 206-26
Rupert Loydell, 'Poetic Revolution: Robert Sheppard's *The Education of Desire* & Ken Edwards' *Good Science*', in *Encouraging Signs* (Bristol: Shearsman, 2013), pp. 135-42
Scott Thurston, ed., *An Educated Desire: Robert Sheppard at 60* (Newton-le-Willows: Knives, Forks and Spoons Press, 2015)
Andrew Duncan, *A Poetry Boom 1990-2010* (Bristol: Shearsman, 2016)
Mark Scroggins, 'The 'net/(k)not-work(s)' of *Twentieth Century Blues*', in *The Mathematical Sublime: Writing about Poetry* (The Mad Hat Press, 2016), pp. 111-20
Simon Perril, 'High Late-Modernists or Postmodernists? Vanguard and Linguistically Innovative Poetries since 1960', in *The Cambridge Companion to British Poetry, 1945-2010*, ed. by Edward Larrissy (Cambridge: Cambridge University Press, 2016), pp. 82-98

Articles

Adrian Clarke, '*Returns* and After: The Recent Work of Robert Sheppard', *Angel Exhaust*, 7 (Summer 1987)

Scott Thurston, '*Angel Exhaust* Magazine: New Poetry from Cambridge and London', *Cascando*, 2 (1993), pp. 105-08

Alison Mark, '"Flashlights Around a Subjectivity": Melting Borders and Robert Sheppard's *The Flashlight Sonata*', *First Offense*, 9 (1994), 60-66

Tim Woods, 'Memory and Ethics in Contemporary Poetry', *English: Journal of the English Association*, 49.194 (Summer 2000), 155-65 <https://doi.org/10.1093/english/49.194.155>

Scott Thurston, 'The Poet as Critic, Criticism as Poetics: On Barrett Watten and Robert Sheppard', University of Salford Library, 2009 <http://usir.salford.ac.uk/2384/1/The_Critic_as_Artist_Scott_Thurston.pdf> [accessed 9 October 2018]

Scott Thurston, 'Innovative Poetry in Britain Today', *Revista Canaria De Estudios Ingleses*, 60 (April 2010), 15-30

Lytton Smith, 'From the Other Coast', *Los Angles Review of Books*, 2 December 2011 <https://lareviewofbooks.org/article/from-the-other-coast/> [accessed 10 September 2018]

James Keery, 'A Fine Bold Wicked Thing to Do' [*When Bad Times Made for Good Poetry*], *PN Review* 209, 39.3 (January-February 2013), 44-46

Reviews

Jeff Nuttall, 'In the beginning was the word' [*Dedicated to You But You Weren't Listening*], *Guardian*, 6 October 1979

Jeff Nuttall, 'In praise of Northern Pigs' [*The Frightened Summer*], *Guardian*, 21 March 1981

Tony Baker, '*The Frightened Summer*', *Angel Exhaust*, 4 (1981), unpaginated

Norman Swinburne, 'Making Bacon...' [*The Frightened Summer*], *Angel Exhaust*, 4 (1981), unpaginated

John Lees, 'Robert G. Sheppard' [*The Frightened Summer*], *Iron*, 37 (September-November, 1982)*

Ken Edwards, 'Robert Sheppard: *Returns: Texts 1980-84*', *City Limits*, 17-23 January 1986, p. 52

John Lees, '*Rock Drill...*' [*Returns/Rock Drill*], *Iron*, 49 (June-September 1986), 70-71

Michael Horovitz, 'More New Brits' [*The New British Poetry*], *Poetry Review*, 31 October 1988

Peter Porter, 'New vamps for old', *Observer* [*The New British Poetry*], 22 January 1989

Martin Bright, 'Robert Sheppard...' [*Letter from the Blackstock Road* and *Internal Exile*], *City Limits*, 4-11 May 1989, p. 64

Peter Conway, 'Strange Days...' [*Daylight Robbery*], *Flesh Mouth* (March 1991)

Mark Robinson, [*Daylight Robbery*], *Scratch*, 5 (April 1991), 42

Norman Jope, '*Daylight Robbery*', *Memes*, 5 (May 1991), 44

Jeff Nuttall, 'Bookends' [*Daylight Robbery*], *Time Out*, 19-26 June 1991, p. 51

Jeff Nuttall, 'Bookends' [*Floating Capital*], *Time Out*, 18-25 September 1991, p. 49

Mark Robinson, [*Floating Capital*], *Scratch*, 6 (Autumn 1991), 51

Norman Jope, '*Codes and Diodes*' (and *Cannibal Club*), 6 (December 1991), 37-38

Andrew Duncan, 'Pulse strings out beat of intermittent presence' [*Daylight Robbery* and *Floating Capital*], *Fragmente*, 4 (1991), 91-97

Martin Stannard, [*The Flashlight Sonata*], *The Wide Skirt*, 24 (1994), 54-55

A. C. Evans, 'The Memory, The Sensation, The Sonata' [*The Flashlight Sonata*], *Stride*, 36 (1994)*

Norman Jope, 'Reviewed by…' [*The Flashlight Sonata, Transit Depots/Empty Diaries, net/(k)not/-work(s)*], *Memes*, 10 (1994), 25-26

Kerry Sowerby, listings and reviews [*The Flashlight Sonata* and *Twentieth Century Blues*], *Ramraid Extraordinaire*, 3 (1994)*

Tim Allen, '*The Flashlight Sonata*', *Terrible Work*, 3 (Spring 1994), 34-35

Keith Jebb, 'Reviews' [*net/(k)not/-work(s), Icarus, Logos*], *Odyssey*, 17 (1994), 50-52

Steve Sneyd, [*Logos on Kimonos*], *Data Dump*, 10 (1994), 4

Keith Jebb, *Strategies for Syntax* [*Fucking Time* and *Free Fists*], *Poetry Quarterly Review* (Winter 1995)

Paul Donnelly, '*The Flashlight Sonata*', *Ambit*, 139 (1995), 62-63

James Keery, 'Twentieth Century Blues' [*The Flashlight Sonata, Pages 219-238*, and *Transit Depots/Empty Diaries*], *PN Review* 107, 22.3 (January-February 1996), 49-51

Anonymous, *The Lores, The Buzz*, 10 (1998)*

Sam Smith, Untitled review of *Empty Diaries, Zine*, 17 October 1998, 26-27

Scott Thurston, 'Robert Sheppard: *Empty Diaries*', *Tears in the Fence*, 23 (Summer 1999), 102-03

John Goodby, 'Barnadine's Reply' [*The Thing About Roy Fisher* and *News for the Ear*], *Poetry Review*, 90.4 (Winter 2000), 67-70

John Mingay, 'Plato, The Sculptor and the Syntactical Guerrilla' [*The Lores*], *Stride*, 2003 <https://www.stridemagazine.co.uk/2003/may/plato.htm> [accessed 13 August 2018]

Edmund Hardy, '*The Lores*', *Terrible Work*, 2004*

Scott Thurston, 'Indoor Utopia Welfare Pastoral' [*The Lores*], *Tears in the Fence*, 37 (Spring 2004); reposted on *Litter* <http://www.leafepress.com/litter5/sheppardThurston/thurstonSheppard.html> [accessed 13 August 2018]

John Muckle, 'Like a Potato' [*Tin Pan Arcadia*], *Poetry Review*, 94.4 (Winter 2004-5), 93-99

Nate Dorward, 'Two from Salt' [*Tin Pan Arcadia*], *The Gig*, 18 (May 2005), 63

David Kennedy, 'Open and Shut' [*The Poetry of Saying*], *PN Review* 168, 32.4 (March-April 2006), pp. 62-63

Alice Lenkiewicz, [*Complete Twentieth Century Blues*], *Neon Highway*, 13 (2006), 24

Cliff Yates, '*The Poetry of Saying*', *The North*, 38 (2006), 58-59

Scott Thurston, 'In Dialogue with Materials that Bleed' [*Tin Pan Arcadia* and *Hymns to the God in which my Typewriter Believes*], *Stride*, July 2006 <https://www.stridemagazine.co.uk/2006/July%202006/Tin%20Pan%20 Arcadia%20rev.htm> [accessed 13 August 2018]

Sam Rennes, '*A is for Apple for Teacher*' [*Risk Assessment*, with Rupert Loydell], *Stride*, 2007 <https://www.stridemagazine.co.uk/Stride%20 mag%202007/Feb%202007/risk%20assess%20rev.htm> [accessed 21 September 2018]

Patrick James Dunagan, 'No monster' [*The Salt Companion to Lee Harwood*], *Jacket*, 2008 <http://jacketmagazine.com/36/r-harwood-rb-dunagan. shtml> [accessed 13 August 2018]

Ian Davidson [*Complete Twentieth Century Blues*], *Poetry Wales*, 44.3 (2008-9), 64-66

Todd Nathan Thorpe, '"To educate desire," "to repurpose kitsch"' [*Complete Twentieth Century Blues*], *Jacket*, 2008<http://jacketmagazine.com/36/r-sheppard-rb-thorpe.shtml> [accessed 13 August 2018]

Paul Wright, '*Complete Twentieth Century Blues*', *Writers in Education*, 47 (Spring 2009), 93-96

Keith Jebb, 'Destabilising Poetries' [*Complete Twentieth Century Blues*], *Poetry Salzburg Review*, 16 (Autumn 2009), 106-113

John Muckle, 'A Ton of Feathers' [*Complete Twentieth Century Blues*], *PN Review* 187, 35.5 (May-June 2009), 67-69

Alan Baker, '*Warrant Error*', *Litter*, 2009 <http://www.leafepress.com/litter2/litterbug02/litterbug-sheppard.html> [accessed 13 August 2018]

Benjamin Keatinge, [*The Poetry of Saying*], *European English Messenger*, 18.1 (Spring 2009), 75-76

Steve Spence, 'An Assault Upon the Citadel' [*Warrant Error*], *Stride*, October 2009 <https://www.stridemagazine.co.uk/Stride%20mag2009/Oct%20 2009/Warrant%20Error%20.htm> [accessed 10 September 2018]

Rupert Loydell, 'Quiet Subversions' [*The Given*], *Stride* <https://www. stridemagazine.co.uk/Stride%20mag2010/Sept2010/Given%20review. htm> [accessed 10 September 2018]

Mandy Bloomfield, '*The Poetry of Saying*: British Poetry and its Discontents', *Journal of British and Irish Innovative Poetry*, 2.1 (2010)

Scott Thurston, 'Innovative Poetry in Britain Today', *Revista Canaria De Estudios Ingleses*, 60 (April 2010), 15-30

John Muckle, 'Muckle on Rowe and Sheppard', *Eyewear*, 30 August 2010 <http://toddswift.blogspot.com/2010/08/guest-review-muckle-on-rowe-and.html> [accessed 10 September]

John Challis, [*The Given*], *Hand + Star*, 2011, nla

Sean Colletti, 'Wandering Around' [*Berlin Bursts*], *Stride*, May 2011<https://www.stridemagazine.co.uk/Stride%20mag2011/May%202011/Klein-zahlerSheppard.htm> [accessed 10 September]

Alan Baker, '*The Given*', *Litter* 5, 2012

Christopher Madden, '*Berlin Bursts*', *The Wolf*, 26 (Spring 2012), 74-79

Ben Hickman, 'As One is Moved and Moves' [*Berlin Bursts*], *PN Review* 204, 38.4 (March-April 2012), 74-75

Lyndon Davies, [*A Translated Man*], *Poetry Wales*, 49.2 (Autumn 2013), 68-70

Michael Blackburn, 'Tradition, Traduction, and Truth' [*A Translated Man*], *Poetry Quarterly Salzburg*, 25 (Spring 2014), 148-55

Tom Jenks, [*A Translated Man*], *Tears in the Fence*, 59 (Spring 2014), 54-56

Andrew Oldham, 'Three Recent Poetry Collections' [*A Translated Man*], *Eyewear*, 1 May 2014 <http://toddswift.blogspot.com/2014/05/three-recent-poetry-collections.html> [accessed 10 September]

Ian Brinton, 'History or Sleep by Robert Sheppard (Shearsman Books)', *Tears in the Fence*, 23 November 2015 <https://tearsinthefence.com/2015/11/23/history-or-sleep-by-robert-sheppard-shearsman-books/> [accessed 10 September 2018]

Billy Mills, 'Three Shearsman Books by Mark Weiss, Robert Sheppard and Peter Philpott' [*A Translated Man*], *Elliptical Movements*, November 2015 <https://ellipticalmovements.wordpress.com/2015/11/01/three-shearsman-books-by-mark-weiss-robert-sheppard-and-peter-philpott-a-review/> [accessed 10 September 2018]

Steve Waling, 'Linguistic Transfiguration' [*The Drop* and *Unfinish*], *Stride*, 2016 <http://stridemagazine.blogspot.com/2016/08/lingsuistic-transfiguration.html> [accessed 10 September 2018]

Steve Waling, 'History or Sleep: Robert Sheppard, Shearsman', *Write Out Loud*, 29 January 2016 <https://www.writeoutloud.net/public/blogentry.php?blogentryid=54007> [accessed 10 September 2018]

Clark Allison, 'The Advert of Itself: Some Notes on Robert Sheppard's *History or Sleep*', *Stride*, November 2015 <https://www.stridemagazine.co.uk/Stride%20mag%202015/Nov%202015/Clark.Sheppard.htm> [accessed 10 September 2018]

Ian Brinton, 'The Drop by Robert Sheppard (Oystercatcher Press)', *Tears in the Fence*, 8 January 2016 <https://tearsinthefence.com/?s=The+Drop> [accessed 10 September 2018]

Anna Cathenka, 'Vaguely Repulsive Realism' [*History or Sleep*], *Stride*, 2016 <http://stridemagazine.blogspot.com/2016/10/vaguely-repulsive-realism.html> [accessed 10 September 2018]

Alan Baker, 'Two Oystercatchers' [*The Drop*], *Litter*, 8 (2016) <http://www.leafepress.com/litter8/baker/baker.html> [accessed 4 October 2018]

Nikolai Duffy '*History or Sleep* by Robert Sheppard', *The Wolf*, 33 (Spring 2016), 64-69

Charles May, 'Best British Short Stories 2016: Part I', *Reading the Story*, 1 August 2016 <https://may-on-the-short-story.blogspot.com/search?q=Robert+Sheppard> [accessed 10 September 2018]

Ian Brinton, 'The Meaning of Form in Contemporary Innovative Poetry (Palgrave Macmillan)', *Tears in the Fence*, October 2016 <https://tearsinthefence.com/2016/10/21/the-meaning-of-form-in-contemporary-innovative-poetry-palgrave-macmillan/> [accessed 10 September 2018]

Clark Allison, 'Perennial and Multifarious Forms: A Brief Response to Robert Sheppard's *The Meaning of Form in Contemporary Innovative Poetry* (Palgrave)', *Stride*, November 2016 <http://stridemagazine.blogspot.com/2016/11/perennial-and-multifarious-forms.html> [accessed 10 September 2018]

Callum Gardner, [*History or Sleep*], *Poetry Wales*, 52.3 (Spring 2017), 88-89

Alan Baker, '*Petrarch 3* – a derivate [sic] dérive', *Litter*, 2017 <http://www.leafepress.com/litter9/petrarch/petrarch.html> [accessed 4 October 2018]

Ian Brinton, '*Atlantic Drift* edited by James Byrne & Robert Sheppard (Arc Press & Edge Hill University Press)', *Tears in the Fence*, October 2017 <https://tearsinthefence.com/2017/10/01/atlantic-drift-edited-by-james-byrne-robert-sheppard-arc-press-edge-hill-university-press/> [accessed 10 September 2018]

Hilary Davies, 'What is the Wind Doing?' [*The Meaning of Form*], *PN Review* 237, 44.1 (September-October 2017), 69-70

Steve Waling, '*Atlantic Drift*: edited by James Byrne and Robert Sheppard, Arc', *Write Out Loud*, February 2018 <https://www.writeoutloud.net/public/blogentry.php?blogentryid=74386> [accessed 10 September 2018]

Peter Riley, 'Translation, Expanded Translation, Version, Mess', *Fortnightly Review*, 13 May 2018 <http://fortnightlyreview.co.uk/2018/03/translation-expanded/> [accessed 10 September 2018]

Billy Mills, 'Poetry after Brexit' [*Twitters for a Lark*], *Elliptical Movements*, 13 May 2018 <https://ellipticalmovements.wordpress.com/2018/05/13/poetry-after-brexit-some-recent-reading/> [accessed 10 September 2018]

Gareth Farmer, Review of *The Meaning of Form in Contemporary Innovative Poetry*, *Journal of British and Irish Innovative Poetry*, 10.1 (June 2018), 7 <http://doi.org/10.16995/biip.73>

Mary Jean Chan, [*Atlantic Drift*], *Poetry London*, 90 (Summer 2018), 46-7

Miscellaneous Responses and References

Michael Hoffman, 'The Prudence Farmer Award', *New Statesman*, 24 August 1984, pp. 21-22

Michael Horowitz, 'New Poetry', *The Independent*, 30 January 1987, p. 111

Ken Edwards, 'Some Younger Poets', introduction to 'Some Younger Poets', in *The New British Poetry 1968-88*, ed. by Gillian Allnutt, Fred D'Aguiar, Ken Edwards, and Eric Mottram (London: Paladin, 1988), pp. 265-70

'Responses to "Smokestack Lightning"', (by Glyn Purseglove, Stephen Pereira, Steve Vine, Judith Stevens, CJPS, Tony Rollinson, Kate Hodgkin, anon, in *Complete Responses,* February 1992, nla

Patricia Farrell, 'Material to the Event', in *Artist's Book Yearbook 1996-97* (London: Magpie Press, 1996), pp. 19-22

Keith Tuma, 'Robert Sheppard (b. 1955)', head-note in his *Anthology of Twentieth Century British and Irish Poetry* (Oxford and New York: Oxford University Press, 2001),

Johan de Wit, 'A Response to Robert Sheppard's *The Necessity of Poetics*', *Pores*, January 2002 <http://www.pores.bbk.ac.uk/1/index.html> [accessed 21 September 2018]

Iain Sinclair, comment in *Corridor8*, 2011*

Stephen Burt, 'LIKE: A speculative essay about poetry, simile, artificial intelligence, mourning, sex, rock and roll, grammar, and romantic love, William Shakespeare, Alan Turing, Rae Armantrout, Nick Hornby, Walt Whitman, William Carlos Williams, Lia Purpura, and Claire Danes', *American Poetry Review*, 2014 <https://dash.harvard.edu/bitstream/handle/1/22686179/BurtSelf2013.pdf?sequence=2&isAllowed=y> [accessed 10 September 2018]

Steve Spence, 'Finding Your Way', *Stride,* March 2016 <https://www.stridemagazine.co.uk/Stride%20mag%202016/March2016/PoetryBoom.Spence.htm> [accessed 10 September 2018]

John Seed, 'Six on the best: Some of Britain's top poets tell Andy Croft which collections impressed them over the last 12 months' (10 December 2018), *Morning Star* <https://www.morningstaronline.co.uk/a-1e85-Six-on-the-best> [accessed 10 September 2018]

Joey Francis, 'Conference Report: Robert Sheppard Symposium', *Journal of British and Irish Innovative Poetry*, 9.1, 2017 <http://doi.org/10.16995/biip.40>

Carol Rumens, 'Poem of the Week: "Prison Camp Violin, Riga"', *Guardian,* 23 July 2018 <https://www.theguardian.com/books/booksblog/2018/jul/23/poem-of-the-week-prison-camp-violin-riga-by-robert-sheppard> [accessed 17 August 2018]

Interviews

'An Interview with Robert Sheppard' [with Stephen Pereira], *Angel Exhaust*, 7
(Summer 1987), 17-24

'An Interview with Robert Sheppard' [with Jane March (Alice Lenkiewicz)],
Neon Highway, 7 (2003), pp.

'Signature and Ethics' [with Edmund Hardy], *Intercapillary Space*, 2006
<http://intercapillaryspace.blogspot.com/2006/06/signature-ethics.
html> [accessed 17 August 2018]

'The Postman Below the Window' [with Tim Allen], in *Don't Start Me Talk-
ing: Interviews with Contemporary Poets*, ed. by Tim Allen and Andrew
Duncan (Cambridge: Salt Publications, 2007), pp. 335-57

'Literary Netscapes: Web Poetry and Blogging: Graeme Harper Interviews
Robert Sheppard', in *Authors at Work: The Creative Environment, Essays
and Studies 2009*, ed. by Ceri Sullivan and Graeme Harper for the
English Association (Woodbridge: Boydell and Brewer for the English
Association, 2009), pp. 101-05

Alan Corkish Interviews Robert Sheppard (about the Edge Hill Poetry and
Poetics Research Group), *Erbacce*, 18 (2009), 3-9

'Even the Bad Times are Good' [with Rupert Loydell], *Stride,* January 2012
<http://www.stridebooks.co.uk/Stride%20mag%202012/Jan%202012/
rupertandrobertint.htm> [accessed 10 September 2018]; reprinted in
Rupert Loydell, *Encouraging Signs* (Bristol: Shearsman, 2013), pp. 188

'*The Wolf* Interview' [with Christopher Madden], *The Wolf*, 29 (Winter
2013), 59-68

'An Interview with Robert Sheppard' [with Anamaría Crowe Serrano],
Colony, 2014, nla

'On *Pages*: An Interview Between Robert Sheppard and Joey Frances',
Jacket2, 2017 <https://jacket2.org/commentary/pages> [accessed 17
August 2018]

Contributors

Gilbert Adair co-founded (with John Gibbens and Patricia Farrell) Sub-Voicive poetry reading series in 1980 and curated it until 1992. He has published fifteen books / chapbooks of poetry, most recently *Syzem* Book One (2014), a formal / cultural translation of Blake's *Milton*; Book Two is due in 2019. He is currently working on *h c e*, a nod to Joyce but also to the pidgin spoken in Hawai'i, where he currently lives: Hawaiian Creole English.

Joanne Ashcroft won the *Poetry Wales* Purple Moose Prize for poetry in 2013 and her pamphlet *Maps and Love Songs for Mina Loy* is published by Seren. She is currently a research student at Edge Hill University where she has also taught poetry and fiction. She is interested in poetry in which sound manifests as the dominant textual register. Her research explores the work of Geraldine Monk, Bill Griffiths and Maggie O'Sullivan as sound-rich poetry. She organises the Poetry and Poetics Research Group at Edge Hill University.

Charles Bernstein is the author of *Near/Miss* (University of Chicago Press, 2018), *Pitch of Poetry* (Chicago, 2016), and *Recalculating* (Chicago, 2013). He is Donald T. Regan Professor of English and Comparative Literature at the University of Pennsylvania, where he is co-director of PennSound.

James Byrne is a poet, editor and translator. He edited *The Wolf* from 2002-2015. With Robert Sheppard, he co-edited *Atlantic Drift: An Anthology of Poetry and Poetics* (Edge Hill University Press/Arc, 2017). His poetry collections include *Everything Broken Up Dances* (Tupelo, 2015) and *White Coins* (Arc Publications, 2015). *The Caprices*, his next book, includes creative responses to the works of Francisco Goya and will be published by Arc in September 2019. Byrne has taught with Sheppard at Edge Hill University since 2015.

Adrian Clarke was first published by Eric Mottram in the *Poetry Review* and re-emerged in the 1980s with collections from Actual Size and Writers Forum, co-editing *Floating Capital: new poets from London* with Robert Sheppard and subsequently the wildly irregular AND magazine with Bob Cobbing. He is now a member of the Veer Books editorial collective.

Ailsa Cox is a short story writer. She is widely publishing in magazines and anthologies, including *Best British Short Stories 2014*, *The End* (Unthank Books) and *The Mechanics Institute Review*. Her collection, *The Real Louise*, is published by Headland Press. Other books include *Writing Short Stories* (Routledge) and *Alice Munro* (Northcote House). She is Professor of Short Fiction at Edge Hill University where she taught, for many years, with Robert Sheppard.

Nikolai Duffy is the author of *The Little Shed of Various Lamps* (Very Small Kitchen), *Up the Creek* (Knives Forks and Spoons), *Notes for a Performance* (Wild Pansy

Press) and *Relative Strangeness: Reading Rosmarie Waldrop* (Shearsman). He is also the editor of Rosmarie Waldrop's *Gap Gardening: Selected Poems* (New Directions). He has written numerous articles on experimental poetics and literary theory. He is the founding editor of Like This Press, a small publishing company specialising in limited edition handmade books. At Manchester Metropolitan University he is Assistant Head of the Postgraduate Arts and Humanities Centre and Senior Lecturer in American Literature.

Patricia Farrell is a poet and visual artist. Her work is published in magazines and collections, as well as individual pamphlets: most recently, *High Cut* (Leafe Press). She completed a PhD thesis in 2011 on poetic artifice in philosophical writing. Her collection, *The Zechstein Sea*, was published by Shearsman Books in 2013. Her next collection, *Logic for Little Girls*, is forthcoming from Knives Forks and Spoons Press.

Allen Fisher is a poet, painter and art historian, he lives in Hereford. He performed and printed with *Fluxus* in the 1970s, published New London Pride editions and co-published Aloes Books and edits the journal *Spanner*. He studied drawing and colour with the Thubrons at Goldsmiths' College, taught at Hereford College of Art, was head of art at Roehampton and head of contemporary arts at Manchester Metropolitan University where he is Emeritus Professor of Poetry & Art. His recent publications include essays in *Imperfect Fit: Aesthetics, Facture & Perception* (University of Alabama)*; loggerheads,* a book of poetry, prose and drawings, the complete poetry of *Gravity as a consequence of shape* (Reality Street Editions)*;* a second edition of the collected poetry of the *PLACE* books (Reality Street Editions) and a reprint of *Ideas of the culture dreamed of* (The Literary Pocket Book).

Alan Halsey's *Selected Poems 1988-2016* is published by Shearsman. *Winterreisen,* a collaboration with Kelvin Corcoran, is forthcoming from Knives Forks & Spoons. He lives in Sheffield from where he runs West House Books.

Robert Hampson is Professor of Modern Literature at Royal Holloway, University of London. In addition to his work in Joseph Conrad studies (as the author of three monographs on Conrad, former editor of *The Conradian*, and the editor of various editions of works by Conrad), he has also been active for many decades as editor, critic and practitioner in contemporary poetry. In the 1970s, he co-edited the influential magazine *Alembic*; he subsequently co-edited the pioneering critical volume *The New British poetries: The scope of the possible* (1993) and more recently co-edited *Frank O'Hara Now* (2010) and *Clasp: late modernist poetry in London in the 1970s* (2016). His poetry publications include *Assembled Fugitives: Selected Poems 1973-1998* (2001) and, more recently, *Seaport* (2008), *an explanation of colours* (2010) and *reworked disasters* (2013), which was long-listed for the Forward Prize.

Adam Hampton is a poet and Graduate Teaching Assistant at Edge Hill University in the United Kingdom. He is completing a Ph.D concerning textual superimposition and illegibility in the poetic text, particularly in the work of Nathan Walker, Susan Howe and Rosmarie Waldrop.

Edmund Hardy writes essays and poems. He also curates the online poetry journal *Intercapillary Space* (www.intercapillaryspace.blogspot.com)

Tom Jenks has published thirteen books of poetry and shorter prose. He has worked extensively with procedural methods, particular involving digital technology, which was the subject of his Ph.D. research at Edge Hill University, where his supervisor was Robert Sheppard. His procedural work includes a synonymical spreadsheet 'translation' of the Book of Genesis and a database-driven reduction of John Stuart Mill's *On Liberty*. He edits the small press zimZalla, specialising in literary objects.

Christopher Madden is an independent scholar, critic, and writer specialising in narrative studies, poetry and poetics, queer theory, and psychogeography. He has published articles on the queer chronotopes of Annie Proulx's 'Brokeback Mountain', and Holocaust humour in Woody Allen, Shalom Auslander, and Howard Jacobson. Titles in which his reviews have appeared include *The Wolf*, *PN Review*, *Holocaust Studies: A Journal of Culture and History*, and *Textual Practice*. His review of Robert Sheppard's *Berlin Bursts* and subsequent interview for *The Wolf* led to his involvement in the Robert Sheppard Symposium and indeed to the present volume.

Alison Mark is a former academic, now psychoanalytic psychotherapist based in London. Her PhD thesis was on Veronica Forrest-Thomson, subsequently published as *Veronica Forrest -Thompson and 'Language' Poetry*. She is an editor of *Women: a Cultural Review*, and co-editor (with Deryn Rees-Jones) of *Contemporary Women's Poetry: Reading / Writing / Practice*.

Chris McCabe has published five poetry collections the most recent of which are *Speculatrix* and *The Triumph of Cancer* (both Penned in the Margins). He has been shortlisted for The Ted Hughes Award and has recorded his work for the Poetry Archive. He is the co-editor of *The New Concrete: Visual Poetry in the 21ˢᵗ Century* (Hayward Gallery, 2018) and his novel, *Dedalus*, is published by Henningham Family Press. He works as the National Poetry Librarian.

Geraldine Monk was first published in the 1970's. Her main collections of poetry include *Interregnum,* Creation Books, *Noctivagations* and *Escafeld Hangings* both published by West House Books. In 2012 she devised and edited the collective autobiography of selected British poets *Cusp: Recollections of Poetry in Transition*, Shearsman Books. Her latest collection *They Who Saw the Deep* was published by Parlor Press / Free Verse Editions.

Sandeep Parmar is Professor of English Literature at the University of Liverpool where she co-directs Liverpool's Centre for New and International Writing. Her books include *Reading Mina Loy's Autobiographies: Myth of the Modern*, an edition of the *Collected Poems of Hope Mirrlees* (Carcanet, 2011), and two books of her own poetry published by Shearsman: *The Marble Orchard* and *Eidolon*, winner of the Ledbury Forte Prize for Best Second Collection. Most recently she edited the *Selected Poems of Nancy Cunard* (Carcanet, 2016). She is a BBC New Generation Thinker.

Mark Scroggins is a poet, biographer, and literary critic. His books of poetry are *Red Arcadia* (Shearsman, 2012), *Torture Garden: Naked City Pastorelles* (The Cultural Society, 2011), and *Anarchy* (Spuyten Duyvil, 2002). He is the author of *Louis Zukofsky and the Poetry of Knowledge* (University of Alabama Press, 1998) and *The Poem of a Life: A Biography of Louis Zukofsky* (Shoemaker & Hoard, 2007). He has edited *Upper Limit Music: The Writing of Louis Zukofsky* (Alabama, 1997) and a selection of uncollected prose for *Prepositions+: The Collected Critical Essays of Louis Zukofsky* (Wesleyan University Press, 2000).

Zoë Skoulding is Director of Creative Writing at Bangor University; her main interests lie in sound and performance, ecopoetics and urban space, and translation as a creative practice. Much of her work has centred on how place shapes and is shaped by language. Her poetry collections include *The Museum of Disappearing Sounds* (Seren, 2013) and *Teint: For the Bièvre* (Hafan Books, 2016). Translation is another important area of Skoulding's practice-based research, with translations of the work of Luxembourgish poet Jean Portante into English. She also co-translated the American poet Jerome Rothenberg into French.

Scott Thurston has published a number of books and chapbooks of poetry, including three full-length collections with Shearsman, and most recently *We Must Betray Our Potential* (The Red Ceilings, 2018), as well as many essays on innovative poetry and poetics. He co-founded the *Journal of British and Irish Innovative Poetry* with Robert Sheppard in 2009, the Open Access version of which he currently edits with Gareth Farmer. He was co-organiser of the long-running poetry reading series and online archive The Other Room in Manchester and edited *The Salt Companion to Geraldine Monk* (Salt, 2007). He first met Sheppard at the age of sixteen at an FE college in Surrey, and was later supervised by him during his doctoral research. Thurston is currently a Reader in English and Creative Writing at the University of Salford.

Index

Lightning Source UK Ltd.
Milton Keynes UK
UKHW010439250419
341587UK00001B/49/P